AL NORTE

Mexican American Monographs, No. 13
Sponsored by the Center for Mexican American Studies
The University of Texas at Austin

AL NORTE

Agricultural Workers
in the Great Lakes Region,
1917–1970

BY DENNIS NODÍN VALDÉS
ILLUSTRATIONS BY NORA CHAPA MENDOZA

UNIVERSITY OF TEXAS PRESS, AUSTIN

First Edition, 1991

Requests for permission to reproduce material from
this work should be sent to Permissions, University
of Texas Press, Box 7819, Austin, Texas 78713-7819

⊗ The paper used in this publication meets the
minimum requirements of American National Standard for Information Sciences—Permanence of Paper for Printed Library Materials, ANSI Z39.48-1984.

Library of Congress Cataloging-in-Publication Data
Valdés, Dennis Nodín.
   Al norte : agricultural workers in the Great Lakes
     region, 1917–1970 / by Dennis Nodín Valdés.
     — 1st ed.
     p.   cm — (Mexican American monographs ;
     no. 13)
   Includes bibliographical references and index.
   ISBN 0-292-70413-5 (alk. paper). — ISBN 0-292-
     70420-8 (pbk. : alk. paper)
   1. Migrant agricultural laborers—Lake States—
     History. 2. Alien labor, Mexican—Lake States—
     History. 3. Puerto Ricans—Lake States—
     History. I. Title. II. Series.
   HD1527.A14V35   1991
   331.5′44′0977—dc20   90-21831
                                     CIP

Contents

Illustrations

Preface

Literature on Latinos in the Upper Midwest has addressed principally urban settings. It has examined the lives of people who worked on the railroads and in stockyards, automobile plants and steel factories. This emphasis has led to the view that the midwestern Latino historical experience has been almost entirely urban, in contrast to that of the Southwest, where ranches, farms, and orchards have also played a decisive role in Latino life.[1] In fact, since the initial entry of Spanish-speaking people into the Midwest, the sugar beet industry has hired more people of Mexican and Puerto Rican birth and descent than any other employer in the region. Moreover, other agricultural interests have also hired thousands of these workers. This study is a history of Latino agricultural workers in the Upper Midwest from the time of their entry into the region during World War I until 1970.

This book focuses primarily on the class struggle between capitalist employers and seasonal farmworkers. It is a social history of work, the labor process, and the world of farmworkers. Its emphasis is on work, which attracted people to the region, dominated their waking hours, and shaped their lives more profoundly than anything else. This study questions commonly held beliefs that labor relations in agriculture lagged behind the factories, that farmworkers' lives were more traditional and changed more slowly than in other sectors, and that, because of political powerlessness and a passive culture, farmworkers were helpless victims of unscrupulous employers.

These assertions in the literature ignore the fact that employers engaged in ongoing experimentation in technology, crops, and relations with their field-workers throughout the period. Agricultural corporations continually altered the work process and replaced established workers with others in an effort to maintain more effective control. As a result, the agricultural work process and the composition of the labor force changed as rapidly as in any of the most advanced industries in the region.[2] Farm employers in the Midwest created an ethnic laboratory in the twentieth century that employed immigrants from Europe, people of Mexican birth and descent, southern Euro-Americans and African Americans, German and Italian World War II prisoners, Nisei, Puerto Ricans, and people from the British West Indies. Although their national, regional, and racial backgrounds differed, they all shared experience as farmworkers. This ethnic laboratory is an ideal setting to compare the impact of national, regional, and racial differences over time, since class is held constant.

Organized efforts to challenge the exploitative relations workers encountered almost always ended in failure. Only a few unions ever appeared and, until recently, they disappeared quickly. Because the union experience in the Midwest was more sporadic than in California or Hawaii, it has not been possible to write a history of farmworkers by studying the unions that tried to organize them. A work-focused examination of the class struggle does, however, make it possible to fill in the gaps left by union lethargy.

Many terms are used to identify the Spanish-speaking population in the United States. In this volume the term "Latino" will be used to refer to them collectively. "Mexicano" is a self-referent, whose English-language equivalent is "Mexican." "Tejano," "Mexican American," and "Texas-Mexican" apply to people of Mexican descent born in the United States, while the term "Chicano" became popular in the 1960s. In conformity with popular usage of the time, I will refer to the first generation of farmworkers of Mexican origin in the Midwest as Mexicanos (World War I to the Great Depression), the second generation as Mexican Americans (the Great Depression to the 1960s), and the third generation as Chicanos (the 1960s).

I wish to thank many former and present farmworkers who shared insights into their work and lives in the rural Midwest and made this book possible. I am grateful to former and present staff of the Chicano Studies Research Center of UCLA, particularly Juan Gómez-

Quiñones, Emilio Zamora, Carlos Vásquez, and Roberto Calderón, for making my life more comfortable during my stay with them. I also thank other colleagues and friends who discussed this subject and read all or parts of the manuscript and offered other kinds of assistance, particularly Rodolfo Acuña, Víctor Nelson-Cisneros, Devón Peña, Ricardo Romo, Juan García, and Jesse Gonzales. I thank Delfín Muñoz for help interviewing and Juan J. Castillo for opening personal files for my use. To my colleagues at the University of Minnesota, Guillermo Rojas, Stuart Schwartz, Bob McCaa, and Clarke Chambers, I am particularly grateful for intellectual stimulation and support. For the beautiful illustrations, which capture the story visually, I thank Nora Mendoza. I wish to acknowledge the financial support of the Rockefeller Foundation and the UCLA Institute of American Cultures, which gave me time to write this manuscript. I thank the staff of the University of Texas Press for their efforts. I am grateful to Guadalupe Luna for invaluable assistance in criticism, editing, and interviewing and for being there.

CHAPTER 1

Factories and the Fields,
1898–1917

At the end of the nineteenth century the Upper Midwest was a vast region of rolling prairies, undrained swamps, and cutover forests. The most successful agriculture in the region, known as "the breadbasket of the world," involved grain cultivation. Other parts of the Upper Midwest were sparsely inhabited, scarred by mines and tree stumps left by loggers. If left alone this area probably would have reverted to its forested state in a few generations.

A new form of agriculture, scientific and research-oriented in approach and controlled by corporations, however, quickly descended on the stumplands and the swamps. The sugar beet industry led this industrialized agriculture. From the start sugar beet production and the beet corporations were closely linked to the region's powerful agricultural colleges and depended on state and federal government subsidies.

With research and experimentation in crop growing largely resolved before the corporations appeared, the major problems the industrialists faced involved establishing a relationship with traditionally independent farmers and locating a source of labor for a region that lacked a tradition of intensive crop production. Writing in 1904, sugar beet expert Charles Saylor from the United States Department

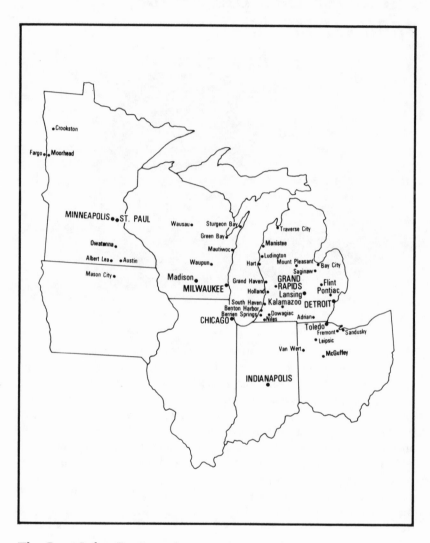

The Great Lakes Region

of Agriculture (USDA) observed, "The single problem that confronted the capitalists . . . was: where are we going to secure labor to grow beets? It was certainly the hardest problem they had to solve." The capitalists' experiments, described at the time as "developing a class" of workers for the sugar beet fields, ultimately turned to Mexicano *betabeleros* (sugar beet field-workers).[1] Mexican workers became the core of the agricultural proletariat in the Upper Midwest following World War I, and have remained so. This chapter examines the industry and its concerns with production and field labor before Mexicanos arrived.

The success of the sugar beet industry in the Midwest hinged on a combination of circumstances: an expanding market, a publicly financed research network, available investors, and cheap land. Market expansion also coincided with rapid demographic growth in the nation. Between 1865 and the mid-1920s, sugar consumption in the United States rose from 18.5 pounds to 109 pounds per person, while the nation's population more than quadrupled.[2]

The research network of the agricultural college system that became entrenched during this same period was in effect a public gift to the industry. Beginning in the 1870s, state agricultural colleges engaged in experimental research on the sugar beet and its by-products, soils, climatic conditions, and cultivation practices. University researchers promoted sugar beets by making public appearances, writing articles, and distributing free literature and seeds to local farmers. They also encouraged potential investors, many of whom had enriched themselves from the earlier lumber boom and now sought another enterprise in which to invest their profits. They discovered that available cheap land in the low-lying cutover areas and river valleys that had largely been avoided by established grain farmers was ideal for sugar beet growing. Here the companies built refineries and less-established farmers planted sugar beets.[3]

Five distinct areas of sugar beet production appeared in the Upper Midwest during the early twentieth century. The most important were in Michigan, referred to by some Mexicano workers as "Michoacán del norte," (Michoacán of the North). The major sugar beet—producing zone in the state included and extended beyond the Saginaw Valley in Eastern and Central Michigan. Another growing area in Southern Michigan extended into neighboring Northwestern Ohio and Northeastern Indiana. A third and less-important section covered the Southwestern part of the Upper Peninsula of Michigan and Eastern Wisconsin. A fourth zone included the Minnesota River Valley in Southeastern Minnesota and extended into Northeastern Iowa. The final beet-producing area in the Upper Midwest centered around the Red River Valley in Northwestern Minnesota and Eastern North Dakota, an area that entered commercial sugar-beet growing in the early 1920s.[4]

All these zones entered commercial farming comparatively late in the agricultural history of the Midwest. Some of them originally were swampy, and earlier Anglo-American and European settlers avoided them until they were drained. Others were part of the forests that first had to be cut down before they could be farmed. These settings also tended to be located far from important population centers.[5]

The success of the sugar beet industry stemmed also from public support. Most research continued to be performed at the agricultural colleges, supported by public, not beet company, funds. During the 1890s federal and several state government decrees established special tariffs and bounties to encourage the beet sugar industry and to protect it from foreign competition. Throughout the twentieth century the industry has continued to maintain close ties with the agricultural colleges and local politicians. The beet industry also enjoyed steady support from the rural press, "the advance agent of progress," which promoted the industry vigorously since its inception.[6]

Sugar beet production expanded rapidly. In 1897 there were only four operating sugar beet factories in the nation and none in the Great Lakes States. Between 1898 and 1913, eighty-six new factories were constructed in the Upper Midwest. Michigan led the way, with twenty-four factories appearing by 1903. Similar expansion occurred on the Great Plains, in the Intermontane–Rocky Mountain area, and on the Pacific Coast. For the next half century Michigan, Colorado, and California dominated the industry and typically produced between 50 and 75 percent of the nation's sugar from beets each year.[7]

The sugar beet industry rapidly became vertically integrated. In the Midwest two large corporations, the Michigan Sugar Company and the American Beet Sugar Company (later the American Crystal Sugar Company), quickly gained control over a majority of regional production. There were only two other important corporations active in the Great Lakes states, the Columbia Sugar Company (later the Monitor Sugar Company) and the Continental Sugar Company (later the Great Lakes Sugar Company), in addition to a handful of small, typically short-lived, operations. Major owners held stock in different companies and sat on a number of executive boards. Moreover, personnel shifted frequently between refineries and companies. In the political arena, cooperation rather than rivalry characterized corporate actions. The industry as a whole sought political solutions to its problems, whether on the local, national, or international level.[8]

The midwestern sugar beet industry owned the factories but had to contend with two groups of human actors to ensure production in the fields: farmers and workers. The industry made no serious effort to purchase large tracts of land, as it was able to induce local growers to plant beets. The farmers it encountered had moderate-sized holdings, averaging roughly 90 acres in Michigan and Ohio, increasing to 170 in Minnesota, averages that held constant through the early twentieth century.

For grain crops, farm families were able to perform most planting and cultivating tasks. They required large numbers of outside workers only during harvest. Sugar beets, by contrast, demanded intensive hand labor for much of their seven-month growing season. Because of the risks involved, particularly in acquiring labor, the corporations made a special effort to convince growers to plant the crop. They had to offer inducements, including a guaranteed price before planting, low-interest loans, and free use of or cheap rent for costly machinery. Most important, the companies had to take the responsibility for recruiting field-workers. Established farmers in the Midwest, the "most considerable area in the world in which agriculture is uniformly prosperous," were hesitant to accept company inducements, but less-established ones were more willing to devote a few acres each season to beets.[9]

Midwestern farmers remained an important group with which the industry and the field laborers had to contend. Farmers formed sugar beet growers' organizations as early as 1899 to protect their interests and later formed a special beet growers' committee within the American Farm Bureau Federation. On decisions pertaining to the industry, however, their organizations were dominated by beet companies, which determined policy on planting, cultivation, harvest, and payment.

The growers did resist corporate efforts to make them perform unpleasant labor in the fields. While they often labored long hours, farmers' work involved riding on machines or standing, not walking stooped, kneeling, or crawling along the ground. One sugar beet expert commented, "Our farmers were not accustomed, inured or disposed as a rule to perform in the hard, laborious duties required in growing sugar beets." The growers refused to do fieldwork and allowed the corporations to control recruitment of workers and the work process.[10]

During the first two decades of the twentieth century the beet industry experimented frequently in its search for the ideal field labor force. Its first efforts focused on groups, or "gangs," of local women and children. Most were foreign-born Europeans or their children and were paid by the day or the week. In 1900 Clinton D. Smith, director of the Michigan Agricultural Experiment Station at East Lansing, praised the beet industry for its efforts: "It has furnished employment to a large number of boys that would otherwise have been idlers, and to a possibly still larger number of women, who were sorely in need of the money thus earned."[11]

As production expanded, industry recruiters turned to immigrant neighborhoods in nearby cities, where they found available single males. The most important among them were Belgians, who in the later years of the first decade of the 1900s became the most important group of workers in the Michigan, Ohio, and Wisconsin sugar beet areas. Working also in gangs, they were commonly hired for specific tasks that lasted several weeks. As production expanded, company recruiters searched in ever-widening circles. Soon they turned to eastern European immigrant families, who first entered the midwestern fields in the early years of the twentieth century and dominated the work force in the 1910s and early 1920s. The most numerous among the Europeans were Germans from Russia, people of German origin who had lived for several generations in Russia, a majority in the Volga region of Russia, recruited largely from Nebraska and Kansas. Hungarians, Poles, Serbians, and other Slavic groups from several midwestern cities also worked in the fields.[12]

Family labor altered the organization of work in several ways. First, supervision became primarily the responsibility of parents instead of corporation overseers. Second, families contracted for the entire season rather than by the day, week, or task. Consequently, beet fieldwork became the workers' principal source of sustenance during the year. Third, wages changed from payment by time to piecework, typically based on the number of acres worked. Frequency of payment fell from daily or weekly to payment at the end of specific tasks, typically, four times per season. Fourth, with the entry of families, employers had to provide more durable housing and related perquisites. The sugar companies responded by building standardized units disparagingly called "hunky houses." These small portable shacks of one or two rooms, typically twelve by sixteen feet, were commonly set on wheels for easy movement from one field to the next.[13]

European immigrants found certain attractions in family beet labor. Urban factories usually hired only men and most offered unsteady employment. The beet fields offered secure employment for several months. Because women and children worked, large families could earn a higher income than could male household heads alone in the factories. During breaks between tasks in the beet fields, fathers often secured temporary employment on railroad gangs or in shops or factories in nearby cities. The families also received a plot of land to grow a garden. This provided fresh vegetables in the summer and canned food for the winter. The families were most attracted because fieldwork was a stepping-stone, as it had been for hired hands. Companies encouraged many of these families to become growers by providing tools, advice, and low-interest loans. The range of paternalistic corporate inducements enabled many immigrant families to become farmers by first renting and later purchasing land they had previously worked under contract.[14]

This pattern of upward mobility among European immigrants is consistent with their experiences in urban settings during the late nineteenth and early twentieth centuries, as discussed by Stephan Thernstrom and others.[15] When Mexicanos entered the beet fields in World War I, neither they nor their children could expect a similar future.

CHAPTER 2

Mexican Entry, 1917–1929

World War I accelerated opportunities for European immigrant beet workers and strengthened their bargaining position with employers. The rising wages of wartime industry drew many families to the cities and the war forced wages up in agriculture. Other Europeans began to rent and purchase land and like other farmers they soon refused to work in the sugar beet fields. Employers were concerned about beet workers' reactions to the organizing efforts of the Industrial Workers of the World (IWW). In response to these challenges, the industry turned to Mexico to find a new source of cheap labor.[1] This chapter examines the influence of the Mexican workers on the work process during and immediately after World War I and compares their lot with that of their predecessors.

Wartime Emergency Workers

Organized agricultural interests in the Southwest and sugar beet producers throughout the United States joined forces to insert a special clause in the Immigration Act of 1917. This clause allowed Mexican citizens to enter the country under prior contract and exempted them from the literacy test and the eight-dollar head tax required of permanent immigrants.[2]

The companies and their lobbyists argued that Mexicanos were their last resort. In fact, sugar refiners in parts of Colorado and California had been using Mexican field-workers for many years and found them satisfactory. Most employees resided in nearby *colonias* (settlements) in Northern New Mexico, Southern Colorado, and Southern California. In the Midwest, when European immigration was cut off, urban industry began recruiting hundreds of thousands of rural African Americans and Euro-Americans. In Detroit, the closest large city to the heart of the beet fields, the African American population mushroomed from under six thousand in 1910 to one hundred thousand by 1930.[3]

The rural, poverty-stricken southerners appeared to be logical candidates for the midwestern beet fields. They were closer to the fields than the Mexicanos and cheaper to recruit. Beet companies throughout the nation, however, had already decided to recruit Mexicanos for work in California, Colorado, Michigan, and elsewhere. This decision largely explains why African Americans never formed a significant fraction of the beet labor force. Although later they performed agricultural labor, African Americans were lured mostly to urban locations in the Midwest, whereas Mexicanos found employment in both urban and agricultural tasks.

Recruitment of Mexicanos to the midwestern beet fields became formalized in the 1918 season. The corporations hired *enganchistas* (recruiters) and sent them to the Mexican border and into Mexico with promises of seasonal work in the beet fields, good working conditions, and high pay. *Enganchistas* facilitated arrangements, often informal, that induced thousands to enter the United States and sign work contracts. The beet companies, moreover, succeeded in convincing the secretary of labor to continue to apply the 1917 exemption after the war ended. By 1920, the Michigan, Holland–Saint Louis, Columbia, and Continental sugar companies had recruited more than five thousand Mexican workers, mostly single males, for the Michigan and Ohio beet fields.[4]

The attractive newspaper advertisements and promises of *enganchistas* did not represent what the Mexican workers encountered. Investigators concerned with working conditions discovered that company *revisadores* (field men) placed Mexicanos in the roughest and most poorly cultivated fields, fields often abandoned by other workers. The corporations' failure to abide by promises of good pay and working conditions convinced many Mexicanos to break their contracts and seek employment elsewhere. Company representatives complained that workers deserted for Toledo, Detroit, Saginaw, and other cities, attracted by higher pay and better working conditions.[5]

The formal recruitment of Mexican *braceros* (contract workers) allowed by the Immigration Act of 1917 halted after the 1920 season because of the postwar depression. The recruitment program soon ground to a halt and urban midwestern employers released thousands of their Mexican workers. They had considered them very satisfactory during the wartime emergency but, faced with rising unemployment, claimed that "these Mexicans could not compete with the workmen of the northern races."[6]

The depression also led to the first concerted attempts to repatriate Mexicanos from the agricultural and urban settings of the Midwest. Beet companies sponsored a majority of the "repatriation" simply by complying with the promise to provide workers with transportation to the Mexican border. In addition, the Saint Vincent DePaul Society, other church groups, and the United States Department of Labor (USDL) devised a limited repatriation plan centering mostly in Detroit. U.S. authorities arranged with the Mexican government to transport workers from the border to their homes in the interior.[7] The beet companies' experience with Mexicanos in the 1918–1921 period convinced them that they had found the best group of workers to date. They were abundant, did not have an established presence or political voice in the region, and could easily be removed with the assistance of the government when not needed.

Recruitment and Contracting

The postwar depression ended quickly and company recruiters turned again to the Mexicano labor pool. This time they focused on the rapidly growing Mexicano population residing in the cities and small towns of South Texas. Later in the decade, as midwestern *colonias* expanded, recruiters also followed Mexicanos to the urban Midwest.

The recruitment mechanism involved beet company representatives working with private employment agencies, the most important being the Sunshine Agency in San Antonio and Aldrete in Dallas and Fort Worth. Workers from Mexico and South Texas were lured by newspaper advertisements, fliers and word-of-mouth. *Enganchistas* also visited small towns, labor camps, and mines on both sides of the border. Max Handman observed that "Texas is the corridor and clearing house for most of the Mexican casuals that are distributed over the country." Workers who went to the far western states typically passed through El Paso, while those who went to the Midwest were more likely to enter through Laredo and smaller cities to the east.[8]

Company recruiters, operating through the agencies, arranged transporation, advanced funds, and assigned workers to specific locations and farms. They did not compete with the newly created United States Employment Service (USES), which initially devoted attention to agricultural placement in the early 1920s. The USES operated mostly on the Great Plains and in the West and remained peripheral to the beet companies' recruitment efforts until World War II.[9]

Almost all Mexicans recruited to the Midwest were born in Mexico. Most were recent arrivals to Texas who had been in the state for periods ranging from a few days to a few years. While in Texas they worked in a variety of unskilled jobs, including coal mining, chopping and picking cotton, grubbing farms, chopping wood, and in unskilled casual labor in the cities. They were lured to the North by stories of its attractiveness, the lack of *distinción* (discrimination), and especially by promises of high wages.[10]

The recruitment of urban midwestern Mexicanos for the beet fields first took place from the older railroad centers of Saint Louis and Kansas City. Recruiters soon found workers closer to the fields as *colonias* appeared after the war in Des Moines, Saint Paul, the Chicago area, Detroit, Saginaw, Toledo, and smaller towns. The shorter-distance recruitment saved transporation and other expenses for both the companies and the workers.

The midwestern recruitment mechanism functioned in a variety of ways. In Chicago, private agencies on Halstead, Madison, and Clark streets announced job opportunities. In Detroit a less-formal system operated, as company agents placed placards and notices in the Mexicanos' favorite pool-rooms, restaurants, and other public places with information about wage rates, whom to contact, and when work would begin. In smaller places, recently settled Mexicano beet workers who knew potential workers often served as informal recruiters in exchange for small favors from the companies and growers. These informal mechanisms became increasingly popular.[11]

Recruitment in the mid-1920s far exceeded that of the World War I period. In 1924 midwestern corporations recruited at least six thousand workers from Texas. By 1926 more than twice that number came, and *betabeleros* displaced Eastern Europeans in the Midwest as they displaced European and Asian beet workers in other parts of the country. According to a 1927 survey they formed an estimated 75 to 90 percent of the total labor force in all of the beet-growing regions. In 1927 USDL expert George Edson estimated that there were about fifteen thousand Mexican workers in the Midwest. Including "non-working" children ages six through sixteen, younger children, and adult women, more than forty thousand people spent six to eight months of the year in the upper midwestern beet fields.[12]

The sugar beet migration of World War I and the 1920s was not related to the Great Plains wheat belt migration that moved north from Texas to Canada each year at harvest time. The Great Plains phenomenon began earlier, peaking between the 1890s and the 1920s. It was mechanized out of existence quickly at precisely the time Mexicanos first entered the beet fields, not only because machines were available, but also because farmers feared the organizational efforts of the IWW (the Wobblies). The Wobblies' efforts to organize workers through strikes peaked around 1915. In the end the IWW could not overcome the combined onslaught of blacklists by local farmers, reprisals by sheriffs' deputies, and the machines.[13]

The labor processes in the wheat and the beet fields differed sharply in the early twentieth century. The former involved frequent but short-distance movement as the crop ripened, whereas sugar beet labor required long-distance movement only twice per year. The typical wheat harvester usually worked no more than two or three months per year, as opposed to six to eight months for beet workers. The wheat harvesters were largely native-born single Euro-American males, whereas by the 1920s the beet workers were predominantly Mexicano family units. Wheat belt migration on a large scale ended by the 1920s, but sugar beet migration continued for several more decades. The wheat fields did not employ workers for a long enough period each year to make up the major source of their earnings; the sugar beet industry created a permanent agricultural work force in the region.

The companies regulated working arrangements and details of the work process, as evident in the work contracts of the 1920s. Although they tried to obscure their dominating role, they drew up the agreements without direct input from farmers or field workers. Work contracts designated the farmer as the employer and the company as agent of the farmer. It was a technical formality, as George Edson observed, for farmer and worker "merely sign on the dotted line indicated to them by the sugar manufacturing company." The corportions recruited, provided transportation, supervised work in the fields, arranged credit, owned the dwellings in which most workers resided, and signed the workers' paychecks.[14]

Contractual arrangements evolved rapidly during the first three decades of the industry. The earliest arrangements involving adult female and child workers were informal; they were typically hired by the day and paid by the hour. As male gangs increasingly entered the fields, written contracts appeared, typically detailing arrangements for each specific task. The contracts became even more detailed in the second decade of the century as European immigrant families came to dominate field labor. In addition to stipulations regarding work and pay, contracts now contained provisions for transportation, free housing, furniture, kitchen utensils, tools, and garden plots.[15]

By the 1920s the contracts had become even more detailed and restrictive. Payments declined to three and then two times per season, in effect increasing worker indebtedness and reliance on the corporation. Payments for harvesting were based not only on acreage, but also on yield. The corporations claimed that earlier workers were fast but careless and purposely pulled out plants during cultivation so they would have fewer to harvest. Consequently, they forced Mexicanos in the 1920s to work more slowly and thus to contract smaller acreages than their European predecessors. (In later years researchers disproved these company arguments, finding no relationship between immaculate fields and high yields.) Corporations also popularized the "hold-back" during the 1920s, withholding several dollars from each pay period to ensure that workers remained the entire season. Final paychecks did not come until early winter, long after the harvest ended. The corporations also introduced the "bonus" to reward workers for fields with high yields. Bonuses were mostly an illusion, as 1926 figures showed that they totaled less than 1 percent of seasonal income.[16]

The contracts also obscured who actually worked, as they included only the corporation, the farmer, and the head of the family. The corporations granted acreages based on the number of available workers, including children, but did not want to provide evidence that they employed child labor. A 1920 Michigan study determined that more than 20 percent of the children of beet worker families at age six, 60 percent of those aged eight, and almost all of those aged ten worked alongside their parents. The relative importance of child labor was demonstrated in a 1924 Wisconsin study. It determined that 52 percent of field-workers were fifteen years of age or less, and only 21 percent were twenty-one years of age or more. These studies showed that child labor was an implicit part of the sugar beet field labor contracts.[17]

The companies frequently advertised that transportation was free, but contracts showed this to be a misrepresentation. Transportation costs were an advance on wages and were later deducted from paychecks. During most of the 1920s workers from Texas who provided their own transportation received twenty-three dollars per acre, five dollars more than those who did not. Those recruited from nearby cities typically earned one dollar more per acre (twenty-four dollars) for arriving at the fields unassisted.[18]

The midwestern beet contracts also provided free housing, which included tables, chairs, blankets, dishes and kitchen utensils, a cooking stove, tools for work, and often a nearby garden plot. Housing in Minnesota, Iowa, and North Dakota usually was provided by farmers who made room in storage sheds, parts of barns, or abandoned farmhouses. In Michigan and Ohio the corporations typically rented portable one- or two-room frame houses. Company houses followed Henry Ford's production principles—they were all alike. A worker for the Isabella Sugar Company in Mount Pleasant, Michigan, recalled that the house in which she lived was furnished with porcelain dishes, knives and forks, straw mattresses, and a standard wood stove. The houses had wooden folding tables built into the walls, benches for sitting, and bunk beds. In another Central Michigan house, a labor investigator observed, "The Mexican family whose house was exceptionally clean and tidy had been provided only two beds, one without any mattress, a rough board table, three tree stumps for chairs and a few rough dishes."[19]

Contracts further stipulated that dwellings were to be located near a source of clean water for cooking and bathing. Yet workers regularly had unsafe and improperly maintained wells, surface pollution, tin cans and other debris floating in muddy or sandy water. Complaints that the water "had a bad odor or made them ill" found no remedy. Some workers in the sugar beet areas were fortunate to find many still-pristine lakes and rivers nearby, commonly the only places to bathe.[20]

Contracts also reveal changes in planting practices. The average plot size devoted to beets expanded from one or two acres at the turn of the century to about five or six in the 1920s. This meant that families commonly worked three or four neighboring farms simultaneously during the season. The contracts neither revealed that staggering of plantings was being eliminated, supposedly to maximize the growing time for beets and to ensure higher yields, nor that the change did not affect yields. Furthermore, the contracts did not show that the acreages per worker declined. The average male European adult before World War I contracted about twenty acres of beets, compared with roughly ten for Mexicano men in the 1920s.[21]

These contract changes in the 1920s forced Mexicanos to rely more on credit than had their predecessors. Their first paychecks arrived between three and four months after they arrived in the beet region. Until that time they had to run up a tab at the local general store, guaranteed by the company. They were allowed one dollar per month per acre credit, to be deducted from the first paycheck. In conjunction with hold-backs, credit helped companies bind workers to their jobs for the entire season.[22]

Labor and Its Fruits

Beet field labor typically began in April or early May, by which time most workers had been in the region about a month. They traveled from Texas in Pullman coaches chartered by the sugar corporations. The cars were well maintained, clean, and afforded workers the same comforts provided other private users of the rail service, including food and drink en route. The units were self-contained, so there was no need for rest stops. On arrival they usually met growers, who loaded workers and their belongings onto farm wagons and took them to the beet shacks. If farmers failed to show, workers had to walk several miles to their dwellings, with their belongings tied to their backs and the younger children in their parents' arms.[23]

The family was a single working unit, typically composed of young Mexican-born parents in their twenties and thirties with only weak ties to Texas. Most families were small nuclear units with both parents present. Frequently, working units were made up of a mother and her children or several young adult brothers and sisters. The families performed several tasks within a period lasting between 180 and 200 days, with an average of 60 to 80 days in the beet fields. The actual number of working days varied according to the degree of overhiring, the size of the family unit, acreage contracted, weather conditions, and whether growers staggered plantings. The working day sometimes lasted sixteen hours. During the long periods of idleness, *betabeleros* tried to find employment with local farmers or worked their garden plots.[24]

Before the first tasks in beet cultivation, some people were fortunate to find employment helping local farmers with odd jobs, including cutting trees, chopping wood, preparing fields, and cleaning up orchards and gardens. In the 1920s there was little outside work, for other forms of labor-intensive agriculture were not yet well developed in the region. Beet workers spent most of their time preparing their garden plots, planting tomatoes, garbanzos, pinto beans, peppers, onions, squash, and other vegetables. A few made arrangements to purchase and care for pigs and cows.[25]

The first cultivation tasks—blocking and thinning—lasted from May until early July. Blocking entailed removing unnecessary clusters of plants from each row, leaving plants roughly ten to twelve inches apart. It was one of the most time-consuming tasks and had to be performed quickly. Because of increased daylight hours of late spring and early summer, the working day averaged from eleven to fifteen hours. Before the 1920s workers usually blocked with long-handled hoes. Agricultural researchers then declared that the short-handled hoe was more effective, although it forced workers to walk stooped over or on their knees. The simultaneous introduction of the short-handled hoe and Mexicano workers linked the two in the popular and academic mind. In 1927 University of Nebraska geographer Esther Anderson suggested that blocking with short-handled hoes was "characteristic of Mexican and Japanese workers." *El cortito*, the short handled hoe, became the symbol of stoop labor for two generations.[26]

Workers without exception had harsh words for *el cortito*. Manuel Contreras recalled the 1920s in Southern Minnesota: "I must have walked on my knees from here to Mexico and back." Another worker complained that "all day long you crouch, bend over, and at night when you go to supper you feel as if you were dead." Later the president of the United Farm Workers of America, César Chávez spoke more forcefully about the short-handled hoe and beet work, the task he dreaded most: "I think growers use short-handled hoes because they don't give a damn about human beings. They look at human beings as implements. If they had any consideration for the torture that people go through, they would give up the short-handled hoe."[27] Later studies confirmed that the short-handled hoe caused ruptured discs, arthritis of the spine, and torn back ligaments. Earlier researchers' contentions that the short-handled hoe led to higher yields were already disproved when mechanical cross-blocking first was introduced to the Upper Midwest in 1930. Yet growers continued to insist that the hoe was necessary and successfully prevented its elimination until mechanical blockers were perfected.[28]

Thinning immediately followed blocking and involved removing all but one in the cluster of plants that grew from the same seed. It also required workers to walk stooped or on their hands and knees, but was not as demanding in physical terms as other cultivation and harvesting tasks, so young children could perform this task adequately. Beet companies and growers defended thinning by children on the basis of their "nimbleness," "small fingers," and "stature closer to the ground."[29]

Hoeing followed blocking and thinning by only a few days in staggered fields, with a gap of two or three weeks in those planted simultaneously. It required removing weeds to within six or eight inches of the young plants. Employers considered it men's work, partly because it was performed with long-handled hoes too large for children to handle, and because fewer workers were required and the pace was less frantic. The workday in hoeing lasted about nine hours except in the rainy season, when the fields were unusually weedy. Hoeing usually ended in early August and was followed by a break in the beet fields until harvest in late September or early October.[30]

During this break Mexicano families typically faced a long period of idleness. Some were fortunate to find brief employment topping onions, harvesting celery, picking melons, digging potatoes, or harvesting other vegetables. In the grain belt some worked in the corn or wheat harvests. In rare cases men found summer work on extra gangs on the railroads or in factories and shops in nearby cities. As structural unemployment rose in the later 1920s they were less able to find work outside the beet fields in the late summer. During this period Mexicanos devoted most of their time to their garden plots, harvesting, and canning. Women dominated the garden work and the canning, forms of household economy labor that contributed an important portion of family subsistence. Some families canned hundreds of quarts of tomatoes, hot peppers, squash, and other vegetables that filled their plates throughout the year.[31]

After the late-summer interim, workers turned to the harvest, a two-stage process. The farmer first "lifted," or cut, the taproot of the beets with a mechanical lifter attached to the back of his horse-drawn wagon. Then the field-worker, equipped with a long knife with a hook at the end, picked up two beets, knocked them together to remove dirt, and topped them, cutting the leafy crown from the rest of the beet. Children were an important part of this phase of the work process. They often gathered and piled the lifted beets so that older workers could top them more quickly. After topping, the children piled the beets in rows and covered them with the leafy tops to prevent rain and frost from penetrating them, thereby reducing the sugar content. Many children also topped beets, because the task had to be done quickly to beat the heavier fall freezes.

Topping often took place in the least pleasant climate of the season. Because light frost hastened maturation, *revisadores* delayed topping as long as possible. The task was often performed in heavy rain, high winds, and freezing temperatures, which numbed, cramped, and chapped workers' hands and made the topping knives difficult to grip. Furthermore, as daylight hours shortened in October and November, *betabeleros* had to use lanterns and other forms of artificial light to extend working hours. Under these conditions, workers frequently suffered cuts and gashes on hands and legs, and many lost fingers. They were forced, however, to complete the task or forfeit pay held back from earlier tasks.[32]

In the late 1920s male adults in the Upper Midwest averaged $160 per season in the sugar beet fields. This represented a sharp decline from the earnings of European adults, which averaged $280 in 1920. Based on company calculations, women performed about 75 percent as much fieldwork as men, and children under sixteen could handle between 50 and 90 percent as much as an adult male. Although earnings compared favorably with earnings in Texas, the decision to head "*al norte*" involved many risks.[33]

The Rural Setting

The Mexicano families who went to the Midwest in the 1920s found a much more highly differentiated population of European descent than in the Southwest. They encountered citizens of English descent and several self-conscious ethnic groups that retained their language and many of their customs. The Mexicanos were the last of the immigrant groups to go to the Midwest and, unlike their experience in Texas and elsewhere, they found no prior Mexicano presence in the region.

Were they treated as the last of a long line of European immigrants or as a non-Caucasian group kept apart from the majority? Initially, they fit the second pattern. The beet companies recruited them and kept them isolated, promising local residents that they would ship all Mexicanos out at the end of the season. Local politicians, farmers, sheriffs, and other permanent residents also tried to ensure that *betabeleros* did not mingle with them. The efforts to isolate, however, were not entirely successful.

Despite its ethnic diversity, the midwestern population at the time of World War I had few residents of non-European descent. Mexicanos already suffered widespread negative stereotyping from several sources. The stereotypes were reinforced by the experiences of thousands of young midwestern soldiers who accompanied Gen. John J. Pershing on the infamous Punitive Expedition into Mexico in 1916 and 1917. The soldiers invaded Mexico in an unsuccessful effort to capture its best-known revolutionary leader, Francisco (Pancho) Villa. Popular novels and Hollywood movies further nurtured the negative stereotype. As one expert observed, "Many people have had their hair stand on end from the thrills they get in reading novels or seeing Western films in picture shows, where the villain was a treacherous greaser." Local politicians shared the negative local attitudes. Michigan congressman Roy O. Woodruff of Bay City explained that "everybody looked upon them with apprehension. [We] had been led to believe they were a worthless and dangerous lot, a bunch of brigands." Local farmers expected knife fights and brawls, and some expressed fear for their lives. Even the most recent European arrivals, the Germans from Russia, had strong anti-Mexican feelings and tried to prevent their children from associating with those of the *betabeleros*.[34]

The small-town press reinforced these negative images. It portrayed the newcomers from Mexico as incomprehensible and dangerous, often engaging in knife fights, lovers' quarrels, drinking, and marijuana cultivation. Such fears led to de facto segregation of *betabeleros* from rural churches, restaurants, theaters, and classrooms throughout the region.[35]

Sugar beet officials tried to create countervailing opinions. Aware of the image of the lazy Mexican peon, one Michigan official claimed, "They are not lazy here as they are in the hotter climate of the south. This atmosphere seems to put pep in them." The beet companies also felt compelled to create a rationalization that Mexicans were particularly suited for beet field labor. Beet company official Harry Austin commented, "Much of the Mexican population is descended directly from the Indian. He has by nature the inherent traits of that race. He is fundamentally rural. He prefers outdoor life to the confinement of industrial pursuits."[36]

Other company representatives contended, "For monotonous work as beet work . . . they seem to be tireless," and "few whites have the patience to do the detailed hand work necessary" in the sugar beet fields. Austin himself concluded, "It is a weird complex he seems to have in his make-up . . . that he is migratory."[37]

Stereotyping continued after *betabeleros* arrived, in part because few local residents came into contact with them. Workers seldom had cars and traveled infrequently in the sparsely populated farm areas where they resided. The beet fields were a very isolating world. Contacts were limited to immediate families, the *revisador*, farmers for whom they worked, and occasionally law enforcement officials. Their confinement was the result of the material conditions surrounding beet production, not legal segregation. Nevertheless, workers like Trinidad Moreno, a young girl in Central Michigan in the 1920s, concluded that "there was no freedom for the Mexicano."[38]

The only regular contacts workers made involved sugar company *revisadores*. The field men arranged credit at the nearby country stores, supervised work in the fields, and helped cash paychecks to ensure that workers paid their debts. Through the *revisador* the companies sold items like bed ticking, blankets, clothes, tools for work, and bulk food, including pinto beans, lard, and flour. Company officials claimed that they made the sales at cost, as a service to workers.

When disagreements arose between workers and farmers on the measurement of land, housing conditions, or pay, the *revisador* was the final arbiter.[39]

Workers' next most frequent contacts were with local farmers, with whom relations varied widely. Workers typically worked on three to five farms in a single season. Some farmers would not grow beets because they did not want to deal with Mexicanos. A Chaska, Minnesota, farmer refused to drive twenty-five miles to nearby Saint Paul because he was afraid of its supposedly large and dangerous *colonia*. Other farmers, however, carried on forms of exchange to the mutual advantage of both, selling fresh milk, eggs, butter, vegetables, and meat, often in return for non-beet labor. Although many were generous and fair, outside observers agreed that they treated Mexicano workers differently from their European predecessors. One labor expert noted that "it is true that he [the Mexicano] does not mix, nor will he be treated as well as the other nationalities are by the farmers." Many growers accepted Mexicanos for stoop labor in beet fields while contradictorily asserting, "They don't seem adapted to white man's work." The companies had to prod farmers continually to fulfill contractual obligations to provide decent housing and treatment and grant garden plots to workers. An American Crystal publication reminded farmers that "they [workers] are human and respond generally to kind treatment."[40]

The gentle company admonishments were not enough to compel growers to provide adequate housing, uncontaminated water, and garden plots, as required by contract. Yet it was the widespread practice of undercounting acreage that angered workers the most. Crescencia Rangel bitterly recalled an incident fifty years earlier in Minnesota: "I was working with my daughters. The farmer cheated us of 7 acres."[41]

Betabeleros in the rural areas had only infrequent contacts with public officials and civil servants, including law enforcement officers, social workers, schoolteachers, and reform-minded investigators. At the end of the season unwanted *betabeleros* were rounded up by sheriff's deputies and immigration officers to ensure departure. Observers widely agreed that sheriffs and police were harsher toward Mexicanos than toward other foreign immigrants and widely violated their civil rights. George Edson concluded that Mexicanos had "a terror of the law."[42]

Welfare agencies were no more enlightened than other government entities. Influenced by widespread stereotypes, social worker Eva Gibbs in Mason City, Iowa, claimed that "two-thirds of the Mexicans have syphilis." Agency workers, especially in small and medium-sized cities, made it policy to refuse assistance to needy Mexicanos. Beet workers in dire straits sometimes received assistance from *mutualistas*, self-help organizations formed by their compatriots in nearby towns and cities. Welfare agencies frequently turned over workers to police and immigration authorities for shipment to the Texas border, especially if they were destitute or suffering from potentially fatal diseases like tuberculosis and leprosy.[43]

Another public institution, the school system, was expected to be more inclusive than the others. By the 1920s all midwestern beet-producing states had attendance laws that required temporary and permanent residents, typically between the ages of seven and sixteen, to attend school until they achieved an eighth-grade education. Exceptions were made for parents who were granted written permission from school authorities if they could demonstrate the need for their children to help support the family. In practice, however, truant officers and school officials simply refused to enforce mandatory attendance laws for the children of beet worker families. Many authorities believed that the children did not deserve access to the public school system. Even sympathetic school officials commonly were unwilling to confront growers and company officials, who were often school board members, when they removed children from school while there was work in the fields. Lack of money for books, school supplies, and clothes also kept children out of the classroom. Consequently, beet workers' children seldom attended rural midwestern schools.[44]

Reformers addressed the issue of mandatory school attendance at the time the Mexicanos began to enter the region. They prevailed on Congress to pass the Child Labor Law of 1919, which severely restricted child labor in all occupations. The U.S. Supreme Court, however, declared the law unconstitutional in 1922, ruling that the federal government had no right to interfere with matters of state concern. On the state level, reformers also tried to encourage school attendance. Their arguments were based in part on studies that concluded that because of nonattendance, beet workers' children suffered severe age-grade retardation. Some reformers convinced local school districts to establish experimental schools. A Mason City, Iowa, project demonstrated that schools could operate during breaks between sugar beet labor with very positive effects on the children enrolled. The schools also demonstrated that such programs could be financed under the mandate of existing laws. Faced, however, with resistance from corporations, local farmers, and local residents, the projects never went beyond the experimental stage.[45]

Public interest–oriented reformers were also concerned about housing conditions and child labor in midwestern beet fields. Their studies found many shacks, sheds, and partitioned barns with animals on the other side "unfit for habitation." Filthy toilet facilities and polluted water were widespread.[46]

They discovered respiratory problems among children who worked in damp fields and inhaled dusty air. Work also caused injured backs and rheumatism. A Colorado study found that two-thirds of the youths examined had winged scapulae, caused by the awkward stooped working position required by topping: "Their back is held high and bowed over, the chest is dragged downward, and free action in breathing is interfered with." Almost a quarter of the children suffered from a flat left foot, the result of the position they adopted while topping beets. Because of inadequate diets, clothing, and housing, children also had a very high incidence of rickets and tuberculosis. The consequences of child labor in the beet fields compared to those in the worst urban slums and sweatshops of a generation earlier.[47]

The reformers convinced authorities in several midwestern states to conduct their own studies and hearings in the early 1920s, but their efforts were either aborted or inconclusive. John J. Scannel, secretary of the Michigan Federation of Labor, explained that the 1923 legislative investigation in his state was "directed by the sugar beet interests."[48]

The sugar beet corporations thwarted the investigations and tried to discredit the findings of the reformers. Corporate representatives continued to argue that "the worker in the beet fields in the open air is very healthy." Sympathetic academics lent an air of credibility to company claims. In 1927 Michigan geographer and sugar beet expert F. A. Stilgenbauer wrote that "child labor is utilized . . . without any injurious effects." The corporations also "discovered" agitators. One company official claimed that the reformers were linked to subversive Cuban interests, namely sugarcane growers intent on destroying the sugar beet industry.[49]

Industry officials offered their own remedies for health problems. An American Beet Sugar Company brochure in Minnesota suggested that workers get quick medical attention and health checks, fully aware that they had no provisions for health care. It added its own bit of medical advice: "Kissing, especially on the mouth, is a dangerous transmittor of disease, especially tuberculosis. Save the children from this danger. Do not kiss them."[50]

Another potential element in the reform thrust was the Mexican consulate. Mexican consular officials were responsible for protecting the interests of the Mexican government and its citizens. Following

Venustiano Carranza's accession to the Mexican presidency, three regional consular offices were established in the Upper Midwest. The Detroit office was responsible for Ohio and the lower peninsula of Michigan, the Chicago office for Illinois and Northern Indiana, and the Milwaukee office for Wisconsin, Minnesota, and the Dakotas.[51]

Consular officials encountered many impediments in defending their beet worker clients, the first being distance. The Central Michigan beet country ranged from roughly 100 to 170 miles from the Detroit office, and the main thoroughfare was still largely unpaved in the 1920s. The Milwaukee offices were even farther from the production areas under its jurisdiction. The Southern Minnesota and Iowa fields were about 300 miles away, and the Red River Valley was almost twice that distance from Milwaukee.

A second and more serious obstacle was that the Mexican officials, lacking resources, had to make special requests for funds to take trips to the fields. Consequently, few midwestern consuls made such trips. Thus, they could only be of service if workers traveled to the city to find them.[52]

Finally the class and outlook of most consular officials blunted their potential effectiveness. They consciously shied away from issues that appeared to have potentially political overtones and urged their compatriots to do so as well. Typically urban-born and formally educated, they seldom pursued cases with vigor on behalf of workers who were hundreds of miles away. In Milwaukee E. P. Kirby Hade, a Euro-American who lived in Mexico as a mining engineer during the days of Porfirio Díaz, served as consul for several years. He responded infrequently to beet worker complaints and was seemingly more interested in maintaining the goodwill of company officials than in protecting workers. In Detroit consular officials were similarly uninvolved until 1930, when consul Ignacio Batiza inspected the beet zone in Central Michigan after numerous complaints from workers. He described housing as generally "miserable" and added that workers were regularly cheated of their earnings. Batiza reported "various irregularities" committed by judges and law enforcement officials up to the highest level. He emphasized the need to change public officials' behavior toward Mexicanos, but concluded that without constant vigilance, the consulate could do little to change working conditions or to prevent such abuses.[53]

The lack of contact with outsiders among midwestern *betabeleros* suggests a world much more isolated than that of Mexicano farm workers in Texas, Colorado, Arizona, and California. It meant that their families were the organizational focus of working and nonworking life. Because of the isolation, language retention was not an issue, as it was in midwestern cities. One investigator calculated in 1926 that only 2 percent of *betabeleros* in the region were fluent in English. Being separated from the public school system, even children lacked frequent contact with the English-speaking world. Nonetheless, there were some exceptions. Families occasionally went to nearby towns at the end of the season, usually to purchase food, clothing, and other items to take back to their winter homes in Texas or the Midwest. They also planned social gatherings in which several families living near each other met on Sundays to sing, dance, play music, share meals, and in general relax from their demanding week. These experiences often became the basis of close friendships and ties of *compadrazgo* (godparenthood) that lasted a lifetime.[54]

There were rare special functions in the 1920s that transcended the seclusion of the fields. The 1925 celebration of Mexican independence, the 16 de septiembre (September 16), in the town of Shepherd, Michigan, was among the most memorable. It was arranged by Francisco Vásquez, a former *betabelero* who had settled in nearby Mount Pleasant. The three-day celebration, held during the break between beet hoeing and topping, attracted an estimated two thousand people from several counties. It included speeches, dancing, and music provided by a Mexican orchestra from Detroit. The Mexican consul from Detroit managed to find the means to attend this gala event. Isabella County sheriffs, unwittingly challenging stereotypes, reported a polite and well-behaved crowd with no rowdy or drunken behavior.[55]

The isolation, social relations of work, and controls imposed on workers suggest that the world of the beet worker had several features in common with the barrio, the ghetto, and the American Indian reservation. Furthermore, the reality of this world of *betabeleros* has the general characteristics of an internal colony. Workers, nonetheless, perceived several advantages to working in the North. First, they agreed that wages were higher in the North than in Texas or Mexico. Second, discrimination against Mexicanos was not institutionalized, as in the farm counties of South Texas and other locations. Many farmers were fair and just and thought Mexicanos merited the same treatment as U. S. citizens. Economist Paul Taylor concurred that discrimination against Mexicanos in the Midwest was less sharp and that friction with outsiders was less intense than in Texas and other parts of the Southwest. Additionally, many Mexicanos found working conditions in the North less exploitative. Ignacio Vallarta, who spent many years as a *betabelero*, recalled that in the South Texas spinach fields, "they [growers] treated us like slaves." Finally, beet workers did not expect to remain in the fields permanently. Most of them saw the work as an opportunity to reach the North and at the end of the season to head for the big cities.[56]

Automobiles and the End of a Cycle

By the 1920s the Detroit automobile industry achieved a break-through in production techniques that enabled it to produce and sell cars cheaply enough to be purchased by industrial workers. The expanded used car market made it possible for even poorly paid unskilled workers to acquire vehicles. Thousands of Mexicanos migrated to the North and worked in the beet fields precisely to purchase a Detroit-made automobile. Used car dealers flocked to the beet fields. One observer noted, "Increasingly it is found that the Mexican is the man who finally drives an automobile to the junk heap." The sugar beet companies, responsible for the welfare of the workers, expressed concern that they spent so much of their earnings on cars and that salespeople frequently overcharged them.[57]

Yet the *betabeleros* had performed some reasoned calculation. They knew that the price of a used car in the Midwest, much lower than in Texas, often was not much greater than return train tickets for the family. The car also allowed returning migrants to purchase merchandise produced in the North and transport it home. Many did not plan to keep the vehicles, but would purchase them, drive south, and sell them at a profit. Or, like thousands of others in later generations, they traveled to Michigan, bought a car for less than they could anywhere else, and took it back home.[58]

Automobiles also allowed workers more freedom. Those who stayed in the beet region could drive to stores in nearby towns and cities to purchase goods at more competitive prices and free themselves from the credit mechanism of the country store. They could also drive to other farms to seek work if they found none nearby. When they encountered abusive farmers and *revisadores*, they were better able to pack up their belongings and leave. They could also travel to nearby cities to seek higher-paying jobs in the factories, where they faced fewer of the controls that oppressed them on the farm.

Their memories of the work were not pleasant. George Galvín, who eventually settled in Saint Paul, Minnesota, recalled that "the trouble was that every year in the spring, we went out and worked beets. . . . it was a backbreaking job." Manuel Contreras complained, "I think my bones are still healing from the work." Another former Minnesota *betabelero* recalls, "It is terrible. Now that I remember, I get the chills." They left the fields as soon as they deemed it possible.[59]

Those who left often returned to Texas with the assistance of beet company officials, acting in response to pressures from local residents and politicians, who arranged discount fares to return south. Some went to San Antonio, Dallas, and Houston, seeking temporary employment to survive the winter. Still others went to South Texas, particularly to the Winter Garden district, to find harvest work in spinach, asparagus, onions, and other crops. Many worked in Texas in late fall and winter and returned to the beet fields the following spring. They became the first important group to work the midcontinental migrant worker stream. Those who performed satisfactorily received service cards that virtually guaranteed beet work and letters from companies with information on wages and instructions on reporting for work the following season. Despite the seasonal nature of the work, some families saved enough money to purchase homes in South Texas at prices much lower than those available in the North. Yet those who returned south were only a minority. One study calculated that in 1926 only about one-third of the *betabeleros* from the Upper Midwest went south after the season ended.[60]

Midwestern cities offered a second alternative, and investigator Robert McLean observed that "every city located in or near a beet area can be counted upon to develop a Mexican colony." In the cities Mexicanos hoped to find steadier factory employment with higher pay, the chance to support the entire family on adult male wages, and an opportunity for children to attend school regularly. Wages in Michigan cities where *betabeleros* settled—Saginaw, Pontiac, Flint, and Detroit—compared favorably with the average income of roughly $2.70 per working day in the beet fields. Ford Motor Company paid $6.00 a day; Briggs Manufacturing Company, $3.50 to $4.00; the railroad yards, $4.00; and street work, $3.50 to $4.00.[61]

Former *betabeleros* found similar opportunities in other sugar beet-producing states. In Ohio they chose Lorain, Youngstown, and Toledo, the most important settlement in the state. Large numbers settled in the Chicago and Calumet regions of Illinois and Indiana, but represented a lower proportion of the total Mexicano population than in other urban areas of the Upper Midwest. In the Chicago-Calumet district the most visible concentration of former *betabeleros* was the major port-of-entry, Chicago's Hull House district. Milwaukee had a visible Mexicano district, the only important one in Wisconsin. There were also concentrations of Mexicanos who spent their winters in Des Moines and the Twin Cities, where there were Mexican neighborhoods in the Riverview district of Saint Paul and around 6th Avenue and 5th Street in north Minneapolis.[62]

The beet companies often encouraged workers to settle in nearby cities, hoping that they would return to the fields the next summer. There was continuous movement between the cities and the sugar beet fields. Javier Tovar, who lived in Detroit, observed that many workers found some employment in the cities, but in the spring, "in despair [they] would go to the beet fields from here." Others preferred to struggle in the cities rather than return. An unemployed Chicago worker looking for a job complained, "I think the beet fields are too hard on a man and I do not want to break my back." The midwestern cities became the major destination of beet workers at the end of the season and an important source of recruitment the following spring.[63]

A third alternative for *betabeleros* at the end of the season was to settle in nearby rural locations. They found dwellings scattered throughout the countryside or clustered in small towns, often near the sugar refineries. Encouraged by the *revisadores'* promises of work the following season, a few of them rented houses in the country and fewer still managed to purchase them. They remained a visible but very small part of the rural communities in Northeastern Indiana, Central Michigan, Southern Minnesota, Northern Iowa, and the Red River Valley. Many who remained in small towns stayed in housing provided by the beet companies, a phenomenon more common in Minnesota, Iowa, and North Dakota than farther east. The American Crystal Sugar Company in Minnesota built an apartment-style workers' colony in Chaska, a string of cottages at the edge of town in Albert Lea, and several units of apartments in Mason City, Iowa, which were affectionately dubbed "Laredo" by the workers. The company also had an apartment complex for workers in East Grand Forks, Minnesota, where they stayed during the winter.[64]

Unlike their European predecessors in the beetfields, however, relatively few Mexicanos remained in rural areas, and fewer still rented or purchased farms. They usually rented small, inadequate houses or company housing. American Crystal hoped to establish a resident population of beet workers in its midwestern territory as it had in the Great Plains and Rocky Mountain districts. The companies encouraged Europeans to settle and become farmers, but they tried to convince the Mexicanos to settle nearby or in the cities and remain field-workers.[65]

Conclusion

The sugar beet corporations had a greater influence than any other industry on the initial entry and continued presence of Mexicanos in the Midwest. After Europeans left the fields, the industry committed itself to employing a work force of Mexican descent by recruiting from Texas and the Mexican border.

Unlike their European predecessors, Mexicanos had few opportunities to rise above common labor, and as a group they remained farmworkers, the core of an agricultural proletariat that would expand in later years. During the early twentieth century the corporations responsible for their proletarianization created a mechanism of labor relations that appeared increasingly "backward." They created a highly paternalistic system using the *revisador* as a go-between and allowed nonwage inducements that tied workers to the fields. Furthermore, they fostered an ideology, in conjunction with academia, that Mexicanos rather than Euro-Americans were destined to perform stoop labor because of inherent cultural traits that resulted from the way they resolved the work process.

The midwestern Mexicano presence in the early twentieth century was both an urban and a rural phenomenon and thus parallels the early twentieth century southwestern experience. The story of the Midwest is one of labor migration created by corporation recruitment. Another similarity with the Southwest is that Mexicano farmworkers functioned as family units. Employers hired families for agriculture because protective child labor laws did not apply as they did in industry. In both locations Mexicano farmworkers formed essentially a new class segment integrated into the industrial capitalist economy but largely excluded from mainstream culture.

There were also many ways in which Mexicano life in the Midwest contrasted with that in the Southwest. First, there was no significant Mexicano presence in the Midwest prior to World War I. Those who came to work in the northern states had to forge a cultural presence largely in a vacuum. During the 1920s they succeeded to a certain extent in the cities, but the organization of work and daily life in the countryside made contacts beyond the family more difficult. The midwestern cities and the beet fields formed a symbiotic relationship that enabled workers to survive and to develop a fragile social and cultural presence.

Second, the Mexicano experience in the Midwest was much less diverse than in the Southwest. Mexicanos in Texas, New Mexico, and California had a long history and a great variety of working experiences and social relations with non-Mexicanos. The workers who came to the Midwest were mostly foreign immigrants and their young children and were hired by corporations to perform unskilled labor, both in cities and on farms.

A third difference between the two regions was that there were generally weaker barriers to participation in social and institutional life in the Midwest for Mexicano immigrants after they settled. Because of the greater diversity of the European-descent population and their prior struggles for acceptance, public officials and local citizens in the cities were less hostile to Mexicano workers than they were in the Southwest. In South Texas, as David Montejano notes, former midwestern farmers successfully pushed for laws that barred farmworkers from participating in mainstream civic affairs and precluded them from enjoying many of the rights of citizens.[66] In the Midwest, the farmers' attitudes were not necessarily more enlightened, but they were less able to push for such laws. Furthermore, most Mexicanos who settled in the Midwest wound up in the medium-sized and large cities. They were not segregated in residence and their children attended public schools alongside the students of European descent.

The importance of the sugar beet industry to the Mexicano presence in the Midwest can be illustrated further by comparison with their compatriots farther east. Thousands of workers from the Mexican border were recruited to work in factories and railroads in New York, Pennsylvania, and West Virginia after World War I. A number of large *colonias* appeared in many parts of the region during the 1920s. Those eastern settlements declined and disappeared by the early years of the Great Depression. The urban industrial base alone would not sustain them. In the Midwest, the beet fields offered them employment during hard times in the cities.

CHAPTER 3

Crisis and Resistance, 1929–1938

The Great Depression that ravaged the United States beginning in 1929 affected midwestern industry and its workers profoundly. The decline of production in urban industries threatened many recently settled former *betabeleros* and other Mexicanos. Those who lost their jobs became targets of coordinated local drives to remove them from the country. The effect of the crisis in agriculture was more complicated, for although it jarred production in some crops, it provided an opportunity for others. In both urban and rural settings, employers used the crisis to try to increase their control over workers, who met them with various types of resistance.

Economy and Repatriation

During the late 1920s and the early 1930s nativist pressures in the Southwest and the Midwest, from the press, organized labor, and government service agencies called for the removal of Mexicanos from the country. Intellectuals provided a justification for these actions. Indiana educator and lawyer Oswald Meyer, for example, asserted that Mexicanos were an "unassimilable mass" and a "political and social problem of the utmost gravity to our country." Academics identifying themselves as "Learned Americans," including C. C.

Little, president of the University of Michigan, and Edward A. Ross, William H. Kiekhofer, and John R. Commons of the University of Wisconsin, also expressed reservations about the Mexicano presence. They asserted on supposedly scientific grounds that Mexicans threatened the homogeneity of the population of the United States and its "civilization." [1]

In 1930 and 1931 private and public employers in the Midwest, responding to the pressure, engaged in mass layoffs that often singled out Mexicanos. Unemployment generally ranged from 20 percent to 33 percent of the working population, whereas among urban Mexicanos it commonly reached 80 and 90 percent. For the first time Mexicanos became a burden on urban relief coffers.

In several midwestern cities federal immigration officials, state and city authorities, and local police departments resolved to lower welfare costs by removing Mexicanos from their midst. They also tried to enlist the cooperation of Mexican consuls by convincing them that repatriation was preferable to unemployment in the United States. They offered to pay transportation costs to the border and to convince Mexico to cover the remainder of the journey to the interior. Typically, the Bureau of Immigration attempted to use "friendly persuasion" to encourage Mexicanos to leave. By 1931 the pressure increased, with well-publicized roundups to locate those who were deportable. Immigration and welfare officials hoped that these efforts would convince others to leave voluntarily. [2]

The best-organized repatriation effort in the region took place in Detroit and involved famed Mexican artist Diego Rivera. Rivera spent much of 1932 and 1933 painting his famous mural "Man and Machine," at the Detroit Institute of Arts. While in Detroit, Rivera created an organization called the *Liga de Obreros y Campesinos*, (Workers and Peasants League), composed of industrial workers, many of whom were former *betabeleros*. He created the League to educate workers and to assist in the repatriation of thousands of them from the Midwest to colonization projects in Mexico. Although the League sought to attract workers from cities and rural areas throughout Michigan and Ohio, it was ineffective beyond Detroit. While it had the cooperation of U. S. and Mexican federal, state, and local officials, its efforts to remove unemployed Mexican workers were much less successful than bureaucrats had expected, even in Detroit. Other formal repatriation efforts took place in Indiana, Illinois, and Minnesota. As in other parts of the country, repatriation programs typically involved coordinating the efforts of local public and sometimes private officials with the Bureau of Immigration, but had only limited effect. Most repatriation from the Midwest was the result of uncoordinated or informal efforts involving mostly urban Mexicanos.[3]

Repatriation did not threaten *betabeleros*, who were protected by the sugar beet industry. By continuing to hire Mexicanos the companies were able to reduce wages so sharply that the work was not attractive even to unemployed Euro-Americans. Between 1930 and 1934 field wages fell by 60 percent, from twenty-three dollars to thirteen dollars per acre. Acreage allotments also declined. These conditions were consistent with a general deterioration of agricultural wages throughout the country to 29 percent of urban wages by 1934, compared with 47 percent ten years earlier. During the nadir of the depression, one sugar industry official pleaded, "God help the sugar industry in Michigan if the Mexican is kept out of the state."[4]

During the depression *betabeleros* commonly worked in the fields in the spring and returned to the cities in the winter to take advantage of less-restrictive welfare policies and greater employment opportunities. Those who worked in Michigan and Ohio wintered most often in Saginaw and Detroit, whereas those in Minnesota, Iowa, and North Dakota commonly chose Saint Paul. Officials in the cities were more sympathetic than county officials, yet adopted an explicit policy of removing Mexicanos from the welfare rolls in the spring to ensure that they would return to the beet fields.[5]

The impact of urban unemployment and smaller field allotments reduced the proportional Mexicano dominance as *betabeleros* during the early years of the depression. Urban Europeans and Mexicanos returned to the fields to reclaim jobs they had abandoned earlier. Between 1929 and 1932 in the American Crystal zone of Iowa, North Dakota, and Minnesota, the proportion of Mexicano workers fell from 80 to 90 percent to slightly more than 50 percent. In the Michigan and Ohio region the variation was greater, as their numbers declined to about 60 percent in Central Michigan, and roughly 25 percent in Southern Michigan and Ohio.[6]

Mexicanos who could not find employment in the cities and were unwilling to repatriate when pressured found opportunity in the beet fields. The companies, intent on maintaining a large surplus population to keep wages down, encouraged them to stay. In 1932 the director of the Michigan State Welfare Department observed that enough Euro-Americans would work in the beet fields if they were paid what he considered "a living wage." Nonetheless, the industry preferred Mexicanos to that more costly alternative. Welfare policies also influenced work patterns. Public assistance offered a level of subsistence roughly equivalent to, but steadier than, wages in the beet fields. Urban Mexicanos were cut from the welfare rolls in the spring, while in rural areas and small towns they were denied welfare outright. On the other hand, Europeans and United States–born citizens in many locations were cut from the rolls if they accepted temporary employment in the sugar beet fields.[7]

The number of beet workers rose sharply in the early years of the depression. Company acreage allotment policies increased the total number of field-workers by 30 to 40 percent. Furthermore, the companies pressured the federal government to raise tariffs on foreign sugar and increase their share of the national market. Acreage allotments in the early 1930s rose by 30 to 40 percent. According to a 1933 estimate, the Mexican beet worker population totaled fifty-five thousand, a third more than in the late 1920s.[8]

Reorganization and Expansion of Production

The depression had an uneven effect on different agricultural enterprises. The sugar beet industry initially went into turmoil and the companies turned to the federal government for help. In 1930 they convinced President Herbert Hoover to issue a special directive raising the duty on foreign sugar and guaranteeing a quota for local factory districts. They led legislative efforts on behalf of the Jones-Costigan Act of 1934, which amended the Agricultural Adjustment Act and granted sugar beet growers direct crop subsidies.[9]

The industry also reorganized. In Minnesota, Iowa, and North Dakota, the American Beet Sugar Company became American Crystal in 1935. The industry in Michigan and Ohio experienced a more complicated reorganization. All factories in Michigan except those of the Michigan Sugar Company went into receivership between 1931 and 1934. The Monitor Sugar Company, formerly Columbia, appeared in 1932, and the Lake Shore Sugar Company, previously Holland–Saint Louis, began in 1933. Continental Sugar of Michigan and Ohio reincorporated in 1934 as the Great Lakes Sugar Company.[10]

The corporations also altered their relations with growers. In 1932 sugar beet corporations in Michigan, Ohio, and Indiana organized beet growers' associations for each of their factory districts. Designated grower and corporate representatives served on the Farmers and Manufacturers Beet Sugar Association (FMBSA), an umbrella organization representing sugar beet interests. One FMBSA goal was to resolve long-standing grower and corporation conflicts. Another was to enhance the industry's political clout. The FMBSA also encouraged and supported research at Michigan Agricultural College (later Michigan State University), whose Agricultural Extension Service experts helped formulate technical innovations, including blocking and planting machines. On the advice of researchers the FMBSA popularized the so-called fifty-fifty contract between company and grower. The plan shifted part of the risk of unprofitable seasons to the farmers by sharing the "net proceeds" equally. In earlier years the companies had guaranteed prices to farmers.[11]

The growers' associations took over responsibility for field-worker relations in principle while the companies maintained control in fact. The associations ensured that the interests of the companies came first, those of the farmers, second, while the field-workers, who had no voice, continued to come out last. The clearest indicator of the new arrangements was that wages fell from approximately 30 percent of farmers' receipts in 1930 to only 23 percent by 1934.[12]

Like the sugar beet industry, the midwestern onion industry had an erratic history during the early 1930s. The heart of onion production in the region before the depression was the Scioto Marsh in North-Central Ohio. The rich marsh in its natural state had muck (decomposed organic matter) averaging five to ten feet thick. Sporadic draining of the marsh began in the late nineteenth century and accelerated in the 1910s. By the early 1920s more than five thousand acres of marshland were devoted to onion production. The largest single tract belonged to the Scioto Land Company, owned by W. C. McGuffey. He and a handful of growers, including John B. Stambaugh, Veril Baldwin, and Carl Krummery, owned two-thirds of the Scioto Marsh.[13]

In the first decade of the twentieth century a handful of workers drifted into the region from the isolated hill country region of Southeastern Kentucky, particularly from Floyd and Magoffin counties. In the 1910s and 1920s, as production soared, growers and their agents recruited and transported workers from Kentucky to the onion fields. They hired smaller numbers of people from nearby West Virginia to complement the local work force. Workers and their families entered the region in April or early May and usually stayed until October, planting, weeding, and topping onions. They resided in makeshift cabins made of plywood, tin, and other scrap materials. One group worked on sharecrop arrangements, with an average family responsible for three to five acres for the season. A second group was paid by the hour, a less-stable arrangement used by employers to supplement the work of sharecroppers.[14]

With the onset of the depression, former Kentuckians and West Virginians increasingly began to settle in the marsh area permanently. They stayed in the shacks on the marshlands or moved into the tiny nearby communities of McGuffey, Alger, and Ada. Many had lost their land in the hill country and had little reason to return. By the early 1930s between four hundred and five hundred families settled on the marsh itself. In the onions they also faced deteriorating work conditions. Poor cultivation practices and overdrainage in earlier years had caused the muckland to dry, and in the early 1930s winds blew away much of the rich topsoil. As a result of the oversupply of labor, wages fell from approximately fifteen cents per hour in 1932 to between five and twelve cents in 1934.[15]

The commercial production of fruit also became an important source of employment for seasonal workers in the Great Lakes region. Production concentrated along the Lake Michigan coast of Western Michigan. Smaller growing areas appeared on the Lake Erie islands and the coast of Northwestern Ohio, and on the Door Peninsula between Sturgeon Bay and Lake Michigan in Northeastern Wisconsin. Prior to the depression the fruit industry had relied almost entirely on local labor. In the late 1920s and 1930s production expanded rapidly, stimulated by low land prices, rising urban demand, and a mild climate moderated by the Great Lakes. Much of the region was cutover forest that first came into cultivation only after the turn of the century, when independent small farmers initially purchased lands. During the depression the midwestern industry benefited from a successful advertising campaign that increased the sales and consumption of commercial fruits and vegetables and put the Midwest in a competitive position compared with many other fruit-producing locations. It also enjoyed cheap labor.[16]

Strawberries were the first of several commercial fruit crops in the region that eventually attracted thousands of migrant workers, mostly single Euro-American men, for the annual harvest. In the early twentieth century most strawberry cultivation in the region still took place on small truck farms located near urban markets, mostly in Louisiana, Arkansas, and Missouri. During the 1920s, particularly in good years, strawberry harvesters, largely single Euro-American men whom local observers almost invariably identified as hoboes migrated northward in the spring as the fruit ripened and occasionally reached Michigan.[17]

By the early 1930s strawberry production had expanded rapidly in Western Michigan, and employers had to begin more systematic recruitment of workers. In 1931 Berrien County growers formed the Benton Harbor-Covert Relief Expedition, a heavily advertised campaign that sent several truckloads of food and clothing to starving workers in Phillips County, Arkansas. The next year they sent trucks to recruit and transport several hundred workers from Arkansas to Berrien County to pick fruit. Their efforts stimulated the expansion of the earlier, sporadic migrant stream. By the middle of the decade thousands of people, both single men and entire families, most of whom were Euro-American, migrated north with the strawberry harvest. They began in Louisiana and Arkansas in April and moved to Missouri in early May. They entered Southern Illinois around Vermillion and Farina and Southern Indiana near Borden in the middle of May and reached Southwestern Michigan by early June.[18]

In the 1930s Western Michigan also became an important location of seasonal work in the so-called stretch crops, the result of a flurry of tree plantings during the 1920s. Cherries were the most important of the tree fruits grown in the region, which included peaches, plums, pears, and apples. The heart of cherry production was in the Grand Traverse Bay region and neighboring counties in Northwestern Michigan. Traverse City quickly proclaimed itself the country's cherry capital. Two smaller zones of production in the region also appeared: Door County on the western shore of Lake Michigan in Wisconsin, and the islands and the northwestern Ohio shore of Lake Erie. The cherry harvest season lasted roughly six weeks during July and August. By the end of the decade an estimated nine thousand to twelve thousand workers had entered Western Michigan to harvest the crop.[19]

During the 1930s blueberry growers also became an important employer of thousands of field-workers. The first midwestern blueberries to enter the market were not grown on commercial farms. As late as 1940 almost three-fourths of Michigan's large crop consisted of wild blueberries harvested from the cutover timberlands of the Upper Peninsula, particularly on the plains of Seney, Cook, and Strong. Most wild blueberries grew on property that the state and the national governments had acquired through tax delinquency.[20]

Blueberry pickers in the Upper Peninsula were not hired or recruited as they were for other commercial crops, but were essentially independent operators. In the early years of the depression families commonly came from other parts of Michigan, particularly Detroit. Later in the 1930s they were joined by migrants from farther south— Ohio, Indiana, Kentucky, and Arkansas. Workers drove their battered cars to the blueberry region to harvest the fruit for a month to six weeks in late summer. They lived in makeshift dwellings, including tarpaper shacks, trailers, and tents, in primitive camps lacking running water or sanitation facilities. One journalist observed, "Lake Superior is the community bathtub." During harvest season squatter communities sprouted up almost overnight. In the mid-1930s Hoar's Head, near Whitefish Point on the shore of Lake Superior, had three thousand temporary residents at its peak. Each day truckers came to the camps, purchased fruit from the pickers, and drove it to midwestern cities. In 1931 twelve million quarts of wild blueberries entered the market, approximately 90 percent of the state's total production.[21]

In the 1930s commercial blueberry plantings increased in Southwestern Michigan. Growers from Berrien, Van Buren, and neighboring counties soon drove the wild blueberries off the market. Keefe's blueberry plantation near Grand Junction, established in the late 1920s, soon became the largest producer of blueberries in the nation, employing several hundred migrant workers every season. With 360 acres Keefe's was one of the few large holdings in the fruit belt.[22]

During the Great Depression, fruit production in Western Michigan increased along the Lake Michigan shoreline. The Benton Harbor Community Fruit Market, formed in 1931, became one of the largest distribution points for fruit in the nation. Fruit growing in the Midwest, as in other parts of the nation, was an intensive activity of small farmers who employed migrants only during the harvest peak. In the 1930s, 63 percent of the fruit orchards in the region were under fifty acres. Local growers preferred to hire Euro-Americans from states to the south. A 1939 study indicated that about 40 percent of the migrants who picked fruit in Western Michigan came from Arkansas, and another 20 percent from Southeastern Missouri. By the end of the decade an estimated fifteen thousand to twenty thousand workers had entered Michigan to work in the fruit crops for the season, more than 80 percent of them Euro-Americans. Many were small farmers and former sharecroppers displaced during the depression. Most of the rest were African Americans from the South. In the late 1930s a small number of Mexicanos from the beet region began to enter the fruit zone, mostly for harvest work in the rapidly expanding cherry industry.[23]

In the 1930s canning crops also expanded in the region. Tomatoes were the first important crop among them, because they lent themselves well to canning and were versatile for cooking. In the 1930s Indiana was the leading grower of canning tomatoes in the nation, with production concentrated in the south-central part of the state around Indianapolis. Agricultural college research perfected a strategy of planting seeds farther south and transporting seedlings to richer soils in more northern locations after the danger of frost ended. Production gradually shifted north and east, eventually concentrating in Northwestern Ohio.[24]

Small local canneries still dominated the tomato industry in the 1930s. During these years of rapid growth canners contracted with local farmers to purchase tomato plantings that averaged one to five acres. The canneries typically operated during and shortly after tomato harvest, from August until November, or slightly longer if they also canned peas and corn. At this time corporations, including Libby, Hunt, and Heinz, operated only a handful of canneries in the Midwest. The rapid growth of multinational corporate canneries in the region dates from the 1940s.[25]

As tomato production expanded, growers and canners recruited field-workers largely from the nearby Kentucky hill country. Later in the decade this group of mostly single males came to Indiana informally, driving old cars, hitching rides, and hopping trains. Sometimes local farmers or canneries provided housing, but usually workers created makeshift camps and slept in tents or in their cars. They usually worked from August until the first frost in October and were paid piece rates. Employers also began to recruit Mexicanos from the sugar beet areas to pick tomatoes in the later years of the decade.[26]

The economic crisis lowered land costs and wages and thus stimulated the rapid expansion of many commercial crops in the Midwest. At the same time governmental reforms threatened to end the availability of cheap labor and make possible farmworker unionization. Organizational activities of factory workers in the 1930s offered an opportunity for the agricultural labor force to join with the urban union movement. The prospects for agricultural unionism in the Midwest during the middle years of the Great Depression were more favorable than at any time in the century.

Organizing in the Fields

Agricultural unionism in the Midwest was stimulated by federal efforts to assist industry, growers, and farmworkers via New Deal legislation in the 1930s. The National Industrial Recovery Act of 1933 granted workers the right to organize, but was soon declared unconstitutional. The Jones-Costigan Act of 1934 empowered the secretary of agriculture to determine minimum wages for beet field labor. The 1935 Wagner-Peyser Act, popularly known as the National Labor Relations Act, confirmed workers' rights to organize with the protection of the federal government. The position of agricultural employees under this legislation remained nebulous until later in the year, when Franklin D. Roosevelt issued the Re-Employment Agreement as an amendment to the National Labor Relations Act. The amendment deprived farmworkers of the constitutional protection of the right to organize granted most other workers. By that time, however, the agricultural worker unionization movement in the Midwest was already in motion.[27]

Between 1930 and 1935 agricultural workers thro   country engaged in a rash of strikes. They were most active in California, where organizing efforts preceded New Deal legislation. The strikes were led by Mexicano unions, leftist organizations, and trade union sympathizers and represented the most intense strike action in agriculture yet in the century. Farmworker organizing efforts did not lag behind those in urban factories. In some cases farmworker efforts preceded and in others coincided with the unionization struggles taking place in mass-production industries in the cities.[28]

One early effort, a Mexicano- and Mexican American–controlled organization called the Beet Workers' Association, reached the Great Lakes region. It began in 1929 in Great Western Sugar Company territories in the Rocky Mountain and Great Plains states. The association planned to organize and educate workers and growers before it initiated massive strikes. Although its greatest activity took place farther west, it established several tenuous locals in beet-growing areas in Minnesota, North Dakota, and Michigan. It collapsed, however, with the onset of the depression.[29]

A more important indigenous organizing effort began in 1934. On June 20 onion workers in the Scioto Marsh of Ohio called a strike. Paul Taylor called it "one of the bitterest and most violent agricultural labor strikes the country had yet experienced." It was initiated by local workers and led by Okey Odell, a poorly educated former industrial- and farmworker from West Virginia who had settled in the nearby town of McGuffey. The strike began as a protest against recent wage cuts from 12.5 cents per hour in 1933 to 6 cents per hour for children and 12 cents for adults in 1934. Workers were angered because the prices growers received for onions rebounded modestly in 1933 and 1934 from their nadir in 1932. On July 5 the workers received a charter for Local 19724 of the Agricultural Workers Union (AWU), the first AWU local in the United States chartered by the AFL. Local 19724 gained important financial support from the Toledo Central Labor Union and many AFL locals in Northern and Central Ohio, and the AFL sent organizer Jacob Rizor to assist the strikers.[30]

A conflict between local and federal officials determined the course of the strike and its eventual outcome. Local authorities, often related to powerful growers and beholden to them for their jobs, were consistently hostile to the strikers. Hardin County sheriff Morton Anselm hired more than fifty inexperienced deputies from among local residents to patrol the fields and "protect" the growers' private property and the strikebreakers from the strikers. County judge Alexander Hoge granted an injunction requested by growers to prevent workers from congregating in groups of more than two and sentenced several strikers to prison for violating the injunction. Hoge issued a second injunction permitting the deputy sheriffs to expel strikers from their rented homes on the Scioto Marsh if they "refused to work," and the deputies, most of them local farmers, eagerly complied.[31]

Federal officials, who were not native to the region, attempted to remain neutral in the conflict. When the strike began, workers applied for assistance to the Federal Employment Relief Administration (FERA). Relief director Allen Ochs determined that the workers were eligible for assistance while on strike. He contended that it was his responsibility to prevent them from starving and admitted that "without relief the strike would have been broken long ago."[32]

As the confrontation intensified and gained national attention, the federal government was pressured to mediate. The USDL sent Robert C. Fox to the strike area as mediator. Fox talked with growers and workers separately but was unable to convince the growers to discuss the workers' demands with them. He reported that growers Veril Baldwin and Carl Krummery vehemently refused to deal with the strikers on the grounds that they were "illiterate and were of bad character . . . not trustworthy, drunkards." As the federal government failed in its mediation efforts, the level of violence escalated.[33]

Following a mysterious bombing of the house of the mayor of nearby McGuffey in late August, the local sheriff called strike leader Odell into his office for questioning. During the conversation a hostile mob gathered outside the sheriff's office. As Odell stepped outside the crowd attacked him while the sheriff watched. Between seventy and eighty people in the party, among them many sheriff's deputies, then kidnapped Odell, tied him up, and took him for a "ride" to the Hardin County line in a truck owned by grower Veril Baldwin. There they again beat Odell, broke four of his ribs, dumped him, and threatened his life if he came back. The undeterred Odell returned on foot to his home in McGuffey. Soon a mob armed with shotguns, rifles, and clubs gathered outside his house. Odell, with rifle in hand, dared them to try to remove him and the crowd backed down.[34]

Local law enforcement authorities continued to influence the course of the strike. A local grand jury refused to indict sixty-seven people positively identified as part of the mob that kidnapped and beat Odell. Meanwhile, a local judge tried and convicted Odell of pointing a weapon at the armed crowd that had gathered outside his house. The court also sentenced him to ninety days in jail and a one hundred dollar fine. Several outside groups quickly entered the fray in support of Odell, including the Socialist party, the Unemployed

League, and the American Civil Liberties Union. Although the strike was waning, in September Socialist party leader Norman Thomas appeared in the McGuffey area to rally the strikers. The support enabled Odell to appeal the initial sentence, though without success.[35]

The onion workers tried to continue their activities in the marsh during the 1935 season while growers devised a strategy to thwart the strike. First, they turned most of their holdings over to tenants on sharecropping arrangements, thereby enabling them to claim that the workers were independent operators and not hired employees. Second, they switched to other crops, including potatoes, corn, and sugar beets. Third, they acquired better lands for onion production in Southern Michigan. They also began draining potential onion-growing areas, including Gun Marsh in Allegan County and the swampy lands around Stockbridge in Ingham County. They also brought mucklands around Grant and Hudsonville in Southwestern Michigan into production. In 1935 W. C. McGuffey acquired extensive properties on Gun Marsh and Veril Baldwin and Carl Krummery purchased large tracts in the Stockbridge area. These Ohio growers also imported Kentucky-born migrants and their families from the Scioto Marsh. As a result of their efforts, onion production in Michigan more than doubled between 1930 and 1940, and Michigan replaced Ohio as the most important onion-growing area in the Midwest.[36]

Although the Scioto Marsh strike failed, midwestern organizing efforts initially led by Odell did not collapse shortly afterward, as Bernard Sternsher incorrectly suggests. In 1935 Odell began organizing onion and beet field workers in other parts of Northwestern Ohio and in Southern Michigan. He appeared at several meetings near the onion fields and throughout the district controlled by the Great Lakes Sugar Company in both states. He emphasized the need to unionize all farmworkers to deal effectively with employers. He asserted that "workers in industry are organized to fight for their rights. Industrialists and capitalists are organized. The farmers themselves are organized. I believe that those who work on the farm should also be united."[37]

In 1935 Odell faced additional pressures in his struggle. He failed in his efforts to clear himself in court and was forced to serve time in the Toledo workhouse, from which he ultimately walked away and disappeared. Odell also had to contend with heightened Red-baiting, which led to an AFL ouster of Local 19724. The AFL defended its action on the dubious grounds that the onion workers' local had "come under communist influence."[38]

The beet worker organizational movement in Northwestern Ohio and Southeastern Michigan continued after Odell's departure, led by Jacob Rizor of the Toledo Central Labor Union. Beet workers in the area were the best candidates among midwestern farmworkers for union organizing. Most were permanent residents with urban work experience. They lived close to Detroit and Toledo, which at the time were the sites of several important struggles centering in the mass-production industries. Many enthusiastic AFL unionists in the area offered additional financial support for their efforts. Local beet workers included Germans from Russia, Belgians, Hungarians, and a large colony of Mexicanos in Blissfield, but ethnic diversity did not prevent the workers from uniting. Mexicanos, a minority of the beet field employees in the area, were enthusiastic union members. Several of them, including Jess Ramírez, Narciso Rodríguez, Aurelio Ruiz, Joe Durán, and Salvador Sánchez, were elected officers in Michigan and Ohio AWU locals. The organizing campaign was encouraged by the increase in industrial employment in 1935, accompanied by a "movement of people from farms to the cities," providing workers greater leverage in negotiations with employers. The Detroit and Chicago Mexican consuls agreed that conditions for Mexicanos were improving, stimulated by more available employment in the beet fields.[39]

The first and most important unionization effort among beet workers occurred in the Blissfield area, just north of the Ohio border. About seven hundred workers formed AWU Local 19994 in 1935. In May the workers struck against a recently announced Great Lakes Sugar sliding wage scale that paid $15.60 per acre based on average yields. They demanded a flat rate of $23 per acre, company recognition of the union as bargaining agent, and a closed-fields provision prohibiting the company from hiring non-union members. Strike organizers claimed that 98 percent of the workers in the district stayed out of the fields in support.[40]

The growers' association was dismayed at the success of the walk-out and turned to the USDL conciliators to contain the workers' demands. One grower representative, sugar beet expert C. P. Milham of Michigan Agricultural College, called in a conciliator. Milham assured local growers that the conciliator would accept rates offered by the company, because they were the rates established in other districts. "I feel certain that the mediator will not permit any higher prices for labor in this area." Milham erred, as mediator J. E. O'Connor recommended a compromise of $19 per acre for cultivation and harvesting tasks. Both Local 19994 and the Blissfield Growers Association accepted the rates suggested by O'Connor and agreed to larger acreages for union members. Allotments per worker in the district rose from 6.8 acres in 1934 to 12.6 in 1935, the highest in the Midwest. The contracts further prohibited outside labor recruitment when local union workers were available. Last, the contracts prohibited discrimination "by the fieldmen or the growers as to color or creed." These last two stipulations implicitly referred to workers of Mexican descent from Texas who the union feared would be imported to break the union, and to discrimination against Mexicanos already settled in the Blissfield area who had long suffered abuses at the hand of representatives and farmers.[41]

The Blissfield victory inspired beet workers in other districts. Findlay-area workers quickly organized AWU Local 20007, with nine hundred members. After the growers refused to negotiate for provisions identical to those in the Blissfield contract, Local 20007 called for a "beet workers' vacation," and 97 percent of the workers joined in support. Growers still refused to respond, so the local requested a federal mediator, and the USDL sent in R. T. Fox. In contrast to O'Connor in Blissfield, Fox suggested a less-favorable compromise, specifically, that workers who had already signed contracts abide by them while others should negotiate arrangements based on the Blissfield union contract. He did not accept the union's request for a closed-fields agreement. Considering the late start of the strike, the local could still consider it a partial victory.[42]

In 1936 midwestern beet workers continued to expand their organizational efforts. They formed AWU locals in Fremont, Ohio, and Saint Louis, Michigan, and unchartered locals in Ottawa, Ohio, and Alma, Michigan. This represented union penetration into territory controlled by the Michigan and Monitor Sugar companies in Central Michigan. Meanwhile the locals at Findlay and Blissfield maintained their still-precarious footholds and negotiated contracts with growers.[43]

In late 1935 and 1936 two important outside decisions placed agricultural union organizers on the defensive. First, because the National Labor Relations Act of 1935 did not apply to farmworkers, federal sympathizers were less supportive than earlier. Second, by 1936 the AFL curtailed most of its financial support to the small, weak, and unprofitable agricultural worker unions in the Midwest. This business-oriented AFL strategy forced AWU locals to look beyond the union movement to survive.[44]

In 1937 the Sugar Act appeared, ostensibly written to assist grower and worker alike. The act prohibited government benefit payments to growers who hired children under age fourteen. One sugar beet expert calculated that annual benefit payments in 1939 were $365 for the average Michigan farmer's 8.8 acres of sugar beets, more than double the cost of field labor. The act also set up a system of regional public hearings to allow representatives of corporations, growers, and workers opportunities to provide evidence on wage and working conditions in each locality. The USDL used this evidence to determine minimum wages.[45]

The first sugar beet wage hearings under the act were held in the winter and early spring of 1937 and 1938. Almost all the witnesses represented corporations and grower associations. Among the few exceptions were Albert Markva and Salvador Sánchez, representatives of AWU Local 19724, who expressed hope that the companies would negotiate a contract in good faith before the season began. In Saint Paul, Minnesota, Mexicanos Herman Rosenthal of the CIO, Jacinto Rodríguez, and Ezekiel Marino of the AFL spoke on behalf of the local workers. The union representatives documented grower abuses such as underpayment and undercounting acreage, which technically disqualified growers from benefit payments authorized by the 1937 Sugar Act. They also detailed the American Crystal practice of firing and blacklisting union sympathizers. Beyond their appearance at the hearings, the AFL and CIO did not make a concerted effort to organize the field laborers of Minnesota, Iowa, and North Dakota. At the Milwaukee hearings no workers' representatives spoke, and at Saginaw, there was only one. That worker, according to USDL official Stanley White, "disputed several company charges that outside work was available or housing conditions [were] adequate." White also reported that the company-grower representatives in Saginaw met before the hearings and set uniform rates for the district, adding that "the techniques of figuring out the amount to go to the worker was something they could not explain."[46]

The few workers who spoke at these hearings consistently complained of widespread abuses and the need for unions as the only protection for workers' interests and the only means of assuring compliance with the law. Yet neither White nor other government representatives challenged the hearings mechanism as inadequate. The hearings did not fulfill the Sugar Act's expressed intent of allowing growers, corporations, and workers to provide information for the USDL on which to base its wage recommendations. Despite the failure of the hearings in their first year, the USDL used an identical format for the next thirty years to determine wage rates. As in the first year the companies continued to set "prevailing" rates in closed meetings before the hearings began and the USDL accepted their recommendations without question. The system thus lessened the opportunities for future worker organization.

In the spring of 1938 the sugar beet corporations took the offensive, waging a concerted effort to break beet workers' unions throughout the nation. In the Midwest they focused particularly on the strongest link, Local 19724 of Blissfield. First, they created organizations ostensibly composed of corporation and grower representatives to deal with labor. The Michigan Sugar Company established the Beet Growers' Employment Committee (BGEC), and the Great Lakes and Lake Shore Sugar companies formed the Great Lakes Growers Employment Committee (GLGEC). The committees' stated purpose was "the rendering of service and assistance to the sugar beet growers in connection with the obtaining and employment by them of field labor and in general, to do any and all things necessary, advisable and expedient to assist beet growers in the employment of field workers."[47]

The companies automatically deducted fees from each grower, for whom committee membership was mandatory. Corporation officials who also served as officers of the employment committees determined labor policies. P. G. Beck of the Farm Security Administration (FSA) explained the purpose of these organizations succinctly: "The sugar beet companies do not want to be implicated in the hiring of labor."[48]

A second element in corporate strategy was to provoke the union by reducing wages and withdrawing union recognition. Through its Employment Committee, Great Lakes reduced wages in 1938 from nineteen dollars to eighteen dollars per acre and refused to recognize the closed-fields agreement. The company claimed that the lower rate was based on the minimum determined at the recent sugar beet hearings. The union demanded either twenty-three dollars per acre plus one dollar per ton over ten tons or eighteen dollars per acre and half the benefits the Sugar Act paid to growers, plus the closed-fields provision.[49]

Finally, the company offensive recruited strikebreakers from Texas. During the nadir of the depression, between 1930 and 1934, there was little outside recruitment of beet field workers into the Midwest. The companies recruited several hundred Mexican-descent workers from out of state in 1935, when the beet worker union movement began. That year the press and several local politicians expressed outrage at the corporations' importing workers when unemployment was so high and at their providing such miserable transportation. Opposition in the Midwest to importing outside workers did not reach the intensity it did in California and Colorado, where dramatic, highly publicized blockades were set up to prevent the entry of out-of-state migrants. Nevertheless, the corporations recruited modest numbers of nonunion, nonresident migrants from Texas again in 1936 and 1937.[50]

In 1938 the corporations, claiming a shortage of workers, used their newly formed committees to initiate massive recruitment of Tejano (Texas-born) *betabeleros* to Michigan and Ohio. Available evidence contradicts corporation claims of increased labor shortages that year. According to USDA statistics for Michigan, the agricultural supply/labor demand ratio in April 1937 was 79/100; in April 1938 it rose to 126/100. The companies also renewed the familiar chant that "native labor can not compete with Mexican labor in the beet fields." They brought more than five thousand Tejanos to the Michigan and Ohio fields in 1938 to ensure an available force after they provoked the union to go on strike. Several company officials admitted that they were recruiting Tejanos to break the union.[51]

The Blissfield workers struck in late May. Nine hundred union members left the fields and an outside reporter observed that "work is completely at a standstill." Meanwhile, antiunion elements around Blissfield and Adrian formed the Lenawee Protective League, a vigilante group. Led by members of the American Legion and composed largely of farmers who grew beets, it was inspired by the Associated Farmers (AF) of California, an organization criticized by many for its fascist features and created to prevent farmworker unrest in that state. In early 1938 AF representatives visited many parts of the Midwest to help growers organize against farmworker unionization. As part of the grower effort in Southern Michigan, Blissfield sheriff Fred Seager deputized four hundred Lenawee Protective League members to assist him in patrolling the beet area to prevent union members from keeping "willing" workers from entering the fields. A league representative commented, "The whole idea is to avoid trouble with a showing of force."[52]

In June USDL mediator Robert Pilkington visited the area at the request of Local 19724 in an attempt to mediate the dispute. Shortly after arriving he wrote, "Sugar companies are in collusion with the growers of southern Michigan and Ohio and attempting to destroy the AFL union by using the minimum wage determination of the Secretary of Labor as justification to deny collective bargaining rights to workers."[53]

After Pilkington discussed the strike with corporate representatives, growers, and strikers, he suggested a compromise. Local 19724 president Samuel Isard quickly agreed to the compromise; corporate and grower representatives refused, claiming that the Sugar Beet Wage Hearings set wages. Pilkington, apparently intimidated by the vigilantes, then suggested a second "compromise," identical to the growers' original offer of eighteen dollars per ton for the seven-ton minimum, no union recognition or closed fields. The determination was a defeat for the strikers, for it removed the weak federal support that had made agricultural unionism possible in the region for three years. After the strike the AFL withdrew its remaining assistance and Local 19724 collapsed.[54]

Meanwhile, several hundred beet workers, angered that the AFL had backed down so quickly, turned to the recently formed United Cannery and Packing Workers of America (UCAPAWA) of the Congress of Industrial Organizations (CIO). They received a charter for Local 279 and threatened a strike in the fall if the growers refused to negotiate. Like AWU leaders in the spring, CIO leaders requested a negotiator, and the USDL sent Stanley V. White. White discussed the situation with both sides separately, but could not convince the employers to negotiate. Company representatives justified their actions by asserting that the union did not have worker support, the workers had already signed contracts in the spring, and there was already an agreement with the AFL. White reported that all of these claims were false. He also asserted that the company, not the GLGEC, was responsible for recruitment, transportation, and wages, and that the formation of the GLGEC was a pretext to break the union. Yet he urged the CIO not to strike. CIO leader Donald Henderson heeded his advice, placating the workers with a philosophical statement that such a strike would "hold up the education of the farmer and confirm him in his detestation of the CIO." In fact, there were no future chances to educate farmers, because Local 279 in effect collapsed as the workers abandoned it for its refusal to support a strike. A few sympathizers remained in the area in 1939 and 1940, but the surrender by CIO leader Henderson in 1938 ended concerted organizing drives in the midwestern beet fields for a generation.[55]

Conclusion

The Great Depression created a crisis in both urban and agricultural industry in the Midwest. Production in the cities declined sharply, while in agriculture the effects varied greatly. The sugar beet industry was in turmoil in the early 1930s but quickly reorganized and recovered. In many other agricultural activities the depression encouraged expansion due to low land prices, growing consumer demand, and cheap labor. The effects on workers were uneven. In the cities they generally faced sharply declining employment and wages. Urban Mexicanos, often former beet workers, were singled out among foreign workers, fired by employers, and subjected to repatriation pressures. Most resisted, refusing to heed the admonitions of public and private officials, and returned to the beet fields to work.

During the 1930s changes in agricultural production altered the organization of the industry and relations with the field-workers it employed. The sugar beet industry developed new arrangements involving the corporations, growers, and field-workers. Through the growers' associations it created, the industry sidestepped the possible legal implications of recruiting workers for strikebreaking and other purposes.

The federal government might have altered the power relations between workers and their employers. The Jones-Costigan Act and its successor, the Sugar Act, were written to assist processor, grower, and worker alike. Although few observers deny that the legislation helped the first two groups, the suggestion that it proved "slightly beneficial" to the workers has only a shaky foundation.[56] The government simply ignored its responsibility to balance power relations between the contending parties while it maintained a façade of impartiality in the wage hearings.

The expansion of commercial agriculture in the Midwest during the 1930s led to the articulation of two distinct branches of the migrant worker stream from the South. The first consisted of people of Mexican descent who came from Texas to the sugar beet fields. Unlike the Mexicanos of the 1920s, the Tejanos were largely U.S. citizens, children of immigrants who settled in Texas during the early years of the century. The second branch of the stream was composed of people originating mostly in Arkansas and Missouri, with smaller numbers from neighboring states. Most were Euro-Americans, but a small portion were African Americans. Many of them were former small farm owners and sharecoppers who had lost their farms and migrated during the early years of the depression. They worked primarily in the fruit crops, beginning with the strawberry harvest, which reached Michigan by late May or early June, continuing with bush and tree fruits in the summer, and ending with tomatoes in the late summer and fall.

The reorganization of the midwestern agricultural industry resulted in still another challenge by workers, who sought to organize in unions. They chose onions and sugar beets, crops that were relatively conducive to worker organization and controlled by large corporate owners. They were far removed from the traditional midwestern farmer-hired hand relationship that obscured class differences and smoothed over potential conflicts. Further, both crops offered relatively long employment seasons and allowed workers residential stability. Worker efforts began with the strike in the onion fields of the Scioto Marsh in 1934. Although the onion workers' AWU local was defeated, its leader, Okey Odell, carried the struggle to the beet industry of Northwestern Ohio and Southern Michigan. Beginning in 1935 beet workers organized locals in several locations, won several strikes, gained recognition by growers, and survived until 1938. An organized counterattack by the sugar beet corporations, however, convinced the AFL to withdraw. The more youthful and radical CIO immediately entered the fray, but almost as quickly also lost interest. Without the support of organized labor, the workers' unionization efforts collapsed.

The midwestern agricultural workers' failure to organize in the 1930s was not, as one expert has recently noted, because they were "the victims of flaws fatal to all migrant organizations—namely the financial and political impotence engendered by rootlessness."[57] The unionists of the 1930s were already for the most part settled residents of the communities where they worked. The failure of unionism in their case was the result of other factors. Most important, the corporations had a decided advantage because they controlled local government and its judicial and police apparatus. They successfully channeled farmer, police, and conservative resident antipathy into a unified opposition via their growers' employment committees and vigilante groups and thereby maintained a virtual monopoly on violence and repression. In addition, the corporations eventually gained control of the crucial labor-oriented agencies of the federal government. More neutral in the early years of the New Deal, federal administrators soon succumbed to corporation-grower pressures to turn against agricultural unionism. By 1938 neither the USDL nor the USDA was willing to abide by the letter of the law provided by the Sugar Act. Furthermore, the corporations had the financial resources to tap a new source of strikebreakers from Texas after provoking a futile strike.

Finally, organized labor failed miserably. Still in the midst of a euphoria caused by recent victories in mass-production industries in the Midwest, its very cool response to agricultural workers represents one of the earliest of a series of retreats that it made in coming decades. The CIO was even less successful than the AFL. In its first year of activity in the Midwest it simply backed down and refused to support a strike, consistent with its response in Colorado under similar circumstances. As one informed observer noted, CIO organizers did not "know the first thing about beets."[58] Organizing farmworkers was difficult and did not appear to be a good short-term business proposition. Other than a few scattered local efforts by workers, the agricultural union movement in the Midwest remained moribund and would not be resuscitated for a generation.

The failure of agricultural unionism in the 1930s was particularly important because it represented an unusual opportunity to join agricultural and mass-production workers. The two segments of the working class had much in common—diverse ethnic backgrounds, militancy, the security of relatively stable residence, and common urban work experiences. Afterwards, the two groups became increasingly separated. The urban unions became more conservative and the industrial workers more complacent, willing to accept the trappings and rhetoric of middle-class living. Midwestern agricultural workers became increasingly migratory, non-European, culturally separated from urban union members, and unable to find allies to assist their challenge to the deteriorating relations they encountered in the fields.

CHAPTER 4

A Midwestern Grapes of Wrath, 1938–1942

In the 1930s the expansion of the cotton, fruit, and vegetable industries in the United States was accompanied by an expanded field labor force of hundreds of thousands of seasonal workers, referred to as migrants. The workers received attention in California from such reformers as John Steinbeck and Carey McWilliams, and in the mid-South largely because of the success of the Southern Tenant Farmers Union. The transformation of agricultural labor in the Midwest at the time has been underestimated and misunderstood. Walter Stein, for example, has suggested that Michigan "did not receive large interstate migrations during the Depression." He failed to detect the rapid expansion of a migrant stream to the Midwest composed of African Americans, Euro-Americans, and Mexican Americans during the 1930s. By 1940 more than sixty thousand workers annually entered the Great Lakes region for employment in agriculture, the majority migrating to Michigan. To correct distortions and gaps, this chapter examines the formation, work, and social relations of this rapidly growing midwestern proletariat.[1]

Formation of the Migrant Stream

There were two distinct regional sources of the migrant stream. The first, U.S. citizens of Mexican descent, came from South and South-Central Texas. The second, Euro-American and African American workers, originated from the mid-South, particularly the northern fringe of the Mississippi Valley cotton-growing region of Southeastern Missouri and Northeastern Arkansas. The two branches formed what later became known as the midcontinental migrant stream.

In the 1930s South Texas had a large population of descendents of the Mexican immigrants who had entered the region during the earlier decades of the century. Many outsiders could not distinguish between them and the earlier generation of Mexicanos and referred to them collectively as Mexicans. The Tejanos, however, had social, economic, and cultural networks and family ties to Texas. Unlike the earlier generation, their lives and their memories were rooted in the United States, not in Mexico.

The Great Depression affected many of the Texas industries that employed the residents of Mexican descent. The coal industry was in the last stages of a long-term decline. As the mines gave out, thousands of workers were displaced. A few repatriated to Mexico, some moved to nearby cities, still others took up agricultural work in the Southwest and the midwestern sugar beet fields.[2]

A greater number of South Texas residents already worked in agriculture. Many lived in the Winter Garden district around Crystal City, where agricultural production had expanded rapidly during the 1920s and early 1930s. Later in the 1930s, a sharp decline in spinach and onion planting resulted in high levels of underemployment. Conditions worsened as Euro-Americans from Dust Bowl territory in North Texas, Oklahoma, and Arkansas migrated into the area and displaced Tejano residents in several occupations, particularly the higher-paying packing-houses. In 1939 Santos Vásquez of the Pecan Workers Union observed, "In the twenties you never saw an Anglo in the sheds—now you rarely see a Mexican." Local Tejanos encountered additional competition in the late 1930s as employers again began to recruit workers from across the border with Mexico. The Crystal City area became an important source of agricultural workers for other parts of Texas and beyond, particularly the Midwest. Labor agents hired by the sugar companies came to Crystal City and other towns along the border to recruit beet workers in the spring. Most workers returned in the fall, lured by the lower cost of living, family ties, and permanent homes, and supplemented their incomes with fall and winter employment in Texas agriculture.[3]

Conditions were also difficult for the residents of San Antonio and surrounding towns in South-Central Texas. Thousands of people worked in San Antonio's pecan-shelling industry, the largest single employer in the city. Earlier in the 1930s employment had risen when employers decided to deindustrialize and hired workers for less than the cost of running the machines they had introduced in the 1920s. The pecan companies continued to lower wages until early 1938, when pecan workers struck to protest further reductions. The federal government eventually intervened on the side of the workers, ordering owners to increase wages to twenty-five cents per hour. The employers retaliated against workers by reinstalling machines and hiring Euro-American women, who were willing to work for the higher wages. Several thousand pecan shellers lost their jobs and beginning in 1938 many of them took their first trips to the midwestern sugar beet fields.[4]

The beet industry offered an alternative to many low-paying menial tasks in South Texas. Andrew Anguiano grubbed trees in the late 1930s for five dollars an acre; a family of five or six averaged two acres a week. Many former beet workers earned a living by chopping wood, for which they received twenty-five cents a cord. They often had to augment their earnings picking wild berries, figs, peaches, and pears. Futhermore, Texas had a very meager relief mechanism. Federal projects, including the National Youth Administration (NYA) and the Civilian Conservation Corps (CCC), offered temporary support, food, and clothing to some young adults. In contrast, beet company offers of seventeen dollars an acre with transportation provided to the North did appear attractive.[5]

South Texas WPA investigator Selden Menefree, who never visited the beet region but heard enthusiastic stories, claimed that "the beet workers who went north were the aristocracy among the Mexican farm laborers." Although Menefree's perception of work in the beet fields was unduly optimistic and accepted the most generous estimates of earnings, many Tejanos viewed the North and its opportunities as a sharp contrast with the dismal conditions in their own state. Employment in the Midwest expanded rapidly in the late 1930s, but information about the work spread even more quickly.[6]

In the mid-1930s, midwestern sugar beet companies created a new system of recruitment, hiring, and transportation of workers from the South. It had some surface similarities with the mechanism they devised during and after World War I, but there were important differences. First, they had to contend with Texas farmers, who viewed them as competitors for a cheap labor force and tried to constrain the migration of the Mexican-descent workers through various means that included the law. The legislative efforts of Texas growers included the unenforced 1923 Emigrant Agent Act. Their efforts culminated in the Texas Emigrant Agent Act of 1929, which, as David

Montejano notes, was another effort to maintain control over workers. The 1929 law required that employers from other states employing Texas residents recruit through licensed agents registered in Texas. General employment agents were to pay an annual ten-dollar license fee, a one thousand–dollar state occupation tax, and one hundred– to three hundred–dollar occupational taxes to each county from which they recruited workers.[7]

Whereas Texas growers hoped to use the act to limit the departure of workers of Mexican-descent to the midwestern beet fields, the beet companies found ways to get around the law. The most important was a loophole that excepted "private" agents, or those who worked for a single employer, from paying the tax. T. Y. Collins of the Texas Bureau of Labor observed that by 1940 the state had not collected any occupational taxes.[8]

The most important agents were Frank Cortez, S. P. Acosta, Simón Vásquez, Francisco de la Garza, and the Peña brothers, Julio and Mauricio. Some of them, like Cortez, were former migrant workers. The agents made connections to find workers in cities and towns in South-Central Texas and the Rio Grande Valley. Each agency, working for a single company, recruited thousands of workers each year, which indicates a lucrative enterprise.[9]

Another new feature with the agency system involved the *troquero*, or crew leader. Some agents started as *troqueros*, expanded, and eventually hired other *troqueros* to assist them. Troqueros recruited, registered, and transported workers to the beet fields by truck. In the North they were hired as company "translators," intermediaries between workers and company officials and growers. Troqueros dealt with *revisadores* in locating and supervising work, making housing arrangements, measuring land, setting up credit, and paying workers. They exercised a great deal of personal control over workers in their crews and deflected much of the conflict between workers and the sugar beet companies and growers. They took over many of the duties of the *revisadores* of the 1920s and their trucks replaced the trains.[10]

The *troquero* system of the 1930s was a response not only to the availability of trucks, but also to changes in the organization of field labor working units. The Mexicanos of the earlier period came almost exclusively from small, separate, nuclear family units. They traveled by train with dozens of other families, most of whom were strangers. The Texas-Mexican crews by contrast, commonly were composed of several households of adult brothers, sisters, cousins, and their children. They traveled, worked, and lived in close proximity. Even when not related, crews often came from the same town or urban neighborhood, so that workers were likely to be in the company of familiar people.

Crews usually registered at the labor agency offices in San Antonio, Dallas, or the Rio Grande Valley between March and May. The heart of recruitment, the barrio on San Antonio's West Side, had thousands of people ready for registration or departure. While waiting, they stayed in nearby houses if they had relatives or friends, hotels if they had money, or on the streets if they had neither.[11]

Workers paid the troquero a registration fee ranging from one dollar to two dollars, and transportation charges of nine dollars to fifteen dollars one way, with children under fourteen paying half fare. The agents were required to inform workers of wages and acreage before departure. Despite the regulations, however, written contracts were not common. Prospective workers typically had to accept oral contracts or "agreements signed in blank." Because most of the workers did not have money for travel and food, the sugar beet companies advanced them funds, deducted from the first paycheck in mid-summer. As a result, most were in debt before they left Texas and were not guaranteed work for the season.[12]

The most common means of transportation to the North was in open-stake trucks ranging in size from one to two tons. Often used to haul livestock, these vehicles commonly carried between twenty-five and fifty people on the journey. In the truck each family carved out a space for its members and for food, clothing, and equipment. Telesforo Manduján of San Antonio recalled a trip he took to Michigan in 1938 that was so packed that "passengers had to stand all the way, and one man tied himself upright to a stake so he would not fall off if he should happen to fall asleep." The distance one way varied from sixteen hundred to two thousand miles and typically required two or three days and nights of solid driving.[13]

Notwithstanding the discomforts and hazards, employers and government employment officials commonly portrayed the journey as a pleasure trip. Robert M. McKinley of the Texas State Employment Service stated, "Strange to say they like it, that class of people look on that as a sort of holiday or outing, and they will take the trip year after year more for the outing than anything else."[14]

Passengers inevitably remembered the trips much differently. The trucks drove nonstop except when circumstances prevented them, with two drivers generally sharing duties so there would be no need to rest. Their only regular stops were for gasoline at intervals averaging roughly three hundred miles, accompanied by a short break lasting from ten minutes to half an hour. Drivers tried to avoid unscheduled stops, even for serious emergencies, for fear of stopping in unfriendly territory and because of the pressure to deliver workers as quickly as possible. Some headstrong drivers refused to stop even when trucks required repairs or serious illnesses occurred. On rare occasions drivers even tried to force workers to use large cans to relieve themselves. Passengers would not tolerate such demands, however, particularly in the context of public modesty that prevailed within their families.[15]

The trip was further complicated by the 1935 Motor Carrier Act, which provided for the regulation of the interstate transportation of workers. The act required truck registration and announcement of transportation rates with the Interstate Commerce Commission (ICC), inspection of trucks, and keeping a log, and it restricted drivers to a maximum of ten hours driving during any twenty-four-hour period. Nonetheless, the act was not regularly enforced and drivers who were caught seldom received fines. Being stopped, however, often meant a delay of several days, so drivers devised methods to evade law enforcement officers. They switched license plates, drove at night, took more dangerous back roads, and covered the tops of their trucks with tarpaulins so that riders were not visible from the outside. The drivers considered the act a nuisance rather than an effort to ensure the safety of the passengers. In effect it exacerbated the physical dangers, resulting in numerous accidents. Few of these accidents ever received more than brief notice in the local press. One exception was a 1940 tragedy in which a truck departing from Alamo, Texas, on its way to the Michigan beet fields crashed and killed thirty-one people.[16]

Many of the horrors that accompanied such accidents went unreported. In a 1942 accident in Arkansas, an army truck ran into a truck loaded with workers en route from Dallas, Texas, to Findlay, Ohio, killing a woman and injuring several other passengers. The army driver, who had been drinking, was at fault, but police did not issue a ticket. Further, local hospital authorities refused to provide medical attention to more than two dozen of the injured workers for two days while attempting to contact the Great Lakes Sugar Company to arrange for train fare. Only one local restaurant on the edge of town was willing to serve the travelers food, on the condition, however, that they eat it outside. Finally, while the workers were waiting at the local train station to leave, local police placed several of them in jail, contending that another railroad customer had reported his wallet stolen. The charges proved unfounded, yet the workers were not released until the intervention of the Mexican consul from San Antonio the next day.[17]

Because of haste and fear, drivers often refused to stop for serious illnesses, seizures, and heart attacks and ignored the health of pregnant women packed onto crowded trucks. Dr. E. V. Tubbs, Blissfield, Michigan, health officer, testified that in 1937 Estela Torres, in the late stages of pregnancy, was forced to stand during the entire trip from San Antonio. The jostling and abuse of her body resulted in the premature birth and death of the baby. As Mrs. Torres could not afford a formal burial, the infant was buried in a shallow grave in Michigan.[18]

Each spring as the trips north began, people in the Midwest became aroused about the beet workers' arrival, not because of the hazards of the trip but because they perceived the workers as taking jobs from local residents. In response police, using the Motor Carrier Act as their justification, frequently staged highly publicized drives to detain and search all trucks entering the state from Texas. The Michigan State Police were particularly active throughout the late 1930s. On apprehending a truck, they took drivers and passengers to police station jails, "pending a fingerprint check" and communication with sugar beet companies to ensure that the crew already had contracts to work. Investigations sometimes took several days, which workers spent waiting in jail. Truck drivers in violation of the Motor Carrier Act typically received suspended sentences on condition that they leave the state. The drivers returned the crews to the Indiana line, and the companies then arranged public transportation for the remainder of the trip. As a result, the police got their quota of apprehensions, the companies got their quota of workers, and the workers got more than their quota of abuse. For them, the trip up north was not a holiday.[19]

Troqueros also evaded the registration requirements of the Emigrant Agent Act of 1929, in response to orders from their corporation bosses. In 1941 only one midwestern agency even registered workers. The companies hired individual agents and *troqueros* to recruit for them "informally," in clear defiance of the act. Harry Maddox of the Central Beet Growers' Association of Decatur, Indiana, defended such recruitment, asserting that the *troqueros* "merely informed them where work would be." The corporations' encouragement of "free wheelers" loosened the control that Texas growers had over workers while it offered the beet companies a greater labor surplus and saved them the cost of registration.[20]

The recruitment and transportation of fruit workers from the upper Mississippi Delta cotton-producing region was less complicated than that of the beet workers. Most migrants to fruit-growing areas were experienced agricultural workers, formerly tenants, sharecroppers, or day laborers. They lost their jobs in the 1930s as owners sought to reap the benefits of the Agricultural Adjustment Act's Soil Conservation Program. The program paid benefits to cotton producers—defined as landowners, tenants, and sharecroppers—but not to wage earners. It encouraged owners to plant smaller acreages, curtail contracts with tenants and sharecroppers, purchase tractors, and hire wage labor. The major challenge to the program came from the Southern Tenant Farmers Union, but it failed to reverse the accelerated displacement of cotton workers. Many of them found seasonal work in the strawberry harvest that passed from Louisiana up the Mississippi River Valley to Tennessee, Arkansas, Missouri, and Southern Illinois before moving into Michigan.[21]

The fruit workers were referred to as "free wheelers," reflecting their independence from crew leaders or other formal recruitment mechanisms. They went north in response to radio announcements, advertisements in local newspapers, posters on fences and utility poles, and word-of-mouth. They typically traveled as individuals or nuclear families, hitchhiking, riding trains, or driving their old cars loaded with most of their belongings. A few still traveled north in their old horse-drawn farmers' wagons.[22]

In the late 1930s the fruit and vegetable industry of the Upper Midwest was not dominated by corporations. Fruit farmers had small orchards and diversified crops they sold on the open market or to one of a plethora of small canners that still dominated production in the region. The only centralized mechanism was the Public Fruit Market established by the City of Benton Harbor. It was open to any grower who was willing to rent a stall and to any purchaser. Compared with beet workers, fruit pickers traveled shorter distances and their facility with the English language reduced the need for a crew leader.[23]

Some observers have portrayed the migrants to the fruit-growing areas of the Midwest as the same workers who went to California at the same time, the workers from Steinbeck's *Grapes of Wrath*. Although they came from the same general region, their origins were somewhat different. Almost three-fifths of the migrants to California came from Oklahoma and North Texas, whereas less than 1 percent of those to the Midwest originated from those states. By contrast, three-fifths of those who came to the Great Lakes region were from Arkansas and one-fifth from Missouri. While slightly more than one-tenth of the migrants to California also came from Arkansas, most were from the western portion of the state, whereas those who went to the Upper Midwest came from the northeastern counties bordering the Mississippi River. Another important difference was the role they played as workers. The better-known "Okies" and "Arkies" of California displaced a settled resident worker population and worked mostly in cotton. The people who went to Michigan worked principally in the fruit harvest, which did not have a substantial outside labor force prior to the depression.[24]

Other observers have suggested that migrants to California intended to settle while those who came to the Midwest remained migrants, often heading north to make mortgage payments on their homes in the Mid-South. In fact, few owned any land or had employment ties to encourage their return. Like those who went to California, they worked in agriculture with the ultimate hope of settling in nearby towns and cities.[25]

The migrants who came to the region to pick fruit generally came as single males or small families. In 1940 more than four-fifths were Euro-American, the rest African American. Roughly three-fourths of the Euro-Americans but only one-fourth of the African Americans came as family units. The mean size for the former was 4.0 persons, for the latter, 2.3 persons. More than 90 percent of both ethnic groups had experience in agriculture but represented different class segments. Roughly three-fourths of the African Americans were former wage workers, whereas about half the Euro-Americans were former tenants and a quarter were wage laborers. Eleven percent of the Euro-Americans but none of the African Americans owned land. For the journey north, most Euro-Americans came in automobiles and brought supplies and camping equipment with them; few of the African Americans had cars or brought equipment other than a change of clothes. By contrast, the Mexican American beet worker families had an average of four to five working members over fourteen years of age and more than six people, including children. Furthermore, the beet workers came from a much greater variety of occupational backgrounds, including farm labor, mining, shop work, and urban industry.[26]

The vast majority of fruit production concentrated in Michigan, with other important clusters in Indiana, Ohio, Illinois, and Wisconsin. The Tejano beet workers were less concentrated. Most of them also found employment in Michigan, and small numbers worked in fruits or vegetables in all the states between Ohio and the Red River Valley in North Dakota. The combined number of interstate workers rose from an estimated nadir of five thousand in the early 1930s to twenty thousand by 1938, forty thousand by 1940, and sixty thousand by 1942. Approximately 60 percent of the total came to Michigan; Indiana had slightly more than 10 percent. The number of older resident Mexican-born beet workers declined in the late 1930s, yet there were still an estimated six thousand permanent resident adult Mexicano workers in Minnesota alone in 1940.[27]

Work and Pay

Shortly before World War II economists, employment officials, and agricultural researchers popularized the term "unorganized labor market" in reference to farmworker migration and work patterns. This term referred to a lack of centralized mechanisms to plan and coordinate workers' movement from one crop to another. Workers spent much time and money waiting for crops to ripen and traveling haphazardly in search of work, even during harvest peak. The notion of "disorganization," however, obscures the chronology of the formation of the migrant stream, patterns of hiring and recruitment, and the presence of surplus labor.

First, employers were responsible for the disorganizing, successfully breaking farmworker organizing efforts throughout the country. Next they introduced a new labor force from several pools to keep workers divided and to maintain a labor reserve. They saw no need for further planning or coordinated worker movement, which could have threatened their control and increased their labor costs. When labor shortages during the war reduced the size of this labor reserve, workers had a better bargaining position and their wages increased. They bargained for other benefits as well. In 1942 a Home Missions Council volunteer in the Sodus area in Southwestern Michigan observed, "The migrants are refusing to live in hog houses, chicken coops and corn cribs because they can get other jobs." That same year a Moorhead, Minnesota, volunteer wrote, "For the first time, the laborers are recognizing their economic independence and refuse to quibble with the farmer about the wage or size of the field—rather they will move on."[28]

Corporate actions exacerbated unemployment and disorganization in many ways in the late 1920s and the 1930s. In response to the large labor pool in the early 1930s, corporations reduced acreage per worker by a third. Meanwhile they introduced tractors and cross-blocking, accomplished by using a tractor-driven blocker instead of field workers with hoes. As a result, employment per acre fell from an average of ninety-five hours each season in the 1920s to sixty-five in the late 1930s. Spring blocking and thinning declined from an average of six to four weeks, July hoeing from three weeks to ten days, and fall topping from two months to five or six weeks. The work process did not change significantly and the number of people employed did not decline. Consequently, the corporations arranged for their employees to work elsewhere during the increasingly long slack periods in the beets.[29]

Traveling in crew leaders' trucks, workers could travel one hundred miles or more for shorter periods. To encourage this outside employment, the companies also cut out the garden plots, making workers entirely dependent on wages for subsistence. Simultaneously, the companies ensured the workers' return by maintaining "bonuses" at the end of the season of approximately two dollars per acre, and by prohibiting *troqueros* from arranging work during busy times in the sugar beet season.[30]

Although beet work was still organized around the family, household organization, affected by changes in the law as well as by technology, differed from the earlier period. By prohibiting labor by children under fourteen, the 1937 Sugar Act encouraged the formation of two types of working unit: one comprising families, including adult women and small children; another comprising adult males. Some mothers stayed behind in Texas with their young children while the rest of the family went north. Roughly 62 percent of adult beet workers were male. Family units headed by women did occur, but were usually obscured by statisticians, who subordinated them in units they thought were headed by older sons or other male relatives. The presence of children under age fourteen in the sugar beet fields gradually declined because of the Sugar Act, but it increased rapidly in other crops.[31]

Within the two work units, the division of labor differed both within and outside of the fields. When mothers and younger children were present, there was a sharper division of labor by gender and age than in the earlier generation of beet workers. In the Mexicano families of the 1920s, everyone over age five or six worked in the fields and tended to share other responsibilities as well. In the Tejano families mothers or older daughters and young children stayed out of the fields more frequently. They performed other necessary and time-consuming household tasks, including caring for the very young, cooking, washing clothes, and hauling and heating water. The all-male work units demonstrated a more communal tendency, as fathers and sons shared tasks in the field and at home. When they worked fruit and vegetable crops, all able-bodied children, women, and men usually worked in the fields, despite the division of non-wage labor by gender. The partial withdrawal of women from wage labor suggests a continuing degradation of their position in the workplace paralleling to many other tasks early in the twentieth century.[32]

Betabeleros found employment outside the beets in three periods of the season. In the early spring a small number who came north worked at cleaning fields, woods, sheds, and other preparatory tasks. During the break between blocking and hoeing in June and July there was more work, particularly in cultivating crops, especially beans and pickling cucumbers. The final gap, between hoeing and topping in July or early August until October, was the most important. Through a variety of arrangements involving *revisadores, troqueros,* local farmers, and distant employers, workers labored in a succession of fruit and vegetable crops and earned important cash income. Most of the *betabeleros* in the Central Michigan and the Saginaw Bay zones and those of the Southern Michigan–Northwestern Ohio areas went to Western Michigan. Their major destination was the cherry harvest in the Grand Traverse Bay area. Many of them also went to the onion fields in several muckland locations in Southern Michigan. Later in the summer, along with beet workers from Wisconsin, they often went to Northern Indiana and Ohio to pick tomatoes and detassel corn. At this time Minnesota and North Dakota beet workers commonly harvested potatoes in the Red River Valley or canning vegetables in Southern Minnesota.[33]

The majority of midwestern fruit production concentrated in western Michigan along the Lake Michigan shore. There were smaller areas in Northwestern Ohio along the shore of Lake Erie and in Door County in Northeastern Wisconsin, along the Lake Michigan shore. Another fruit-growing area was in Southern Illinois in Anna, Pulaski, and Union counties. Still smaller areas of local truck crop production were located near larger cities, but these hired mostly local resident children and adult women. In the 1930s another group augmented the nonlocal work force and were identified by growers and bureaucrats as "vacationists." Several thousand residents of nearby cities supposedly combining vacation with fruit picking, went to the Western Michigan cherry harvest in the 1930s and 1940s.[34]

By 1940 seasonal workers in the midwestern fruit belt were entering the strawberry region of Southern Illinois in late April or May. Most of the three thousand workers lived fewer than one hundred miles southwest, in Arkansas and Missouri. They stayed until early June, when they headed to the strawberry fields of Southwestern Michigan. At least ten thousand people found employment in Berrien County alone, remaining to pick blackberries, raspberries, dewberries, and other bush fruits in the early summer. By mid-July there was a lull, and most of them moved out to pick other fruits and vegetables, to return later in the season.[35]

Most went to the cherry district of Northwestern Michigan between early July and mid-August. It was already the most concentrated area of work in the Great Lakes region, and Grand Traverse County soon became the largest user of out-of-state migrant labor in the nation. By 1940 Tejano beet workers formed about 17 percent of the ethnically diverse harvest labor force in the cherry harvest. The cherry-producing locations along the southern shore of Lake Erie and the western shore of Lake Michigan were still small enough to employ predominantly local workers. In Ohio local workers were supplemented by urban African Americans, Kentucky onion workers, and beet workers from Northwestern Ohio and Southern Michigan. In Door County, youth from nearby towns and cities supplemented local residents.[36]

After cherry harvest ended, the two branches of the migrant stream again separated. Most fruit pickers returned to Southwestern Michigan. Commercial blueberry harvesting provided employment beginning in early August, soon followed by a wide variety of crops, including peaches, pears, grapes, tomatoes, melons, and apples. The late summer and early fall harvest peak in Southwestern Michigan required even more workers than in June. Meanwhile the Tejanos went in three directions. One group returned to the beet areas to harvest beans and pickling cucumbers, a second went to the onion areas, and the largest traveled to Northern Indiana, Southern Michigan, and Northwestern Ohio for the tomato harvest until the first frost in October. In the tomatoes they encountered single Euro-American workers from the mid-South who moved from the fruit to the vegetable harvest and the canneries. When the tree crops and the tomatoes were over, the fruit pickers typically left the Midwest, while the Tejanos returned to the beet fields for topping.[37]

Relations between worker and employer in fruit and vegetable crops differed in important ways from the sugar beets. First, the farmers were the employers. The elaborate corporate recruitment mechanism had not yet penetrated the area. Second, the harvest in any crop was organized by the hamper, bushel, lug, quart, bucket, or pail, with little standardization in size of container or price paid. Furthermore, anyone strong enough to carry the container was old enough to work. Another feature was the wide variation in periods of employment, partly due to weather. In abundant years the pickings were good and workers enjoyed long hours of work and short intervals of unemployment. Uncontrolled factors—frosts as late as June, wind and hailstorms, unusually cool temperatures, heat waves and occasional drought—did not affect all crops equally. Cool, wet weather might delay or destroy some crops but enhance yields in others. There was much less control over water than in the irrigated farming of the West. Under normal growing conditions in the Midwest, as in other parts of the country, workers faced long periods of unemployment during the season. Despite their constant complaints of worker shortages, growers overhired, held unnecessarily large work forces by curtailing the working day early, and instituted holdbacks and bonuses. These grower policies exacerbated unemployment much more than the weather.[38]

The seasonal income of midwestern migrant workers fluctuated widely. A useful comparison can be gleaned from detailed government studies conducted in 1939 and 1940. According to the USDA the Texas-Mexican sugar beet workers averaged roughly $152 for the six-and-one-half-month season, of which all but $30 came from sugar beets. The fruit pickers earned more, despite greater variation in wages. A Farm Security Administration survey determined that adult African American workers averaged $256 and Euro-Americans earned about $317 annually. Texas-Mexicans, whose low incomes were partly offset by larger work units and slightly lower costs of reproduction in South Texas, brought up the rear.[39]

Camps and Communities

With the sharp increase in production and the growth of the migrant stream, the demand for temporary worker dwellings also expanded. The housing contrasted sharply with that in the stable, homogeneous communities nearby, and the generally makeshift conditions engendered criticism. To avoid attracting attention, corporations and growers tried to keep the camps and their occupants isolated, but this was more difficult than in the 1920s. The recent arrivals were more numerous, more mobile, and as U.S. citizens, more aware of certain rights. Consequently, tension between farmworkers and local residents based on class and cultural differences were greater than before and were never resolved.

In the sugar beet areas, as Tejanos arrived to displace the largely resident labor force in the late 1930s, a massive housing shortage occurred. The older portable beet shacks had not been maintained; thus corporations resorted to tents, old barns, shacks, chicken coops, and abandoned houses often without screens or windows. Great Lakes Sugar Company housing was described as dilapidated, overcrowded, and "full of vermin and without sanitation whatever." In several cases, the companies failed to provide housing, as in 1940, when Great Lakes Sugar Company employees in Blissfield "camped out in the open." Furthermore, the corporations often failed to provide water for drinking, cooking, and washing, forcing workers to spend several hours each week hauling it themselves.[40]

Increasingly, the beet companies placed workers in camps rather than on isolated farms, with an entire crew in an old farmhouse, a shed, a barn, or a cluster of old beet shacks. New camps commonly consisted of a handful of cabins, each constructed to accommodate one or two families, located close to each other so they could be serviced by a common well and outhouse. The small camp was a response to the larger crews and provided a basis for community life not available to Mexicanos in their isolated dwellings in the 1920s.[41]

In the 1930s the companies constructed the first large camps in the region, typically near sugar beet factories or heavy concentrations of beets. In the Saginaw Valley the Michigan Sugar Company established a camp at Prairie Farms with nineteen housing units for thirty-five beet worker families, or approximately two hundred people. The occupants departed daily in cars and trucks to nearby beet fields. Many large camps gradually adopted a permanent character. In Michigan, Blissfield's Horkeytown had more than three hundred permanent residents in the late 1930s. In Mount Pleasant, the sugar company built a camp popularly known as El Pozo, located next to its factory on the edge of the Chippewa River. Workers traveled to farms as far as fifteen or twenty miles away each day and returned in the evening. By 1940 about five hundred residents remained in the camp, working sugar beets during the season and seeking employment elsewhere at other times. Many of them eventually found permanent employment in shops and factories in Mount Pleasant, Midland, and Bay City.[42]

While the housing of beet workers in the 1930s left much to be desired, conditions in the fruit and vegetable areas were even worse. There was no central element of control, and individual fruit growers initially resisted providing any accommodations. They argued that the season was short, the weather was warm, and workers were content to find housing for themselves. They could sustain the arguments throughout the 1930s because of the labor surplus, which weakened the workers' bargaining position.

The early camps in the fruit and vegetable areas were characterized by their lack of organization and their temporary nature. Many were referred to as "jungles." Some were former railroad camps and were closely associated with the trains their occupants commonly used for transportation. The camps appeared in many places, in boxcars on the side of the tracks, under trestle bridges, in abandoned buildings, and sometimes out in the open. Occupied mostly by single men, the jungles were sharply separated from permanent communities nearby. Instead of being located "across the tracks," they appeared along the tracks, a short distance from town yet accessible to both workers and farmers.

The jungle at Villa Ridge in Southern Illinois straddled the tracks. It lacked water and toilets and unlike many such communities had both male and female occupants during harvest season. It was little more than a brush patch in the open, without protection from inclement weather. One observer noted that many people went into the depot when it rained. A jungle near Decatur, Michigan, occupied by men who came to the area to work in the onion fields, functioned also as a hiring hall. Farmers who wanted help simply went to a small shack on the side of the railroad tracks and asked one of its occupants for a specific number of workers on a set date. Men appeared as requested, usually bringing their own lunches. They worked hard and "when their day's labor was done they were paid and they disappeared." Still another jungle appeared near Lawton, Michigan, during strawberry harvest. Single men previously staying near Hartford arrived via the Pere Marquette railroad. Lawton farmers drove their trucks or wagons to town to procure the workers, who supplied their own needs. After work they would "demand to return to their jungles at night."[43]

The jungles disappeared in the late 1930s and early 1940s, as farmers began to set up worker camps in their orchards. The growers acted not from altruism but from fear. Permanent residents viewed the jungles as dangerous and were particularly apprehensive about their expansion. They would not tolerate concentrations of thousands of people near their small communities without an adequate means of control. Workers also exerted pressure, particularly those who came with their families. As their bargaining position improved in the early 1940s, they refused to work if not offered housing. Growers soon realized that they could avoid friction if they allowed employees to stay on grower-owned property, usually in the woods and out of sight of their neighbors. These growers found that isolation proved the best policy.[44]

The transition from jungle to camp in the fruit belt occurred gradually. Riverside, Michigan, near Benton Harbor, had a jungle with one-hundred-forty inhabitants until disbanded by the local sheriff. In response, local farmers permitted the equivalent of jungles to appear on their own property. These early camps consisted largely of tents, automobiles, chicken coops, lean-tos, and toolsheds. Many of the workers simply slept out in the open, without water or toilet facilities.[45]

Former Michigan secretary of labor and industry Daniel O'Connor reported in 1940 that the most common dwelling for farmworkers in Van Buren County was "a brooder house or chicken coop that the hens are not using for the season," followed by barns, toolsheds, and abandoned farmhouses. Fifty workers were assigned to "what formerly had been a pig pen." Another two hundred stayed in two sheds measuring seventy-five by ten feet that faced each other, each with eight doors, without floors, windows, or chimneys. The camp had only two open privies, located next to the hogpen. Sanitation and water quality seldom concerned farmers in these early camps. In some instances growers dug wells for their camps, but in others the occupants had to travel to farmhouses or towns for water. In Berrien County only 4 percent of all privies built for migrants were of the closed type; if maintained, closed privies would have prevented the entry of disease-carrying flies and mosquitoes. O'Connor observed, "The worst conditions I encountered in industry do not compare with the unfortunate conditions under which the migrant pickers work and attempt to live." [46]

In the cherry region of Northwestern Michigan the rapid expansion of production also led to severe housing shortages. As in other areas, camps usually appeared on each grower's property. Typically, they housed from ten to fifty people, while a few had more than one hundred residents. Similar makeshift arrangements also appeared, most frequently the tent. Workers, crew leaders, or growers provided the tents, which usually could accommodate an entire family sleeping on cots or the ground. Growers typically justified the arrangements by pointing out that thousands of people vacationed in the area in tents. [47]

In the tomato areas of Ohio and Indiana, migrants also had to fend for themselves. Workers from Kentucky stayed in old buildings and farmhouses, barns, an abandoned slaughterhouse, on the side of the road in their cars, in open fields, and even in strawstacks. Not unlike migrants in most other locations, they had to cook outdoors. Being single, they were less inclined to partake of elaborate meals and consequently ate mostly canned and packaged foods, beans, chili, and hamburgers. [48]

One universal characteristic of this seemingly disorganized pattern of housing was the nearly absolute segregation of workers of different ethnic backgrounds. In Southern Illinois, African Americans concentrated in Anna and Pulaski counties; Euro-Americans worked in neighboring Union County. African Americans who passed through Union County were "told not to stay overnight." In Berrien County there were two major centers of production, both located within eight miles of Benton Harbor. African Americans concentrated in areas to the southeast of the city, especially around Sodus, with 300 permanent residents, Eau Claire, population 324, and Berrien Center, population 134. An estimated 1,500 to 2,000 workers stayed within a three-mile radius of each of those small towns. Euro-American workers clustered around three villages to the northeast of Benton Harbor—Riverside, Coloma, and Watervliet. At harvest time more than 8,000 Euro-American workers lived in the vicinity of these three villages.[49]

In the Michigan cherry region the three groups were clearly segregated. Workers of Mexican descent concentrated on the Grand Traverse Peninsula along Highway 37, a strip of land roughly eighteen miles long and one mile wide. African Americans clustered around Northport, on the northern tip of the Leelanau Peninsula. Euro-Americans worked in the other locations.[50]

Local residents and growers typically asserted that Euro-American southerners demanded segregation and claimed that they refused to work alongside African Americans or Mexicans. Yet the growers organized the work force and chose to segregate, in line with established customs. A local hotel manager, when questioned about why he refused to rent a room to a family of Euro-American workers from Arkansas, asserted, "Oh, you must be talking about some of those migrants. . . . I can't have them dirtying my sheets."[51] Tejanos were more isolated, because of both structural factors and personal preferences. Their movement was largely restricted by the *troquero* system and language. Furthermore, they needed the outside less, as they enjoyed social and cultural life in the close circle of family and crew members in their midst. They were also hesitant to mix or allow their children to socialize with others. A Saginaw resident noted that "they had no effect on the community as they live and associate nearly entirely with themselves."[52]

Permanent community members vigorously sought to maintain the isolation. One observer noted that Scandinavian residents in Minnesota acted as though "these people do not belong here." In East-Central Michigan, a church worker wrote that local growers felt that the Mexicans were "treacherous" and "cannot be trusted." The lack of trust meant that for beet workers in Albion, Michigan, "everything they buy has to be paid for in advance."[53] Mexicanos also had reason to be suspicious. They faced widespread discrimination throughout the region. In many locations employers refused to hire them for work outside of agriculture. Employers and store owners cheated them constantly. Gertrude Herman, who taught Mexican American children around Alma, Michigan, stated that a field man in the area boasted of cheating them on field measurement. The *revisador* bragged, "These Mexicans don't know enough to understand measurements and we can cut off three or four acres without their realizing it." Michigan State College sociologist John Thaden concluded that they were "preyed upon by local merchant, auto dealer and farmer" alike.[54]

Compounding suspicion was the nearly universal reality of segregation, which, as one Ohio observer noted, "has been the rule rather than the exception in most areas." Mexicans were excluded consistently from public movie theaters, restaurants, motels, barbershops, and dances, even in the larger cities. They were welcomed to work and spend their money as long as they stayed in their place and accepted the limitations that communities placed on them.[55]

Permanent residents' apprehensions toward African Americans were expressed differently because of the structure of the work force, demographic, cultural, and linguistic factors. Most of the African Americans were single males and not part of organized traveling groups. Unlike Tejanos they did not encounter language barriers with local residents. Furthermore, they had more opportunities to find familiar and welcome territory in African American neighborhoods in many nearby towns and cities. Being alone, they were more likely to go to stores, restaurants, and other public places to eat and to socialize. As a result of their greater visibility, antagonisms with Euro-Americans often were much sharper. A Villa Ridge, Illinois, observer noted that some growers established amicable relations with African Americans, but that "others regard them as animals and treat them as such."[56]

Local residents often vigorously worked to prevent African Americans from entering an area even to work. In 1938 a Van Buren County grower hired an African American crew to weed and harvest onions. A local journalist reported that, in response, segregationist neighbors "staged demonstrations to frighten away the negroes. They descended on their camp one night with shotguns and lanterns and fired a few shells into the air." The camp residents quickly scattered. As they fled, many suffered injuries "running headlong into surrounding fences, but none turned up for medical care. In fact, by next morning only a few remained, and they were with harassed and frightened looks on their faces. Probably next year local labor will be used entirely."[57]

Permanent Euro-American residents in the fruit belt also manipulated deeply ingrained stereotypes to control and terrorize African Americans, including the fear of their men molesting Euro-American women. In South Haven, Michigan, local Euro-Americans spread unfounded rumors that an African American man had accosted a Euro-American woman in a local park. On hearing the rumors, the workers departed just in time to escape a lynch mob. Unfortunately, one unsuspecting worker entered the park, and the mob quickly apprehended him and beat him severely. When the crowd was making preparations to tar and feather him, he fled to a nearby hotel and hid there until local police came to put him in jail for his own safety. The next day he fled town.[58]

Farmworkers of all ethnic groups encountered problems with local police, whose attitudes reflected those of their constituents. It was a story of ongoing and constant surveillance and harassment without regard for the Fourth Amendment (protection against unreasonable search and seizure). Concerned about a possible burden on welfare rolls, in 1938 and 1939 Michigan ordered its police to check all Tejano workers entering the state. Following orders, the police detained every entering vehicle with Texas license plates or carrying passengers who appeared to be of Mexican descent. The Berrien County Board of Supervisors devised a similar plan to use its police force to check out-of-state farmworkers. A local grocer noted that a county police officer who did not like migrants in general always stopped them simply to "check them." The Reverend Ernest Culpepper, an African American minister holding a church picnic in Eau Claire, Michigan, reported that the Berrien County sheriff intruded on the group and without knowledge of what they were doing ordered them to disband immediately. When the Reverend Mr. Culpepper explained who he was and that the group was about to hold religious services, the sheriff backed off and allowed them to continue, but "walked away muttering something about thinking it was a crap game."[59]

The police function in social control appeared again when employer demand for workers dwindled. Farmers regularly called sheriffs to chase workers from the fields, out of town, and from their own camps when they no longer wanted them. The police "forcibly invited them to leave when the crops were over," threatening them with jail if they were not gone in twenty-four hours.[60]

Although local residents were seldom concerned about police infringement of workers' constitutional rights, outsiders often were shocked. The Indianapolis press commonly criticized sheriff Nelson Pangborn, who restricted the free movement of thousands of tomato pickers from Kentucky into Johnson County, Indiana, each year. In 1939 Pangborn considered wages lower than normal and unemployment unusually high. He decided to resolve these problems by arresting the workers on minor charges, including vagrancy, then took their fingerprints, jailed them, and ordered them to leave the county. He claimed that workers came to the tomato harvest as a pretext for going on relief: "It gave the bums and the moochers a good excuse to come here." He justified his actions on the grounds that "the very sight of wanderers in their ancient battered cars, thumbing rides, seeking handouts at back doors, parked aimlessly by roadsides was disturbing Johnson County residents." He adopted a broad construction of his own police power: "a candidate for jail is a transient without visible means of support seeking harvest field or canning factory work in a market that's glutted." Local residents were surprised at the stir over Pangborn's actions. One commented, "Is there anything peculiar to this year?" Because rural police in the Midwest disregarded farmworkers' constitutional rights freely, as they did elsewhere, workers were not able to organize and effectively challenge many such abuses for several decades.[61]

In spite of these tensions, midwestern farmworkers were beginning to create a social and cultural life of their own, one that contrasted with the isolated, nuclear family–oriented world of the 1920s. They were surrounded by relatives and other familiar faces at work and in camps every day. In the evenings many of them found familiar programs on their radios. They often gathered to listen to stations that reached them from as far away as Ciudad Acuña, Coahuila, to hear programs they had known in South Texas. They also engaged in recreational activities by themselves and enjoyed some activities in nearby communities. Many small towns with large temporary populations began to sponsor free movies once or twice a week that migrants could attend. One in Riverside, Michigan, attracted over fifteen hundred workers. A Breckenridge, Michigan, church member noted, however, that "the presence of Mexicans is resented at organized community gatherings such as the free show at Wheeler, or the livestock auction every Tuesday at Breckenridge."[62]

Because of their numbers and freer movement, workers and recent settlers began sponsoring social and cultural events to attract farmworkers throughout the region. At this time the first Saturday night *bailes* (dances) began. Many workers brought their own instruments and formed *conjuntos* (musical groups). Increasingly, professional musicians from larger cities in the region and even from Texas began to tour the farmworker circuit. Hundreds of people gathered for these largely family events. Easier access to transportation also made possible closer links with established ethnic neighborhoods in towns and cities. On Saturday nights workers in Michigan, Ohio, and Minnesota often visited larger cities such as Saginaw, Toledo, and Saint Paul for activities sponsored by local Mexican communities. As the network between farmworkers and settlers continued to develop, information about employment and other services spread, further encouraging permanent settlement.[63]

Settlement by Euro-Americans was proportionately greater, largely because they faced less discrimination in hiring. Those who settled often became part of the growing communities referred to as "Little Arkansas" or "Little Missouri" that sprang up in the industrial towns and cities of Michigan, Ohio, Illinois, and Indiana. At the time some scholars questioned whether they could integrate with longer-established Euro-American residents because of visibly different backgrounds and cultural ways. Such concerns did not last for long, for they soon became an accepted part of the Euro-American urban working class. Even where they were most densely congregated, they were not sharply segregated.[64]

African Americans from the fruit belt settled most often in larger cities, including Chicago, Gary, Benton Harbor, and Detroit, where they found established communities and greater employment opportunities. They were the smallest group among the migrants, but they faced the greatest hostility and the most overt discrimination from the majority population. Yet the industrial boom that began in 1940 attracted them to urban settings, where they quickly met other former agricultural workers from the South. They became part of a visible and highly segregated segment of the midwestern urban working class.[65]

The Tejano workers also began to settle, largely in areas where Mexicano beet workers had preceded them. They found work on railroads, in foundries, packing plants, and automobile factories throughout the region and stayed in older neighborhoods close to work. Dr. Mudd of the Chevrolet foundry in Saginaw preferred to hire them because he claimed that "Mexicans stand the heat better than any other group." As they settled into established Mexican communities, there was tension between them and the Mexican immigrants who preceded them. Despite the minor differences, however, they stayed together like family, and outsiders could seldom distinguish the two groups.[66]

Their entry into midwestern cities added diversity to a Mexican community flavored by Texas-Mexican culture, food, and music, which were becoming increasingly articulated in the 1930s and 1940s. When they settled their children attended school, played with local children, and quickly learned the subtleties of midwestern English. Yet even the youngest children, who became immersed in the local setting, could not free themselves from an awareness of being different from the longer-established Euro-American residents.[67]

Many parents preferred to settle in midwestern cities, where they found overt violence and discrimination against them less pronounced than in Texas. Some parents decided to remain in the northern communities because, as one asserted, they did not want their children to experience "the inferiority that was inevitable in Texas." They were also lured by the promise of higher-paying and more stable jobs. The regional economy began to boom as war production accelerated. By 1940 Texas State Employment Service representative J. H. Bond estimated that approximately 25 percent of those Tejanos who went to the midwestern beet fields never returned. Like other former migrants, they became part of the midwestern industrial working class in towns and cities near the fields. Considering their small numbers, these recent settlers were visibly clustered and occasionally segregated in poor neighborhoods.[68]

The Politics of "The Migrant Problem"

The appearance of thousands of migrant farmworkers throughout the country quickly emerged as an issue during the New Deal. Concern about farmworkers occurred throughout the nation, but its manifestations in the mid-South, the Southwest, and California are more familiar. John Steinbeck's *The Grapes of Wrath,* a story of Dust Bowl migrants to California, reflected the turmoil that emerged with the appearance of millions of new interstate seasonal farmworkers during the 1930s. The unrest was articulated by farmworker union organizers in the early and mid-1930s as a class struggle against employers in many parts of the nation. By the late 1930s, the unions were defeated, but many outside sympathizers continued efforts aimed at legislative reform. They faced powerful opposition in the farm lobby, led by the Farm Bureau Federation, State Extension Service professors, a diverse group of local farmers, and public officials. Farmer interests generally controlled the rural press and local school boards. Politically, they dominated small midwestern towns and were well represented in state legislatures. As a group the new farm bloc lacked the paternalism that distinguished farmers of an earlier generation.

The reformers included liberal urban politicians, women's groups, elements in the church, and a handful of urban newspaper reporters and labor union representatives. The reformers were appalled at the brutality of the process by which the migrant stream had grown so rapidly. They were dismayed by the degree of human suffering that growth engendered, unparalleled in the recent history of the Midwest. They attacked the laissez-faire approach of the farm lobby and sought to apply the welfare "net" of the New Deal to agricultural workers in the same way that it had recently been applied to urban workers. Whereas the farmer group claimed the "community" as its constituency, the reformers posed as the "conscience" of the nation. Neither group tried to bring farmworkers into the debate. Both considered them to be an intractable "migrant problem."

The political struggle in the Midwest peaked in Michigan between 1937 and 1941. During that time state and federal agencies conducted several studies on agricultural workers. Their conclusions were supported by John F. Thaden, who was engaged in field research on Mexican sugar beet workers. The reformers used the information to justify bringing farmworkers under the protection of New Deal legislation, but they lacked the direction and leadership of their well-organized opponents, led by the sugar beet corporations. As Max Henderson, executive secretary-treasurer of the Michigan Sugar Company, observed, "The industry fought them tooth and nail." Undaunted, the reformers addressed such issues as transportation, housing, health, welfare, and education.[69]

The struggle over transportation centered on the *troquero* mechanism and the abuses it engendered. In addition to the dangers of traveling by truck, the role of the *troqueros* drew attention. Many were honest, capable, and dedicated. The corporations, however, had created the system to save money and to avoid responsibility. Companies hired *troqueros* to circumvent transportation laws, the Interstate Commerce Commission (ICC) code, and the cost of formal registration of workers. The *troquero* system removed growers and companies from direct involvement with fieldworkers and it redirected worker conflict from the real employers, the companies and growers, to the hired *troqueros*. Worker complaints went through the *troquero*, who tried to resolve them. In effect, the *troquero* changed the location of conflicts, reduced the possibility of strikes, and masked the control maintained by the corporations. The function of the *troquero* also helped clarify why company representatives and growers alike frequently asserted that Tejanos were "docile," "compliant," "reasonable," and "uncomplaining."[70]

Troquero abuses were also serious matters and, despite the frequent public statements by corporation officials and growers, workers did complain. Worker Ben Vargas testified before the Texas State Employment Service (TSES) in 1941 that *troqueros* commonly failed to allot workers the acreages promised. He cited several families around Findlay, Ohio, who worked much smaller acreages than expected and consequently were stranded and broke at the end of the season. *Troqueros* often pocketed money intended as company advances, made unauthorized charges for transportation and equipment, and cheated workers on payment for work. Remijo Rodríguez was part of a crew of twenty workers who went to the fields near East Grand Forks, Minnesota, in 1940, at an agreed wage of $9.50 per acre for thinning and hoeing two hundred acres. The troquero paid them $7.50 an acre, pocketing the $400 difference for himself. Troqueros and field men also cheated on field measurement. Frank Zamora testified that he worked around Blissfield, where "we always had trouble with the fieldman because he short measured our acreage and he would not go with us to remeasure."[71]

Reformers' efforts to change the troquero system resulted in a lawsuit that ended up in federal district court, following an investigation of how workers were transported from Texas to the Midwest. Federal officials filed suit against the Great Lakes Sugar Company and labor agent Julio de la Peña. The case detailed the simultaneous expansion of Great Lakes operations in Texas and the rise of de la Peña as a company agent. He began working for Great Lakes as a troquero in 1934, transporting workers from South Texas. As the corporation's demand for workers increased, his operations expanded. In 1940 he opened a licensed employment agency in Realitos, seventy miles east of Laredo. At the time he owned two trucks and recruited approximately four hundred workers for Great Lakes to Michigan and Ohio every year. The suit was based on violations of several provisions of the 1935 Motor Carrier Act. Investigations showed that neither the company nor de la Peña had filed transportation rates with the ICC. He did not insure the trucks properly or file logs of the trip, as the law required. In addition, company drivers consistently violated the ten-hour daily maximum per driver rule, and the vehicles failed to comply with numerous safety regulations.[72]

Investigations surrounding the lawsuit revealed that the trip from South Texas to Findlay, Ohio, took three days and nights, with stops of thirty minutes every three hundred miles. The trucks were loaded with an average of forty-eight workers per trip, affording de la Peña very respectable profits. In 1940 Great Lakes paid him $7,077.66 for transporting laborers, $435 for hauling beets to the factory, plus $90 per month as interpreter from May to December. In a separate investigation the ICC determined that the Great Lakes Growers Employment Committee (GLGEC), supposedly responsible for arranging transportation and hiring the workers, "was merely an intermediary" that was "controlled and operated entirely by the Great Lakes Sugar Corporation" (GLSC). For example, the corporation performed routine paperwork "at no cost to the committee," advanced funds, and signed paychecks. The ICC Summary of Investigation concluded that

GLGEC was created "as a device to defeat regulation" and was "controlled and operated entirely by the Great Lakes Sugar Corporation." Yet GLSC president James E. Larrowe bluntly denied the assertions: "Our company has nothing to do with the field labor." Although de la Peña cooperated with the court, he admitted involvement but pleaded ignorance to infractions against the act. The district court held against Great Lakes and de la Peña and fined the company $2,000 plus court costs, and the labor agent $1 plus court costs.[73]

The lawsuit against Great Lakes Sugar represented the first serious investigation and punishment for violation of the Motor Carrier Act as it applied to the transportation of farmworkers to the Midwest. In earlier years police had caught many *troqueros* who violated the act, but the companies and their drivers escaped with token fines at most. The lawsuit against Great Lakes was intent on reducing unsafe truck transportation of farmworkers in the future. In 1941 more than eighteen hundred workers went to the midwestern beet fields in safer and more comfortable trains, for fifteen dollars each direction. The lawsuit also laid bare the role of the Great Lakes Growers Employment Committee as a paper organization created to cover up corporate irresponsibility.[74]

Despite this modest victory, the reformers could hardly claim that it forced corporations to improve worker transportation. Trucks continued to be the dominant mode of transportation, and the 1941 experiment with trains was quickly abandoned. The companies determined that the truck was faster, more convenient, and cheaper. Furthermore, *troqueros* could transport migrants from one place to another during the season and deal with immediate conflicts involving workers.

The lawsuit against Great Lakes only touched the surface; it failed to address a seamier side of the de la Peña–Great Lakes operation. Information uncovered during the investigation revealed that de la Peña, like other labor agents, transported more workers than necessary because he was paid by the head. He granted them smaller acreages than originally promised and engaged in other petty schemes to cheat workers. One worker, Ben Vargas, admitted that de la Peña offered him a bribe of two hundred dollars to tell President Larrowe of GLSC that accusations about his cheating workers were untrue.[75] Meanwhile, the operations of Julio de la Peña and his brother Mauricio continued to expand. The brothers became among the most successful of the entrepreneurs in the network of hiring and transporting beet workers to the Midwest. The corporations also continued to use the growers' committee mechanism to hide their involvement in recruitment. The following year a new organization,

Michigan Field Crops Incorporated (MFCI), was created to replace the disgraced GLGEC. It continued to cover up the dominant role of the corporations.[76]

A final failing of the investigation was that it did not include a monitoring or compliance mechanism, which might have prevented further abuses. The reformers were unable to change the company's newly created troquero mechanism and abuses continued unabated.

The reformers also addressed the issue of housing, which was acknowledged as inadequate throughout the region. In the beet areas the older shacks had deteriorated badly and were gradually replaced by chicken houses, garages, toolsheds, barns, and shanties in equally poor condition. Roofs leaked, screens were missing, and the dwellings were filthy. Furthermore, growers often levied unauthorized charges for stoves, beds, tables, and benches. Conditions in the fruit- and vegetable-growing areas often were worse, as workers commonly had to sleep in the open. After a 1937 investigation, Michigan commissioner of labor and industry George Krogstad declared that "the full weight of the Department of Labor will be used to bring decent and humane methods to the fields, and we will see to it that the evils are corrected and never return."[77]

Yet neither Krogstad nor any other agency representative made serious efforts until a 1940 study by the FSA proposed to construct two large government camps in Berrien County, paid for by federal funds. The FSA had already constructed successful camps in the South and the Southwest and hoped to provide modest but adequate housing in other places where needed. Growers and their representatives in the state legislature reacted unfavorably. In 1941 they introduced Michigan House Concurrent Resolution 14, opposing government construction of any migratory workers' camps in the state. Represented by the Farm Bureau, the Berrien County Horticultural Society, and the Michigan State Grange, they argued that there was no need for housing. They asserted that the workers regarded their time in the region as a "vacation" and, like other people on vacation, "prefer to live in tents." They added that construction costs were prohibitive, considering the short harvest season. The underlying basis of their opposition, however, was control. They knew that workers in government camps functioned much more democratically and were less subject to direct and indirect pressures and threats from corporations, growers, and troqueros. The employers were particularly afraid that workers in government camps were much more likely to organize and successfully form unions.[78]

Reform elements led by women's and church groups offered a counterproposal, Michigan State Concurrent Resolution 26, to support the construction of camps by the federal government. These groups discounted growers' contentions, arguing that existing housing was inadequate, dangerous, and unhealthy. To build such housing was not uneconomical because, although employment in specific crops was brief, workers stayed in the region and could occupy the housing from March or April until November. Furthermore, they claimed, growers fears about unionization were unfounded. Darrell Smith, legislative representative for the CIO, admitted that unions had "no organizational interest" in the pickers, for "our groups must pay their own way. We can't afford to send organizers there every year."[79]

The state legislature determined the fate of the housing legislation in the winter of 1941, passing the bill opposing the camps while allowing the favorable supporting bill to die in committee. Although the decisions were not binding on the federal government, they helped convince the FSA to back down on its plans to build worker housing.[80]

The debate over providing health and medical services was based on costs. Even the reformers did not expect coverage for expensive injuries. Reformers wanted employers and government to encourage preventive health care for illnesses such as rickets, caused by vitamin D deficiency, and sinus infections, caused by staying in unheated cabins and wearing inadequate clothing and footwear. Local studies detailed the consequences of malnutrition and poor health care. In a Berrien County survey, 12.5 percent of the workers had health-related disabilities that had prevented them from working at some time during the previous two months. A Saginaw County study showed that among Tejano beet workers the infant mortality rate was five times higher than that of permanent residents.[81]

The reformers' greatest concern was that communicable diseases, among them typhoid fever, malaria, tuberculosis, diphtheria, dysentery, and smallpox, might spread to permanent residents. Most of these diseases had been eradicated or could have been controlled by basic preventive health care—adequate diet, clean surroundings, and inoculation.[82]

Midwestern health officials typically did their best to avoid treating workers who were ill. As Dr. L. H. Gaston of the Sanilac County, Michigan, Department of Health, reported, "We do not look for problems. . . . we hesitate to spend the money on residents of Texas." Health officials justified their actions by citing increased costs to taxpayers. They often blamed the workers for their conditions. Speaking of Texas-Mexican beet workers, C. C. Slemans, of the Michigan State

Health Department, stated, "As a people they do not understand the matter of the spread of disease nor do they appear greatly concerned. They do not call physicians for diagnosis nor are they inclined to obey quarantine when communicable diseases are discovered among them."[83] Public officials became concerned only when communicable diseases gained the attention of local permanent residents. Shigella dysentery appeared frequently. In a 1941 outbreak, eleven cases were reported and two-year-old Harold Gobell died on the Otis Klepp farm in Keeler Township in Western Michigan. The health department traced the outbreak directly to poor sanitation, filthy camp privies, and a pump in which surplus water drained back directly into the well. A local investigator noted that the well was a center of activity in the camp: "The entire colony bathes, washes dishes, clothes and diapers at the well." The health department concluded that flies and dirty water at the camp, not the workers, were responsible. Klepp promised to repair the privies and to make a concrete top for the well "if possible."[84]

Several diphtheria outbreaks also occurred in the late 1930s and early 1940s. A 1939 epidemic in Michigan killed three Tejano children. As a result the state began an immunization program in 1940 and established centers to inoculate children for diphtheria and smallpox. The program was not continued after 1940, and there were two new outbreaks in 1941. More than a dozen people became ill near Hemlock, and one-year-old Pauline García died of laryngeal diphtheria. A second and even more serious outbreak occurred in the Great Lakes Sugar Corporation labor camp in Blissfield, where fifteen people became ill and three children died. Doctors' reports claimed the Mexicans were responsible for the outbreaks because they maintained dirty habits. As a result of the 1941 epidemic, the State Health Department conducted another immunization program and inoculated more than five thousand Mexican American beet worker children.[85]

Tuberculosis was even more frequent and serious among the beet workers. It came to the attention of the state legislature in 1937 when Dr. V. K. Volk conducted a study in Saginaw, Michigan. He discovered that Mexican residents accounted for 25 percent of the tuberculosis cases in the Saginaw County Hospital, although they formed only 1 percent of the city's population. Legislators were concerned, for state law required all tubercular patients, whether residents or not, to be placed in state- or county-run tuberculosis sanatoriums at public expense. Hospitalization cost roughly one thousand dollars annually per patient. Volk concluded that the high rate of tuberculosis was "a menace to local citizens and an expense to the tax-payer." He cooperated with the sugar companies and the State of Michigan to resolve the problem.[86]

The following season Volk arranged to have the Saginaw County Health Department conduct tuberculosis examinations on Tejanos brought into the area by the Michigan Sugar Company. If they were found to be tubercular, the company had to pay for their return to Texas. More than five hundred Mexicans were examined in Saginaw and approximately sixty-five were sent back.[87]

Volk also worked with the State Health Commission to set up a study committee and determine policy regarding tubercular beet workers entering the state. The committee decided on fluorscopic tests for tuberculosis for all prospective beet workers. The workers' examinations were to take place in Texas when they registered at the employment agencies. The U.S. Public Health Service and the beet companies agreed to share the cost of the examinations. The Texas tuberculosis examination program began in 1939 and continued un-til 1942. Each year the State of Michigan sent a doctor to Texas to conduct the tests. The physician simply lined workers up by sex and took a chest X ray, for which each person paid twenty-five cents. The companies rejected workers who had positive reactions. The others were photographed or fingerprinted for identification as part of their "Beet Worker Permit." The corporations used the permits to keep out both tubercular patients and as a blacklist of those whose work or behavior was deemed unsatisfactory (including the expression of union sympathies).[88]

Tuberculosis examination data indicate a rapid growth in Tejano migration to Michigan, from 4,271 in 1939 to 14,462 in 1942. Dur-ing the period a total of 32,083 workers were examined, of whom 677, or about 2 percent, were rejected. The creators of the program considered it a great success. They assumed that about one of every three of the tubercular workers would have been hospitalized at a cost of one thousand dollars per person, for a total savings of about $225,000.[89]

Both the state and the federal governments considered this a model program. Dr. Allen D. Moyer of the Michigan Department of Health stated, "We are glad to be spared the expense of caring for tubercu-lar men and women among Mexican migrant workers." At one point Dr. T. M. Koppa, of the Michigan Department of Health, who con-ducted the X-ray program in San Antonio, described how it operated to members of the U.S. House of Representatives. In response to Dr. Koppa's presentation Congressman Claude V. Parsons (Illinois) commented, "It is only recently that we have been looking into the human equation. . . . I want to congratulate you, Dr. Koppa . . . for the splendid work you have done."[90]

Although funding for the program was to have been shared equally by the federal government and the sugar beet companies, it was not. In 1940 the Public Health Service paid 56 percent of the total. Through the twenty-five cents each worker paid for being examined, the companies recovered more than their portion of the costs. As the number of workers examined increased and as less expensive finger-printing replaced photographs, company costs declined further. In fact, the companies made a profit on the tuberculosis X-ray examination program.[91]

Health officials, legislators, and beet companies congratulated themselves on the program, yet did not consider the fate of the hundreds of people they discovered with tuberculosis. When questioned about what happened to them, Koppa cynically responded, "We do tell the individual to see his private physician." Trinidad Moreno explained that those discovered to have tuberculosis, whether in Michigan or Texas, ended up without treatment, "to die at home."[92]

The subject of relief for farmworkers also entered the reformers' agenda. Growers opposed it on contradictory grounds. First, they asserted that Works Progress Administration (WPA) recipients did not want to do farm work because they sometimes had trouble getting back on relief. Usually, the agencies and growers resolved problems mutually. W. R. Sullinger of the Ohio State Employment Service (OSES) observed that employment officials cooperated when growers demanded workers: "We have had to go to the regional director of the district and get them to shut down a project to get the labor we needed. We have always been able to get it then." Growers also opposed relief because they claimed that the WPA made workers lazy and unwilling to perform agricultural labor. The government calculated that WPA wages provided workers with mere subsistence incomes, which in the rural Midwest in 1938 meant steady work for thirty-five hours per week at thirty-five cents per hour, or approximately forty-nine dollars per month. Government studies thus confirmed that most farmworkers in the Midwest earned a lower hourly wage than the official subsistence wage in addition to unsteady employment.[93]

The sugar beet companies, unlike the farmers, encouraged the efforts of workers to get relief, particularly in the winter. They were pleased that long-settled Mexicanos who resided in larger cities occasionally received basic items like coal, foodstuffs, milk, and clothing from the government, although public officials complained that relief enabled companies to pay wages below subsistence. When farmer and administration complaints became too loud, the beet companies provided relief, typically in the form of loans on the coming season's earnings.[94]

Policies for fruit pickers were somewhat different and depended more on individual circumstances. In an illustrative case from Berrien County, a pregnant woman from Arkansas requested permission from the relief administrator for hospitalization costs to deliver her baby. Although she was destitute and weakened, the administrator tried to convince her to return home. She insisted that she was not healthy enough to travel. He then threatened her, stating, "I can call the sheriff out here and then you can go whether you want to or not." She finally persuaded him that she was in no condition to travel, and he allowed her to enter the hospital. Such expenses were part of the more than $13,000 Berrien County paid in 1940 for relief to migrant workers, about half for direct relief and the remainder for hospitalization and burial expenses. This contrasted with the $1.5 million the workers earned during the season, most spent on goods purchased in the county.[95]

In contrast, county welfare officials consistently denied relief to the Texas-Mexican beet workers. Home Missions Council director Dorothy Fox reported that in the 1933–1939 period Sanilac County, a major beet-growing area, did not provide relief funds to a single nonresident agricultural worker. Relief administrator O. B. Moore of Clinton County wrote that "at no time in the history of this office have we extended relief to any of these people." Other major beet-producing counties, including Arenac, Lenawee, Midland, Monroe, Muskegon, and Ottawa, also refused any winter relief to beet workers.[96]

Public assistance for permanent resident beet workers also became increasingly difficult to obtain during the late 1930s. State relief administrator William Haber announced a tougher policy that would deny relief to workers employed by companies "that cannot pay a living wage." As a result resident *betabeleros* were denied the support available to other unemployed citizens in need. Furthermore, in many locations state and county officials tried to redefine residency. In 1939 a Minnesota relief administrator referred to the roughly six thousand local Mexicano beet workers as "a residual group of nonresidents who have lived in the state for many years." Relief agencies excluded both nonresident and resident Mexicano sugar beet workers more effectively than the southern Euro-Americans of the fruit belt.[97]

The final subject of interest to midwestern reformers was education for farmworkers' children. State laws explicitly required all children of school age to attend, even those only temporarily in the state. Furthermore, high unemployment levels during the 1930s discouraged the employment of children and contributed to a rise in school attendance in urban areas. Finally, the Sugar Act of 1937 prohibited child labor under age fourteen in the sugar beets if farmers were to receive benefit payments.

Many growers opposed the child labor legislation because of its potential impact on labor costs. Beet grower C. E. Ackerman of Durand, Michigan, admitted a preference for children over adults because he could pay them less. Others obscured their personal economic interests by asserting the priority of parental rights. Grower E. R. Erwin of Bay City, Michigan, stated, "The man of the house . . . has got the right to employ them to make a living." He observed that in his own fields there were children six and eight years old; "they were picking the beets up, and they were helping the family do the work, and at the same time they were really not working." Grower Joseph Schuller of Mount Pleasant, Michigan, bluntly stated his opinion that young Mexican Americans did not merit schooling: "We believe that it would be better for these children to be helping their parents in the beet fields than to be spending their time [in school] doing nothing and learning nothing."[98]

The growers found widespread support among professional educators. One Michigan county school commissioner defended nonattendance from a different angle: "We've got to let the Mexican children help earn some money or the family will be left at the mercy of the public." In many places school officials discouraged them from attending and teachers constantly complained about them. John Thaden reported that at Crawford, Michigan, "teachers would rather not have Mexicans in school." Instructors were upset that the Mexican children "usually necessitate a lot of extra work and extra classes." They apparently hoped to maintain small classroom size by refusing to allow the children in school. Others were more open in their opposition. One teacher claimed that Mexicans were a "bloodthirsty lot," and another asserted that their presence would result in the "lowering of educational standards." These attitudes confirm a 1940 report that concluded, "There is a strong racial intolerance prevailing in the north . . . toward the Spanish speaking and the negroes."[99]

The only time during the year that officials encouraged children to attend school was at the end of May, when the state primary school census was conducted. For every child listed, the school received $11.20 from the state's primary school fund. Approximately five hundred school districts in Michigan received money from this fund because of the Mexican children in migrant beet-working families on the census rolls. Yet at other times, most districts found it impossible to comply with mandatory school attendance laws.[100]

To enforce the child labor provisions of the Sugar Act, the Children's Bureau of the USDL operated in conjunction with the State Department of Public Instruction. The state agency was required to issue proof-of-age certificates for all children who worked in the beet fields as a precondition to farmers' receiving benefit payments. Government officials rarely issued the certificates, yet farmers never failed to receive their benefit payments. The hostility of growers and the refusal of educators and government agencies to enforce laws effectively kept thousands of migrant children in the Midwest out of school for several months each year.[101]

Nonattendance was the norm among children in both seasonal fruit- and sugar beet–working families. A study in Berrien County revealed that 25 percent of all migrant children under age fourteen had not attended school in the previous twelve months. The percentage among Mexican American children was even higher. In Michigan only 100 of 288 Texas-Mexican migrant children were attending school during a survey conducted in October 1939. Investigators reported "several communities that children living near and even next door to the school building and in sight of teachers and principals daily had not yet enrolled." In many places workers' "children do not pretend to start school in the fall." As Dr. V. K. Volk of Saginaw concluded, "The Mexican children do not attend the rural schools as they are put to work in the beet fields."[102]

The reformers' efforts to achieve universal school attendance failed almost as completely as their efforts to introduce a limited number of the "safety net" reforms of the New Deal. The reformers were on the defensive in the struggle, for their numbers were small, their demands were inconsistent, and their opposition was well organized. Beginning in the mid-1930s, church groups stepped into the vacuum to offer migrant programs in the region. The first and largest church program was conducted by the Home Missions Council (HMC), an umbrella organization of Protestant churches conducting missionary work throughout the nation. The HMC began its migrant agricultural worker programs in 1920 on the East Coast. During the next several years it expanded to other parts of the country. It first entered the Midwest at the invitation of the Methodist church of Mount Pleasant, Michigan. In 1931 the Methodist church first conducted religious services for recently settled Mexicano beet workers who continued to work in the fields. In 1936 the HMC and a local church opened a summer school at the Gulick Church near Winn, Michigan. It served children from infancy to age fourteen, conducting classes in traditional subjects, nutrition, and religion, and also provided free health care and meals. The church program served a function neglected by the state and offered an alternative to parents' taking their youngest children into the fields.[103]

The first staff of four instructors included three Euro-American females and the Reverend Alberto Moreno. Prior to coming to Michigan, he had served as minister to Mexicano congregations in several small towns in Texas. Volunteer support included a visiting doctor and nurse to attend to medical needs, and supplies from Mount Pleasant businesses. Donations included food, clothing, medicine, recreational equipment, and a 1929 Essex coupe that picked up the children in the morning and returned them to their camps in the late afternoon. The summer session lasted two months.[104]

The Reverend Mr. Moreno remained in the area permanently and opened a nondenominational church, popularly referred to as the Mexican church, in nearby Shepherd. He also held religious services for Mexicanos in towns in the area. During the lull in sugar beet work in the summer he went to Western Michigan to conduct services. Although trained as a Methodist, he always carried Catholic and Protestant bibles and his services were ecumenical. In addition to his sermons, he attended to workers' problems as they affected health, education, work, and other matters. He frequently intervened in conflicts involving local farmers and workers. The Reverend Mr. Moreno also revealed the frequent failure of state officials to perform inspections and their cover-ups of dangerous health conditions. He stated that it was necessary to change conditions for workers, "so they will be less exploited by the growers, merchants and other people with whom they come into contact." [105]

Programs similar to the one in Mount Pleasant soon appeared throughout the Midwest under the auspices of the HMC and in conjunction with local coalitions of womens' Protestant church organizations. By 1942 one project in Ohio, three in Minnesota, and twenty-two in Michigan focused on the instruction of migrant children. Only a few employed a permanent Mexicano minister who was willing to challenge local abuses. Most reflected the conservative local Protestant congregations and tended to be much more cautious because of potential grower opposition and criticism. HMC minister Orlando Tusler reported that growers around Hart, Michigan, confused the HMC with the Council of Social Action, which they criticized as "communistic." Many ministers refused to support the program. A Wesleyan minister in Western Michigan would not participate in a local program because he "thought that all migrants are bums." In order to avoid controversy local groups increasingly emphasized the spiritual thrust of missionary work. An HMC staff member in Tuscola County, Michigan, complained, "This is essentially a holiness area," concerned with saving the souls of workers but not interested in their physical needs or legal rights.[106]

As the war approached, another concern, "Americanization," altered the earlier material emphasis. The missionaries set up "Americanization Schools" for these children born and reared in the United States. One teacher explained, "The big problem that had to be faced was that these children were not Americans, just Mexicans." Bogged down in matters of spirituality and identity and again blaming the victim, the program subordinated its earlier mission. By the mid-1940s even the Reverend Mr. Moreno had become frustrated and resigned his post at the church to take a job as a factory worker. From there he continued to attend to the physical needs of local Mexicanos after work and on weekends.[107]

The final effort at reform occurred within the university community. John Thaden of Michigan State College, probably the largest and most important agricultural institution in the region, addressed the lack of balance in the college's research. When it was created in the mid-nineteenth century the mission of the agricultural college network included research on agricultural production as well as on the needs of rural people. Thaden noted that Michigan State spent thousands of dollars and conducted numerous studies every year on different crops, but never in its history had it conducted a serious study on farmworkers. To alter the imbalance, between 1939 and 1942 he researched and produced a detailed manuscript more than one hundred pages long on the transportation, housing, and working conditions of beet workers in the state. He also documented abuses by corporations, growers, and permanent residents of communities toward their seasonal workers. The readers of the manuscript were E. B. Hill of the Farm Management Department, H. C. Rather of the Farm Crops Department, George A. Brown of Animal Husbandry, and R. V. Gardner of the Michigan Agriculture Experiment Station; no sociologists reviewed it. They criticized its length, its harsh portrayal of working and housing conditions, and its focus on the mistreatment of workers by growers, local merchants, and the sugar beet companies.[108]

Thaden, who needed the publication for tenure, removed material that offended the reviewers and ended up with a forty-two-page booklet, *Mexican Beet Workers in Michigan.* The agricultural interests of Michigan State College had thus thwarted internal criticism of a system they helped create and in which they had a heavily vested interest. Serious attempts at internal reform of the content and conclusions of research within the agricultural college system were stalled for yet another generation.

Conclusion

The transformation of agricultural labor that began in the mid-1930s went through several stages. In the first, increased production created a greater demand for workers. In the second, resident farmworkers attempted to organize but were defeated, making possible the introduction of a nonresident work force that scholars and growers alike described as disorganized.

Corporations and growers preferred the new workers, who lived in areas where the cost of subsistence was much lower. The two branches of the newly emergent migratory stream had much in common. Migrants were largely rural and agricultural in background and came from the poorest parts of the nation. They were recruited to work in the North, attracted in part because of economic and political forces that made survival in their homelands more tenuous.

Their entry into the region led to greater tensions with permanent residents than existed in earlier years, partly because the newer arrivals came in greater numbers, were more mobile, and had the potential political power of citizenship. Their presence was a defeat for repressive labor policies and represented a freedom of movement and expression that was not possible in the mid-South and Texas. Furthermore, as farmworkers they were able to re-create many social and cultural forms that their predecessors had not.

Yet they also faced important constraints. For one, unlike in California and many rural locations in the Southwest, there were few opportunities to settle and remain active as farmworkers. Jobs in the rural sector were not increasing rapidly enough to ensure a permanent place for them. Those who wanted to settle had to find a place in larger towns and cities.

Reformers in the union movement, the church, and liberal politicians were also unable to overcome cultural differences and accept the need for farmworkers to have their own voice. The reformers did not include them in the struggles concerning their exclusion from politics and the social and cultural life of the small communities where they worked and lived for much of the year. As long as political reforms were attempted from above they were doomed to failure.

The final stage of the transformation in the agricultural work force took place with the outbreak of World War II. The war enabled growers to reintroduce foreign workers and create new mechanisms of control. This resulted in more complicated social relations in midwestern agriculture.

CHAPTER 5

Foreign Workers and Control,
1942–1950

In the 1940s employers of agricultural labor took several initiatives to gain greater control over their workers. Their efforts completed a transformation of the work force that had begun in the previous decade. The most important feature, the permanent entry of government into farm-labor relations, made possible the introduction of large numbers of foreigners into the seasonal work force. It was, as Linda and Theo Majka have observed, "the greatest coincidence of government and the interest of agribusiness to date."[1]

The changes in the 1940s have been interpreted in different ways. One view suggests that because of the disruption in the labor supply caused by wartime demands, the government decided to assist private employers for the benefit of the country.[2] A second interpretation was offered by Carey McWilliams, that is, "planned chaos" in the labor market. McWilliams suggested that private and public groups joined purposely to keep the work force disorganized.[3] The third view, a derivation of the second, was presented by scholar and labor organizer Ernesto Galarza. Based on his experiences in California, he referred to the process as "using race blocs" against each other. This interpretation suggests that government and capitalists were not equal partners, but rather that employers manipulated the government and created divisions in the work force to keep workers at odds with each other, thereby impeding organizing.[4]

Agencies and Associations

During the 1940s government agencies and private grower associations became increasingly involved in agricultural labor recruitment, hiring, and employment. The U.S. Employment Service first began recruitment for agriculture during World War I, but until the late 1930s it operated in only a few locations. Before World War II, private employers in the Midwest outside the sugar beet industry lacked a formal recruitment mechanism.

Alan Clive considers the expansion of production in the Great Lakes region during World War II "a momentary pause in the decline" of production. In fact, it was part of the growth and diversification of specialized crops that had been taking place for several decades. Federal price supports and purchases were a direct stimulus during the war. The most important growth was in the labor-intensive fresh fruits and canning vegetables industries.[5]

Canning vegetables were produced in a wide area running from Northwestern Ohio and Southeastern Michigan through Northern Indiana, Illinois, and Southern Wisconsin into Minnesota. The most important canning crops were asparagus, corn, peas, string beans, and tomatoes. Prior to World War II the canning industry was characterized by hundreds of small, independent canners who employed mostly local youths and women for harvest and canning operations during the brief season.[6]

The expansion in the 1940s was the result of massive investment by major corporations including the Green Giant Company, Libby, McNeill and Libby, the Campbell Soup Company, California Packing Corporation (later Del Monte), the H. J. Heinz Company, and Stokeley Foods. They constructed large canneries and purchased many of the already-established smaller enterprises. Adapting a pattern established in the sugar beet industry, the companies contracted with local farmers to purchase crops for their factories. They attracted growers by offering contracts that guaranteed the purchase of a determined acreage at set prices before the season began. They also provided growers with seeds or plants, rented machinery, and commonly had field men direct the planting, cultivation, and harvesting operations. As a further inducement, they also created a recruitment and hiring mechanism for field-workers, a task made more difficult because of the tighter wartime labor market.[7]

The labor shortage in the United States was greatest in places where industrial activities were most intense, among them the urban Midwest. War industries attracted workers from the ranks of the unemployed in the cities, nearby small towns, and farms. It also attracted many more African American and Euro-American citizens from the South than before World War I. Urban industrial employment threatened to reduce the annual migration of farmworkers, including those from Texas, to the midwestern beet fields. It induced agricultural corporations to organize growers and associations into pressuring federal and state governments to assist in recruiting labor.

The federal government first became active in recruitment in the region because of a minor crisis in the fall of 1942, when many Mexican Americans from Texas departed prior to beet topping because they feared being stranded after the government announced gas-rationing programs. Employers in the Midwest took advantage of the shortage to demand Mexican *braceros*, but the Farm Security Administration instead recruited single men from Kentucky. Complaints from growers that the Kentuckians were not adequate put additional pressure on the USDL and further contributed to the abolition of the Farm Security Administration in 1946. Employers also were able to shift responsibility for farm labor recruitment to the War Food Administration (WFA) of the U.S. Department of Agriculture in 1943. It set up the Emergency Farm Labor Program (EFLP), which lasted until the end of the 1947 season. The EFLP was responsible for operating a new version of the Women's Land Army, the Victory Farm Volunteers, youth employment, and foreign worker recruitment from Mexico and the British West Indies.[8]

The most important foreigners were Mexican *braceros*, who first came to California in 1942 under FSA regulations. The Bracero Program became official in 1943 when Congress passed Public Law 45. The law included an authorization for worker transportation, a grant to the Agricultural Extension Service for recruiting labor, job training, housing, and experimentation with labor-saving devices.[9]

The WFA and college extension services shared administrative responsibilities. Extension agents devised recruitment, training, distribution, and placement schemes. Their county farm labor advisory committees and wage boards, composed of a handful of "the leading farmers of the county," also determined need and set prevailing wages. In effect, the new EFLP handed control over to local corporate representatives and large growers.[10]

Beginning in 1948 farm placement was transferred to state Farm Placement Service (FPS) administrators of the U.S. Employment Service, under the auspices of the USDL. Local FPS administrators handled labor demands as determined by corporate officials and large growers, with the assistance of the Extension Service. The switch to the USDL did not alter control; worker representatives still were not involved in determining need, prevailing wages, or recruitment and hiring decisions.[11]

During the 1940s control of farm labor recruitment was further refined by the formation of new private employer associations, often created at the behest of government officials. The most important in the region, Michigan Field Crops, Incorporated (MFCI), was formed in the fall of 1943. It united established beet growers' employment committees in Michigan, Indiana, and Ohio, which had been embarrassed by the recent federal investigations of worker transportation and housing. MFCI, formed "through prodding and guiding on the part of the extension service" of Michigan State College, dealt with all phases of recruitment, hiring, and employment of beet field labor in Michigan, Ohio, and Indiana. "Acting as agents for their farmers," MFCI staff included corporate officials and major growers in the region. Unlike the earlier committees, MFCI also worked with employers in other crops, including cherries, pickling cucumbers, sweet corn, tomatoes, and snap beans, to transfer workers when there was no work in the beet fields. Based on California Field Crops, Incorporated, also formed at government urging a few months earlier, MFCI claimed that if it organized worker movement from one crop to another, workers would be "assured of continuous employment." In Minnesota, American Crystal helped form the Red River Valley Beet Growers Association in 1943. Both associations continued to recruit workers from Texas and to arrange transportation and placement through private employment agencies.[12]

Smaller associations representing growers formed in the 1940s, including the Michigan Cooperative Farm Labor Services for fruit and vegetable growers, the Eastern Michigan Growers' Association, the Wisconsin, Minnesota, Michigan, and Indiana Canners' associations, the Cherry Growers' Association in Michigan, and the Cherry Growers' Cooperative in Wisconsin. These organizations worked more closely with state employment services than did the beet industry. Government representatives traveled to other states to work with their state employment services and to coordinate the recruitment and hiring of workers. The associations were also active in determining wages. In the case of sugar beets, "public" wage hearings continued to be held annually. In the case of fruits and vegetables, "prevailing wages" were determined in private meetings of county wage boards appointed by extension service personnel. The recruitment, hiring, and employment system elaborated during the mid-1940s remained essentially unchanged until the late 1960s.[13]

Special Farm Labor committees, composed solely of local "grower" representatives, determined local needs, and their recommendations almost invariably were accepted by the FPS. Their haphazard decisions commonly contravened regulations, and they consistently sought to replace available domestic workers with foreign workers. A. W. Siebenand, of Green Giant and the Minnesota Canners' Association, testified in 1950 to the need for foreign workers as "a nucleus around which to build the domestic supply." The Illinois Canning Company in Hoopestown, Illinois, in 1945 employed several hundred Jamaicans, "whom it is hoped will replace the Texas-Mexicans next year." In 1947 MFCI representative Clarence J. Bourg testified that the FPS allotted Michigan 3,500 *braceros* for beet topping, "leaving 10,500 workers to be recruited locally and from domestic sources." The new recruitment mechanism created by and on behalf of the corporations made "hardly a dent" in domestic workers' unsuccessful search for employment while it further obscured employer responsibility. As the president of a Michigan growers' association admitted, "We have lost, through this set-up, the personal relationship between the grower and his employee." [14]

Worker Segmentation

The expansion of specialized crop production, the increased numbers of workers, and new forms of control were accompanied by a sharp segmentation of the agricultural working class. Some scholars see the roots of worker division in cultural differences among the workers, whereas others suggest that capitalists were primarily responsible for such divisions. The nature of these divisions and their causes among farmworkers in the Midwest will be addressed in this section.

Foreign contract workers were the major new addition to the region in the 1940s. The most important, Mexican *braceros,* came as a result of an international agreement between the United States and Mexico. The initial contracts granted workers free transportation to and from Mexico and between places of residence and work. They guaranteed hygienic housing, water, and facilities inspected by the WFA, and either cooking privileges or prepared meals of sound nutritional value at cost, not to exceed $1.40 per day. Workers were to be paid the "prevailing wage" as established by local wage boards or regional sugar beet wage hearings, but never less than 30 cents per hour, and wages were never to undercut domestic wages. The contracts guaranteed employment during 75 percent of the contract period, excluding Sundays, with subsistence provided on days with less than four hours' work. The contracts also entitled workers to a formal grievance and mediation procedure in case of disputes. In 1948, when the Department of Labor took over the program, the enforcement procedure was weakened. It added new stipulations punishing workers, but not growers, who violated the agreement.[15]

Braceros first entered the Midwest in 1943, working in the formerly Tejano-dominated sugar beet cycle. Unlike their predecessors, they were guaranteed paid transportation, a minimum wage, and inspected housing. The organization of work also differed, as they were employed in male crews ranging in size from four to ten. Crew members resided together, ate together, worked on assignments as a unit, and, consequently, were paid the same. Increasingly, *braceros* were housed in larger camps, makeshift arrangements of shacks, barracks, trailers, or specially constructed dormitories. The mutual obligations and dependence on the output of other crew members served as a form of discipline reminiscent of the factory production line.[16]

Most of the British West Indians who came to the Midwest under the Emergency Farm Labor Program were Jamaicans, but some came from Barbados, the Bahamas, and British Honduras (Belize). Their contracts were similar to those of the *braceros* in many ways. The men were guaranteed employment at least three-fourths of the time at prevailing wages, with housing and food stipulations similar to those of the Bracero Program. There was, however, no minimum wage set and after early experimentation the Caribbean governments paid the workers' transportation one way and the workers paid the other as well as transportation between job sites. Furthermore, workers could be deported at their own expense for "an act of misconduct or indiscipline," with no set standard for determining such behavior and no mechanism for worker complaints about employer misconduct or breach of contract. Unlike the *bracero* agreements, these contracts were between individuals rather than governments and lacked clearly specified enforcement or mediation clauses.[17]

During the 1940s approximately one-fourth as many Caribbean men as Mexican *braceros* came to the United States as seasonal agricultural workers. Most of them went to the East Coast and southeastern states, whereas *braceros* went primarily to the Southwest. The two met in the Midwest. Like *braceros*, the Caribbean workers first came to the region in 1943, when almost fifteen hundred worked in the Michigan sugar beet fields. They were expected to work there the entire season, but because of the wet spring they averaged only nine days' work the first month. Unlike the Spanish-speaking Tejanos, whose complaints were largely deflected by crew leaders, the English-speaking Jamaicans quickly protested the failure of the beet companies to provide housing, food, employment, and subsistence according to the terms of their contracts. The companies quickly arranged with WFA administrators to send the workers elsewhere. Some remained in Michigan to work in onions, cherries, celery, and later in the apple harvest. Most were shipped to Indiana, Illinois, Wisconsin, and Minnesota to harvest canning crops and detassel seed corn. The 1943 experience largely shaped their employment in the Midwest in later years. Beet companies did not want them, but the canneries found them acceptable for field labor. Their numbers declined after the 1945 crop season, but increased again in the 1950s.[18]

Midwestern employers were reluctant to employ the English-speaking workers. Dorothy Knowles of the HMC observed that according to growers "they were considered too slow or inefficient with machinery." She added that attitudes were also influenced by "the fact that they are negroid in appearance," a serious concern in many "lily-white" rural communities. In places where migrant workers were more established, employers clearly preferred Tejanos or Mexican nationals. The USES also hesitated to place them in the region, thereby reinforcing a general trend of placing African American workers in the eastern sections of the country and those of Mexican birth and descent in the West.[19]

The Caribbean workers were most numerous where they could be most isolated, especially in newer canning crop areas, where they stayed in large corporation-owned camps. A midwestern canning crop work cycle became established in the 1940s. Asparagus planting and harvesting took place in April and May before sugar beet hoeing and the early fruits. The harvest of the major canning crops—peas, carrots, and corn—was in July and August, following cherries and preceding the late summer and early fall fruit harvest or beet topping. The pea harvest was somewhat different, employing mostly crews of twelve to twenty men who worked long shifts, sometimes sixteen to twenty hours. Pay in these crops typically was by piece rate. Canneries experimented with different groups of available workers, but increasingly turned to single males, whom they housed in central camps on cannery property. Increasingly, these seasonal workers also entered the canneries. A Minnesota report explained that canneries claimed to prefer foreign workers because unlike domestic workers they were "accustomed to year-round hot weather and hard manual work."[20]

The men from Jamaica, the Bahamas, and Barbados typically came to the midwestern canning areas as part of a seasonal cycle. They began in Florida in the winter, went to the Midwest in the late spring and early summer, then to the Middle Atlantic states in the late summer and fall. For Mexican *braceros*, the canneries tended to fill irregular gaps in their employment in the region.[21]

In the early 1940s prisoners of war (POWs) also found employment in midwestern agriculture. Most were Germans; a lesser number were Italians. Through requests to the War Manpower Commission, employers received certification to employ them in "essential" nonwar production industries, especially agriculture. POWs interned in camps throughout the region were given the option of working voluntarily for a daily stipend of 80 cents to spend on goods at the local canteen. They resided in camps or internment centers and each day traveled to work, principally on vegetable canning crops. Like other foreign workers they were single males who worked in crews and were housed primarily in barracks. Their camps were the largest in the Midwest, typically housing more than one thousand. Most worked under guard in crews of ten or more, although farmers often employed smaller groups without a guard.[22]

Japanese prisoners, who were much less numerous, seldom worked in the Midwest. One attempt to employ them in 1944 near Marengo, Illinois, was foiled by residents, who raised "a storm of protest," a reflection of local hostility and racism toward the unfamiliar Asians. By contrast, employers were pleased with the Germans, whom they could hire at the prevailing wage of 30 cents per hour on twenty-four-hour notice. The government used most of the payment it received from the farmer ($2.40 per eight-hour day) to cover its own administrative costs, including armed guards, food, clothing, and shelter, with huge sums remaining for the federal treasury. According to Arnold Krammer, "The relationship between the prisoners and the farmers who employed them was generally one of mutual and genuine admiration." The excellent relations suggest that for employers they represented the seldom-achieved ideal—Caucasian, noncomplaining, willing to work at set rates, and with no chance of becoming a permanent part of the community. Grower attempts to employ domestic prisoners failed, because local prison industries were using them "to the limit." The employment of POWs ended after the 1945 crop season.[23]

A final group introduced into the Midwest during World War II were the Nisei, second-generation U.S. citizens of Japanese descent, formerly interned in concentration camps in Colorado. The WFA made several attempts to bring them into the region. One of its most notable efforts was for sugar beet work around Imlay City, Michigan, in 1943. They were organized as single male groups and housed in special camps in barracks-type dwellings. Several local farmers considered them good workers, but many others "declared they wouldn't have a Jap on the place." State Representative Floyd E. Town of Jackson led an effort to remove them immediately, claiming that their presence "would place our industries in jeopardy." In Minnesota, Nisei also worked, but reportedly resented working in the same fields as lower-status Mexican Americans, whom the Nisei had often employed in agriculture in California and Colorado.[24]

The foreign-born contract workers, POWs, and Nisei of the 1940s lived as single males organized into gangs and typically lived in dormitories or barracks in large camps. The POWs had working arrangements similar to those of other foreigners and were employed principally in canning crops. Most complaints against foreigners, whether contract workers or prisoners, came from small farmers, who expressed not only nativist fears, but also resentment for the favoritism toward the corporations that employed them.[25]

The introduction of foreign workers did not displace domestic workers, who by the 1940s followed three general seasonal work cycles in the Great Lakes region. Southern Euro-Americans and African Americans went first to Ohio, Indiana, Illinois, and Michigan for fruit harvesting; during interim periods they often worked in the canning crop areas in the same states. Two patterns appeared for Tejanos, for whom sugar beets retained a central role. Those who went to Michigan and Ohio frequently started in asparagus planting and snapping in April and May, or else they went directly into sugar beet work. After hoeing, they picked cherries near Lake Erie or Lake Michigan, beans or pickling cucumbers in Central Michigan or muck crops in Indiana, Ohio, and Southern Michigan. Then they returned to beets for topping. Those who worked in Minnesota and Wisconsin filled the gap in beet employment by harvesting potatoes in the Red River Valley, cherries and cucumbers in Wisconsin, and the canning crops in the zone from Northern Indiana to Minnesota.[26]

By the 1940s mechanization had sharply reduced the amount of labor necessary in sugar beets and made workers increasingly migratory. With the introduction of new crops, growers were able to create a much more highly segmented work force, with ethnicity its prominent feature. Legal differences separated domestic and foreign workers, as the former were not protected by the contract guarantees for wages, housing, and employment that the latter enjoyed. There were also differences in crop and work cycles as well as distinct forms of crew organization. A 1946 Indiana study revealed that Tejano crews averaged forty-four persons, those from Arkansas and Missouri thirteen, and the groups from Kentucky and Tennessee six. The Mexican Americans typically worked in moderate-sized crews, Missourians and Arkansans in small groups of two or three nuclear families, and Kentuckians and Tennesseans as single individuals or family units. Furthermore, 95 percent of Tejanos were paid through the crew leader, compared with only 32 percent of the others.[27]

Sharp segregation remained the rule even where different ethnic groups worked the same crops in close proximity. In the most highly concentrated zone of production, the Northwestern Michigan cherry-growing area, domestic and foreign crews were segregated by camps and worked in different parts of the area. The Rochelle, Illinois, vegetable area in the 1940s had Mexican nationals, Tejanos, and Euro-Americans from Missouri. Mexican nationals stayed in a dormitory on the edge of the city, Tejanos on individual farms west of town, and Euro-Americans in a separate and better-maintained camp across the road from the Tejanos. In the tomato-growing areas around Marion, Indiana, southern Euro-Americans resided in camps at Swayzee, Greentown, and Fowler; Tejanos stayed at Phlox, Hemlock, Hartford City, Portland, and Bluffton. In Madison and Tipton counties in Indiana, Jamaicans resided in Point Isabel and at Tipton, POWs at Stokeley, African Americans at Hutchorson's camp, Euro-Americans at Brunson, Hobbs, and Leisure, and Tejanos at Summittville, Warms, near Frankstons, and at Rigdan. Camp managers were instructed to maintain this rigid segregation. Rochelle had Euro-Americans and Tejano camps across the road from one another. One evening a group of Tejanos offered to play softball against the Euro-Americans, who invited them to their larger ball field. The camp manager prohibited the Tejanos from entering, complaining, "They tramp down the grass. Besides, the old man don't allow any of them Mexicans to come over here." Consequently, the two teams played on the smaller field at the Tejanos' camp.[28]

The number of undocumented workers from Mexico increased irregularly in the 1940s. Complaints against them were infrequent and raids by the Immigration and Naturalization Service (INS) were even less common. As in other parts of the country, *troqueros* devised ingenious ways to haul them northward. In 1948 thirty-nine men and one woman were discovered near Chicago in a false-bottomed cargo truck carrying melons. During their five-day journey from South Texas the melons were their only source of food. Undocumented Mexican workers more commonly went to the larger cities of the region, especially Chicago and Detroit, where they encountered more diverse communities and greater employment opportunities.[29]

Labor unionists and domestic workers commonly complained that the movement of Mexican contract and undocumented workers into Texas forced the state's residents into the Midwest. Their views oversimplified and in some ways distorted the history of the Tejano labor migration northward. The earliest flow of Tejanos began in 1935 and expanded steadily until 1942, when movement north from Mexico was relatively slight. Tejano migration to the Midwest declined in 1943, precisely when workers from Mexico were entering the country in greater numbers. Thus the movement of workers from Texas during this period increased steadily but irregularly, without any apparent relationship to migration from Mexico. The Mexican government's blacklist of Texas in the mid-1940s, which contributed to a relative increase in wages in Texas, might be expected to have deterred the movement of Tejanos northward, but it did not. In the late 1940s the entry of undocumented Mexicanos into Texas increased simultaneously with Tejano movement out of the state.[30]

Employers and the government justified the introduction of foreign workers on the grounds of a labor shortage. In relative terms their argument was justified during the period between 1940 and 1945, during which agricultural wages rose from 24 percent to 43 percent of factory earnings. Housing, particularly for foreign workers, also improved. Yet even during the war workers faced long periods of unemployment and underemployment, and agricultural incomes remained far below those of industry.[31]

By 1945 unemployment in midwestern agriculture had begun to rise, in part because of an "alarming increase in the employment of minors." Wages and working conditions began to deteriorate rapidly. In 1947 HMC minister Ellis Marshburn reported "labor surpluses in nearly every crop and generally unsatisfactory earnings." Furthermore, the terms of foreign worker contracts in the late 1940s declined sharply, as many of the earlier guarantees were removed. Meanwhile, the flow of braceros and undocumented workers increased. By 1948, when the Mexican government removed Texas from its blacklist, the influx from Mexico was pushing Tejanos out of the state. As one observer noted, the increase of Mexicans "ignored the availability of domestic workers." Between 1945 and 1950 agricultural wages fell to 37 percent of industrial incomes. By the end of the decade most of the wage gains made during the war were wiped out.[32]

The number of seasonal workers in midwestern agriculture between 1943 and 1950 roughly doubled, from about 65,000 to 120,000, of whom more than half were employed in Michigan. By 1950 the total included an estimated 75,000 Mexican Americans, 30,000 southern Euro-Americans, and 15,000 southern African Americans. The number of contract Mexican workers peaked in 1947, at about 15,000; British West Indian workers in 1946, at about 10,000; and

POWs in 1945, at about 6,000. The corporations' success in maintaining this diverse and highly segmented work force was, according to labor expert Byron Mitchell, "enough to stop most collective bargaining in its tracks."[33]

Workers, Employers, and Midwestern Communities

The only contact most local residents had with midwestern farmworkers was what they read in the newspapers. The two most pervasive impressions that local journalists portrayed appeared in an August 8, 1946, *Detroit News* article. It first stated that "representatives of the Mexican government, the Cherry Land Co-op Crops Association, the Michigan Agricultural Extension Service and the Michigan Field Crops Incorporated, are busy seeing that the Mexican gets paid well, fed well, housed well and returns home with safety and dispatch." It also described men, "women and children, guitars snapping, voices raised in song—a happy people."

Pay included transportation, housing, food, and wages. Mexican *braceros* were the only workers guaranteed free transportation to and from the United States and between places of employment. Yet this advantage was offset by pre-transportation costs. Rito Herrera, who came to Michigan in 1946, had to sell his tools to pay expenses and purchase passports in Mexico that cost him 300 pesos (about $37.50). Other prospective *braceros* had to sell animals and farm equipment, use their savings, and borrow money to pay sums ranging from fifty dollars to two hundred dollars before they departed for the United States; these sums were much higher than transportation for domestic workers. Furthermore, they could not rely on contractual guarantees. Tomás Ledesma spent five miserable days on a truck from McAllen, Texas. Workers had to pay for food en route, and on arrival they were charged for transportation from their barracks to work, and for tools.[34]

Housing guarantees for *braceros* included free dwellings that were clean, potable water, and bathing facilities, all inspected by government authorities. José Pérez Morales and twelve other *braceros* worked in Central Michigan and lived crowded together in a beet shack measuring eight by twelve feet. A crew in Millington, Michigan, had to live in an abandoned farmhouse that leaked badly when it rained. The basement had a standing pool of water two to three feet deep. Water from the well intended for drinking and bathing was too contaminated for either purpose. Moreover, the "bathtub" was a filthy pool formed by the intersection of drains from horse stables. Government inspection of such facilities almost never took place.[35]

Bracero contracts also guaranteed either adequate cooking facilities or healthful meals provided at cost, with the latter being more common. On arrival men often went long periods without being fed, and commonly had inadequate and unhealthful meals. A crew of a dozen men dropped off on a farm in Michigan were neglected for six days before they were fed. In the interim they scraped up thirty cents among themselves to buy two loaves of bread, which they ate with water. The workers were not passive, however; one government report described "frequent work stoppages and other means of protest," another, "open rebellion over food." [36]

Mexican contract workers commonly were placed in poor fields rejected by domestic workers. In 1944 Edmundo Flores, an inspector for the War Food Administration in the Door County, Wisconsin, cherry harvest, reported that *braceros*, domestic Euro-American workers, and growers all testified to him that *braceros* were purposely excluded from first pickings and the best orchards. In other areas they were placed in beet fields that Tejanos refused. Because contracts tied them to the fields where they were placed and they lacked transportation, they had trouble preventing discrimination in field placement. Flores also revealed that they faced long periods of unemployment and underemployment, cheating by field men and growers on field measurement, piece rates, and subsistence. [37]

Inspector Flores considered the inadequacy of the grievance procedure to be at the root of workers' difficulties. One problem was that the number of complaints made it "almost impossible to do anything about it." A second problem was WFA personnel. In Wisconsin only one other WFA administrator could speak Spanish, yet language difficulties between workers and employers "caused an infinite number of misunderstandings." Furthermore, WFA personnel had a "natural affinity" with growers and sided with them despite recurrent "flagrant abuses by employers." They commonly dismissed worker complaints and accepted grower charges that *braceros* who challenged them were "lazy" or "city boys." A Minnesota WFA investigator answered complaints about lack of work and poor pay by suggesting that "they can easily make eight to twelve dollars a day if they care to work." The WFA agreed with Michigan Sugar Company official Arthur Schupp, whose response to worker grievances on wages was that *braceros* were "taking too many siestas." WFA personnel established a practice of sending workers who complained back to Mexico as quickly as possible, without a hearing and in violation of their contracts. Flores's efforts to defend workers in the Sturgeon Bay, Wisconsin, area resulted in his permanent removal after local cherry growers successfully pressured his superiors. [38]

Worker complaints of low wages and underemployment were confirmed by survey data. A WFA investigation in Wisconsin in 1945, before the sharp deterioration in working and employment conditions, revealed 44 percent unemployment in the sugar beets, 16 percent in the canning crops, and 20 percent in the cherries. Pay abuses were best documented for sugar beet workers. A careful study by one of the few sympathetic Mexican consular officials, Ernesto Laveaga, examined beet hoeing in Michigan in 1945. He calculated that workers had to hoe an average of 22.7 beet plants per minute to earn 75 cents per hour, the wage that Michigan Sugar Company officials claimed was normal for a diligent Mexican American worker. Laveaga determined that the average diligent worker could hoe 9.9 plants per minute and concluded that the company claim that normal workers earned 60 cents per hour "is a demonstrable fallacy." He revealed that the companies' figures were the result of including an entire family's earnings on one pay slip.[39]

Finding no other outlet for grievances, *braceros* often walked out of the fields. In 1946 one group left the fields near Millington, Michigan, and walked about eighty miles to the heart of the Mexicano *colonia* in Detroit. The group of twenty-four men prepared a written complaint at the Most Holy Trinity Parish in the heart of the *colonia* and carried it to the Mexican consul, who forwarded it to WFA compliance officers. Government officials immediately threatened to repatriate them instead of granting them a hearing. The major grievance was low wages, as individuals in the two crews had received only $12.89 and $13.35, respectively, for a four-week, 130-hour pay period, after deductions. These earning were about 40 percent of the minimum pay guaranteed in their contracts.[40]

In 1948 a crew of *braceros* in the beet fields near Akron, Michigan, had filthy dwellings and blankets, water unfit to drink, and a *revisador* who refused to measure their fields. After working forty-one days, each crew member had earned $13.75 after food deductions of $31.83. They were then sent to the cucumber harvest near Marshall, where they averaged $1 per day for an additional six weeks. Unable to file a grievance, the crew finally quit and walked more than one hundred miles to Detroit to find a sympathetic listener. Knowing that government officials would not act on worker complaints, employers commonly refused to abide by contract terms, according to one observer, because they considered the written guarantees "to be preposterous."[41]

Another abuse involved employers who transferred workers to nonagricultural tasks to save themselves the cost of hiring mechanics and other skilled workers. When a *bracero* in Wisconsin complained that the prevailing rate for mechanics was higher, the WFA administrator responded that "he was getting a good deal because being a mechanic was easy work." A group of *braceros* near Sebewaing, Michigan, complained about lack of work, so their employer sent them to a local automobile dealer who had them dig ditches. They filed a grievance on wages and treatment with a WFA compliance officer, who promptly ordered them deported for breaking contract stipulations that prohibited them from working outside of agriculture. They then walked more than one hundred miles to Detroit to complain to the Mexican consul and to halt their deportation. The consul confronted a local WFA administrator, who claimed that the *braceros* were lazy city boys who did not want to work. As a compromise, the workers were transferred to another employer.[42]

The 75 percent employment requirement was regularly forgotten. To ensure compliance, employers were supposed to issue daily time slips for each worker, but they regularly refused to issue them or doctored them by crediting workers with eight hours for ten or twelve hours of work. They also inaccurately filled in the work symbols, S (satisfactory), R (refusal to work), W (weather), M (missing), and O (other). Typically, they marked slips with an R on days of heavy rains and wet fields, an abuse WFA administrator Flores considered "flagrant."[43]

Government administrators also violated regulations enthusiastically. Following established procedure, Minnesota WFA administrator John A. Wright simply branded a crew of discontented workers as "agitators" and ordered them deported. In Wisconsin a *bracero* complained that local officials called them "agitators" for protesting illegal deductions and "isolated us from the rest of the group and put us in different fields." USDA officials then "put us on a blacklist and tried to force us to return to Mexico," after threatening them with imprisonment. As Red-baiting intensified during the 1940s, administrators increasingly called dissatisfied *braceros* radicals and Communists. One church observer commented that a worker was accused of being a Communist, "whose only ideological sin consisted in a repeated complaint having to do with the rather scanty amount of food they were being fed."[44]

The foreign workers were the most isolated of all from the midwestern communities, separated as they were by linguistic, cultural, legal, and organizational factors. Furthermore, unlike Mexican Americans, they were not surrounded by relatives and friends who offered a close-knit and familiar working world. Although their contracts forbade discrimination, local opinion lumped them with Tejanos and prohibited entry into public restaurants, churches, movie theaters, barbershops, and taverns.[45]

Even the foreign consul proved to be of little help. Edmundo Flores reported that with few exceptions "the performance of the Mexican consulate was thoroughly inadequate. Strangely enough they showed a tendency to blame all the irregularities on the workers." Rare individuals like Ernesto Laveaga in Detroit and Emilio Aldama in Chicago worked diligently on behalf of their compatriots. Aldama, after confirming reports of widespread contract violations in wages, inadequate housing and health, poor treatment, and discrimination, tried to convince Mexican consular officials to prohibit *braceros* from coming to the Midwest: "Our government should not permit the departure of agricultural braceros to those regions." Most consular officials, however, were timid before U.S. officials and condescending to their own citizens. When Flores visited the consular offices in Chicago, officials mistook him for a *bracero* and tried to repatriate him.[46]

Employers of workers from the British West Indies also abused contract provisions on wages, housing conditions, and food. Their water was often unhealthy, and one sample was shown to have "small worms and bugs." Compared with other workers the Caribbean men experienced more frequent outbreaks of such communicable diseases as malaria, mumps, and typhoid fever.[47]

Jamaicans and Bahamians had more problems than any other group because of community hostility. They were subjected for the first time in their lives to Euro-American racism as exhibited in the United States against blacks, and they were confused and angered. One group in Wisconsin faced a foreman who strutted around with a .38 caliber pistol and frequently shot it into the air. An FSA investigator reported that the foreman proclaimed that "he was the boss" and that "if any of those black devils would threaten him, he did not intend to die first." The workers feared for their lives; the foreman stated to the investigator that he would get rid of the "ringleaders" who initiated the complaints.[48]

Many permanent residents in the small towns had their first contacts with blacks in the 1940s. A group of Jamaicans near Imlay City, Michigan, who arrived in 1943 suffered not only from a hostile community, which barred them from all public places, but also from constant police surveillance. In Door County, Wisconsin, both Jamaicans and Mexicans were prohibited from entering restaurants, bars, stores, and other public places. Local growers also expressed deep resentment against the Jamaicans and Bahamians, complaining that the foreigners were brought in to work while their own sons had been sent off to war. One Indiana grower, upset that health regulations did not apply to domestic workers, complained to a local health officer that "it seemed damned funny that the board of health was interested in these men." The health official responded that the government was not interested in the health of the workers, but in the possibility that they might spread disease to permanent residents. Yet, other growers were satisfied with the Caribbean workers, who had to tolerate greater abuses than domestics. In Michigan, USES representative Peter Odergard commented, "The Bahamians, you can wipe your hands on them. They come and when you are through you can ship them back and you don't have to worry about them the rest of the year."[49]

Jamaican and Bahamian workers also challenged their employers and complained regularly about "the attitudes of the people in the area." In 1945 Dorothy Knowles of the HMC reported from Minnesota that one Jamaican told her, "Miss Dorothy, you are the only white woman we have found friendly in this country." Discrimination against the Caribbean workers was somewhat different from that against *braceros*. Although Euro-American racism and a fear of the poor affected both, Mexicanos were not as foreign, for they had worked in many locations for several decades. Furthermore, the language barrier between Mexicanos and locals served to shield the latter from many workers' complaints. Not surprisingly, the "city boys" who defended their rights frequently had some facility with the English language.[50]

Like the Caribbean workers, African Americans also faced increasingly overt public discrimination, evident in the signs placed in public places: "White Traffic Only," or "We Cater Only to Whites." African Americans were more likely to complain about such treatment than other domestic or foreign workers. One crew of men and women from Louisiana was recruited for cherry picking in the Sturgeon Bay, Wisconsin, area. Employed by H. L. Miller, they quickly became dissatisfied with the sporadic work and low wages and went on strike. Miller refused to negotiate and called on Door County sheriff Hallie Rowe to order them off his property. Rowe testified that he and two of his assistants loaded the workers onto a truck, took them over the county line, then "dumped them and gave them a chance to start for home." Miller justified his actions in the local press: "Most of these negroes have never been outside the South and are completely illiterate. They can't understand anything but the strict and occasionally brutal measures of control over them. Up here their freedom goes to their head."[51]

The Sturgeon Bay Common Council feared that African Americans and the "foreign element" would drive away the tourist trade and ordered the local district attorney to "deliver them straight to their camps" on arrival; if they didn't "stay within their limits" they were to be "arrested for vagrancy." The council granted them one special privilege following a 1948 growers' petition. It allowed local entrepreneurs to set up a beer stand just outside the city limits.[52]

African American workers complained frequently about low wages and poor working conditions. One group from Georgia recruited in 1948 for the Bay County, Michigan, pickling cucumber harvest was upset about unfulfilled promises. Growers called them lazy and claimed that they passed "their time sitting under trees." Soon they walked off the job and went to Bay City, where the minister of the Second Baptist Church found them places to stay. Church pressure forced an inspection of camp conditions by a county health officer, who agreed that two of the three camps should have been closed, although the third was "almost satisfactory." Fifty of the workers applied for and received county welfare. The United Auto Workers even got involved, renting a bus for those who wanted to return home and helping the others find work in Michigan.[53]

Corporations and employment service personnel experiments to place African Americans in sugar beet and pickling cucumber work in Michigan ceased after the 1940s. This suggests that African Americans were more successful in rejecting poor conditions than were foreigners or Tejanos, partly because of greater access to local public and private assistance. In the ensuing decades, pickling cucumbers and sugar beets remained the nearly exclusive domain of Tejanos and *braceros*.[54]

African Americans in midwestern agriculture appear to have had the highest proportion of permanent settlers. Their principal working base was in Southwestern Michigan, from where they settled in Benton Harbor, the Chicago-Gary area, or the urban areas of Eastern Michigan. A 1948 report concurred that African Americans "hope that migrancy may be the means by which they can relocate and become permanent residents." Those who continued in farm labor remained highly segregated. A Northport, Michigan, missionary reported, "The only time any of the people left their camps was when they went for groceries, to visit another camp, or to attend some of our activities."[55]

For Mexican Americans, the largest ethnic group in the region, leaving Texas did not remove them from the direct competition of foreign workers. Their success can be measured in part by comparing them and their competitors with regard to transportation, housing, health, and general relations with the resident community. The government and employers paid transportation costs for *braceros*, but contracted Tejanos secured free passage only in 1942. *Braceros* often went by train or commercial buses, which were less dangerous than the old trucks and automobiles that typically hauled Mexican Americans. Wayne (later Wayne State) University professor of education Edgar Johnston decried the frequency of "fatal accidents involving workers en route to Michigan." For most Mexican Americans the advance for transportation was the first stage in a cycle of indebtedness. A 1947 study of Tejanos in Wisconsin indicated that 96 percent were in debt from the start of the trip north because of loans for transportation, food, and other essentials.[56]

Housing was implicitly included as part of wages for both foreign and citizen workers, but the latter did not have contract guarantees of safe housing or inspections. Their dwellings were consistently considered worse than those of foreigners. Tragedies such as the 1946 case in which four Mexican American children burned to death in a Michigan shack were more numerous among domestic workers.[57]

Unlike foreigners, Mexican Americans commonly paid for coal or kerosene for heating, cooking, and lighting, and typically they paid for eating utensils, hoes, and other tools, bedding, and work clothing. Their purchases contributed hundreds of thousands of dollars to the economies of the small towns where they concentrated. Suppliers in the Saginaw Valley, for instance, estimated that they purchased 20,000 workshirts, jackets, and overalls in 1945 alone and spent even greater sums on food and gasoline.[58]

Health conditions among both foreign and domestic workers in the Midwest remained abysmal. *Braceros* received cursory health examinations in Mexico and had a minimal health insurance program between 1943 and 1947. The least-healthy foreign workers were likely to be rejected by the screening process. Domestic workers lacked any systematic health services, and officials observed widespread malnutrition among Mexican American children, exacerbated by inadequate water supplies and lack of toilet facilities. A 1947 survey of drinking wells used by Tejanos in Isabella County, Michigan, revealed that more than 70 percent were contaminated, with most classified as "severe." Yet health officials lacked the power to condemn wells or to enforce other health and sanitation standards.[59]

Hygiene remained woefully inadequate in most domestic worker camps. The typical instrument for bathing and washing dishes and clothes was still the galvanized tub, often heated in the sun or on improvised heating units such as pickle box stoves. In good camps, workers got water from nearby hand pumps; in others they had to travel long distances or wait for growers or companies to bring water in barrels. For bedding, Leelanau County growers commonly used fertilizer bags sewn together and stuffed with straw. These were placed on bunks or on the floor. The neglect contributed to illness and mortality from whooping cough, diphtheria, and tuberculosis. In the rare cases when dangerous health and housing facilities were publicized, state and county health officials became involved in elaborate cover-ups.[60]

Health officials issued quarantines when outbreaks of communicable diseases such as meningitis or diphtheria occurred. One quarantine following a diphtheria epidemic in Northwestern Ohio isolated a Mexican American crew composed of several closely knit families. The families lacked funds for food and had to survive several weeks without work, sharing their meager resources. When employment materialized they distributed it among the different family groups so that none would go hungry. The quarantine indicates that they paid for the negligence of the health system and demonstrates that authorities could restrict their freedom of movement as effectively as if they had been prisoners of war.[61]

In the eyes of local residents, Mexican Americans remained almost as "foreign" as Mexican braceros. The isolation was not a simple matter of benign neglect. One survey suggested that growers "cannot seem to see how miserable are the living quarters provided the Spanish-Americans." Growers continued to blame workers when the housing and services they provided led to illness or death, as evident in the actions of Veril Baldwin of Stockbridge, Michigan, president of the Michigan Muck Crop Growers' Association. Baldwin led the growers in the bitter Hardin County, Ohio, onion strike in 1934, and provided the truck a local mob used to kidnap and beat union president Okey Odell during the strike. In 1950 he asked rhetorically, "Do you think it is easy for me to let the Mexicans and other workers that come and live their filthy ways in my homes?" The "homes" were shacks he purchased in 1934 immediately after he fled to Michigan from Ohio to escape worker organizing efforts for decent wages and living conditions.[62]

As with African Americans, public discrimination against Tejanos became increasingly explicit in the 1940s. Braceros were not treated any better, but their contracts prohibited discrimination and on rare occasions the Mexican consul helped them. Signs reading "No Mexicans served," and "We cater only to whites" appeared in towns where they congregated; in other places hostile stares and a simple refusal to provide service were equally effective. Certain towns developed the reputation of being particularly unfriendly. Doctors commonly charged "outrageous prices to discourage their trade," and grocery store owners, growers, and field men continued to cheat them. Children and youths who came to town or tried to enter public schools were singled out by local youths with epithets like "beaner," "beanpicker," and "spic."[63]

Even perennially optimistic Catholic priests and Protestant missionaries became disheartened. The Reverend R. Hughes of Bay City testified that in his parish it was a "common assumption" that "every Texan family has syphilis." In Ohio, HMC programs floundered to a greater extent than in any other state in the region, as the Reverend O. W. Willits noted, because "the local communities were suspicious of these laborers, and not concerned." A church worker in Northwestern Ohio was "discouraged with community prejudices . . . as the field for cooperation is not wide."[64]

Reformers and Settlers

In spite of generally deteriorating relations, reformers continued to be active. Within the church, Protestant missionary efforts expanded. The Catholic church began its first programs for seasonal workers, stimulated in part by humanitarian concern and by the acknowledgment that most farmworkers in the region were Catholics. Much of the pressure to act came from parishioners of Mexican descent, who criticized church neglect, and from the less-than-subtle threat of Protestant missionaries seeking to convert their flock.

Catholic archdiocesan and diocesan officials in Detroit, Lansing, Saginaw, Toledo, South Bend, Chicago, Milwaukee, and Saint Paul started programs during the 1940s. Unlike the HMC, the Catholic church was oriented toward ministry rather than missionary activities, specifically for Catholic farmworkers, both Mexican nationals and Tejanos. It recruited Spanish-speaking priests and seminarians to initiate special programs in their dioceses or parishes.

One of the most important was in Saint Joseph's parish in Saginaw. In 1945 the Saginaw Diocese established the Mexican Apostolate for both resident and nonresident workers in the area. The following year it brought in the Social Mission Sisters of the Holy Ghost from Cleveland, who set up a health clinic. The Detroit Catholic Archdiocese also became active, largely through the efforts of Father Clement Kern, rector at Most Holy Trinity Parish in the heart of the Detroit *colonia*. For more than three decades Father Kern was an activist and an ardent defender of the concerns of Latino farmworkers in the Midwest. Many workers who came to the city immediately went to the Casa María Community House, founded by Father Kern in 1943. More than any church figure in his day, he struggled in behalf of workers, against discrimination, and especially for their right to organize. He was the most visible of a small group who consistently addressed the widespread abuses of corporations and growers in the region.[65]

Catholic programs focused mostly on education through summer schools and a handful of experimental programs. Two of the most notable were boarding schools established by the Moorhead and Crookston dioceses in Western Minnesota. The former was run by the Sisters of Saint Benedict. It admitted children from kindergarten to fifth grade who lived away from their parents for the entire week and returned home on weekends. The children stayed in four classrooms converted into a dormitory and received intensive instruction in academic subjects. The similar Crookston School, run by the priest and sisters of the local Saint Joseph School and Church, admitted children between ages six and fourteen. Approximately two hundred students attended Saint Joseph during the six-week summer session while their parents worked in the fields.[66]

Church efforts were limited for several reasons. Notions of responsibility and philosophical outlooks divided church personnel. HMC staff members disagreed on whether programs should seek structural reform. Many who were sympathetic feared opposition by company and grower interests. A greater number believed that the programs should address only spiritual matters, an attitude that, as one HMC staff member complained, offered "personal insurance for the land beyond, but does not include the life of today." The effectiveness of the HMC was also limited by language barriers, for only a handful of its staff and volunteers understood any Spanish. Exceptions included ministers such as Sam Rocha, Simón Alférez, and R. A. Tolosa, who showed more concern than others about reform and the function of language as a tool of exploitation.[67]

Rivalry between Catholics and Protestants also developed, diverting the energies of many well-intentioned people. In Ortonville, Minnesota, HMC staff complained that their local program was being undermined by "Catholic propaganda." One self-righteous HMC missionary in Beck, Michigan, wrote of Mexican Americans, "It has been observed that these families under the domination of the Catholic church remain subservient, superstitious and non-aggressive, while those who have embraced the Protestant religion, live aggressively and with passion."[68]

The missionary and ministry programs seldom addressed abuses

directly. Even where it might have established intercultural programs and shared facilities when it worked with more than one
group in an area, the HMC kept separate schools to isolate Mexican
Americans, Euro-Americans, and African Americans from each other.
Without coherent direction, church programs resulted in piecemeal
efforts that seldom touched on the underlying issue of control, the
root of farmworker exploitation.[69]

Reform efforts also came increasingly from newly formed organizations of settled Mexican Americans, including the Mexican Civic
Committee formed in Chicago in 1943, La Unión Cívica of Saginaw,
formed in 1945, and La Unión Cívica of Lansing, which began in
1947. These organizations served primarily social and cultural functions, but they also challenged racism and discrimination against
Mexicanos of all backgrounds. Unfortunately, their impact was limited by their small size and weak political bases. Composed largely
of second-generation Mexicans indigenous to the region, they preceded the Texas-based G.I. Forum by more than a decade. Their appearance marked the beginning of Mexican American efforts that
continued to expand in following decades.[70]

These organizations benefited from settlement by Mexican Americans who were still or were former farmworkers. Many new residents
chose the older neighborhoods of earlier Mexicano settlers in Saint
Paul, Milwaukee, Saginaw, Detroit, and the Chicago area. In a 1946
sample of 270 male heads of household residing in Saint Paul, 25
percent still worked in the beet fields. The next logical step toward
their permanent settlement in that city was in the packinghouses. Of
the Great Lakes states, the population of Mexican descent in Minnesota had the highest proportion of former farmworkers. In the
Saginaw–Bay City area many Tejano agricultural workers found employment in the foundries and, to a lesser degree, in other shops and
related industries. They commonly moved into Saginaw's First Ward
around Saint Joseph Parish, where Mexicanos had lived since the
early 1920s.[71]

Mexican Americans also settled in places where few Mexicanos
had settled earlier. Wartime recruitment attracted beet workers to
foundries in Ecorse and Pontiac, Michigan, where they formed small
colonias in housing projects. A new colonia appeared in South
Bend, Indiana, as a result of settlement by seasonal workers from the
expanding crop region in Northern Indiana and Southwestern Michigan. In Northwestern Ohio, Mexican Americans increasingly settled
in Toledo and in nearby cities and towns. In places like the village
of Leipsic, a settlement referred to by outsiders as "Little Mexico"
appeared when farmworkers found employment in the Libby's can-

nery. Thus, in spite of continuing hostility and discrimination, Mexican Americans were more likely than African Americans to settle on the urban fringes and in the smaller towns in the region.[72]

Compared with African Americans, Tejanos faced greater difficulties in settling in the Midwest because of language and lower levels of formal education. Many were restricted by jobs and promotions that required formal applications and written examinations in English. Once employed, not unlike African Americans, they faced employers and supervisors who were hesitant to promote them from menial tasks. Those Tejanos who settled in the Midwest tended to remain in the same place rather than to continue changing jobs. They were tired of the unsettled and unstable life of agricultural labor and were relieved by the security of permanent employment, whether in older *colonias,* on the city fringes and in industrial suburbs close to work, or in smaller towns.[73]

Mexican Americans occasionally faced competition when they encountered *braceros.* Some observers suggested that friction between the two was inherent, caused by cultural and regional differences. The observers, however, overlooked employers' conscious efforts to pit workers against each other. Mexican citizens often believed that they were discriminated against by Mexican Americans, who often served as their interpreters, field bosses, supervisors, and cooks. They saw that U.S.-born workers often got first pickings and better fields. Furthermore, the domestic workers had their families and greater freedom of movement. Mexican Americans also had reasons to develop negative attitudes toward *braceros.* As U.S. citizens, they saw foreigners taking their jobs and causing their wages to decline. They understood that the *braceros'* superior contracts guaranteed better housing and more hygienic living conditions. Nevertheless, the two openly fraternized in the fields, in taverns, restaurants and other public places. As Edmundo Flores noted, when they were not forced into competition there was seldom any friction.[74]

Because the Tejanos were citizens, brought their children, and often settled, some reform efforts were carried out specifically in their behalf, notably in public education. Surveys of Tejano adults and children indicated that many had never been to school, despite strict compulsory education laws, the 1937 Sugar Act, and the school census law. In a 1944 study, Margaret Koopman of Central Michigan College found that not one county commissioner in the state complied fully with the law. In one district she studied carefully, only 27 of 221 school children had proof of age certificates, as required by the Sugar Act. Throughout the Central Michigan beet area she found that only 18 percent of 11,400 school-age children of agricultural workers even enrolled in classes.[75]

The first experimental public educational programs for farmworker children in the region began in the 1940s, financed by school census funds. The Breckenridge, Elkton, and Saginaw, Michigan, school districts hired extra teachers and aides to provide Mexican American children extra attention in the spring and fall. Central Michigan College and Moorhead State Teachers College (later Moorhead State University) also worked with local administrators to establish experimental summer school programs. They demonstrated that high-caliber educational programs were feasible at a modest cost, and using available funds. Yet state aid, compulsory education laws, and other inducements could not counter pressures by growers and their lackeys on the school boards, who refused to comply with the law. Their narrow interests and antidemocratic attitudes toward the pedagogical needs of thousands of youth represented a glaring failure in local control of public education. The meager schooling that took place remained in the hands of missionaries, and most children stayed away from school.[76]

Another arena of reform during this period was the government-sponsored committee and commission created to address public concern over the problems of migrant workers. In 1946 the President's National Citizens' Committee on Migratory Labor appeared. It was succeeded in 1947 by the Federal Agency Committee on Migrant Labor, and in 1950 by the President's Commission on Migratory Labor. These efforts produced a few studies on agricultural labor before they collapsed.[77]

State reformers established similar commissions, the most notable in Michigan, which remained the state with the most seasonal farmworkers in the region. In the late 1930s a handful of state officials and concerned private citizens tried to form such an organization. Their efforts led in 1945 to the formation of the Governor's Committee on the Education, Health and Welfare of Migrant Workers, an interagency organization comprising state, grower, and corporation representatives. It was succeeded in 1947 by the Michigan Governor's Study Commission on Migratory Labor. The only charges of these committees were to make studies and recommendations. The second group suggested that growers and processors establish a mechanism to regulate housing, health, and sanitary conditions. In 1948 Wisconsin created a special migrant committee of the Governor's Commission on Human Rights, and Minnesota formed a Governor's Interracial Commission with a migrant subcommittee. Like the Michigan committees, these commissions accomplished little beyond conducting studies and making recommendations that were never implemented. As the director of the Wisconsin organization, Rebecca Barton, stated, it was merely a "gadfly" organization. Given the lack of worker representation, the low budgets, and the lack of enforcement power, their hopes of changing anything had little chance of realization.[78]

A handful of politicians also sought legislative reform. A bill submitted in 1949 by Michigan State Representative T. John Lesinski to set standards for housing and sanitation in migrant camps was typical. The bill never reached the floor of the House due to the lobbying of the sugar beet and canning companies, the growers' associations, and the Michigan Farm Bureau.[79]

The reformers of the 1940s confronted widespread, organized resistance. A perceptive observer in Michigan noted that "the bulk of public opinion is hostile to migrants." When school authorities tried to open schools, community centers, and youth centers, they often faced strenuous opposition. Even church reformers encountered hostility, though it was often quite subtle. In 1943 a Home Missions Council volunteer observed that in a hardware store a man "confronted me and told me I had no business meddling with the Mexicans for they could never measure up to a white man." In many places Protestant groups had to shelve plans for migrant programs because of local opposition. The Rev. Mr. Hughes of Bay City testified that in 1947 another local minister "had to leave because in his attempt to get something done, the people got aroused and hounded him out."[80]

The opposition of the unenlightened combined with the hostility and feigned ignorance of the supposedly informed and reduced the possibility for reform. In 1949, after more than a decade of experience in farm placement programs involving Tejanos and *braceros*, University of Wisconsin professor and farm labor expert George Hill wrote, "The Mexican is a strange person. He is an extremely emotional individual. . . . The average Wisconsin employer looks on the Mexican as queer, having a peculiar sense of values. He has." Hill frequently tried to discredit reformers concerned with child labor and other farmworker concerns. Father Clement Kern had many encounters with Michigan State College agricultural economist E. B. Love, who directed college-related farm placement programs. The priest observed that the professor "gets very impatient with these people, these crusaders," as Love called the reformers.[81]

Hostile public opinion toward Mexicanos in the 1940s was fanned by press distortions in reports on the Sleepy Lagoon incident, the zoot-suit riots, and the *pachuco* phenomenon in the Southwest. As Louise Año Nuevo Kerr noted, hostility spread throughout the nation, including the largest city in the Midwest, Chicago.[82]

Ill feelings were even more pronounced in rural midwestern communities, where tens of thousands of Mexican-looking people came to work each season. An illustrative case involved a criminal libel lawsuit filed by Marland H. Littlebrant against Swift Lathers, editor of the *Mears Newz*, a weekly newspaper published in the heart of Northwestern Michigan's cherry country. The well-intentioned journalist was indignant when Littlebrant, sheriff of Oceana County, murdered nineteen-year-old José Dávila, a Mexican American farmworker, in cold blood. Lathers editorialized that Littlebrant, who had a reputation as a notorious Mexican hater, was not justified in his actions simply because Dávila had been teasing a new friend, seventeen-year-old Maxine English, and took her glasses in fun. The liberal national press became interested in the incident, another in the wave of hostile actions against Mexicans that occurred during the war.[83]

Carey McWilliams reported that the sheriff justified his actions on the grounds that Dávila had a knife in his possession. Lathers described the incident from trial evidence and other eyewitness testimony. The confrontation began when the sheriff called Dávila, who had his right hand, but no knife, in his pocket. Then,

> when the Mexican started to walk toward the sheriff (literally obeying the command), he was shot down . . . [and] struck several times on the side of his face with a blackjack. [The] defending attorney, [Samuel J.] Andalman revealed: "I'll tell you why this man didn't take his hand out of his right hand pocket all that time. It was because he couldn't. It was because he was paralyzed. When the sheriff hit this man on the left side of the head again and again, the blood began seeping into his brain and affected the right side of his body.[84]

There was a public outcry against Dávila's murder, not only from the liberal press, but from Mexicano communities in the Midwest and from Mexico. The Comité Mexicano contra el Racismo (the Mexican Committee against Racism) in Chicago, and Mexican consuls in the Midwest and Mexico protested vigorously. They understood the international implications of anti-Mexican sentiment in the United States.

Although the reformers could not prevent the rising anti-Mexican sentiment, they did draw a great deal of attention to Dávila's murder, and eventually the jury found Lathers not guilty of slander. Lathers's victory did not vindicate the reprehensible murder, however; Sheriff Littlebrant was neither tried for murder nor reprimanded.

The case also suggests the futility of Mexican and Mexican American reformers trying to find justice. Those who understood the mechanism of discrimination and sought justice, including consular officials, government reformers like Edmundo Flores and Ofelia Mendoza, liberal priests and local community residents, were effectively overwhelmed by their more powerful enemies.[85]

Conclusion

Stimulated by World War II, corporate agriculture in the Midwest established an increasingly sophisticated mechanism to recruit, hire, and employ workers to meet expanding production and offset the tighter labor market. It worked closely with growers, federal, state, and county agencies to set up a comprehensive mechanism to bring a diverse group of workers from different parts of the country and from foreign lands. The corporations could not reverse the relative labor shortage immediately, but they made sure that agricultural wages did not become competitive with those in industry. They were not "planning chaos," but rather flooding the labor market while dividing the agricultural working class in order to maintain control.

The entry of foreign workers was the final stage of a transformation of the agricultural proletariat that began in the 1930s. Specialized production and mechanization created a greater demand for workers; this need was met not by local recruitment but by attracting workers from low-wage, largely agricultural areas to the south. High unemployment levels in the 1930s made formal recruitment hardly necessary, except in the sugar beet industry. As corporations took over the fruit and vegetable crops, they sponsored new "grower" associations and induced the government to finance a nationwide labor recruitment mechanism. By the late 1940s the second generation of the agricultural proletariat in the Midwest was in place.

The situation of these workers was much more complicated than it had been for the generation of the *betabeleros* of the 1920s. Workers of different ethnic and national backgrounds and political statuses were pitted against each other by employers who manipulated the conditions under which they lived and worked. Employers maintained control over them through the recruitment mechanism, isolation in camps, and social ostracism. They created divisions that pitted domestic against foreign workers and maintained distinctions based on ethnicity. The differences were reflected in contracts, placement in different crops, crew organization, camp structures, and the social life of each group. That the group theoretically most isolated, the POWs, was treated better by farmers than other foreign and domestic minorities, indicates the ability of employers to manipulate ethnic differences as barriers to common organization.

The context under which these divisions occurred in the 1930s and 1940s questions Michael Hechter's application of the notion of the cultural division of labor.[86] Hechter suggests that the cultural differences were responsible for divisions within the working class. In the case of farmworkers, employers consciously created divisions and stifled the unity that workers demonstrated on numerous occasions. Growers controlled the instruments of power—the police force, public officials, and public opinion—to keep farmworkers weak, divided, and ostracized. The ultimate meaning was not that segments of the working class occasionally showed antagonism toward each other, but that employers thwarted the class struggle by successfully manipulating cultural divisions.

The significance of cultural division transcends farmworkers. As the second generation of the agricultural proletariat formed in the 1930s and 1940s, industrial workers in the region became unionized. The industrial working class, whose diverse European roots became increasingly undifferentiated, continued to unionize. The agricultural proletariat, increasingly foreign-born and minority workers, remained divided and weak.

The rift separating the two groups became insurmountable during the 1940s, largely because of conscious actions by agricultural corporations and their allies. They used the state to assist them in over-recruitment and the creation of internal divisions among workers. Those who dismiss this manipulation of farmworkers and of the agricultural labor process as primitive misunderstand the creativity of capitalist employers. The failure of organized labor to enter the midwestern fields made the task of the corporations much easier. Organized labor's unwillingness to encourage farmworkers to organize contrasts with its vigorous though unsuccessful support of the National Farm Labor Union in California during the bitter DiGiorgio strike of the late-1940s. In the industrial heartland of the nation, the hush of organized labor resounded throughout the fields.

CHAPTER 6

Operation Farmlift: Bootstrap to the Midwest, 1950

In 1950 the Michigan sugar beet industry initiated a search for a new labor force to replace the Mexican Americans who had been in the fields for more than a decade. Although they did not have a reputation for being contentious, the Tejanos seldom stayed long, as they constantly looked for better employment opportunities. Growers would have preferred *braceros* had they been available, for their contracts and difficulty with English helped keep them under control, and the federal government paid most of the cost of recruitment and transportation. However, the National Farm Labor Union and its allies were pressuring the federal government to abolish the Bracero Program. In 1948 and 1949 the union led efforts to convince Congress that there was no shortage of domestic workers. Thus the Bracero Program was in jeopardy. The ever-resourceful Michigan sugar beet industry turned to Puerto Rico, hoping to find workers as poor and easily controlled as the *braceros*. Because they were U.S. citizens, hiring Puerto Ricans would protect the industry from criticism for hiring foreign workers.

Industry plans meshed with the Puerto Rican government's recently inaugurated Operation Bootstrap. This program aimed at economic development and reducing unemployment through industri-
alization stimulated by tax breaks and other benefits to mainland
industry. The plan sought to reduce the island's reserve labor force
further by encouraging labor migration to the mainland, mostly to
urban industrial employers on the East Coast, particularly New York
City. Puerto Rican officials also hoped to send agricultural workers
to the United States, but until the late 1940s had found few interested employers. This chapter examines its first major effort in this
direction, Operation Farmlift, which sent more than five thousand
Puerto Rican farmworkers to Michigan. It promised to change the
shape of the farm labor force in the Midwest and possibly throughout
the nation.

Background

The sugar beet industry's recruitment of Puerto Ricans in 1950 followed its experiments with European and Mexican immigrants early
in the century and Texas-Mexicans in the 1930s. In 1943 it attempted
to bring in Jamaican, Bahamian, and Nisei workers, but without
success. In the mid-1940s it was able to recruit small numbers of
Mexican nationals, but political pressures threatened to curtail this
attractive work force entirely. In 1948 and 1949 employers experimented with southern African Americans, but neither employers
nor workers were satisfied. In 1950 industry representatives claimed
that Puerto Ricans were necessary because the INS threatened to
expel undocumented Mexican workers from Texas, which would
open up employment to Mexican Americans, who would no longer
be available for the Midwest. The industry's argument about the
shortage of workers from Texas is not convincing for, as HMC director Ellis Marshburn revealed, it confused cause and effect. Marshburn reported that, because of Operation Farmlift, the industry abandoned its recruitment efforts in Texas, and its publicity further
discouraged many Mexican Americans from coming north as freewheelers. The industry thought it could replace them with Puerto
Ricans.[1]

Puerto Rico was a logical source of labor for agricultural employers in the continental United States. The island had almost seven
hundred thousand able workers, a majority with agricultural backgrounds. Unemployment on the mainland was less than a quarter of
the 18 percent rate in Puerto Rico, and its per capita income was
more than four times higher. Furthermore, seasonal employment in

the continental United States could mesh with the sugarcane harvest cycle, as cane cutters, the majority of seasonal farmworkers on the island, were unemployed during the *tiempo muerto,* or dead season, from late spring until December.[2]

Attempts at large-scale hiring of Puerto Ricans by outsiders had been made before. In 1900 and 1901, more than five thousand workers from Puerto Rico went to Hawaiian sugar plantations. They encountered many difficulties with employers, however, and the program dwindled. Smaller numbers of Puerto Ricans worked in sugarcane harvests on other Caribbean islands, typically in sporadic, short-lived arrangements. In 1926 the Arizona Cotton Growers' Association imported more than two thousand workers from the island. The Arizona project was beset by bad planning and poor treatment of workers. Furthermore, racially sensitive southwestern employers were surprised to discover people of African ancestry among the Puerto Ricans. As association official C. M. Achauer commented, "If the Lord will ever forgive us for bringing in these coons, we will never do it again. The Mexican is far superior to the negro in Arizona. He will do as he is told, while the negro always wants to do it his way." The experiments were largely forgotten in later decades, although smaller numbers of Puerto Ricans worked in California agriculture, often after working in Hawaii.[3]

The Puerto Rican government's efforts to include farm labor employment in Operation Bootstrap lagged behind its efforts with regard to urban industrial employment. It complained vigorously to the U.S. government about the British West Indian and Mexican *bracero* programs initiated during the war and contended that they discriminated against Puerto Ricans, who deserved preference because they were citizens. Many farm employers were aware of a major difference, however, namely, that citizens could not be deported. One government official explained, "Obviously the INS have a hold on Bahamian and Jamaican workers that would not apply to Puerto Ricans."[4]

The Puerto Rican government's efforts between 1944 and 1947 to find mainland employers for its farmworkers yielded only meager results. When Luis Muñoz Marín was elected governor in 1948, the effort intensified, led by Puerto Rican labor commissioner Fernando Sierra Berdecia. In 1949 the Puerto Ricans convinced the U.S. Employment Service to consider the island a supply source for domestic labor and to encourage employers to hire Puerto Ricans. More than 2,000 farmworkers went to New York and New Jersey that year, recruited by the Farm Labor Cooperative Association of New Jersey. An additional 186 men were sent to the Michigan sugar beet harvest.

They proved satisfactory and helped set the stage for Operation Farmlift.[5]

The sugar beet industry in Michigan then expressed interest in hiring Puerto Rican farmworkers. The move was led by Congressman Frederick Crawford of the Eighth Congressional District, which included the major beet-growing zones in the Saginaw Valley and Thumb area of the state. Crawford had been linked to the Michigan sugar beet industry since 1917 and for many years was a vice-president of the Michigan Sugar Company. He left in 1932 to form the short-lived but successful Crystal White Sugar Company, and became its president. The next season he and a handful of investors in Crystal White earned more than five hundred thousand dollars in profits. He sold his interests in 1935, and was elected to Congress. As a politician he remained closely tied to the beet industry and spoke on its behalf when the occasion arose.[6]

During his tenure in Congress, Crawford also established close ties to Governor Muñoz Marín. On the surface Crawford and Muñoz Marín appeared to be incompatible: reporter Thomas Hayes described Crawford, a Republican, as a "reactionary" and "a very bellicose man, about as quick to battle with his fists as with words"; Muñoz Marín was the embodiment of Puerto Rico's Popular Democratic party, and had a reputation as a progressive. Crawford learned about Puerto Rico during his long tenure as a member of the House Committee on Insular Affairs. In that capacity he visited the island frequently and sponsored a wide range of legislation pertaining to Puerto Rico. He also established a close relationship with Muñoz Marín, whose political future was tied to that legislation. Crawford became a "bosom buddy" of the Puerto Rican governor. In 1949 Crawford arranged negotiations between his friends in the Michigan sugar industry and the Puerto Rican government that led to Operation Farmlift.[7]

The details of the plan were made public in March 1950, when Michigan Sugar Company secretary-treasurer and MFCI representative Max Henderson met with Puerto Rican labor commissioner Sierra Berdecia. The agreement between MFCI and the Puerto Rican government guaranteed workers a written contract and 160 hours of employment every four weeks. The contract further stated that "in no event shall the employee working on piece-work rates, receive less than 60 cents per hour or the prevailing rate for similar comparable work." In 1948 the USDA set the prevailing piece rate in sugar beets at $5.84 for a 10-hour day, equivalent to 58 cents per hour. The contract also stipulated that the employer pay the worker at least once every two weeks and provide three adequate meals per day at

cost but not more than $1.50 per day, or suitable cooking arrange-
ments. It provided for hygienic housing, clean water, sanitary facilities, and a medical policy for workers to be paid for by employers.[8]

The agreement required that each worker pay $55 for air transpor-
tation from Puerto Rico to Michigan, $1.00 for photographs, and
$1.25 for a birth certificate copy. The Puerto Rican government in-
sisted that all its citizens have work contracts and that certification
of need be verified by the Puerto Rican Department of Labor and farm
employers on the mainland. The Department of Labor was responsible for inspecting facilities and ensuring compliance. It was the
strongest and most specific of recent worker contracts in the midwestern sugar beet industry.[9]

The initial arrangement in March called for one thousand workers
to be sent from Puerto Rico to Michigan for the season. By April
MFCI had decided that it needed fifteen hundred. By May the order
rose to three thousand and in early June the industry asserted that it
needed five thousand workers. Puerto Rico had a seemingly endless
supply, and the workers were scheduled to arrive in Michigan between the last week of May and the middle of June. Sugar beet execu-
tives, growers, and workers alike looked forward to the airlift. Representative Crawford asserted that Operation Farmlift "should open
the way for great benefits for the future," by which he meant that
Puerto Ricans would replace Mexican Americans in the midwestern
sugar beet industry.[10]

Airlift to Disaster

In the spring Puerto Rican radio stations and newspapers throughout the agricultural sections of the island announced the availability
of seasonal employment in Michigan. Those interested were to visit
the offices of the Puerto Rican Department of Labor in San Juan to
interview with labor officials and MFCI representatives. Almost all
who went were experienced agricultural workers, some with prior
experience in New York and New Jersey. Two men who had gone
to New Jersey the previous year had take-home earnings of $1,200
and $1,300, respectively, for six months of employment. One man
brought back $550 after four months' work, and another returned
with $1,000 after six months. Most of the workers traveled by bus
from their hometowns in the interior to San Juan, where they
boarded privately chartered airplanes to Michigan. They did not
know precisely what was expected of them and had no experience in the sugar beets. Many were told that they would pick fruit.

MFCI promises of employment and guaranteed wages were adequate inducements.[11]

MFCI cooperated with the USES on details of the last stage of their trip to Michigan as well, as they arranged for local farmers to meet workers at the airport and drive them to their lodgings. It was a newer version of farmers coming to train stations in their wagons to take Mexicano *betabeleros* to their portable beet shacks.[12]

The flights from San Juan to Tri-City Airport near Freeland took place in two-engine C-46 transport planes owned by Westair, a Seattle-based private charter company. The 2,180-mile trip averaged slightly over ten hours. En route workers received a sandwich or doughnut and a soft drink or coffee. Westair officials packed between sixty and sixty-five workers on each airplane, exceeding the maximum legal weight limitations as established by the Civil Aeronautics Board (CAB). Ruperto Muñoz, who was aboard a June 5, 1950, flight recalled that the plane "was overcrowded, of course." The Puerto Ricans arrived much later than workers normally did, and weeds in the fields were already tall. By June 5 approximately fifteen hundred men had arrived in Michigan.[13]

On the evening of June 5, 1950, disaster struck when a C-46 crashed into the Atlantic Ocean approximately three hundred miles east of Melbourne, Florida. It had sixty-two workers aboard, plus the pilot, copilot, and a flight attendant. A search team of five coast guard ships, two navy planes, and the destroyer *USS Saufly* hurried to the scene of the accident and recovered thirty-seven survivors. Twenty-eight people died, of whom at least three, including Pedro Guzmán, were killed by sharks in sight of other passengers and crew members. After several days of searching, the destroyer pulled into port at Charleston, South Carolina. From the mainland, thirty of the survivors decided to continue north and took a Greyhound bus to Saginaw. Each of them received ten dollars to cover the cost of clothes they lost in the crash.[14]

The accident endangered the future of Operation Farmlift. Governor Muñoz Marín immediately canceled all noncommercial flights between Puerto Rico and Michigan, and the CAB grounded Westair. Company president J. J. Patterson called the actions unfair and claimed that the Puerto Rican government had voided the contract without a fair trial or investigation of the accident. He asserted that the accident was the result of a "mechanical failure." Representative Crawford was even more upset. The *Bay City Times* reported that "in a stinging telegram sent Governor Marín today, Crawford charged the order would cause the loss of 25,000 to 30,000 acres of beets."

Crawford's pressure convinced the Puerto Rican governor to change his mind so that the crop could be saved.[15]

Muñoz Marín agreed to allow Operation Farmlift to continue on condition that the remaining thirty-eight hundred take more expensive but safer commercial airlines. Henderson quickly went to Puerto Rico to negotiate a plan on behalf of Michigan Sugar and MFCI. Together they arranged with Pan American and Eastern airlines to transport men in four-engine DC-4s. The larger airplanes carried an average of fifty-three workers per flight, or ten fewer than the smaller two-engine C-46s. The cost of the one-way trip rose from $55 to $90 per worker. MFCI claimed that the Puerto Rican government should pay the additional cost, since it had broken the previously negotiated contracts, but Muñoz Marín refused. The beet growers finally agreed to pay the difference. The commercial airline phase of Operation Farmlift, which took place between June 9 and June 15, was heralded in the *Detroit News* as "the biggest mass migration in commercial aviation history."[16]

Only scattered criticisms of the accident appeared in the early weeks after its occurrence, none from government representatives or the commercial press of Michigan. The *Saginaw Catholic Weekly* of June 18 was the first to charge wrongdoing. It argued that the arrangements involving Westair "cut rates to a point that imperils proper safety" by overloading the airplanes. By the end of the month Vito Marcantonio, American Labor party representative from the Bronx, from a district with some Puerto Rican constituents, had made similar accusations. He laid blame for the accident on "capitalists for overcrowding airplanes." Meanwhile, other public voices remained silent. The CAB investigation of the accident did not appear for more than a year. Meanwhile, the Puerto Ricans began working in *la remolacha,* as they referred to the sugar beets.[17]

In the Beet Fields

The Puerto Rican men began working almost immediately on arrival in Michigan. They were quickly herded off in trucks to distribution centers or directly to camps. Most stayed in the same housing as the Tejano families they replaced, the small sugar beet shacks, other temporary dwellings, or the surplus army tents that were still being used widely in the region. They typically slept on straw-filled mattresses on small cots or on the floors of their dwellings. Like the Tejanos, they usually did their own cooking, purchasing food and supplies at nearby country stores from the five-dollar advance per week per person. Like the Mexican *braceros* they were divided into crews, commonly of seven to ten men, who resided, cooked, and ate together. They worked as a unit in the fields; consequently, all crew members, including the elected leaders, earned the same wages.[18]

Entering the fields comparatively late in the season, they were very busy for several weeks. They began at six in the morning and worked until seven or eight in the evening, with a one-hour break for lunch, for six or seven days per week. Although new to the sugar beets, they were experienced in agriculture and learned the tasks quickly. MFCI representatives, field men and growers considered them excellent workers who caused them practically no difficulties.[19]

The workers faced many unexpected surprises in the Michigan sugar beet fields. They stated without exception that as workers they were treated poorly. Many of them, including Primitivo Padilla, Rogelio Polo López, and Ruperto Muñoz, complained of being treated like animals. They were not accustomed to being herded to and from the fields in trucks that smelled of the animals the vehicles hauled at other times. The men were universally disappointed over being housed in filthy "small, box-like huts," often infested with rats. Crews of seven to ten men usually shared a single shack, with beds placed even in the kitchen, allowing little room to turn around. Their mattresses were straw ticks or rags, frequently filthy, smelly, and wet when they were issued. Santos Cintrón testified that he was part of a crew of eight men placed in a dwelling twelve by eighteen feet, which was crowded and leaked badly when it rained, forcing the men to crawl under their double-decked bunk beds to escape the leaks. The old tents were worse, as they leaked water from the roofs and had no floors.[20]

The men also found drinking water unfit for consumption. Many complained that the water they were expected to drink was "as salty as the sea." A newspaper reporter confirmed that many pumps "poured out discolored, foul tasting water" that made many men ill. In many cases there were no bathing facilities. After a week in Michigan without a bath, one group discovered a stream nearby. Others were told to use nearby ditches as bathing facilities.[21]

Employer failure to comply with contractual provisions for food caused additional suffering. Many workers did not receive meals or the five dollars per week allowance to purchase groceries for several weeks. Ruperto Muñoz recalls long periods when "we were very hungry." To complicate their difficulties, the workers often had to walk several miles to the nearest store. Others had to resort to ingenious measures to survive. Members of one crew that did not receive its weekly advances raided a nearby potato patch at night, then boiled the potatoes, their only sustenance for several days. A member of the crew, Pablo Tirado, testified that he "went to work but the others were so weak they couldn't leave. To make things worse, the patrón then tried to make me get the others to work, but I just gave him a stare. Only God and my calm saved him." [22]

Adjustment to the northern climate was another problem. In the early weeks, the men from the tropical island faced unexpected "bitter cold," exacerbated by inadequate clothing and a shortage of blankets. Furthermore, because of the pressure to complete hoeing and weeding quickly, they had to work during heavy downpours and in muddy fields. One worker testified that they did not even stop for "rain, thunder or lightning." [23]

The workers' biggest surprise was over wages and terms of payment. When they were recruited in Puerto Rico, the sugar beet company representatives promised a minimum hourly guarantee, with payment every two weeks, and the terms were explicitly stated in their written contracts. On arrival in Michigan, the *revisadores* informed them that they would be paid according to terms traditionally arranged with midwestern beet workers, with the first payment in early August after they completed hoeing. Until the workers received their paychecks, Michigan Sugar granted them five dollar weekly advances for food. They were upset, not only because of company deception, but also because they expected to send part of their wages to their families in Puerto Rico. Donald West of the HMC reported that one man was so depressed about being unable to send money home that he committed suicide. [24]

When the first cycle of beet work ended in July, several hundred workers were sent to harvest apples or pickling cucumbers in Michigan. Others picked peas in Washington state. More than four hundred men were sent to harvest corn and work in the canneries in Minnesota. Sixteen hundred went to New York and New Jersey in an arrangement with the Garden State Cooperative Association. [25]

Most of the workers who remained in Michigan were frustrated. Molly Fraser Durham of the HMC observed that "there were complaints on every side" because of employers' failure to provide meals, adequate housing and bedding, sanitary services, or to pay the workers according to the terms of their contracts. It was, as she described, a series of "broken promises." When the workers protested to anyone about noncompliance with the provisions of their contracts, they met stiff resistance. One group went on strike for a day, but lacking either money or food and threatened with being cut off from their supplies at the local grocery store, they quickly returned to work. A large group of workers unsuccessfully requested an investigator from Puerto Rico. Meanwhile, the farmers in whose fields they worked claimed that they had nothing to do with the workers' conditions or their contracts.[26]

The biggest shock came when the workers eventually received their first paychecks, for their earnings were only a fraction of what they expected. By then, as work was beginning to slacken, many callous farmers asserted that if they did not like the conditions, they could leave. One worker recalled that "many were afraid to give up their jobs, fearing what might happen if they were not employed immediately." Yet they started trickling out of the fields, and soon their numbers became a flood. Ruperto Muñoz expressed the dilemma one crew faced:

> The department's men threatened to throw us in jail if we left. I guess they took advantage of us because we didn't know English. We didn't know what was going on. They told us it was a contract and we couldn't break it. . . . There was one farmer who used to have a blue uniform who used to carry a gun. This guy used to wear a uniform just like the police, but I don't know if he was a policeman or not. He used to come over once a day and check all of us, to see if we were there or not. . . . It was like a prison.[27]

Public Response

Without funds and unable to enforce the terms of their contracts, workers expressed their dissatisfaction by walking out of the fields. Many headed to the nearest large city, Detroit, more than one hundred miles away. One group of four, including Jesús Nieves, Ramón Vargas, Juan Rodríguez, and Pedro Jiménez, left because their written contracts were not honored. The journey took three days and three nights, during which time they ate only bread, drank water, and slept under trees. In Detroit they were directed to the Most Holy Trinity Parish in the Mexican barrio, where Father Clement Kern and assistant priest Father Carlos Talavera, originally from Mexico City, offered them sympathy and support. Once they heard the story of the workers, Father Kern recalls, "we immediately got alarmed."[28]

The priests took action on the immediate concern of lodging and food, the intermediate matter of finding work, and the longer-range goal of worker organization and justice. They housed most of the men who arrived at the parish in the rectory or on the third floor of the adjoining parochial school. They lent the other men small sums of money to rent rooms in older motels and rooming houses in the neighborhood. For food they requested help from Mexican women in the neighborhood. Kern estimated that approximately 450 of the

Puerto Rican workers, or almost 10 percent of the total who came to Michigan under Operation Farmlift, left the fields and came to Most Holy Trinity for assistance during the summer of 1950.[29]

The priests handled employment as a two-stage problem, beginning with language. Father Kern recalls that initially local Mexicanos and the priests had some difficulty conversing with the Puerto Ricans, because they knew Spanish as spoken in Mexico and Texas and were not familiar with the Puerto Rican idiom. Nonetheless, they adjusted very quickly. Soon the priests were able to teach men words and phrases in English that were essential for survival. Eleno Torres quickly discovered the importance of language, for when he walked out of the fields and into Detroit, he first went to a police station to ask for directions. Nobody on the staff understood him, so the police put him in jail for three days, although he was not suspected or charged with any crime. Father Kern also arranged for formal language instruction with the assistance of members of the Detroit Federation of Teachers, with whom he had close ties. Public school teachers came to the parish to instruct the men in basic conversational English.[30]

The second aspect of employment involved helping the men find jobs. The priests contacted personnel people they knew, scoured newspaper advertisements, and made phone calls seeking work for the new Detroiters. Fortunately, it was a good year for the economy of the city, stimulated by Korean War production. Some workers found temporary employment as dishwashers and janitors. The priests were also successful in convincing personnel supervisors to hire the men in several nearby factories, particularly at Kasel Steel, Young Metal and Iron Works, and the Ford Motor Company. The starting pay in most factories was $1.25 per hour, a princely sum compared to earnings in the fields. Workers could send money home to their families, as they had planned when they first came to Michigan.[31]

Operating through the Beet Workers Defense Committee, which they had created the previous year, the priests were also concerned about worker defense and organization. Kern and Talavera visited the beet fields to gather testimony and other documentation. Kern recorded that housing and sanitary facilities, the method of payment, and earnings were "an out-and-out contract violation." His examination of pay stubs of scores of workers revealed abysmally low take-home pay. Individuals in five crews who worked seven days per week during the period from June 18 to July 20 took home $10.19, $16.14, $13.24, $16.15, and $34.27, respectively. The members of one crew got checks for 20 cents, and members of another crew of eight worked two months for absolutely nothing, as their pay slips indicated that they actually owed the company $9.69 each for advances. Kern calculated that average earnings per worker employed by Operation Farmlift were slightly more than 20 cents per hour.[32]

Talavera observed on his trip to Central Michigan that workers were "living like dogs" in the beet fields. He also reported concern about the workers' families in Puerto Rico: "I have seen letters which have come from the wives in Puerto Rico telling husbands that their children are starving to death because no money is coming home." Many families had to sell their furniture and other possessions in order to eat, and others went hungry and became ill.[33]

To attract public attention and organize workers the priests also arranged for meetings with workers and government officials at the Casa María Community House. Workers testified to USDL and state employment service officials, who consistently defended employers. Harry Markle, of the Michigan Unemployment Compensation Commission, suggested that the problem "was mainly one of misunderstanding due to language difficulties. . . . The contract is a fair one. We found that on the whole most of the workers were satisfied." Harold Mann of the USDL also defended the employers, adding that the wages were set at public meetings every year. Both Talavera and Kern attacked the wage hearing mechanism. Kern asserted, "I fail to see the purpose of these meetings, as there are no worker representatives." Furthermore, during the late-winter "public" hearings, the state's beet workers were still in Texas or Mexico.[34]

The priests and the workers also convinced Puerto Rican labor commissioner Sierra Berdecia to investigate conditions in the Michigan beet fields. The commissioner spent nine days in late July and early August gathering information and interviewing workers and beet company officials. His study revealed individual earnings averaging $7 to $18 dollars per week, or roughly 23 cents per hour, consistent with Kern's figures and the 1946 study of Detroit's Mexican consul Laveaga. As a consequence of the low earnings and the hardships, Sierra convinced the Puerto Rican legislature to grant $117,000 for food, clothing, and medical care for the families of the workers.[35]

The investigations helped force the sugar beet companies to renegotiate a contract for those workers who remained. They promised improvements in housing, a 65 cent an hour wage, plus a $1 an acre bonus if workers remained until the end of the season. In return, Sierra refrained from public criticism of employer failure to provide adequate housing, sanitary facilities, or medical services, or of wages roughly one-third the level guaranteed by contract. Representative Crawford criticized Sierra Berdecia's investigation as being motivated by "political reasons." MFCI official Henderson echoed the charge, stating that the labor commissioner was "accusing the employers [apparently only in private] of contract violations that do not exist."[36]

The sugar beet interests did not silence Father Kern, who also tried to encourage the labor movement to become involved in organizing workers. He hoped that the Beet Workers Defense Committee would become a farmworkers' union in Michigan. Despite numerous calls, requests, and petitions to both the AFL and the CIO for help, the priests' requests for organized labor to assist in worker organization went unanswered.[37]

The priests also criticized Operation Farmlift at the President's Commission on Migratory Labor hearings in Saginaw in September. Like other public spectacles, the hearings were unbalanced, more than twenty individuals representing the agricultural industry and canners' and growers' associations and only three workers. Representatives of the public sector again came to the defense of the industry. Markle of the state employment service asserted that wages in Michigan "far exceed those of other states," a frequently expressed argument contradicted by data from several other states in the West, the Midwest, and along the East Coast. Markle did not address several recent studies that consistently showed that beet worker earnings averaged only slightly more than twenty cents per hour. Taking another line of defense, sugar beet official Harold R. Gough asserted that employers could not pay more "until we prove that the sugar beet industry is profitable." Notwithstanding this assertion, the government-subsidized industry showed profits in all but a few years during the previous two generations. Thus the Saginaw hearings were another industry whitewash, supporting Father Kern's argument that conditions for unorganized workers could not improve "in view of the superb organizing of growers and food processors."[38]

Meanwhile industry representatives offered a series of excuses for the poor conditions and low pay among the Puerto Rican workers who came to Michigan. In the press they blamed the workers, asserting that those who complained were troublemakers or "just plain lazy." Henderson asserted that the problems were the result of poor briefings in Puerto Rico and worker negligence. He added that, "without wives to cook and keep house, many laborers spent extravagantly and let their houses become filthy." Crawford asserted that the low earnings were due to "bad weather." Yet Extension Service and Department of Labor agricultural reports indicated that 1950 was a good growing season in the state.[39]

Conclusion

Newspaper reporter Gordon Blake made the following assessment of Operation Farmlift: "This incident will ever remain a blot on the escutcheon of American justice and fair play. While we are fighting to make the world safe for democracy, America, it seems, is becoming less and less safe for Americans."[40] Blake apparently was not aware of the long history of farmworkers in the country and their treatment. In midwestern agriculture, Operation Farmlift was not unusual for the lack of justice that accompanied it, but rather for the publicity that attended that injustice.

Politicians in Congress and the Michigan legislature offered surprisingly few comments on the affair. Representative Marcantonio from the Bronx introduced a resolution to investigate conditions among the Puerto Rican sugar beet workers in Michigan. Yet, as Representative Crawford noted, agricultural interests on the House Rules Committee were able to "quietly pigeonhole" the resolution. In Michigan, state senator Robert Chase of Flint also called publicly for an investigation of MFCI and its violation of contract stipulations, but nothing resulted from his efforts.[41]

The Puerto Rican government's actions were hardly more commendable. Muñoz Marín never sent a compliance officer to Michigan, as the beet contracts stipulated. Even after the plane crash he avoided a confrontation by hurriedly arranging for alternative transportation for the Puerto Rican workers. He responded to complaints about the welfare of workers' families with a special grant, almost identical to the added sum paid by Michigan sugar beet growers for commercial transportation following the Westair crash. Even as evidence of poor working conditions and contract violations mounted, he refused to call for an investigation. Almost two months later, only after intense pressure from workers and their families and the surrounding publicity, he sent labor commissioner Sierra Berdecia to investigate, but the report was never made public. Governor Muñoz Marín, in order to ensure the success of Operation Bootstrap, had to maintain the goodwill of employers and politicians in the continental United States at the expense of the island's workers.

The only public investigation surrounding Operation Farmlift was the mandatory CAB investigation of the June 5 airline accident. The CAB determined that the accident occurred after both engines malfunctioned because of undetermined causes not related to weather. The report revealed that the airplane was loaded beyond maximum legal weight regulations, crews were not properly trained and had failed to take adequate safety precautions. The pilot did not even declare an emergency, although his plane was in distress for more than half an hour before it went down. The CAB report concluded that if Westair had complied with regulations, there would have been at least "a substantial saving of lives."[42]

There were some positive consequences of Operation Farmlift. The fledgling Beet Workers Defense Committee survived for several years, the only semblance of agricultural unionism in the region during the 1950s. Fathers Kern and Talavera continued to attend meetings, help organize farmworkers, and create outside support for them. As Kern stated, "I'm going to be in this thing for a long while. Maybe five years from now it'll be another Presidential hearing." Many people criticized him as a radical and an agitator, but the *Catholic Weekly* of Saginaw editorialized, "One is not a 'communist' or an 'agitator' because one tells the truth."[43]

A more significant consequence of Operation Farmlift was that it resulted in the formation of a permanent Puerto Rican community in Detroit. Almost five hundred men who walked out of the beet fields in 1950 ultimately settled in the city. Some kept the jobs in which they were first placed and others found better ones. They soon sent for their families and relatives and created a network of migration between the island and the city. Other workers who left the fields went to Saginaw, Chicago, Milwaukee, and New York City; some of these later moved to Detroit. Prior to Operation Farmlift the Detroit *colonia* was composed almost entirely of people from Mexico and Texas, with a handful of people from other Latin American countries. By the late 1950s it included a thriving Puerto Rican element as well. The small group of men who left the Saginaw Valley beet fields were the core of the city's Puerto Rican community, which grew to an estimated ten thousand within a generation.[44]

The experiment of 1950 represented still another effort by the sugar beet industry to introduce a new ethnic group into the fields. Despite the problems with Operation Farmlift, in the summer of 1950 Michigan sugar beet officials hoped to recruit even greater numbers of men from Puerto Rico for the following season. In late August Max Henderson visited the island to talk with the governor, "desperately trying to make amends and line up Puerto Rican workers for next year." In the fall MFCI publicized a plan to recruit fifteen thousand beet workers from the island, or three times the number who had come in 1950. They would have been enough to replace most of the Mexican American workers in the state's sugar beet fields. Industry officials did not realize that the Puerto Ricans were indignant over the treatment they received. Many of those who left the state to work elsewhere "vowed they would never come back to Michigan."

Puerto Rican contract workers did come to the continental United States in future years for agricultural labor, but not to the sugar beet industry, the employer that promised them the opportunity to dominate the Midwest.[45]

Operation Farmlift further demonstrates the creative and experimental nature of midwestern farm labor recruitment. The industry suddenly discovered Puerto Rico, an apparently ideal source of workers with a much lower standard of living and higher levels of unemployment than South Texas, plus cooperative public officials. Industry calculations erred first by underestimating the Puerto Rican workers, who had many years of experience in agriculture on the island, who were much more aggressive in defending their rights than were Mexican Americans, and who expected employers to abide by contract terms. They preferred not to work rather than endure the abuses. The employers also failed to consider the high cost that workers had to pay for round-trip transportation. For Mexican *braceros*, transportation was partly subsidized by the government and growers, and Tejanos riding trucks paid less than one-third the rates charged the Puerto Ricans. Finally, the industry did not calculate the importance of family labor, which made it possible for Mexican Americans to earn higher wages than Puerto Rican men could by themselves.

Publicly expressed industry fears of worker shortages in 1951 did not materialize. The Tejano workers were readily available, as they had been the previous year. Furthermore, the outbreak of the Korean War in mid-1950 helped agricultural interests convince Congress to pass Public Law 78, making it possible for the industry to import more Mexican *braceros* than ever before.[46]

CHAPTER 7

Age of Illusions, 1950–1959

In the 1950s midwestern agriculture used more sophisticated technologies and experienced higher levels of production in many labor-intensive crops, due largely to corporate expansion. The success of companies including Heinz, Campbell Soup, Del Monte, Libby, McNeill and Libby, Hunt, Stokeley, and Aunt Jane gave the appearance that agriculture was thriving. The good times were accompanied by accelerated indebtedness and bankruptcy among family farmers, however, and a much larger impoverished seasonal labor force. The contradictions of prosperity and poverty were greater than ever before.

A pervasive feature of the decade was a rapid acceleration in mechanization and the use of pesticides and herbicides in production. Industrial leaders throughout the nation promoted a popular image that mechanization and technology were contributing directly to a better life and improved standard of living.

The agricultural industry suggested several reasons for the emphasis on machine over human labor. First, mechanized agriculture was improving living standards by providing higher-quality, low-cost food. Second, it was eliminating low-paying and unpleasant hand tasks. Third, there was an "insufficient supply" of workers, and the only ones available had unacceptable "migratory habits." The machines would provide cheaper and better food, create a more skilled work force, stabilize work, and reduce migration. This chapter will examine the rhetoric and consequences of mechanization and other changes among midwestern farmworkers in the 1950s.[1]

Machines, Crops, and Workers

Mechanization had a contradictory impact on employment, for although it encouraged expanded production, it reduced the labor time necessary to produce the crops. The sharpest reduction took place in the sugar beet industry, the principal employer of nonresident labor in the region for half a century. Mechanization was already reducing labor demand in the 1930s, when cross-blocking was first adopted in some places. Midwestern companies introduced segmented seed in the late 1940s, which partially eliminated the need for thinners. Mechanical harvesters, first brought into the region in the mid-1940s, handled more than 50 percent of the crop by 1950, and practically eliminated the demand for sugar beet toppers by 1955. In later years new types of seeds, mechanical thinners, blocking machines, weeders, and herbicides continued to eliminate the demand for beet workers.[2]

Sugar beet mechanization in the Midwest lagged behind the Rocky Mountain and California zones by several years. Corporations commonly attributed the slower pace to illogical and uneconomical resistance by midwestern farmers. Yet the farmers seldom acted against their own economic interests. Hand thinning and hand topping were acknowledged to result in higher yields. Mechanical topping also destroyed potential animal feed. The high cost of machinery, artificial fertilizers, fuel oil, and chemicals drove many farmers deeply into debt and forced others out of business. It also concentrated production in fewer locations. By the 1950s most sugar beets in the region were grown in four counties in the Thumb area of Michigan and the Red River Valley of Minnesota. Farmers usually were justifiably cautious but eventually accepted changes of proven benefits.[3]

Mechanical and chemical inputs also reduced the demand for beet workers. In the mid-1940s approximately fifteen thousand adult workers were employed in Michigan for approximately eighty days during the season. By the mid-1950s only about eight thousand workers remained, employed about thirty days each year.[4]

Mechanization affected labor in many other crops during the 1950s. Mechanical snappers were introduced into the sweet corn crop at the beginning of the decade. An Illinois company official admitted that the cost of mechanical harvesting was "a little higher" than by hand, but it offered nonmonetary advantages. The most important were that recruiting a smaller harvest labor force lessened company responsibilities and that harvesting could be completed more quickly. Many farmers resisted mechanical harvesting, however, because their cattle would not eat as much of the stalk pasture as in hand-harvested fields and because the machines were less thorough than hand "jerkers."[5]

Green pea pitching and bean picking were largely eliminated by the use of mechanical pickers in the middle of the decade. In the late 1950s potato combines and loaders rapidly reduced the demand for potato harvest workers in East-Central Michigan and the Red River Valley. In the same period herbicides and mechanical harvesters were eliminating onion thinners and toppers. The mechanical harvest of more fragile and weather-sensitive fruits remained largely in the experimental stage.[6]

During the 1950s increases in production largely offset the impact of mechanization. More hand harvesters worked in cherries, blueberries, black raspberries, and apples. The expansion of cherry production in Door County and the Traverse City area was particularly notable. In July and early August more migrant farmworkers concentrated in Grand Traverse than in any other county in the nation. Snap bean production increased in Michigan's Thumb area. Muck crops expanded in the Willard Marsh of Ohio; Allegan County, Michigan; Saint Joseph County, Indiana; Marquette County, Wisconsin; and the Hollandale area in Freeborn County, Minnesota. In Southern and Central Wisconsin, Southern Minnesota, and East-Central Illinois, vegetable canning crop production also rose.[7]

The most important crop expansion took place in the tomato and pickling cucumber industries. Ohio became the regional leader in tomatoes, second only to California. Northwestern Ohio, neighboring Southern Michigan, and Northeastern Indiana produced very high quality tomatoes and had an advantage over their western competitor in being closer to regional markets. Pickling cucumbers, introduced into many areas in the late 1930s and 1940s, expanded astronomically in the 1950s as pickles and relishes of many varieties became increasingly popular. Michigan State University led the country in pickling cucumber research, developing different varieties of seeds, hybrids, and chemicals for fertilization and weeding. Yields rose from 30 to almost 150 bushels per acre between 1947 and 1958.[8]

In the early years of the industry, farmers planted small plots and they and family members did most of the harvest labor themselves. They turned increasingly to Mexican American *betabeleros* to work during the July–September harvest period. Michigan became the leading pickling cucumber producer in the nation, with production centered in the Saginaw Valley. For much of the period Wisconsin was second, led by Waushara County. There were other important growing zones in South-Central Minnesota and North-Central Indiana.[9]

The corporations controlled pickling cucumber production more thoroughly than any other major crop in the region. They provided seed, fertilizer, insecticides, and fungicides, rented machinery, determined the timing and overseeing of different field operations, and often did planting and thinning for farmers. They also recruited and distributed harvest workers to different farms, maintained payroll records, and often housed the workers. Most of the processors' activities took place through the growers' associations they established. The industry in Michigan also developed close ties with MFCI to obtain field laborers.[10]

The production changes of the 1950s altered the work cycle of most midwestern farmworkers. The principal feature was the decline in sugar beet labor and a greater range of travel and work patterns in the different crop areas. A second feature was a sharp increase in cannery work for Tejanos throughout the Midwest, sometimes linked to work in field canning crops. Mexican Americans often started the season in asparagus cutting or tomato setting in the late spring, followed by sugar beet hoeing. Afterwards they worked in the early summer fruits, followed by cherries, beans, pickling cucumbers, and fall fruits. In Michigan sugar beet employment lost its dominant position, but the state retained its leading place in the region because of strawberries, cherries, and cucumbers. In other states, sugar beet work was replaced principally by cherries, muck crops, tomatoes, and other canning crops. Earlier, Mexican Americans who came to the Red River Valley of North Dakota and Minnesota tended to stay there all season or to move short distances to Southern Minnesota during gaps in sugar beet work. Increasingly, they had to travel to Wisconsin, Illinois, and Indiana for tomatoes and canning crops. Still others came into the area after earlier work in the Rocky Mountain area. Workers who went to Michigan and formerly spent the entire season in the sugar beet region and the cherries increasingly added work in fruits, cucumbers, muck crops, and tomatoes. Throughout the Midwest mechanization accelerated migrancy, counter to corporation claims.[11]

Migration out of Texas was also increasing, especially because of the mechanization of cotton picking between 1957 and 1961. More Tejanos entered the migrant stream, traveling to California, the Midwest, and Florida for citrus fruit harvesting. Despite the pressures

exerted by shorter harvest periods, they tried to remain in a relatively concentrated area while outside their home state. In 1958 more
than 50 percent of the Tejanos who did seasonal work in Michigan
migrated directly from Texas without stopping, and almost 67 percent returned immediately after completing summer work. The
longer gaps between crops allowed many to supplement farm labor
with temporary work on the railroads, in quarries, and in urban
shops and factories. Thus although mechanization accelerated migrancy, workers resisted it by seeking work in a single area and in
more stable nonagricultural employment.[12]

The Work Force

The most visible change in the seasonal farm labor force in the nation during the 1950s was the sharp rise in employment of foreign
workers. By 1959 the Mexican-born formed a majority of the seasonal
farmworkers in many parts of the Southwest. Employers attributed
the increase to a shortage of available domestic workers, but critics
suggested that it was the result of conscious efforts to undercut labor
organizing and drive down wages.

Although less important than in the Southwest, thousands of foreign workers also came to the Midwest. Midwestern agricultural interests contended that there was less reliance on foreigners because
higher wages lured domestic workers. Labor organizers, on the other
hand, argued that U.S. citizens who lived near the border were displaced from their home territories and had to travel north to find
work. According to this view, domestic migrants in the Midwest
served a function similar to that of *braceros* and undocumented
workers elsewhere: flooding the labor market and helping to bring
down wages. Neither of these arguments adequately considers the
recruitment function performed by the Farm Placement Service.[13]

During the 1950s regional and national private employer associations worked closely with the FPS in worker recruitment. State advisory committees for sugar beets and cucumbers in the Midwest
were controlled by MFCI, for fruits and vegetables by the Farm Bureau, by canner and vegetable growers' associations in the canning
crops. Farm Placement personnel functioned, Ernesto Galarza explains, as "staff assistants" for the corporations that created these associations. Together they worked out arrangements that consciously
clustered workers by ethnicity.[14]

During the 1950s the relative numbers of the different ethnic
groups in the region changed slowly. The proportion of Mexican
Americans increased throughout the region and by the end of the

decade formed between 67 percent and 90 percent of the nonlocal work force in Minnesota, Wisconsin, Illinois, Indiana, and Ohio. Farm Placement officials estimated that between eight thousand and thirteen thousand adult citizens found seasonal employment in each of these states, all of which ranked between twelfth and twentieth nationally in the use of migrant workers.[15]

The patterns were more complicated in Michigan, the second- or third-largest user of migrant workers in the country, depending on the year. The Farm Placement Service estimated that approximately 37,500 domestic seasonal farmworkers entered the state in 1950; the number had risen to about 70,000 by 1959. The expansion of the early 1950s was taken up by rural African American and Euro-American workers, who were often displaced in the South by the mechanization of the cotton harvest. Later in the decade the number of Mexican Americans increased more rapidly. Officials estimated that there were about 12,000 adult African Americans in Michigan at their peak in the mid-1950s; Euro-Americans were estimated at between 12,000 and 18,000 adult workers during the decade. The two groups continued to dominate the fruit harvests but were more scattered in cannery and muck crop labor. The number of Mexican Americans increased from about 16,000 to 20,000 adult workers during the decade. Their tasks changed somewhat, for as employment in sugar beets declined, they turned increasingly to strawberries, bush and tree fruits.[16]

The Farm Placement Service consistently underestimated the number of domestic workers. It deliberately neglected freewheelers, who did not register with the service. Its counting procedure was based only on "adult" workers and excluded many women and all children under age fourteen or sixteen, depending on the survey.

The number of children in the migrant stream varied sharply by ethnicity. African Americans more frequently traveled in adult crews than as families, and children probably did not augment their total by more than 20 percent. Euro-Americans frequently traveled in family groups. A Van Buren County, Michigan, study calculated that Euro-American families averaged 4.2 children, of whom 2.4 accompanied their parents northward. Of those surveyed, 42 percent were from Arkansas, 17 percent from Florida, and 9 percent from Missouri. Mexican Americans traveled increasingly as single families, with much higher proportions of children than the others, an average of 5 to 6 children per family, with 1.7 to 2.0 children per adult worker in crews.[17]

The Farm Placement Service considered these people "nonworkers" but they contributed directly and indirectly to household income. As the wife of one Michigan cherry orchard operator wrote, "The children help by picking or sorting fruit. [They] are not overworked. Sometimes they play. They are happy. They have so much time on their hands that they become juvenile delinquents." Children as young as five or six augmented family production by caring for infant brothers and sisters and performing other tasks. Candillo Delgado conceded that "with the family working I can make more money." Because of child labor the Tejanos, who fell into the lowest earning level among midwestern domestic migrants, often could compete with foreign workers.[18]

Although their numbers increased rapidly in the Midwest, foreign workers concentrated in a few crops. Carl S. Kirk of the Michigan Farm Bureau portrayed them as "specialists among migrant workers," contradicting the International Agreement and laws governing the program that stipulated that they were only to engage in unskilled tasks and supplement citizens in areas of labor shortage. British West Indian workers reached a peak of roughly three thousand in the mid-1950s, and were confined largely to the canning areas of Minnesota, Wisconsin, Illinois, and Indiana. Mexican *braceros* increased rapidly after 1954, when Public Law 309, an amendment to Public Law 78, declared that the United States would conduct unilateral recruitment of Mexican citizens if Mexico refused to "cooperate" with U.S. demands for workers. By 1958 about twenty thousand *braceros* worked annually in the Midwest, most in Michigan, the nation's fifth-largest user of Mexican contract labor. They displaced rather than supplemented Mexican Americans in sugar beets and cucumbers, which belies their classification as crop "specialists."[19]

Undocumented foreign workers were less important in the Great Lakes region than in the Southwest. They seldom attracted much public attention other than after infrequent INS raids and occasional statements of opposition from organized labor leaders. Undocumented Mexicans were more numerous in midwestern cities, where they often worked in services, construction, and other seasonal tasks. The INS concentrated principally in Chicago and Detroit for the midwestern phase of its infamous 1954 Operation Wetback. Its sporadic raids on farms typically netted only a handful of workers. Midwestern employers successfully convinced the public that undocumented workers were unimportant, diverting public attention from them. Based on extant information, it is difficult to estimate their importance as farmworkers in the region.[20]

The total seasonal out-of-state farmworker force in the Great Lakes region at the end of the decade included about 20,000 African

Americans, 40,000 Euro-Americans and 140,000 Tejanos. There were also several hundred Puerto Ricans and Native Americans and about 20,000 foreign workers, almost all Mexicans under contract.

Living quarters changed gradually during the decade. The tent and barn continued to lose popularity. Tents often were government surplus from World War II and could not be replaced cheaply. Farmers were not constructing barns as frequently as in earlier generations, but were replacing them with less-expensive sheds and storage buildings. Employers also constructed multiple-dwelling residential units, commonly divided into one- or two-room apartments, a cheap version of the highway motels that became popular at the time. In larger camps they placed several buildings in close proximity, enabling residents to share facilities.[21]

Camps increased in size, but remained small by southern and southwestern standards. Those in cherry orchards typically housed between fifty and two hundred persons; those in the blueberry area often housed more than two hundred inhabitants. Units on vegetable growers' private farms were smaller. Surveys in the late 1950s in the vicinity of Aurora, Illinois, found camps on asparagus farms averaging about thirty people, and on tomato farms roughly forty people.[22]

The larger corporation camps generally consisted of barracks or clusters of shacks, euphemistically called "cabins." Company housing for families in the sugar beet region commonly housed 20 to 80 persons. Foreign worker camps were larger, typically housing from 50 to 250 people. In the cannery areas, where the trend toward centralized housing began earlier, the camps tended to be even larger. Corporation camps in Ohio and Illinois for families commonly had 15 to 60 units, averaging about 5 or 6 people per dwelling, or 100 to 300 people at peak occupancy.[23]

A decline in the size of domestic crews worked against growth. This decline indicated a diminishing reliance on crew leaders, unlike California and much of the Southwest. More Mexican American families had automobiles or pickup trucks, and many younger members could speak English fluently. Workers also had better access to information because of Farm Placement Service bulletins and announcements. Mexican American crews in the mid-1950s typically averaged between fifteen and twenty members, and were smallest in Minnesota, where they averaged fewer than eight persons by the end of the decade. Euro-American crews were fewer, but they continued to be organized by family units. At the same time African Americans increasingly traveled in adult crews with more than one hundred persons.[24]

Many observers suggest that the massive introduction of foreign workers into the Southwest forced domestic workers to migrate to the North. The argument applies only selectively and does not explain the *braceros'* presence in the Midwest or their domination in only selected crops. Midwestern employers offered their own reasons. One admitted that they formed a "reserve" that kept wages down. A Minnesota cannery manager explained that corporations hired foreign workers "to hold a threat over the heads of whites and the Texas Mexicans, to make them work!" Almost all foreign workers in the region worked in the corporation-controlled sugar beet, pickle and canning industries. The pattern paralleled that in the Southwest, where large corporations and their grower associations convinced the Farm Placement Service that they needed Mexican *braceros* most.[25]

Midwestern employers justified their use of foreign workers on several grounds. Carl Davenport, of Lakeville, Michigan, president of the National Pickle Growers Association, explained that the *bracero* was "an excellent worker, and by virtue of his background in agriculture, is suitable and adaptable to the type of stoop labor required." A Michigan employer asserted that Mexican Americans were becoming less reliable: "The Texas-Mexican, who has serviced this area for many years, has smartened up considerable . . . and those who are here are not very dependable. I don't know whether it's the Indian blood in these people or the gypsy instinct that they appear to be constantly on the move." Although the racial implications should have applied equally to Mexicans born in Mexico or the United States the growers admitted less control over citizens, who were not bound by contracts or threats of deportation and were likely to leave when they considered pay and living conditions intolerable.[26]

By the end of the decade, *braceros* performed at least 75 percent of the fieldwork in sugar beets and 90 percent in cucumbers, crops that had been dominated by Mexican Americans in the 1940s. Sugar beets traditionally were the lowest-paying crop and, according to Ernesto Galarza, the sugar beet thinner was "the lowest of the stoop crop laborers." The more youthful pickle industry, which was not important in Galarza's California, was even more exploitative, its rapid expansion made possible by classic speed-up tactics in production that pushed both growers and pickers. Conditions were so bad that in the late 1950s the Farm Placement Service was forced to devise a special formula system to offset the workers' low earnings.[27]

Through MFCI the corporations also controlled the employment of *braceros* elsewhere, as MFCI selectively leased out unemployed *braceros* for snap beans, onions, cherries, and other crops to growers who paid fees recovered from the workers' salaries. This outside employment required a pliant FPS to determine that a "shortage" existed, almost inevitably because of poor working conditions. One group of growers, including circuit judge Charles L. Brown of Traverse City, requested *braceros* for their cherry orchards. They claimed that they needed the foreigners because "domestic labor simply refuses to come in, either because of the size of the trees or the scarcity of the crop." Michigan congressman Alvin Bentley, one of the best friends of corporate agriculture in the Midwest, posed the matter differently: "The farmer cannot afford to pay the wages which are even as high as an unemployed worker would be receiving from state compensation benefits." [28]

Tejanos were displaced selectively from Michigan's pickle and sugar beet industry, but not from those industries in Minnesota, further dispelling the notion that foreigners were the only acceptable "crop specialists." *Braceros* did not have prior experience in midwestern crops, and their turnover was more than 80 percent every season. The largest corporations were the only groups powerful enough to exert political pressure at the national and regional levels to secure foreign workers, and those from Michigan had the most influence because they were the best organized. [29]

Voices in the Wilderness

Farmworker interests in the Midwest found few friends in the 1950s. Politicians, the local press, and even the labor movement were generally passive when confronted with the contradiction between the rhetoric of justice and equality for all and the reality that farmworkers faced. National labor union strategy focused on California as the beachhead of agricultural unionism. The Midwest did not have a parallel to the National Farm Labor Union (NFLU) and the National Agricultural Workers Union (NAWU). There were no other groups to rally around to challenge control of labor decisions by the sugar beet, canning, and pickle company associations, the Farm Bureau, and the Farm Placement Service. Furthermore, at no other time in the twentieth century did the regional press show so little interest in or report so little on midwestern farmworkers. A small group of reformers continued to confront powerful employer interests, typically in forums to which each had access but for which they had unequal resources, on state-based migrant labor committees, in the legislature, in local communities, and within the church.

The most visible state committee was the Michigan Governor's Interagency Committee on Migratory Labor, succeeded by the Governor's Study Commission on Migratory Labor, appointed in 1952 to conduct a special study of agricultural workers in the state. Its most notable accomplishment was to publish a pamphlet in 1954 entitled *Migratory Workers in Michigan.* The report made several legislative recommendations, but none was enacted into law during the decade. A disappointed committee head Craig Mitchell concluded, "Members of the committee have lost their zeal because of their inability to do anything more than engage in discussions of the problem of migratory labor."[30]

Similar committees appeared in other states. Wisconsin established a State Migrant Committee in 1953 under the auspices of the Wisconsin Welfare Council. Lacking a legal mandate, the committee cooperated with other agencies, particularly on experimental educational projects. In 1956 Ohio established the Governor's Committee on Migratory Labor, the composition and rhetoric of which were more thoroughly controlled by growers and canners than in Michigan and Wisconsin. Its heads during the period were David Sutherland, manager of Ohio Northern Sugar, and William Schneider, personnel manager of Stokeley Van Camp. When confronted with information about low incomes and poor working and housing conditions, the committee did not recommend reforms, but instead excused employers on the grounds that they could not afford to provide more.[31]

Other state governments were even less active. The only state-appointed body in Illinois to deal with agricultural workers was the Subcommittee on Migrants of the Illinois Commission on Children. Its stated purpose was to gather data, and it officially adopted a position of neutrality concerning reforms. The subcommittee attended to its mission so poorly that in 1959, nearly a decade after it was created, commission member Naomi Heitt admitted that it did not even know where migrants were located in much of the state. In Minnesota the Subcommittee on Migrant Workers of the Governor's Interracial Commission maintained a low profile, and the State of Indiana did not even create a forum to discuss farmworkers.[32]

The state committees that dealt with farmworkers met irregularly and had a high turnover rate. Members included a handful of volunteers, a larger number of uninformed bureaucrats, and corporate agricultural representatives, who were well informed and usually dominated proceedings. The corporations represented "the other side" of discussions to extend equal protection to farmworkers by means of legislation concerning wages, housing and living conditions, and basic human rights. The committees sponsored few detailed investigations or recommendations for legislative reform and typically were dormant for many years. Yet they did contribute information about transportation, working conditions, income, housing, and schooling. Travel to the North was much faster in the 1950s because of an improved highway system and faster vehicles. Foreign workers most often were hauled in buses or trucks; citizens, who still came in large stake trucks, increasingly traveled by private pickup trucks and personal automobiles. Time for the trip from South Texas fell to an average of thirty-five hours. Despite the potential for greater safety, accidents levels remained high. Few notices appeared of even spectacular crashes, as in the death of a family from McAllen, Texas, near Bloomington, Indiana, in a flaming truck wreck or the tragic overturning of a truck filled with workers near Saint Johns, Michigan. The complacent local and regional press seldom considered such matters newsworthy.[33]

A more conscious veil of secrecy prevented publicizing investigations revealing that workers seldom earned even the manipulated prevailing wages. Investigators documented a pattern of holdbacks, bonuses, refusal to pay previously agreed-upon wages, short weighing, and INS deportation of foreign workers who complained about irregularities.[34]

The most thorough studies of earnings of foreign workers involved the "modern" pickle industry. Although the corporations quintupled production between 1947 and 1958, they abolished hourly wages and reinstituted a form of sharecropping, a modern corporate adaptation of a system long in disgrace. Workers received half the returns paid by corporations to the growers; the amount was based on a complicated scale that paid most for the smallest and tenderest pickles. Workers were further confused because "each company has its own respective number of grades and grade size." Weighing and grading took place at the pickle stations, so workers could not verify measurements.[35]

Lloyd H. Gallardo of Michigan State University investigated "sharecropping" and discovered many reasons why the farmer found it so attractive. The most important was that it "relieves him of a large percentage of the costs of efficient management." The value of the crop was determined by the size of the field and the number and productivity of the vines. Because grower receipts were not influenced by the number of workers or their efficiency, the farmer was "better off with too many workers." Because of excessive hiring, fast pickers had to stop early in the day or intrude on plots designated for other workers. The system was so lax that growers and corporations seldom knew how long workers spent in their fields.[36]

One Michigan study reported that actual earnings for pickling cucumber harvesting fell from nine dollars to six dollars per hundred-weight between 1947 and 1958, while the size of the premium grade decreased. Further, there were widespread illegal employer actions, including inaccurate recording of hours, illegal deductions for fuel, electricity, and other "miscellaneous" unrecorded expenses. The Reverend Joseph Crosthwait reported that in 1958 harvesters averaged between twenty and thirty cents per hour.[37]

In response to worker complaints they could no longer silence, the FPS and the pickle industry agreed in 1958 to allow a "neutral" study of earnings as the basis for a possible revision of the payment system. Conducted by Michigan State University professor Noel Stuckman in cooperation with the National Pickle Packers and National Pickle Growers associations, the study was based on a "representative" sample of farms. Although Stuckman acknowledged that earnings were directly related to yield, over which the worker had no control, yields in his sample were 46 percent above the state average. In spite of this unacknowledged and uncorrected statistical bias, Stuckman concluded that for a worker to earn the prevailing wage, a field had to have yields at least 40 percent above the average. Stuckman also observed that harder work could not improve earnings, because each plot was divided among the different pickers assigned to it. The study recommended the adoption of the Workers' Yield Return Formula (WYRF), an upward adjustment in payments for workers in the lowest-yielding fields. Stuckman optimistically concluded that future increases in production would lead to higher earnings, a view contradicted by the experience of previous years, when sharp increases in yields led to lower earnings. Stuckman unwittingly demonstrated worker resistance by revealing the absence of citizens in the fields. Furthermore, he noted that fewer than 2 percent of *braceros* returned to the pickles for a second season.[38]

The year of Stuckman's study, Michigan pickle industry representative Carl Davenport presented his own report explaining why employers preferred *braceros*. He calculated that a group of African American domestic workers earned 41.4 cents per hour, compared with *bracero* earnings of 63.5 cents, and attributed the differences to lazy U.S. citizens who "lounged, played cards and drank gin." In the study Davenport admitted that the hard-working *braceros* still earned 30 percent less than the prevailing wage. They remained in the fields because they were held captive by their contracts.[39]

Foreign workers fared poorly in other crop areas as well. A 1958 British embassy study in Wisconsin examined three crews of cherry pickers from the British West Indies. It discovered that only 52 percent, 32 percent, and 25 percent, respectively, of the members of the three crews earned the prevailing wage of seventy-five cents per hour. Individual impressions confirmed these studies. An Indiana newspaper reporter observed that "one of our good, respected farmers gives these boys extra work," paying 25 cents an hour. P. H. Evelken, who worked with *braceros* in Wisconsin for many years, concluded that, based on employer treatment of workers and wages, "one would think that this was a slave area," as earnings averaged under twenty dollars per week, and many men ended up broke after a season of work.[40]

Worker income was affected by other grower practices. The associations frequently convinced the Farm Placement Service to provide workers when there were no certified shortages and to distribute them to noncertified growers without authorization. The associations that "lent" them received kickbacks from the nonassociation farmers who received the workers. The Michigan-based Eugene Committee for the Defense of Migrant Workers observed that many employers did not know about or consciously ignored the sanctions in the *bracero* contracts, "due mainly to the fact that they feel nothing will be done if they are caught in violation."[41]

Because domestic workers were not protected by minimum wage regulations, agencies saw no need to conduct detailed studies of their earnings. Agencies more often addressed the problem obliquely, attempting to counter their critics with a "reform" based on the assumption that unemployment and underemployment were the root problems. In cooperation with grower associations, the FPS devised the Annual Worker Plan (AWP), introduced into the Midwest in 1954. It was based on a premise that low earnings were the result of "aimless wandering from job to job." Midwestern and Texas Farm Placement officials cooperated with employers to achieve "continuity and stability of employment for seasonal migrants approaching year-round work." By the end of the decade, they estimated that at least 67 percent of all domestic workers were registered in the AWP.[42]

The AWP saved employers the expense of a recruiting license and setting up recruitment facilities in Texas. It reduced their paperwork and served as a conduit to crew leaders. Even labor leaders applauded the AWP as a positive step toward improving wages and working conditions. Nonetheless, it did little to help workers. Growers continued to dominate recruitment, with the help of passive USES and state officials and no worker representatives on boards. As economist Max Leftwich noted, the presence of FPS officials in the recruitment mechanism remained "a legal formality." The AWP did not even address the problems of low wages, overrecruitment, or the adverse effects of the increasing number of foreign workers. Employers continued to engage in unauthorized activities with FPS cooperation and influenced politicians and provided inaccurate information on the radio and in the press about worker shortages.[43]

Social Security for farm workers was introduced in 1950. To be eligible, individuals had to work for the same employer for two successive quarters during the year to receive one quarter of Social Security credit. In effect the stipulation successfully disqualified more than 95 percent of midwestern migrant workers.[44]

The failure of reform was confirmed by farmworkers' wages, which fell by the end of the decade to approximately 35 percent of industrial workers' wages. Annual income disparities were even greater. In 1957 the average adult migrant worker earned $859 for the entire season nationally, almost identical to the figures in the Midwest. A 1958 study determined that annual family incomes for Mexican American seasonal farmworkers coming to the Midwest, including parents and children, was $2,256. The relative decline in agricultural incomes contrasted with productivity, which rose by 83 percent in agriculture between 1940 and 1958, compared with only 33 percent in industry.[45]

Studies of housing continued to reveal that workers stayed in old shacks and shanties, abandoned farmers' houses, surplus war tents, boxcars, barracks, corn cribs, and hastily vacated chicken coops. These dwellings were largely without screens and were poorly maintained and crowded. The newer multiple-dwelling units, even when built for people, had many of the same problems. In Saint Joseph County, Indiana, farmers put up new buildings fifteen feet square, without windows or screens, to house three or four Tejano families. A machine shed near Stockbridge, Michigan, was partitioned into cubicles for a dozen families, with a narrow passageway in the middle; the unscreened doors on either end were the only source of ventilation. Workers arrived in March and stayed until November, but the dwellings were poorly heated, often with dangerous wood-, kerosene-, or gas-burning cooking stoves. Beds often lacked mattresses, pillows, and blankets, and some people had to sleep on bare floors. Drinking water frequently came from hastily dug shallow wells or from dirty or rusty oil drums. Growers increasingly introduced running water, commonly from an open pipe that stuck straight out of the ground, with no drainage. When it rained, large pools of stagnant water remained for weeks and created additional health problems.[46]

The newer camps were not necessarily healthier or safer than the old. In Minnesota six family members died of asphyxiation from a gas hot plate used for heating their "modern" cabin. Dr. D. K. Volk of Saginaw attributed the continued high mortality rates of Tejano children in the area to abysmal living conditions and lack of access to medical care. An outbreak of bacillary dysentery on Lewis Myers's farm in Livingston County, Michigan, was linked to drinking water from an uncovered pump primed by a shallow well located inside a radish-processing facility. Garbage from the camp and the processing operations simply was dumped on the farm and in the camp. Unscreened privies without doors continued to be built throughout the region and were a major source of epidemics of impetigo, dysentery, and meningitis.[47]

Growers typically defended even the worst conditions by asserting that the housing was free. They did not acknowledge that housing often served to store animals or tools at other times in the year, or that it was old and would have cost them money to destroy or remove. Furthermore, such housing served as a form of control over workers and prevented the entry of unwanted outsiders. They could brand workers who complained as "troublemakers," expel them from their camps, and have them blacklisted by the growers' association. At this time modest challenges to grower arguments that worker housing was the private property of growers and thus was not subject to outside intrusion appeared in Wisconsin and Minnesota legislation.[48]

The Wisconsin law, enacted in 1949, required that the Wisconsin Board of Health register and certify all camps in the state. All dwellings had to have at least four-hundred cubic feet of space per person over age twelve, and two hundred cubic feet for those who were younger. Each camp was required to have separate toilets for men and women, wash basins, showers, and laundry facilities. The next year the State Board of Health inspected twenty-five camps in Door County and found twenty-four of them to be substandard. Its investigation resulted in a 1951 amendment permitting the state to hire two permanent inspectors, but the positions remained vacant for most of the decade. In 1952 more than 400 camps were registered in the state, of which 275 had been inspected and only twenty-six found "reasonably" to comply with the law. In 1957 an amendment to the statute established penalties for noncompliance, ranging from fines of ten dollars to one hundred dollars; however, it added an escape clause allowing temporary permits "if a grower shows good faith" toward compliance. In 1959, ten years after the law was passed, the State Board of Health reported that there still was "no sure way of knowing where these camps were located."[49]

The corporations led the resistance to compliance. Sugar beet and

pickle companies "made very slight attempts to improve their camps."
Many employers evaded regulations by "leasing" camps to crew
leaders or workers. The Board of Health further reported that not a
single camp license had ever been revoked or a single fine levied on
the basis of the strongest migrant housing law in the Midwest.[50]

The Minnesota law was equally as ineffective. An investigation by
the Minnesota Board of Health of nineteen camps in different parts
of the State revealed that all had inadequate window areas, unsani-
tary privies, and poor garbage disposal. Seventeen camps had unsatisfactory water supplies, sixteen had poor storage and garbage containers, and fifteen had liquid wastes close to the surface. There was
only one inspector in the state, and during the first decade of the law
no growers were fined for noncompliance.[51]

Bracero housing was more stringently regulated by worker contracts that guaranteed standards of cleanliness, safety, and comfort. Yet
camp operators commonly falsified reports regarding housing type,
physical conditions, and space. Observers agreed that, although
compliance was "a mockery of regulations," domestic worker housing was even worse.[52]

Midwestern employers commonly claimed that worker housing
was better than elsewhere, but this assertion was widely challenged.
An Ohio church report found that Tejanos were "quite disgusted"
with the housing, "often described by them as the worst they had
seen." An Ohio study by Wade Andrews and Saad Nagi reported that
"no more than one-third of the housing units of any kind are clean,
screened, sanitary and have a safe source of water." Father Clement
Kern asserted that housing "was nearly all bad." Lakeview, Michigan, workers resided in "living quarters most of their employers
would not keep their dogs in." In Minnesota, Robert Henley of the
Home Missions Council concluded that conditions were inferior to
the worst housing of the Great Depression.[53]

Poor living conditions were exacerbated by the lack of medical
services. A study conducted jointly in Texas and Michigan revealed
that 20 percent of farmworkers required medical services for infections, asthma, nervous conditions, fever and vomiting, and poison-
ing caused by campground hazards and exposure to chemicals on
soils, fruits, and vegetables. In a few places, including Curtis in Lucas County, Ohio, and Maple Island in Freeborn County, Minnesota,
local authorities set up mobile health clinics to administer chest
X rays and inoculations and to attend to minor health needs. More
frequently even state-funded public emergency relief systems seldom served migrant workers, who were not informed about them or
were refused services.[54]

Braceros were covered by medical insurance automatically deducted from their wages, but upon succumbing to illness or injury they were frequently deported before treatment. Reformers' attempts to set up medical insurance programs for domestic farmworkers never went beyond the experimental stage, for employers and insurance companies considered them a risk. The president of Michigan Blue Shield concluded that, "at present, we cannot see how we can develop a program for such pickers." A 1958 Ohio study determined that because such services were lacking, 33 percent of the babies of migrant women in Ohio were born outside of hospitals.[55]

The reformers, supported by mandatory attendance laws and the Fair Labor Standards Act prohibiting child labor when public schools were in session, were more active in education. Central and Western Michigan universities and Alma and Moorhead colleges established experimental education programs. The Big Ten schools, many of which spent millions of dollars annually in agricultural and other research on behalf of private investors, avoided such projects.[56]

There were also a number of privately sponsored experimental educational projects in the region. The most successful were in Bay County, Michigan, Waupun and Manitowoc, Wisconsin; and Ottawa County, Ohio. The Bay County school operated in 1956 and 1957, financed by a grant from the National Child Labor Committee. Sessions lasted five to seven weeks, with approximately thirty students per class. Emphasizing arithmetic, language, and writing, they offered many of the younger children their first immersion into English. It was the only important public-supported program oriented toward migrant education in Michigan, where almost fifty thousand school-aged children entered the state to work each season.[57]

The Waupun project, sponsored by the Wisconsin Governor's Committee on Human Rights and local school authorities, was funded by the National Council on Agricultural Life and Labor (NCALL) and contributions. It lasted from 1950 to 1953 and averaged twenty students a year. In 1958 and 1959 the Ohio project was funded by the Elizabeth S. Magee Education and Research Foundation and the United Church Women of Ohio. Held at the Allen Central School in Ottawa County, it concentrated on language and math and included art and music. During the six-week sessions children advanced an average of one to two years in comprehension in reading and math skills and gained one to five pounds in weight. All three projects ceased when private funds dried up.[58]

These efforts had little effect in raising the low levels of formal education among migrants. A 1957 Ohio survey showed that more than 50 percent of elementary-aged children in Mexican American farmworker families lagged in school by one grade, and an additional 25 percent, by two or more grades. The Minnesota Governor's Interracial Commission in 1958 reported that the average age of first graders among migrant children was eight years, and that by fourth grade the average age rose to twelve. Many continued to miss classes several months each year, and others never attended school at all.[59]

The impact of inadequate schooling can be gleaned from Michigan studies conducted in 1954 for Euro-American children in Van Buren County and Mexican American children in Bay County, followed up in 1957 by surveys of parents. Twenty-five percent of Euro-American parents had a fourth-grade education or less. Mexican American parents averaged less than three years of formal schooling, one-fourth had never attended school, and fewer than 40 percent could write and speak English. Among the children, almost all the Euro-Americans attended school, but by age ten they averaged one year behind grade level. Among the Tejano children, 12 percent never attended school, 75 percent were at least one grade behind, and almost 50 percent were two or more grades behind age level. Further, 91 percent dropped out of school by the time they reached the eighth grade.[60]

School and law enforcement officials were largely responsible for nonattendance. Ohio consumer advocate Elizabeth Magee criticized the "lack of cooperation" from local school authorities. The Minnesota Governor's Interracial Commission reported that in 1950 Hollandale school officials "rebelled against the enforcement of compulsory school laws for farm worker children." The superintendent in East Grand Forks admitted that the district made no effort to encourage Mexican American students working on nearby farms to attend classes and that none were enrolled. In many districts public schools would not admit them unless they paid out-of-district tuition. A fall, 1951, study in Michigan and Ohio by the USDL revealed that children were employed on sixty-six of sixty-seven farms surveyed, in violation of the Fair Labor Standards Act. A Red River Valley teacher admitted that she discouraged local migrant children from attending because she was unwilling to go into the basement of the school to find books for them. Educators were not challenged effectively for blatant disregard of attendance and labor laws. Their behavior was rooted in the dominant attitudes of the communities where they lived. Farm Bureau and grower association members, who controlled school boards, contended that existing conditions were adequate because the children did not need or deserve better schooling.[61]

In one case, the Reverend Shirley Greene of NCALL planned to conduct a comparative national study of the education of the children from farmworker families and chose Berrien County to represent the Midwest. He first secured approval for the project from state agencies and county school authorities. He then encountered an unexpectedly hostile reception from Berrien County Farm Bureau president Ray Dewitt, who quickly pressured local principals and school boards to retract their approval. In a private meeting, the Reverend Mr. Greene tried to dissuade Dewitt, but Dewitt complained that such studies "always result in unfavorable publicity for the growers." Dewitt then threatened Greene, asserting that he had just met with "a representative of the FBI to find out about how to go about conducting an investigation" of NCALL. The Farm Bureau leader later noted that "we are very much aware of the many national organizations of socialistic trend that are worming their way into our local governments and organizations."[62]

The Red-baiting forced the Reverend Mr. Greene to transfer the midwestern section of his research to the canning area around Hoopestown, Illinois. In retreat Greene threatened to expose the Farm Bureau: "The record of our experience in Michigan will, of course, be made a part of the report which we publish at the conclusion of our national study." Greene's work, entitled *The Education of Migrant Children*, timidly relegated the unpleasant experience in Michigan to a footnote: "Local opposition in the county first proposed for the study led to the substitution of Illinois." Neither Berrien County nor the Farm Bureau was mentioned. Even the most dedicated educators were afraid to offend the most reactionary agribusiness interests.[63]

The reform effort in the 1950s interested a few national and state politicians and led to two major Senate investigations. The first, a result of the President's Commission on Migratory Labor hearings of 1950, was chaired by Hubert Humphrey (Minnesota), in 1952. It provided valuable information, but its legislative recommendations were not enacted. A more comprehensive Senate investigation began in 1959 and continued through the 1960s. Chaired by Harrison Williams of New Jersey, its leaders included Patrick McNamara of Michigan and Eugene McCarthy and Hubert Humphrey of Minnesota. Sharp battles in committee produced important legislation that appeared the following decade. Committee reforms were challenged or weakened by the Farm Bureau, corporate and association representatives, numerous Republican politicians, and the rural and conservative urban press. The subcommittee, led by Senator Williams, visited Berrien County in 1959. The Benton Harbor *News-Palladium* criticized the visit as a "privy-sniffing, under-the-mattress tour of migrant living conditions."[64]

In state legislatures, politicians sporadically introduced legislation to investigate housing, camp conditions, crew leaders, licensing crew leaders, and transportation; these bills, however, seldom got past initial committee hearings. A not-atypical case involved Michigan House and Senate Concurrent Resolution 25, introduced in 1955 and intended to study migratory labor in the state. Sen. Burch Storey of Belding, a grower, chaired the investigative committee. He called a single one-day session in which a handful of growers, state officials, and corporate representatives painted a rosy picture. Rep. Don Pears of Buchanan, representing a fruit-growing district in Southwestern Michigan, asserted that workers had no complaints and that the only problems were the result of "guile" caused by outsiders. Storey asserted that because he hired both domestics and *braceros* he understood the problems thoroughly. He added that, "as an employer, I feel that we are doing everything possible for these workers, and some besides." His one-page final report confused Mexican nationals with Mexican Americans and erroneously asserted that all workers were protected by written contracts that obviated the need for any new legislation. It concluded that "conditions are improving each year."[65]

John Sweeney, assistant to Governor G. Mennen Williams, complained that "this report represents a complete whitewash." Yet critics did not address the conflict of interest in appointing Storey or the obvious factual errors in the report. The Farm Bureau praised the report, concluding that "seasonal farm labor should be as it has in the past, without interference from unions, committees or other agencies."[66]

Local growers suggested that problems that did exist could be resolved, not by material changes, but by public relations programs to bring workers and the local community into more frequent contact. A report in the Traverse City area suggested that "real progress is being evidenced in the recognition of migrant people as being necessary to the economy." A Wood County, Ohio, missionary claimed that relations were improving because "the farmers realize the workers are necessary." In Oconto, Wisconsin, an effort by merchants to "recognize them [workers] as an economic necessity and for bringing business into the community" included playing Mexican music an hour each day to lure them into stores. Hoopestown, Illinois, merchants initiated a campaign to improve relations with workers as potential customers and adopted the slogan, "Learn 50 words of Spanish and increase your business by 150 percent." Meanwhile the Hoopestown Chamber of Commerce set up a community relations program to encourage acceptance and end segregation in public places. According to the plan, "the first thing to do was to clean them up so when they come into town people wouldn't be prejudiced against them."[67]

Another community relations activity was the harvest time fiesta. The most popular fiestas celebrated cherries in Traverse City and Hart, Michigan; blueberries in South Haven, Michigan; pickles in Waupun, Wisconsin; and tomatoes in Longley, Ohio. Sponsors included local chapters of the Rotary Club, Jaycees, or Kiwanis Club, with enthusiastic support from USDA officials. Initially, the Waupun organizers asserted that the festivities were offered to demonstrate an appreciation for the harvesters, but soon they changed the focus to "publicity engendering," or attracting tourists to make a profit. They were also aware of other "tangible terms," specifically, to attract a "plentiful work force." These community-relations efforts, as former farmworker César Garza of the Minnesota Migrant Ministry observed, were "strictly business."[68]

Public relations efforts, however, did not reduce the underlying class and ethnic tensions. Businesses continued to mark up prices and offer poor-quality merchandise while complaining about their presence. A banker in Grant, Michigan, stated, "The more you do for Texas-Mexicans, the more they demand." The workers were not in fact passive. Former farmworker Bacilio Tijerina, recently settled in Michigan, asserted, "Why should a field man take a truckload of Mexicans who arrive after store hours into the back door of the store instead of the front door?"[69]

Within local communities workers also faced ongoing police harassment and arrests for "alleged" speeding, drunkenness, disturbing the peace, and other supposed misdemeanors and felonies. Exaggerated local fears encouraged police and sheriff's department license. In Stockbridge, Michigan, for example, Mexicano and Mexican American families entered town on Saturday nights. The *Lansing Journal* reported that "the village square is jam packed, a brawling mass of humanity sporting for excitement" who "show an indifferent regard for the law." Police on several occasions showed even less regard for the legal rights of citizen and noncitizen. In the Red River Valley, Clay County sheriff Parker Erikson ordered workers to turn in firearms and knives to growers on arrival in the area. The American Crystal Sugar Company provided him and growers in the area a list of all car owners, car descriptions, and license numbers in case trouble arose.[70]

Community-based church programs for seasonal workers expanded throughout the Midwest in the 1950s. The Catholic church recruited Spanish-speaking priests and seminarians, who worked in areas with high concentrations of Mexican Americans and Mexican *braceros*, including South Bend, Crookston, Green Bay, Grand Rapids, Saginaw, and the Southeastern Michigan–Northwestern Ohio area. The greatest emphasis was on formal schooling. Catholics also set up community centers and health clinics with volunteer staff and trained nurses at Maple Island and Crookston, Minnesota; Racine, Wisconsin; and Arlington Heights and Chicago Heights, Illinois.[71]

The Protestant National Council of Churches, the successor of the Home Missions Council, began its Migrant Ministry (MM) in 1950. The local projects continued under the direction of paid staff with assistance from local ministers and lay volunteers. In the early 1950s the programs turned increasingly toward evangelism. One Michigan staff member asserted, "Important though ministering to the physical needs may be, we believe that the core of the whole program is to present the love of God and Christ the Savior." Staff confusion about doctrine and mission revealed itself in a report on the conversion of former Catholic *braceros* near Sanilac, Michigan: "A number of the Nationals were baptized into the Christian faith." Migrant Ministry projects increasingly emphasized community acceptance. The Fisher, Minnesota, ministry set up a community center for recreation, with a nurse and a child care center. Staff members coordinated public functions to encourage social interaction between farmworkers and permanent residents, including integrated church services, picnics, fiestas, and field trips for children. The Mason, Michigan, project considered its greatest success in community acceptance in the 1956 season was "the use of migrants in the taco sale."[72]

Protestants depended more than Catholics on local support and consequently stayed farther away from issues considered controversial. The new Allegan County, Michigan, staff observed that they were "really on trial as the Migrant Ministry had to be sold to the growers, community and church people." Migrant Ministry penetration was weakest in Ohio, which, one report lamented, "has been very slow to move on the migrant situation."[73]

The ministry was also hampered by internal rifts and the refusal of many staff members and Protestant ministers to concede that the workers were not entirely responsible for their conditions. One MM staff member discussed workers who came to the local community: "We don't look at them as trash, which of course they really are." The Reverend Paul Mumford of Plymouth, Ohio, responding to worker complaints, retorted that "they should get into other work and if they can't they are either naturally dumb or lazy." The Reverend Mr. Esterley of Belmore, Ohio, was reported as "very unsympathetic," while the Reverend Mr. Ringenberg wanted only to "teach the Bible." Wisconsin minister William E. Scholes criticized initiatives by the Reverend Shirley Greene, who "must get better clearance here, or he is going to run into more and more difficulty."[74]

The Migrant Ministry frequently failed to convince local congregations to welcome farmworkers. One Jamaican left services feeling that "everyone stared at us like animals. . . . We left and never went back." In Minnesota the ministry's efforts to run integrated church services and social functions were "practically impossible for the Mexicans." Only the less-controversial recreation programs, sewing classes, softball games, and segregated services in camps did not engender controversy. Workers were unresponsive to local programs, as a Minnesota staff member observed, except the movies, "since entertainment is scarce."[75]

Rivalries between Catholics and Protestants further weakened church programs. In Norwalk, Ohio, a Protestant staff worker complained that there had been problems with Catholics "for the past several years." Protestants became particularly upset at priests who discussed "controversial" topics and criticized growers and working and housing conditions. A Minnesota missionary complained; "Those priests can cause unrest and trouble among the workers—the companies don't like that."[76]

A handful of priests made the only consistent efforts to challenge exploitation and encourage worker organization in the Midwest during the 1950s. They supported workers cheated by employers, forced to live in deplorable conditions, arbitrarily arrested and imprisoned, and, in the case of *braceros*, threatened with deportation. Many refused to back down when pressed by local growers, corporations, or their own superiors. Father Hermes of Saint Johns, Michigan, intervened on behalf of *bracero* pickle workers who complained about wages, working conditions, and poor treatment. The camp manager tried to prevent him and other local priests from entering the camp, but his pressure led to improvements and the removal of the manager. Another activist, Father Neil O'Connor, worked in the Saginaw area. He ultimately saw unionization as the only viable solution, claiming that "the Catholic Church stands behind the organization of all workers to protect their rights and justice." Father O'Connor complained that existing treatment of workers was "one of the major arguments for communism against democracy."[77]

Other priests also exposed mistreatment of workers. Father Peter Miller, of Plymouth, Indiana, responded to a request from a group of Mexican nationals working in the pickles to look into living conditions and pay. When he visited their camp, local police guarding the entrance warned him that it was dangerous to enter, because "agitators" were stirring up the men. On entry he learned that the men were earning three dollars to four dollars per week. Some had blank paychecks for a month's work after paying for food, insurance, and unauthorized deductions for tools and "miscellaneous" items. In addition, the cucumbers were downgraded and workers were short-weighted. Father Miller first notified the USDL, which had only one compliance officer to handle farm labor complaints in the Midwest. The official "insisted that no wrong had been done to them [the workers]" and concluded that because the men were unwilling to work, they would be deported at their own expense. Miller then turned to a Chicago-based priests' group, the Catholic Labor Alliance, and to Chicago's Mexican consul. Together they again met with the USDL representative, who continued to defend the company and insist that it was established and correct procedure to deport the *braceros*. The parties finally achieved a compromise in which workers were granted the option of remaining with the same employer and guaranteed seventy cents per hour plus incentives, honest weight, and fair grading, or being sent to an employer in Michigan.[78]

The most visible priests in the region, Fathers Clement Kern, Carlos Talavera, and Gabriel Torres, continued their struggle from Most Holy Trinity Parish in Detroit. They tried to strengthen the Migratory Workers Defense League (formerly the Beet Workers Defense Committee), the only midwestern organization concerned with social justice and issues that other groups hesitated to address. The priests uncovered a consistent pattern of low wages, poor working conditions, ill treatment, and illegal detentions and imprisonment; they addressed these issues in public meetings and hearings but they were alone in their efforts to challenge agricultural interests. Fathers Kern and Talavera also supported one of the few recorded midwestern farmworker strikes of the decade, initiated in 1951 by *braceros* and Mexican Americans who stopped working for the Croswell Pickle Company. The priests confirmed and publicized such abuses as poor housing, leaky tents, lack of beds, and large crews of workers sharing one filthy, open privy. Earnings averaged less than two dollars per day, despite contract guarantees of sixty cents per hour and forty-eight hours of work per week. With the help of the priests the workers won wage concessions and housing improvements.[79]

Through the Migratory Workers Defense League the priests and workers tried to enlist the support of organized labor to engage in union organizing in the state. Representatives of the National Agricultural Workers Union made brief visits to the region, but there was little interest from organized labor or elsewhere, beyond rhetoric, for creating a farmworkers' movement in the Midwest. Many union leaders in the Midwest were openly hostile, in fact. Michigan AFL-CIO Council representative Ernest Bennett complained that migrant conditions were better than portrayed by "one-sided" newspaper articles.[80]

A few organizations did show increasing interest and became more involved at the end of the decade. One of the most visible was a group of Mexican Americans affiliated with the United Packinghouse Workers of America (UPWA) in Chicago, who formed the Comité de Habla Hispana (the Spanish-Speaking Committee). The committee defended the Spanish-speaking community and protested the deportation of undocumented Mexicanos. It charged that "the arrests of Mexicans are going on without authorization, [they are] being imprisoned and deported like animals." Although not an agricultural union, the committee frequently came to the aid of farmworkers.[81]

Other midwestern union activists spent most of their energies writing resolutions and criticizing conditions in the Deep South and the Southwest, where national union policy saw a more promising organizational base. At the time they did little to challenge the false illusions created by employers about the farmworkers in their midst. Meanwhile, more important changes were taking place among the workers.[82]

Taking Up Roots

The size and number of settlements of former farmworkers throughout the region increased rapidly during the 1950s. Many observers have suggested that their settlement represented upward mobility similar to that of European immigrants who earlier settled in the region. In reality the process was much more complicated. Unlike the Europeans' reasons for migrating, the farmworkers of Mexican descent originally moved not to settle, but to find work. As workers they developed a network that eventually promoted settlement.[83]

In places where work was concentrated they gained access to information and developed their own larger social and cultural world. Radio stations increasingly offered programs of the music of Texas and Northern Mexico, news of local events, activities of interest, and information about work and families in need of emergency assistance, especially early in the morning, late afternoon, and on weekends. Workers created their own church and community groups, which sponsored social events, and local merchants increasingly catered to their special needs. In many places city recreation departments or private groups ran Spanish-language movies. The local theater in Blissfield, Michigan, for example, which normally closed for the summer, showed Spanish-language movies that drew people from a wide area.[84]

Local orchestras and Tejano *conjuntos* played the familiar music of South Texas and Northern Mexico at weekend dances often sponsored by settled Mexicanos. These dances typically were family affairs and attracted hundreds of people to dance, listen to the music, and socialize with relatives, friends, and new acquaintances. On the weekends many small towns and urban neighborhoods briefly took on a Tejano appearance. The network linking migrants and recent settlers thus encouraged further settlement.[85]

Young adults with fewer economic ties to Texas most frequently chose to remain in the Midwest, especially where the working season was longest or where work ended near the canneries that increasingly hired migrants at harvest time and sometimes afterward. In the late 1950s settlement also accelerated because of the decline of seasonal employment in Texas caused by cotton harvest mechanization. Settlement was motivated by more attractive opportunities, but was also the result of being stranded with no prospects for employment.

The Tejanos settled in older *colonias* in the large and medium-sized cities, in new *colonias* on the urban fringes, in medium-sized cities, and in small towns and rural locations. Their first dwellings were often transitional, reflecting desperation more than opportunity. Many were old farmhouses or beet shacks with little insulation and inadequate and dangerous heating; some were even reconverted barns with strips of paper pasted to the walls as insulation. A 1952 survey of recent settlers in the Alma, Michigan, area indicated that only 8 percent had private indoor plumbing. In Rossville, Illinois, a group of recent settlers stayed in war surplus barracks. Settlers in Perrysburg Heights and Gibsonburg, Ohio, had no running water. Despite high rates of colds, sore throats, arthritis, pneumonia, and asthma, the settlement process continued and the communities grew.[86]

In Western and Southern Minnesota clusters of settlers appeared on the fringes of many small towns in Clay, Blue Earth, and Dakota counties. Saint Paul and, to a lesser degree, Minneapolis remained magnets for most former agricultural workers in the state. The Twin Cities offered a wide range of employment, particularly in the meatpacking plants and the railroads. In Wisconsin settlement occurred principally in the southeastern part of the state, near important agricultural communities and industrial towns. Waukesha, Sheboygan, Racine, Kenosha, Oshkosh, and especially Milwaukee had important concentrations of Mexican Americans.[87]

In Illinois most recent settlers went to the Chicago area. On its southern fringes, people concentrated in Chicago Heights, South Holland, Harvey, Lansing, and Blue Island. To the northwest, smaller clusters appeared in Alcove, Arlington Heights, and Des Plaines. In this rapidly expanding area, where suburbs were swallowing up the farms, there were many recent settlers "living in extremely precarious circumstances . . . completely isolated from the urban centers." A group of former agricultural workers remained in the Belle Grove area, where they found employment as unskilled laborers in factories, gas stations, and in carpentry. Another settlement of former Tejanos appeared in East-Central Illinois around Rossville and Hoopestown, where many people found employment in local canneries.[88]

Settlers in Indiana most often went to the industrial settings in the Gary and Fort Wayne areas. They also took up roots in smaller cities where there were canneries, including Kokomo, Peru, and Decatur. A large settlement also appeared in the South Bend area, where people settled both in the city and in the countryside, often continuing to work in the rich mucklands nearby for several years. In the winter many were fortunate to find two or three days' of work. Local authorities made it difficult for them to qualify for township relief or government surplus. The only regular outside assistance came from charities and school lunch programs for children. Like many other ethnic groups, they faced a gradual and difficult transition from farm work to city life.[89]

The most significant settling of farmworkers in the Great Lakes region took place in Michigan and Ohio. In the former, the automobile and feeder industries attracted Mexican Americans to Detroit, almost every medium-sized city in the state, and many smaller industrial communities. Some people found jobs in the automobile plants, but more worked in foundries, shops, and canneries. Settlements in Muskegon, Holland, Grand Rapids, and smaller communities appeared near work. In the Alma area, former beet workers found employment in most of the fifteen factories in town. There was very rapid settlement in Lansing, where people found employment in a range of factory and menial occupations and often returned to farm labor in the summer. The Saginaw and Bay City area still was the single most important zone of settlement outside the metropolitan Detroit area. There were also large numbers of settlers in Flint, Pontiac, and Port Huron. The Mexican American population of small cities in the southeastern part of the state, especially Adrian and Blissfield, also grew. In many locations recent settlers formed chapters of the American G.I. Forum, clubs, and church-related groups.[90]

In Northwestern Ohio there was a very rapid growth in settlement, largely the result of the southward shift of agricultural employment at the end of the season. People found work in automobile plants, factories, and shops in Fostoria, Defiance, and Findlay, and in canneries in smaller towns, including Curtis, Bono, Perrysburg Heights, and Leipsic. Gibsonburg and Woodville offered erratic employment in local gypsum and lime quarries, and Mexican Americans often lived so close that lime dust covered "the entire area" around their residences. The major settlement was in the largest nearby city, Toledo, where they clustered in several neighborhoods, the most important on the South Side. They found unskilled work in nearby canneries, quarries, railroads, and small shops and factories. As in other midwestern cities, a handful of small businesses appeared to offer them services, and they formed clubs, including a chapter of the American G.I. Forum, the Sociedad Mutualista, and *conjuntos* and *orchestras* for social functions. These recently transplanted farmworkers continued to retain ties with family, friends, and former neighbors who had come to the region from Texas for agricultural work, social, and family visits.[91]

The former farmworkers who settled in the Midwest in the 1950s were primarily a second-generation immigrant population of largely unskilled workers. Surveys of recent settlers in Alma, Michigan, and in Toledo, Ohio, revealed that about 90 percent of the adults were born in Texas, the rest in Mexico, and more than 75 percent of their parents were born in Mexico. They had fairly large households, averaging almost six persons. In the Toledo study, formal education averaged 6 years for men and 7 for women, somewhat higher than among the migrant population nationally but well below the county average of 10 years and the national average of 9.3 years. The Toledo settlers remained at the bottom of the working class. More than 75 percent of their parents had worked in unskilled or farm labor, and over half the settled workers in Toledo remained in that category, compared with the overall Toledo average of 7 percent. Their upward mobility was very restricted in comparison with that of earlier European-descent settlers.[92]

The limitations on their acquisition of better jobs was in part a reflection of lower levels of formal education and English language skills compared with Euro-Americans and African Americans. Like the latter, they also had to deal with potential employers who refused to hire them and with employers who refused to promote them even when they were highly qualified. Mexican American women faced problems in obtaining sales and clerical positions. In one case, a young woman experienced as a sales clerk in Texas settled with her family in Minnesota. Her efforts to find similar employment in the Twin Cities met with a flood of refusals. She discovered what was wrong when she applied at a branch of the same chain store for which she worked in Texas. The manager informed her, "You are obviously neat, attractive and smarter than many of my clerks, but I can't hire you. You might be taken for a negro. My customers would not stand for that." Such hiring patterns in the Midwest tracked Mexican Americans into a much narrower range of occupations than in South Texas and other parts of the Southwest. In those locations there was a demand for a Spanish-speaking middle class to serve a much larger working-class clientele in the barrios and the *colonias*. This class function did not yet exist in most of the Midwest.[93]

As farmworkers settled, the rest of the population had difficulty realizing that they were there permanently and that the original residents could no longer treat them as they had before. In Gratiot County, Michigan, a report called people who had first settled in the area decades earlier "migrants that live here year round." Negative stereotyping was evident in a 1958 survey of landlords in the Toledo area. Only 19 percent stated that they would willingly rent to Mexicans. A Northwestern Ohio schoolteacher observed that "generally when people in this area think of Mexican people, they think of dirty, lazy, irresponsible people." Such attitudes reflected underlying community hostility. In Minnesota the Governor's Interracial Commission investigated the case of two young boys from the first Mexican family in Hollandale to purchase land. They were expelled from school for alleged misconduct. The commission determined that school authorities did not conduct a fair investigation and that "the boys were used as scapegoats to appease community pressure" and anti-Mexican sentiments in the predominantly Dutch community. In the end the boys returned to their places in school.[94]

Conclusion

The 1950s were an era of unquestioned acceptance of the inevitable link between technology and progress. The mechanization of planting, cultivation, and harvest tasks in midwestern agriculture occurred more rapidly than ever before. It increased employment by producing a wider variety of foods for commercial consumption but continued to reduce the labor required for specific tasks.

The decade was a time of strong nativist sentiment, yet corporations recruited thousands of foreign workers. The rhetoric of democracy abounded, but corporate success was predicated largely on the denial of the rights of workers. Technology was supposed to make life easier and more secure, but employers used it to displace workers and to accelerate migrancy.

Workers responded to their declining position in society in many ways. They abandoned farm work and established permanent residence, which offered not only greater stability and security, but also more power. The increasing use of machines had the unintended result of sending workers to more places and affording them more employment options and places to settle.

Settlement was in part a response to opportunity, but it was also a response to desperate conditions. As opportunities in agriculture declined both in the Midwest and in Texas, thousands of farmworkers decided to drop out of the migrant stream, even though they saw few prospects of employment. They were somewhat more upwardly mobile than Mexicans new to the region had been in the previous generation.

Furthermore, they only gradually severed the ties they had made in the fields and maintained links with relatives, friends, and former neighbors who came north from Texas. In the process they exchanged information and encouraged others to settle nearby. In spite of the hostility engendered by class, cultural, and physical differences, gradual accommodation occurred, made easier by the growing but still small numbers of settled former farmworkers. The act of settlement itself was a necessary first step that made possible the more energetic efforts of the 1960s.

As the 1950s demonstrated, the few sympathetic outsiders were often misguided and easily distracted. They needed direction that could come only from those established in the new settlements and able to shatter false illusions about what was happening in the fields.

CHAPTER 8

Breaking Chains, 1960–1970

In the 1960s relations between midwestern farm-workers and their employers changed dramatically. A more vigorous reform movement than at any time in the century included legislators, civic and religious groups, and the national press. Growers reacted vigorously. Part of their response was to accelerate the rate of mechanization. In the Midwest, it outpaced expanded production and helped alter the composition of the work force. Grafton Trout described its effect on workers in the migrant stream: "There's a chain of crops. If any piece in the chain is broken, the whole chain falls apart."[1] Thousands of people were left without work, and many of these decided to settle.

Workers and Corporations

The 1960s witnessed intensified discussion of the "death of the family farm." Smaller holdings were absorbed, and many farms were disappearing altogether. In Michigan, for example, the average farm grew from 111 to 153 acres between 1950 and 1965, and much larger holdings became common. These units were increasingly operated by professionals and university-educated managers and were closely linked to the corporations that contracted for the crops. Family farms were following the pattern of independent artisans of earlier generations. Pressured to adopt factory techniques and corporate business practices to survive, some succeeded but many failed and went bankrupt.[2]

Corporate decisions further altered relations between growers and workers. Larger, more impersonal camps became increasingly common. The sugar beet companies, pickle packers, and canneries had the largest camps in the region. The Morgan Packing Company camp in Austin, Indiana, had a capacity of 450 workers, and camps at the Fettig and Elwood canneries in Elwood could hold 400 and 990 workers, respectively. By the end of the decade the average midwestern camp approached fifty inhabitants. As camps grew, personal relations between farmers and workers were further strained. A Wisconsin worker recalled that in the 1950s many farmers were still giving his family milk and extending other favors; this practice stopped in the 1960s. The corporations also induced growers to introduce labor-saving machinery to reduce field labor. The impact of mechanization was partly offset by the hiring of more migrant workers in the canning plants in place of local residents.[3]

The corporations were not responsible for another change, the end of the Bracero Program. J. Craig Jenkins suggests that credit for eliminating this program belongs to those who spearheaded the "elite reform and realignment" in national politics that began in the late 1950s. In fact, the earliest efforts to eliminate the program date from the late 1940s, and were initiated not by elites but by the National Farm Labor Union in California. Anti-*bracero* sentiments were even more vigorously expressed among elements in the labor movement and the Mexican American population, on the verge of its own transformation and heightened involvement through the Chicano movement in the 1960s. The effort to eliminate the program intensified in the late 1950s and 1960s as other groups joined the movement.[4]

Opposition to the Bracero Program in the Midwest was less intense than in the Southwest. Regional agribusiness interests, represented by the Farm Bureau, the sugar beet corporations, and the pickle industry, defended the program staunchly to the end. Their use of *braceros* reached its peak in the early 1960s and did not diminish significantly until the abrupt end of the program in 1964.[5]

In the early 1960s, as the abolition of the Bracero Program neared, midwestern corporate employers' "efforts to recruit domestic workers . . . were quite limited." As a result they faced a short-lived crisis in 1965. In Michigan, where almost all the *braceros* in the region were employed, efforts continued unsuccessfully to renew the program. Growers and corporations complained that domestic workers could not tolerate the summer heat, were unwilling to work, or simply could not be recruited. A field manager of Saginaw's Daily Pickle Company argued that "nobody works like a bracero." Robert H. Ford of the National Pickle Growers Association asserted that *braceros* were necessary because the pickling cucumber harvest was "the most difficult job in agriculture." Finally, as William P. Moore of the Pickle Packers International admitted, the *bracero* "took a lot of brow beating that the domestic workers just won't stand for." In similar circumstances, domestic workers could still leave.[6]

In 1964 and 1965 the pickle and sugar beet industries experimented with replacements. Their efforts to use local high school students on summer vacation did not succeed, for they found the youths unreliable, lacking in diligence, or simply unwilling to perform the work. They also tried African American workers from southern states. These workers received an unfriendly reception from growers, local residents, and Farm Placement officials, who portrayed them as unreliable, heavy drinkers, violent, and even prone to murder. Cucumber grower Harold Raab of Bay County, Michigan, stated that "drunkenness among the new migrant workers will cause them to lose half the crop this year." Pickle processor Harold Janicke concurred, charging that the African American crews he hired were drunk all weekend and few of them reported to work on Mondays because of hangovers.[7]

Employers even experimented with Puerto Ricans again. In 1964 the Miller Pickle Company of Edmore, Michigan, recruited 260 men to work in the fields of local growers and in its plant. Unfortunately, the company went bankrupt and the owner fled the state just before final payday. The workers had already worked for thirteen weeks, but were paid for only four. The local press reported that the men "nearly rioted" because the employer owed them more than forty-one thousand dollars in back pay plus return transportation to Puerto Rico. The timely intervention of a local priest calmed the workers, "preventing possible disorders." Local charities and volunteers donated food and money for their return fares. The Edmore affair repeated on a smaller scale the experience of Puerto Rican farmworkers in Michigan in 1950.[8]

The failure of these experiments turned the sugar beet and pickle industries' attention increasingly to Mexican Americans from South Texas. The group had dominated those crops two decades earlier and were again a success. Moreover, because Euro-Americans and African Americans abandoned the fields so rapidly in the late 1950s and 1960s, Tejanos dominated the field labor force in Western Michigan for the first time. By the end of the 1960s, they composed between 80 and 90 percent of the migrant labor force in the Upper Midwest, a higher proportion than any other ethnic group had reached in the century.[9]

A majority of the farmworkers who migrated to the Great Lakes region still went to Michigan. Official estimates for the state at harvest peak in 1965 exceeded 80,000, excluding children, "non-working adults," and an undetermined number of freewheelers. In most seasons Michigan was second behind California in the number of interstate domestic migratory workers it received. Ohio, the only state where there was a net increase in workers in the 1960s, had more than 20,000 adult workers by the end of the decade. Other midwestern states ranged between 9,000 and 19,000 working adults. By adding both nonworking household members and freewheelers, a cautious estimate of 250,000 farmworkers entered the region for farm labor in the middle of the decade.[10]

There were important changes in the composition of the work force during the 1960s. In 1964, 60 percent came to Michigan as family groups, 35 percent as adult crews, and 5 percent as singles. The proportion of families increased and adult crews declined the following season due to the halt in the Bracero Program. Household size remained constant at about six persons, but the age composition appeared to be changing. A 1969 Michigan study calculated that 62 percent of the workers were under twenty years of age, and 30 percent were over thirty-five. This suggests that young workers traveled with their parents, but those between ages twenty and thirty-five were dropping out. A Wisconsin survey indicated that recent settlers had lengthy ties to the stream: 80 percent of adults had done farm work as children, as had 66 percent of their parents.[11]

The Politics of Reform

The 1960s were characterized by important political successes in behalf of the nation's farmworkers. Two explanations have been offered for this success in California. First, because farmworker discontent has been relatively constant over time, the key is a shift in public opinion to a greater concern with farmworkers. In the 1960s a wave of liberal public opinion swept the nation and made possible the organizing successes in California. A second view suggests that the changes of the period lie in the success of farmworkers in organizing and articulating their struggle to other farmworkers and to potential supporters, including the public and the government. The following examination contributes to this discussion of political reform and the farmworker movement from a midwestern vantage point.[12]

The surge of interest in farm labor reform dating from the late 1950s even forced agribusiness, described by then-secretary of labor James P. Mitchell as "the toughest lobby" in the country, to change its appearance. Agricultural interests were less able to control the national press or Congress than they had been in the past. One of their responses was to create "reform" organizations in an effort to improve their public image. In Michigan they formed the Farm Labor Management Committee (FLMC) in 1961. Sponsored by the Michigan State Horticultural Society, it was supported by the Michigan State University Agricultural Extension Services, the State Department of Agriculture, and the Michigan State Police. Its stated goal was better cooperation among growers, workers, and the public and improved conditions for workers through proper management techniques. With assistance from the Michigan Department of Public Instruction, it even conducted a management training program where growers learned the proper ways to maintain labor camps and treat workers. The FLMC spent most of its energies, however, lobbying against major reform bills dealing with agricultural workers. It contended that such legislation was costly and counterproductive. As one FLMC member admitted, the real purpose of the group was "to keep our own house in order."[13]

The Wisconsin Better Government Committee (WBGC), was created to speak on behalf of employers and to oppose legislation that might increase costs. Like other grower groups it engaged in public relations efforts intent on improving the image of farm employers. A WBGC secretary asserted that the average migrant had "more freedom than the average American" and that such work had "the whole aspect of going up north for a two month vacation and getting paid for it." In Michigan the State Farm Labor Council was formed in 1965, sponsored by the Agri-business Committee of the Chamber of Commerce. Participants included the State Extension Service, the State Police, and local sheriff's departments. Growers also controlled new "public interest" committees like the Michigan Commission on Agricultural Labor. Technically under the Michigan Department of Labor, it was an advisory committee created to investigate and suggest legislative reforms. It had four members representing growers, three representing the public, none representing workers, and was largely dormant from its inception.[14]

Growers dominated the governor's advisory committees of each state. One of the most active, the Ohio Governor's Committee on Migratory Labor, was chaired by E. E. Richards, manager of the Heinz processing plant in Bowling Green. His successor, Paul Slade, was a Libby, McNeill and Libby official and head of a Farm Bureau affiliate, the Ohio Agricultural Marketing Association (OAMA), voice of the state's tomato industry. The public interest and union representatives had little voice, and their positions on the committee remained vacant for long periods. Pressure to place a farmworker on the committee led to the appointment in 1968 of a labor recruiter for Buckeye Sugar. The committee understandably made no serious proposals for legislative reform in the 1960s.[15]

The moves by agribusiness to get its house in order did not deter reformers, who had strong representation within the church. Church people were motivated by the tenor of the era, internal reforms, including the Second Vatican Council, the increasingly vocal Chicano movement, and the direct pressure of farmworkers. Established interests in the church opposed changes they perceived to be damaging, however, leading to an internal struggle over church policy.[16]

Conservative church and community leaders often tried to remove these reformers. In 1962 the Migrant Ministry in Leelanau County, Michigan, reported that two summer staff members were "good social workers," but were not acceptable for the program. It was necessary to find people "more concerned with the spiritual needs of the migrants." Many people long involved in migrant programs were frustrated by the new environment. In 1965 Michigan Migrant Ministry director Mildred Gladstone found herself unable to adjust to the changed attitude by more progressive elements within the church and decided to quit. She wrote, "We are at the end of an era and I haven't the qualifications to put the new thinking and action into the work. I am so concerned for fear social action is going to take precedence over the religious program that has been the core of the Migrant Ministry for many years."[17]

In the midst of the ongoing struggle between the spiritual and the social reform factions, many local churches established screening centers, health clinics, and experimental schools, often with federal antipoverty and educational program funds. Their old "Harvester" programs, which emphasized handicrafts, recreation, and babysitting, were replaced by "worker friend" and "community worker" projects. Worker friends lived and worked alongside farmworkers, attempting to set an example of Christian behavior while informing them of their rights; they were anathema to growers. One Migrant Minister reported that "some were dismissed by the employer because they pressed questions that were crucial to the life of the camp." Community workers administered educational and resettle-ment programs and advocated workers' rights, often disturbing pub-lic agencies and growers who refused to comply with the law. By the end of the decade the Migrant Ministry explicitly declared that its major responsibilities were to end rural poverty and to support the poor in their struggle for human dignity. The ministers appeared at public hearings, in camps, and on picket lines on behalf of midwest-ern farmworkers and the California-based United Farm Workers Or-ganizing Committee (UFWOC), currently the United Farm Workers of America.[18]

There was greater interdenominational cooperation between Ca-tholics and Protestants, including the earliest Office of Economic Opportunity (OEO) migrant projects and campaigns supporting re-form legislation. Church members also created and participated on citizens' advocacy committees, including the Indiana Citizens' Ad-visory Committee on Farm Workers, the Wisconsin Citizen's Com-mittee for the Support of Agricultural Workers, and the Michigan Committee to Aid Farm Workers.[19]

Joining the church were several midwestern politicians, including Senators Patrick V. McNamara and Philip Hart of Michigan, and Hub-ert Humphrey, Eugene McCarthy, and Walter Mondale of Minnesota. Through the Senate Subcommittee on Migratory Labor, their efforts to promote federal legislation set the trend in health, education, and economic reforms for agricultural workers.[20]

The Migrant Health Act of 1962 made federal funds available for local migrant health clinics that offered treatment for injuries and illnesses, immunization, pre- and postnatal care, emergency hospi-talization, and, occasionally, dental clinics. Federal funds paid for public health nurses, health aides, dentists, medical doctors, and a portion of the workers' bills. The clinics were located in city hospi-tals, private offices, and churches. The Bay City General Hospital clinic, like dozens of others, offered health services two evenings per week and served several thousand farmworkers each year.[21]

A handful of state-funded schooling projects preceded the pro-grams funded by the federal government. The Ohio legislature first allocated funds in 1960 to reimburse local school authorities, but hesitant local officials were reluctant to get involved, and most of the available money was never spent. Michigan and Illinois had similar unfulfilled educational plans. In addition, in 1963 the Department of Health, Education and Welfare (HEW) was entrusted with a program to set up child care centers for migrant workers, to be administered by state welfare departments. Set up in local schools, orchards, and camps, these centers took care of children while parents worked.

The program started slowly, and in Michigan there were only 165 children involved during the first year of operation.[22]

Summer education projects expanded rapidly under Title I of the Elementary and Secondary Education Act of 1965. Title I provided federal funds to reimburse almost all the cost of these jointly administered OEO and state educational programs. Certified teachers, assisted by bilingual teachers' aides and teachers' helpers, taught classes in traditional subjects during harvest peak, usually from six to eight weeks. By 1969 there were forty-three educational projects serving more than seven thousand children in Michigan and similar though smaller efforts in the other midwestern states. Title I also financed local agencies and schools that wished to set up day care centers and Headstart programs. The educational projects involved at least 25 percent of all school-age children who came to the Midwest in the late 1960s. A 1969 Ohio survey indicated that participation would have been much higher if more diligent efforts at communication had been made. Eighty-seven percent of parents who knew about the programs placed their children in the summer schools.[23]

The 1964 Economic Opportunity Act, Title III-B, was the major economic legislation passed on behalf of farmworkers during the decade. Sponsors of the act and much related legislation in behalf of farmworkers in the 1960s and early 1970s accepted the view that the culture of poverty was a way of life for farmworkers. They also assumed that the workers would soon be displaced by mechanization. They concluded that the culture of poverty could be eliminated by encouraging workers to settle out of the migrant stream and learn new skills.

The lack of formal training was evident from surveys indicating, for example, that 75 percent of adult Chicano settlers in Michigan had not gone beyond the sixth grade, and over half of those in Wisconsin had not gone beyond the third grade. These levels were much lower than the national average of 7.9 years for migrant workers, 12.2 years for the total population. In addition, 85 percent of the families of recent Wisconsin settlers earned less than two thousand dollars per year.[24]

The programs offered year-round adult education and job training, counseling, and housing services. Nonpublic corporations in each state were created to administer the migrant programs: Michigan Migrants for Opportunity, later called United Migrants for Opportunity (UMOI); Associated Migrant Opportunity Services (AMOS) in Indiana; United Migrant Opportunity Services (UMOS) in Wisconsin; the Illinois Migrant Council (IMC) in Illinois; and Migrants, Incorporated, in Minnesota. Ohio did not have a statewide agency, but most of its local projects eventually coalesced under La Raza Unida de Ohio.[25]

The early histories of these equal opportunity projects have much in common. Initially, they emphasized the service orientation of government agencies and were dominated by public and grower representatives. AMOS had a citizens' advisory committee chaired by Warren R. Spangle, executive secretary of the Indiana Canners' Association. Spangle tried to restrict implementation of reforms and to prevent activists, particularly Chicanos, from being represented in the agencies. Yet farmworkers and former farmworkers increased their presence as the OEO program expanded and required bilingual and bicultural staff. In the late 1960s recent settlers, who often had begun as aides or student assistants, became agency directors. They quickly put the agricultural interests on the defensive.[26]

These new directors benefited from a 1967 amendment to the OEO act that expanded agency responsibilities to include "5-year migrants," that is, recent dropouts from the migrant stream. It offered two to six months of coursework and practical training in adult basic education and vocational skills and paid a stipend to the participants. It also encouraged settlement by offering practical training in house construction and renovation, plumbing and electrical work, and arranged special terms to purchase construction materials and land. In Wisconsin alone several hundred families built their own houses. The projects also assisted those interested in settling to locate housing, inexpensive furniture and appliances, and jobs. By the end of the decade several thousand recent settlers had participated in various OEO-sponsored programs, thereby enabling the projects and their staff to build up a larger base of support.[27]

As Chicano reformers took over the OEO programs they engendered more opposition from conservative agricultural interests and their allies. UMOI initiated the University-Affiliated Information and Service Program, employing eighteen college students to provide workers with information about and assistance in gaining access to public services. Twelve of the students were Chicanos from Michigan and Texas. They entered camps to inform workers of their rights, confronted abusive growers, and dealt with public employees who were not accustomed to serving farmworkers. As part of the War on Poverty, the OEO also sponsored the Migrant Legal Action Program (MLAP), designed to ensure that the rural poor, particularly migrant farmworkers, also had advocates.[28]

Growers, corporate managers, and public agency personnel used to uninformed, intimidated workers were angered by the changes and criticized the programs and particularly their highly visible Chicano leaders. They found some relief under the Nixon administration and immediately attacked the OEO projects, reduced their funding, transferred their functions to other agencies, and removed most of the activist leaders in one way or another. By the mid-1970s project administrators, many of them now part of the USDA, were much less willing to challenge local interests.[29]

The improvement of worker housing remained the states' responsibility. The earlier Minnesota and Wisconsin laws were amended several times during the decade, and new ones were passed in other midwestern states. Their collective fate paralleled that of the Michigan law. Its first Migrant Housing Law, passed in 1965, called for mandatory inspection, licensing, and regulation of all farm labor camps of five or more persons. It required two annual inspections, one before workers arrived, to allow growers to make corrections, another during the season. The 1966 inspections located camps housing ninety-two thousand persons, with an average of 5.9 violations per camp. Only 15 percent of the camps were inspected a second time, and only half the defects were corrected. A loophole in the law allowed provisional licenses to be issued if there were no "serious deficiencies." In 1967 inspectors found more than 6,000 violations, but took only seven cases to court. They won five and operators paid fines ranging from ten dollars to fifty dollars. The law was amended in 1968, ostensibly because it was causing a backlog in the courts. The amended law transferred cases from the more impersonal circuit courts to local courts, thereby increasing opportunities for cronyism.[30]

The weak laws and weaker enforcement mechanism allowed hundreds of unlicensed camps to remain open and licensed housing still had serious violations. Workers were still forced to stay in overcrowded, filthy cabooses, chicken coops, old barns and cowsheds from which animal waste was not removed. Buildings lacked screens, drainage and trash disposal were inadequate, and many even lacked outdoor privies. In 1970 Indiana state senator Thomas Teague observed, "I've seen worse conditions in migrant camps than anything I ever saw in Vietnam."[31]

Swamps, waste ponds, and garbage dumps bred mosquitos and flies that spread disease. The inspected Berrien County camp of Walter Schoenfield had frayed electric wiring that "spews sparks in the dry wood" and "an outhouse so infested with rats [that] children from the camp are afraid to use it." An inspected camp in Carson City, Michigan, had polluted drinking water, which caused an epidemic among children and forced their parents to spend most of their earnings on hospital bills. Drinking water in the Buckeye Sugar Company camp near Pandora, Ohio, was "so full of purifying chemicals that it varies in color from cloudy to orange, smells bad and makes . . . children sick." Cabins in one Michigan camp that was granted a provisional license had no windows, and a fire broke out in one and killed five children.[32]

Widespread violations of state housing laws were the norm. More than a third of the wells in Door County, Wisconsin, and over half of those in Lenawee County, Michigan, produced unpotable water. Sanitarian Sid Bowman reported that "few if any of the migrant worker camps in Lucas County [Ohio] measure up to specifications" of the state law. In 1967 Wisconsin inspectors reported that 60 percent of the camps in the state were substandard, with an average of six violations per camp, 80 percent of them major. Michigan studies in 1969 found that 20 percent of dwellings had leaky roofs and lacked bathing facilities, 75 percent lacked refrigerators, and more than 90 percent violated state or federal housing codes. Inspectors in Wisconsin, with the oldest housing law in the region, admitted difficulties finding many of the worst camps, conveniently hidden from sight by the north woods.[33]

A more hidden concern, health and medical conditions, also attracted attention during the 1960s. A 1960 survey found that children of the nation's migrant population were five times as susceptible to diseases as children of the permanent residents of the communities where the migrants worked. Infant mortality among seasonal workers in Michigan was double that of the resident population, prenatal care for mothers was almost nonexistent, and 33 percent did not have a doctor in attendance at birth. More than 75 percent of those surveyed had never visited a dentist and almost 66 percent had not received regular medical care. High incidences of colds, intestinal diseases, arthritis, diabetes, skin rashes, and related afflictions resulted from the lack of care.[34]

Local medical authorities exacerbated the problems, as the following Michigan cases reveal. A man suffering pains and diagnosed as having appendicitis was refused admission to a local hospital for several days and subsequently died. A sick boy was taken by his father to a local hospital, but was refused admittance by the nurse, who finally gave him a shot of penicillin. The next day the father again brought the child to the hospital, but the nurse argued that he looked healthy, despite his diarrhea and vomiting. He died the next morning at home, "choking in his own vomit." A three-year-old boy was refused admittance to a Traverse City hospital because his father could not pay for services beforehand, although the nurse administered oral medicine before sending him away. The next day the father returned and the boy was admitted, diagnosed as having meningitis. He was placed in intensive care, but soon died.[35]

A health problem new to the period resulted from a sharp increase in the use of pesticides and other chemical inputs, which flooded the commercial market after World War II. Few studies of the medical consequences of these toxins appeared before the 1970s, and workers were exposed to untested and unregulated substances. The dangers were made worse by corporation field men and growers, who commonly sent uninformed workers into the fields, contrary to warnings on the pesticide containers, and often under the threat of being fired. In 1969 a crew of cherry pickers in the Traverse City area complained about eye and skin irritations caused by pesticides, but were brushed off by the grower, who asserted, "It wasn't harmful, only painful." Another Michigan worker commented, "one of the crew members is completely swollen stiff from the spray. My eyes were almost swelled shut when I woke up. . . . about half our crew has a rash or swollen eyes." In still another instance an orchard worker reported, "The spray on the trees was really thick—a sulfide compound. We were itching, breaking out in rashes. My eyes were so bad I quit picking until they cleared. . . . Everyone was concerned about the spray. The farmer said it was not poisonous."[36]

Exposure to pesticides resulted in serious accidents, illness, and even death. In a pickle company camp in Eastern Michigan, chemicals spilled from a broken vat near where children were playing, causing a young girl to lose an eye. In DuPage County, Illinois, parathion sprayed in tomato fields contracted by the Campbell Soup Company killed two-year-old Ernesto Pérez, who had accompanied his parents to work. The first serious attempts to regulate pesticides in the Midwest began with the Occupational Safety and Health Act (OSHA) in 1970. Agriculture, however, was its lowest priority. Indiana OSHA director Fred Keppler admitted that agricultural inspections had "never taken place" and conceded that public health officials had "no idea" which chemicals were being applied to the water, soil, fruits, and vegetables on the farms.[37]

A final area of concern to reformers was income. State legislatures in the early 1960s became the scene of debates on whether or not to include farmworkers in minimum wage legislation and how to write laws to appease opponents. Most states eventually passed vaguely worded, confusing statutes filled with loopholes and lacking adequate enforcement mechanisms.[38]

The history of wage legislation can be detailed in Michigan, where there were more workers and a greater variety of wage rates than elsewhere in the region. Its first minimum wage law for agriculture, passed in 1964, applied to all employers who hired four or more workers. It raised the minimum wage in three stages from $1.00 per hour in 1965 to $1.25 per hour in 1967. It had no overtime provisions.[39]

Pressure exerted by the Farm Bureau resulted in a 1965 amendment to the law permitting growers to make allowances for costs, including deductions of eight cents per hour from a single worker for lodging, four cents for water pressure, two cents for the toilet, and ten cents for showers. It also established "piecerate equivalents" to the minimum wage and delayed implementation of the law until those equivalents were determined by a Wage Deviation Board. The rate equivalents were based on the pickings of the "average, diligent worker," meaning that the "minimum" wage became the average wage, with half the workers below the minimum. Furthermore, it calculated earnings at harvest peak, so that even the most "diligent" workers were not likely to earn the minimum early or late in the season. The board farmed out the task of investigating rates to agricultural experts at Michigan State University, who did not complete their work until the summer of 1967, thus delaying implementation for three years. The experts eventually recommended different piece rates for more than thirty fruit and vegetable crops, subject to private hearings at which growers could respond to the recommendations. In the representative case of blueberries, the board set a rate of 13.8 cents per pound as the piece rate equivalent of $1.25 per hour. Employers criticized the rates, and a Western Michigan grower offered compelling testimony: "Blueberries are as American as Thanksgiving Day, and paying somebody 14 cents a pound to pick them is a radical idea." The board then determined that 9 cents per pound was the piece rate equivalent of the hourly minimum.[40]

Still another compromise with growers resulted from the law's designating very little money for inspectors. Compliance rested largely on the goodwill of growers, who were not required to keep records of workers' earnings. Very few inspectors understood Spanish, thus making communication with workers difficult. Cronyism further limited the effectiveness of the inspectors, who because of long years of acquaintance and personal ties could be convinced of growers' good intentions. As Elmer Anderson, Western Minnesota compliance officer, stated in 1968, he rarely received any complaints from the more than five thousand workers in his district. "Two years ago we had two complaints. I went out and had the growers pay them while I watched. Most of the growers appreciate their Mexicans. They treat them real well, and they get them back year after year—which is a darned good sign everyone is happy."[41]

A 1969 study by the Michigan Civil Rights Commission (MCRC) determined that wages fell below the $1.45 per hour legal minimum 80 percent of the time in strawberries, 71 percent in hoeing beets, 57 percent in blueberries, and 30 percent in cherries. During the early and later parts of the seasons piece rates fell to an average of 30 cents per hour. Furthermore, workers were not employed eight hours per day in 100 percent of cases in picking blueberries, 50 percent in hoeing beets, and 30 percent in picking cherries.[42]

Midwestern farmworkers' earnings continued to deteriorate compared with those of other workers. Industrial incomes and the cost of living in the Midwest were among the highest in the nation while farmworkers' wages, according to a 1964 USES study, were only 2 cents per hour above the national average. Midwestern workers earned 20 cents per hour less than workers in the Pacific Coast states, 12 cents below Northeast levels, and only 12 cents above the low wage state of Texas, which suffered chronic competition from undocumented Mexican workers. In Wisconsin in 1964 farmworker earnings were lower than in 66 percent of the other states they worked. The USDL calculated that during the period from 1951 to 1964, earnings for farmworkers rose by 21 cents per hour, compared with 98 cents per hour for industrial workers. Wisconsin Governor's Migrant Committee head Elizabeth Rauschenbush determined that in the six-week Wisconsin cucumber harvest in 1964, family earnings averaged less than $4.00 per day, or only $19.52 per week. In Michigan total annual income in 1965 was $855 per individual agricultural laborer and under $1,800 per family, rising to $2,021 per family by 1970. Earnings rose in 1965, the year the Bracero Program ended, but stagnated afterward. The wage laws thus did not have a significant influence on earnings.[43]

Another income-related reform, Workers' Compensation, applied to many farmworkers for the first time. The 1961 Wisconsin law covered all employers hiring six or more workers. In the pickle industry, the largest employer in the state, growers evaded the law by "sharecropping," that is, determining that workers were "independent contractors." Furthermore, information regarding the minimum wage was not widely distributed, as only 8 percent of farmworkers in the state knew they were eligible. The Michigan Worker's Compensation Law provided full coverage only to full-time hired hands and partial medical care and burial benefits to those hired by a single employer for thirteen consecutive weeks. The restrictions excluded more than 99 percent of the state's seasonal farmworkers. Not surprisingly, implementation of the law, first passed in 1965, was delayed through efforts led by the Farm Bureau until 1967, ostensibly for "further study."[44]

A final income-related reform, Social Security, already applied to some workers in the 1950s. Expanded coverage the following decade did not increase eligibility substantially. Workers had to earn more than $150 a month and work more than twenty days for a single employer. A more important problem, however, as a 1964 Wisconsin survey indicated, was that only 16 percent of all employers in the state even asked workers for their Social Security numbers. Many workers thought that Social Security was deducted from their earnings when in fact it was pocketed by growers and crew leaders. Furthermore, with an average life span of only forty-nine years, few farmworkers would have lived long enough to recover the small sums they might actually have contributed to the fund.[45]

To minimize the impact of the reforms further, midwestern corporations, growers, and rural legislators organized lobbying campaigns. The Farm Bureau, Vegetable Growers Association of American (VGAA), and corporations often operated through front groups like HELP (Help Establish Legislative Protection) to lobby and organize letter-writing campaigns. They tried to keep issues out of newspapers and off radio and television public interest programs.[46]

In an effort to sway public opinion they argued that workers did not need, want, or deserve the benefits of reform legislation. The president of the Indiana Canners Association and head of the Governor's Committee on Migratory Labor, Warren Spangle, opposed flush toilets on the grounds that many Indiana state parks had outdoor privies. Minnesota grower Orville Haught asserted that workers "ain't got no experience [with flush toilets]. They use these facilities and break them up." Indiana State Representative Earl Wilson of Bedford responded to one local case when workers complained about plumbing: "Why these people won't even flush the toilets!" Further investigation revealed that workers could not flush them, because the toilets had been broken for several weeks. Michigan grower Elizabeth Munger wrote that additional legislation was harmful and unnecessary for migrants, for "they appreciate the fact that even small children can work," adding that midwestern conditions were "better than what they have at home." John S. Kramek, revealing further misconceptions, concluded that "the migrant, just like a nomad, is a happy-go-lucky wanderer, who refuses to take on the responsibility of ownership, work, and upkeep of the community."[47]

These public relations efforts also asserted that the reforms endangered "freedom" and the "American way of life." Michigan Farm Bureau representatives claimed that proposed changes threatened "free agriculture" and were "another step to limit free enterprise in our country. . . . you must first take over agriculture and then the rest of the country will fall." Farm Bureau member Arthur Thomas warned that, "if government continues to throttle private initiative, then Khruschev will not have to carry out his threat that he will bury us." As part of a Farm Bureau–sponsored campaign, Michigan growers Arthur C. and Lillian Thade wrote to Senator Patrick McNamara complaining that outsiders were stirring up all the trouble and asked him "to help frame a law to outlaw the communists."[48]

Growers also tried to brand reformers as disloyal citizens. When Indiana legislators visited the Red Gold camp in Anderson and reported substandard housing, inadequate ventilation, and swarms of flies, they were criticized on the grounds that "you people do more harm than good around here." Grower Lena Holsta of Traverse City complained that "we never had trouble with the migrant labor until the government started to tell them we were to blame." Others complained about ministers and priests who got involved "without really understanding" what they were doing. Michigan grower Rankin Lyman criticized Father James Vizzard of the National Catholic Rural Life Conference: "You priests and preachers have a very bad habit about being very reckless with the truth. . . . Why don't you keep off our backs and go talk with the processors and learn the facts before you write these wild stories. . . . If you don't like the American way of life, why don't you go back to one of the communist countries and quit trying to wreck us?"[49]

Growers and camp managers also prevented workers from talking to outsiders and participating in migrant programs under threats of losing their jobs. Asserting private property rights, they posted "no trespassing" and "keep out" signs and hired workers, crew leaders, and guards to prevent contact between workers and reformers. Dr. Gorden Harper of the Field Foundation for Hunger was forcibly evicted from a Van Buren County camp by a grower. In Wisconsin inspectors from the State Board of Health were "denied admission to camps." Growers hoped that the "invisible minority" would remain out of the public eye until the reformers' interests were diverted to another cause.[50]

One of the most revealing cases involved Joe Hassle, one of the largest growers in Southwestern Michigan. By the late 1960s he owned more than three thousand acres and fifteen camps, all poorly maintained. He regularly violated minimum wage, housing, and social security laws. He also refused to substantiate claims when workers were eligible for food stamps. For many years he prevented members of the Lansing Catholic Diocese from conducting a migrant program in his camps. In 1969 he denied Sister Betty LaBudie access to a camp to inform workers about a family member who was hospitalized. When two employees of the Dowagiac School District entered a Hassle camp to inform occupants of a summer school for children, "Hassle held a knife to the throat of one and later threatened the other with a shotgun." In 1969 John Bowers, a University of Michigan law student in the Michigan Migrant Legal Action Program entered Hassle's Decatur camp to inform the residents of available local services, day care and Headstart programs, food stamps, and social events. Hassle broke Bowers's car windows, then called the local sheriff's deputies to evict him from the camp.[51]

Hassle had more serious problems with UMOI employees Don Folgueras and Violadelle Valdez at his Krohn camp near Keeler, run by crew leader Andrés García. Hassle instructed García to inform him when anyone entered. The camp was overcrowded, had numerous housing and sanitation violations, swarms of insects originating from a nearby swamp bordering the camp, inadequate toilet and bathing facilities, and contaminated water. A group of workers contacted UMOI for assistance after several children in the camp fell ill from dysentery, and Folgueras and Valdez were sent to help the parents.[52]

Krohn camp residents George and Alicia Gutiérrez wanted transportation assistance to visit their infant daughter, who contracted amoebic dysentery at the camp and was in a hospital twenty-five miles away. Crew leader García refused to help them, forcing George Gutiérrez to make several trips to the hospital on foot. The first time Folgueras came to help Gutiérrez, Hassle ordered him out of the camp. The next day Folgueras and Valdez returned to take several children who were ill to a nearby health clinic. When Hassle learned they were in the camp, he recklessly drove his pickup truck to the site of the cabins, jumped out, and physically attacked Folgueras, calling him a "long-haired bastard," punching him several times in the face and body and knocking off his glasses. When Folgueras reached down to pick them up, Hassle repeatedly kicked him in the ribs until Valdez intervened. Hassle then broke the windows of Folgueras's car with a pipe, took out his shotgun, ordered "everyone not to move and if they moved he would shoot them," and kept Folgueras pinned on the ground for two hours with the weapon while his wife summoned the Van Buren County deputy sheriffs. The sheriffs charged Folgueras with illegal entry and placed him in jail. Although he was stained with blood, they denied him medical assistance, pain killers, and the advice of counsel or permission to use the telephone. Alicia Gutiérrez later testified that the police told the workers that Folgueras and Valdez "were only there to rob them."[53]

Hassle soon dropped charges against Folgueras for illegal entry, but the Gutiérrez family, UMOI, and Folgueras filed a countersuit against Joe and Harriet Hassle, the county deputies, and crew leader García for violating their constitutional rights of free speech, association, and assembly and for injury to lease, hold, and enjoy the full benefits of property. In 1971 Michigan attorney general Frank Kelly wrote an advisory ruling that the state's criminal trespass law could not be used to prevent the entry of visitors to camps where farmworkers resided. He based his decision on a Mississippi law and the First and Fourteenth amendments to the Constitution. He wrote that "the right of the tenant to the undisturbed enjoyment of the leased premises carries with it" all the constitutional freedoms enjoyed by other tenants. The federal district court in Grand Rapids subsequently ruled against Hassle. In spite of the ruling, growers continued to challenge the tenancy rights of farmworkers.[54]

Grower behavior confirmed the reformers' belief in the need for changes. As Anderson Hewitt of the Michigan Migrant Ministry testified, "most migrant workers were consistently cheated" by employers who paid less than minimum wages and did not return holdbacks or bonuses. Growers commonly failed to honor promises to pay return transportation to Texas or to send workers their final payment by mail. Others pocketed Social Security payments, made unauthorized deductions from paychecks, and refused to honor other written and verbal agreements.[55]

Local business leaders also denied farmworkers equal protection of the law. Even at the end of the 1960s, farmworkers were refused service in many small-town restaurants, stores, bars, and other public places. Some claimed a fear of the loss of Euro-American customers; others were more explicit. One business owner asserted, "We don't want any niggers or Mexicans here." On entering a local store in rural Michigan, a Euro-American staff member of the Migrant Ministry observed that "the grocer was very friendly, unlike the way he is when we got with the Mexicans." Myrtle Reul observed that many store owners did not post prices, but determined them by the color of the skin and the accent of the customer. She noted how the price of a dozen eggs in the same store varied from twenty-five to fifty cents.[56]

Local officials also refused to respect the rights of farmworkers. The director of the Gratiot County, Michigan, Department of Social Services denied eligible underemployed farmworkers welfare, stating that "it appears that someone is stirring up the migrants to get in and get their share." A 1968 Michigan law providing for a state fund to reimburse hospitals for the treatment of migrant workers was hardly used because welfare and medical personnel, with absolute power to accept or reject applicants, turned down hundreds of eligible and needy workers.[57]

Additionally, workers continued to encounter law enforcement officers who levied fines for nonexistent or minor infractions and assessed higher court costs and longer jail terms than for local residents. Reul, whose fieldwork involved actually working in the fields and orchards, testified that she "was constantly warned by her fellow workers not to get in any difficulty with the law because as a migrant she would have to pay a fine or serve a jail sentence" for the slightest offense.[58]

Community hostility extended from small-town to urban residents in resort areas, suburbs, and cities. A 1960 report in Manistee County, on the Lake Michigan shore noted, "It is a miracle that we have been able to have migrants and resort people in the same community." Resorters criticized the farmworkers for the dirty camps and for bathing in lakes and bays, yet were oblivious to the much greater environmental damage caused by their own recreational vehicles and motorboats, and the untreated sewage they dumped into the northern lakes, rivers, and streams. They ignored the underlying reality that conditions in camps were the result of growers' violations of federal and state laws. In suburban South Cook County, public officials refused to provide social and medical services, school authorities did not enforce attendance laws, and inspectors did not compel growers to abide by laws governing housing and working conditions. Wherever the farmworkers went, the majority of the community was reluctant "to cross the color line."[59]

The rhetoric of reform was in the air when the Ohio Governor's Committee on Migratory Labor in 1965 stated, "When the migrant comes to Ohio, we try to put an umbrella of protection over him." Yet the reformers encountered problems, the Detroit Free Press explained, because "the same silent conspiracy in rural Michigan undercuts the state's efforts to enforce the law. And agriculture, here and elsewhere, goes on enjoying the same compensation from society that permits such scandalous mistreatment to continue." Yet the limited reforms of the 1960s were greater than in any previous decades, most importantly because Mexican farmworkers and settlers also participated in demands for change.[60]

Farmworkers and Settlers

The increased settling out from the migrant stream in the 1960s resulted from several factors, including government policy. OEO-funded programs throughout the region established training centers, such as Indiana's Centro Cristiana de la Comunidad in South Bend and the Grand County Migrant Council in Marion, that placed individuals with local employers once they completed training programs. The formal programs did not alter prior settlement patterns, but they did increase the number of settlers in large and medium-sized cities as well as small towns.[61]

The lure of urban industrial wages attracted workers to factories, foundries, and small shops. Hundreds of Chicanos found work with such employers as Motor Wheel in Lansing, General Motors in Saginaw, and Great Lakes Steel in Ecorse, mostly in unskilled positions and as operatives. A smaller number found work in service-oriented tasks, particularly as janitors and guards. Tejanos were more likely to stay in medium-sized cities or the industrial suburbs and Mexican nationals in the older *colonias*. In the larger cities former farmworkers congregated in several neighborhoods, one of which typically stood out as the heart of the *colonia*. The rapidly growing Mexicano population in Toledo included important concentrations in the North Toledo corridor, East and South Toledo. South Toledo was the center of most Mexicano services—markets, stores, restaurants, the Guadalupe Center, and later, the Farm Labor Organizing Committee (FLOC) headquarters. This settling strengthened the Tejano influence in established Mexicano communities.[62]

In smaller towns recent settlers commonly worked in agriculture-related industries, finding employment in canneries, pickle-processing plants, sugar refineries, and similar pursuits. They remained isolated socially and culturally from established groups, as a report on small towns in eastern Michigan concluded: "The general attitude of the community is not good. Most people think of the migrants as dirty Mexicans, and treat them as such." Recent settlers' principal ties were with immediate family members, relatives, and other former farmworkers, particularly in rural towns.[63]

The settlement process for Chicano farmworkers throughout the Midwest had several common threads. Most worked for several seasons before attempting to settle out of the migrant stream. Alvar Carlson found that Ohio settlers spent an average of six years in the region as farmworkers before they decided to settle. Recent settlers, particularly women and children, continued working in the fields an average of four to six seasons longer. Furthermore, despite inroads made by evangelizing Protestant missionaries, they remained roughly 85 to 90 percent Catholic. Their first residences included single rooms, shacks, boxcars, and dilapidated farmhouses that lacked running water and indoor lavatories. Growers in East Chicago Heights "agreed that conditions were intolerable and workers were overcharged for their living quarters." In many locations they were reported as "living on the fringe of society," underemployed and isolated from the majority population by language, class, and cultural differences. Surveys in South Bend, Indiana, and Racine, Wisconsin, in the early 1970s found more than 40 percent of recent settlers unemployed and living below the poverty level.[64]

The new residents also strengthened Mexican influence and social and cultural life. They made possible more radio programs, dances and fiestas, Spanish-language movies, and larger chapters of established Mexican American organizations like the American G.I. Forum. They also participated in new organizations, including Latinos Unidos in Toledo, United Mexican-Americans in South Bend, and the Latin Americans United for Political Action (LAUPA), in several cities in Michigan. La Raza Unida, a coalition of Spanish-speaking organizations begun in El Paso, Texas, in 1967, was also active in Michigan and Ohio. It criticized state governments for not having Spanish-speaking personnel, pressured the church to teach Mexican American history in its schools, and set up a scholarship fund for young migrant workers. Another group that sprouted from national roots was the Midwest Council of La Raza, formed in 1970 in South Bend with several former farmworker members. As a representative of Chicano interests throughout the region, it helped organize programs for recently settled farmworkers that offered training, housing, medical, and social services.[65]

Recent settlers also became involved in the church, challenging its historical paternalism and neglect. Among Protestants, a handful of conservative sects became very active in proselytizing, typically through a Spanish-speaking minister who formed a congregation. The larger, established Protestant denominations tended to be less interested, although some, like the Christian Reformed Church in Holland, Michigan, formed a Hispanic Reformed Church. Recent settlers also vigorously criticized Migrant Ministry programs and helped alter their "cookies, Kool-Aid and clothing" approach into one of advocacy for justice and unionization.[66]

Within the Catholic church, at the end of the 1950s the National Catholic Council for the Spanish-Speaking formed the Bishop's Committee for the Spanish-Speaking (BCSS). The BCSS took over the Mexican Apostolate and gradually expanded its focus to include medical, educational, and public relations issues and to assist in resettlement. There were also changes in leadership. In 1967 former farmworker Rubén Alfaro of Lansing was named head of the Midwestern Division of the Bishop's Committee. Alfaro became an advocate not only within the church, but also in the public arena.[67]

Mexican American pressure helped alter Catholic church policy and led to the formation of more parishes and organizations for Spanish speakers. Groups within the Catholic church, among them the Centro Cristiana de la Comunidad in South Bend, formed in 1964, became involved with farmworkers. Later it received OEO funding to establish more complete family day care, educational, and training programs. The Cristo Rey Community Center, begun in Lansing in 1961, performed a wide range of services for farmworkers and recent settlers in Central Michigan. Chicanos involved in the Thomas Merton House, established in Saginaw in 1969, set up headquarters for the Saginaw Brown Berets, the Saginaw Grape Boycott Committee, and the Erie Farm Workers' Organization.[68]

Former farmworkers also participated in coalitions to gain public attention and promote legislation. One such group was the Michigan-based Concerned Citizens for Migratory Workers, formed in 1967, later called the Michigan Committee to Aid Farm Workers. It pressured politicians to pass laws on wages, working conditions, workers' compensation, better housing, and education for farmworkers in the state. It supported union organization efforts in the Midwest and the California-based UFWOC boycotts. It also sponsored seventy-mile Easter weekend marches in 1967 and 1968 from Saginaw to Lansing, patterned after the famous *peregrinación* (pilgrimage) in California from Delano to Sacramento in 1966.[69]

Chicano activists also attacked public school and government bureaucrats for their failure to act responsibly or to abide by federal and state laws. Kalamazoo city manager Joseph Caplinger claimed that the educational problems of recently settled farmworkers stemmed from their "undocumented status." Chicano students frequently faced uninterested Euro-American teachers who showed favoritism toward others in class, social activities, and sports. An Ottawa County, Michigan, report observed, "Teachers are not too happy about them in the classroom." OEO-funded programs were ineffective, and, as one Michigan study concluded, "migrant children often fail to receive educational benefits from this funding." Teacher aide

Esmeralda Sáenz in Carrollton, Michigan, observed that unqualified and insensitive instructors and administrators were only interested in the money; "teachers don't like the children . . . [and] the cooks force Mexican children to eat food when they don't like it." María Castellanos, who taught in another Michigan program, testified that it was "a super-duper baby-sitting project . . . not even good at that."[70]

The activists also confronted government bureaucracy, often at their only points of access, appearances at legislative forums and public hearings. They observed that few if any public agencies had Spanish-speaking employees, which caused problems for many farmworkers and recent settlers who were trying to obtain basic services like obtaining a driver's license. One complained, "The agencies were mostly hesitant to help the migrants." They were frequently denied welfare, food stamps, and other services, although they met eligibility requirements. Chicanos also detailed cases of public agencies' refusal to investigate violations of housing, Social Security, and minimum wage laws. They also demonstrated that public employment agencies hesitated to place Chicanos in jobs other than farm labor. An Indiana report on the State Employment Service verified that "the state was unable to document a single case where a migrant farm worker was referred to any available job outside of farm labor."[71]

Residents of Mexican descent also revealed the failure of local residents to grant them the rights and privileges of others. They verified that many barbers refused to cut hair, restaurants denied service at the counter, and owners refused to rent dwellings. Established residents occasionally tried to prevent permanent settlement and strongly resisted the construction of cooperative housing projects.[72]

The activities of former farmworkers defy contemporary assertions that they were held back by a passive culture or hindered from progressing by "family ties" or a "respect for authority." Recently settled farmworkers' actions were essential to understanding the organizing and reform movements of the period. They challenged stereotypes, revealed the hypocrisy of elected officials, and exposed the consistent pattern of abuse of farmworkers by growers, corporations, and long-established residents. Furthermore, they accepted the responsibility for reform that organized labor in the Midwest had long abdicated.[73]

Farmworker Unionization

Organizing of farmworkers in the Midwest in the 1960s was largely overshadowed by the effort associated with César Chávez in California, the independent National Farm Workers Association (NFWA), begun in 1962. In 1966 the NFWA affiliated with the AFL-CIO and became the United Farm Workers Organizing Committee (UFWOC). Its strategy fit in with the long-standing national AFL-CIO strategy to organize California before making major investments organizing in other states. Both the UFWOC and organized labor extended their efforts to other parts of the country during the decade, principally through the boycotts of California wine and table grapes. Labor and UFWOC representatives also made independent though halting probes intent on organizing midwestern farmworkers. The greatest successes in the region were local drives, led by midwestern Chicanos, that were organized by unaffiliated, independent groups.

Before that time, there were a number of scattered but largely unrecorded strikes throughout the region. One of them, a 1964 blueberry strike near Grand Ledge, Michigan, was union-related. It began as an independent walkout of about 110 workers at Hodgman's Blueberry Farms on July 21, and it was soon declared a bona fide strike by the Michigan Farm Labor Office. The strike expanded over the next several days, with help from union organizers from Chicago associated with the Industrial Workers of the World. The workers sought an improvement over their piece-rate earnings of 8 cents per pint, which they claimed averaged about 50 cents per hour. They voted to affiliate with the long-moribund IWW Agricultural Workers Industrial Union Local 110, which had not staged a strike since 1939. The dispute lasted more than a week, and workers won at least temporary wage hikes and some improvements in camp conditions. After the strike ended, the Wobblies vanished as quickly as they had appeared, leaving the field of farmworker organizing in the Midwest to other organizations.[74]

The first serious campaign in the Midwest linked to the AFL-CIO in the 1960s was conducted by the Laborers International Union (LIU), of Charlotte, North Carolina. The LIU planned a drive in Michigan early in 1966, before the NFWA affiliated with the AFL-CIO. LIU organizers were able to secure more than five thousand authorization cards signed by workers in Oceana and Grand Traverse counties, three thousand more in the Saginaw Bay and Thumb areas, and smaller numbers in Southeastern Michigan and Northwestern Ohio. Despite the apparent enthusiasm of farmworkers in the two states, the LIU soon withdrew from the Midwest. It considered the cost of organizing more than it could afford without additional support from organized labor.[75]

Later that same year, discouraged by the efforts of its affiliates in Texas, Florida, along the East Coast, as well as in the Midwest, the national AFL-CIO adopted a strategy to contain the organizational efforts of midwestern farmworkers and tried to direct the labor movement's efforts toward organizing California's farmworkers first. National policy was based on two central premises. First, the AFL-CIO feared that labor would overextend itself by supporting farmworkers' organizing efforts everywhere. It considered California as the most likely place for success and it had an affiliate active there continuously since the mid-1940s. Second, the AFL-CIO leadership viewed organizing essentially as a business operation. It considered organizing in the Midwest, with its shorter growing seasons and pattern of workers scattered on small farms, as more costly than organizing the large ranches of California and the Southwest. In 1966 AFL-CIO organizer Dan Healy, after touring Indiana, wrote, "It was a rather shocking revelation for me to see the number of camps throughout the state for migrant workers with the largest being slightly in excess of 200 workers. I can readily understand how easy it would be for the AFL-CIO to get bogged down in this type of operation, moneywise and man-power wise."[76]

In keeping with AFL-CIO strategy, director of organization William Kircher repeatedly denied requests for assistance from Chicanos in Ohio, Michigan, Illinois, and Indiana; volunteers were directed to get involved in the UFWOC boycott. To make sure that the AFL-CIO maintained a low profile, Kircher assigned local staff to develop expertise and keep abreast of the midwestern efforts. In 1969, one of those "experts" did not know about Baldemar Velásquez or the FLOC, which had been organizing in Michigan and Ohio for two years. Eugene Boutilier of the National Campaign for Agricultural Democracy (NCAD) concurred that national policy should focus on Chávez: "He must mop up Delano before he can move on . . . expectations might be raised that could not be fulfilled."[77]

Farmworkers in the Midwest did not wait for the labor movement to come to them, but began to organize their own independent unions, as Chávez himself had done. The first organization was started by Jesús Salas in East-Central Wisconsin, a diverse crop region that hired thousands of workers each summer and fall, principally for cucumbers and potatoes. Libby, McNeill and Libby, Heinz, Dean's Food and a few potato processors controlled the recruitment and hiring of most migrant workers in the area. The heart of production was Waushara County, a conservative area with three active chapters of the John Birch Society. Hundreds of farmworkers and their families settled in the region, including Salas, originally from Crystal City, Texas. His father, Manuel, had been coming to the region since the early 1940s, first as a worker and later as a recruiter for Libby. Jesús, who was born in 1944, began traveling to the Midwest in 1951, and continued the annual trek until the family settled in Wautoma in 1959. The Salas family decided to set up a small Mexican restaurant in town, having had experience in the same business in Crystal City. They attracted local clientele in the winter and farmworkers in the summer. After Jesús Salas graduated from high school in 1961, he began working in state-sponsored educational and health programs for migrants, and published and distributed a bilingual newspaper, *La Voz del Pueblo* (The Voice of the People).[78]

He remained active after he entered college at Wisconsin State College at Stevens Point (later the University of Wisconsin–Stevens Point). In August, 1966, he staged an eighty-mile "March on Madison," which began in Wautoma. The immediate goals of the publicity-engendering four-day march were to build public restrooms in Wautoma, to place migrants on the Governor's Commission on Migratory Labor, to enact a state program to advise workers of their rights, to enforce the existing state housing code, and to pass legislation setting the minimum wage at $1.25 for all workers. Salas at the time did not state publicly that unionization was an immediate priority, but the march moved him in that direction.[79]

He was soon engaged in a more concerted organizing drive, hoping to build a solid base of support through local crew leaders. He was pushed into action in early October, when migrant workers struck the Almond plant of James Burns and Sons, the largest potato grower and processor in the state. Burns owned eight thousand acres of land, processing plants at Almond and Plainfield, a fertilizer-blending plant, a motel and restaurant, and a farm implement dealership in the area. More than 75 percent of the roughly one hundred employees in the Almond plant were Mexican American seasonal workers who sorted, filled and sewed potato sacks, and loaded them for delivery. The strike began after Burns publicly reprimanded a worker for taking a drink of water. When the worker complained about the incident in private, Burns threatened him with a gun. It was the tip of the iceberg for irate Chicano workers, who worked twelve to sixteen hours per day without overtime, faced inequalities in job classification, and were not paid the same as local Euro-Americans for comparable work. The workers approached Salas, who suggested that they sign authorization cards and force Burns to negotiate with the new union, Obreros Unidos (OU).[80]

OU promptly notified Burns that a majority of his workers had signed authorization cards. Following Wisconsin Employment Relations Board (WERB) guidelines, which, in effect, extended National Labor Relations Act privileges to all workers including those in agriculture, the union requested that the two parties begin negotiations over wages, working conditions, and terms of union recognition immediately. Burns countered by raising wages by 25 cents per hour, to $1.50, firing twenty-seven union supporters, and refusing to negotiate. OU immediately led a walkout.[81]

The union met with members of the Wisconsin AFL-CIO during the annual state convention in Madison. Salas gained enthusiastic support from John Schmitt, head of the Wisconsin AFL-CIO, and collected small contributions. The state organization continued to provide OU with much-needed monetary and legal assistance, but the amount was trifling compared with budgets common in urban labor-organizing campaigns, or even the funds allotted to UFWOC in California. AFL-CIO representative Charles Heymanns complained that the proposed OU budget for the 1967 season, $11,000, based largely on contributions from the national federation, was not "realistic."[82]

The propitious circumstance of the Wisconsin AFL-CIO convention was offset by the unfortunate timing of the strike, which began with less than two weeks remaining in the season. The peak demand for workers had passed, and Burns was able to complete work and avoid a sanctioned election. Although OU lost the strike, Salas filed a complaint against Burns for unfair labor practices with both the National Labor Relations Board (NLRB) and the WERB. The former refused to hear the petition, claiming that the plant ran an agricultural enterprise. The WERB accepted the case, and in December, 1966, declared that Burns's operation was guilty of "interfering, restraining, or coercing its employees in the exercising of their right to organize" and ordered Burns to cease and desist from such actions. Unfortunately, the order appeared too late to reverse the events of the fall.[83]

The legal victory strengthened moral resolve as the union faced harassment by local John Birchers, the Farm Bureau, and county district attorney Howard Dutcher, who publicly announced that he would investigate "confidential" complaints of the misuse of funds donated to the union. Such an investigation was unwarranted by law and never took place. OU was a private organization and was not obligated to reveal publicly how it spent its six thousand–dollar budget.[84]

In 1967 OU organized fieldworkers employed by the Libby plant in Wautoma. A majority of them signed authorization cards and OU requested an election. WERB guidelines placed the state's farmworkers in a relatively favored legal position and meant that Libby was obliged to allow an election. The workers voted 405–8 in favor of OU as their bargaining agent. Libby, however, refused to negotiate.

OU consequently called a strike and pulled most of the workers from the fields. Libby replaced many of them with strikebreakers, and although production fell sharply, the company held out.[85]

OU promptly filed an unfair labor practice charge with the WERB against Libby for failure to negotiate. The union also complained that a recent Libby decision to introduce harvesting machines was made solely to injure the union. Evidence included the testimony of Joseph Darprawn, president of the Wisconsin Growers Co-op, a farmer who grew cucumbers under contract for Libby. Darprawn stated, "The board of directors have already discussed this problem and we've agreed that we just won't stand for unionized labor."[86]

Subsequently, the WERB ruled that Libby had to appear at the hearing and produce records concerning mechanization. The company claimed that it had no responsibility to the workers and that its decision to mechanize was based on cost and feasibility. The union challenged its bookkeeping techniques, including the failure to include depreciation, the cost of repair, and training costs in its calculations. The WERB determined that Libby was guilty of an unfair labor practice in refusing to negotiate with OU. It also ruled that mechanization was a company prerogative. To break the union, Libby could run its operations as it pleased and mechanize, although it might be less profitable.[87]

These legal victories were not sufficient to ensure OU's success. Financial insecurity left it on the brink of collapse and it did not launch any further aggressive organizing or legal campaigns. Furthermore, its organizing in the canneries conflicted with that of the International Brotherhood of Teamsters and the Amalgamated Meatcutters and Butcher Workers. The Teamsters were prompted to organize several canneries where OU first stimulated interest, however.[88]

OU leadership also faced outside distractions in its organizing effort. Salas met César Chávez, who offered a cooperative working arrangement in exchange for help on the California boycott. Then in 1968 Salas accepted a full-time job with UMOS in Milwaukee and began organizing urban Chicanos and working on the grape boycott while his brother Manuel took over OU leadership. Faced with financial difficulties, the loss of its original leadership, and outside distractions, OU became ineffective. Soon the AFL-CIO retreated, in part because it was upset about continued OU interest in the canneries and the jurisdictional problems that interest engendered. In 1970 both the federation and UFWOC cut their affiliations and OU collapsed.[89]

The second indigenous organizing effort in the Midwest, FLOC, was led by Baldemar Velásquez and other recent settlers in Northwestern Ohio. Velásquez was born in 1947 in Pharr, Texas. He traveled with his family to the Midwest for several seasons. In 1954 they were stranded and decided to remain. The family took up permanent residence in Pandora in Putnam County, and like many other families, continued to work in the fields after settling.[90]

Velásquez began organizing as a college student. He entered Ohio Northern University in 1965 and transferred to Pan American University in Edinburg, Texas, the following year. He transferred again in 1967 to Bluffton College in Ohio, where he completed his studies. As a student he participated in the free speech and civil rights movements and anti–Vietnam War activities and became an accomplished folksinger. In the summer of 1966, while working as a volunteer for the Congress of Racial Equality (CORE) in Cleveland, he realized that local farmworkers did not have the attention of local political activists. "Even the flaming radicals . . . nobody wanted to touch the farm worker situation. . . . there was a lot of resistance, maybe because it was such an embarrassment . . . just talking about it, that it's in their state, and they've swept it under the rug for so long."[91]

When FLOC formed in September 1967, Velásquez hoped to make the organization "the official coordinating committee" for local farmworkers. Its goals included improved housing facilities, education, enforcement of minimum wage laws, and informing workers of their rights, including the right of collective bargaining. FLOC did not consider unionization an immediate priority, largely on the advice of sympathetic local union leaders, who suggested that it would be suicidal. As Velásquez stated, "we just want to unify our people and help them understand what rights they have." FLOC also gained public air time from a nearby Lima radio station and established a local newspaper, *La Voz del Campesino* (The Voice of the Farmworker).[92]

The push for unionization accelerated when Velásquez encountered employers who impeded his efforts to distribute the newspaper. Libby management at the Leipsic camp would not let Velásquez enter to distribute the paper unless company representatives first read it, "to make sure it says nothing damaging." Velásquez challenged the corporation and was arrested for trespassing. He claimed that camp residents "ought to be allowed to be visited by anyone who wishes to see them. This is a right to which all citizens are entitled." Libby never pressed charges, fearing that it would lose in court. Nonetheless, its actions convinced FLOC members that organizing workers should be their top priority.[93]

In 1968, after Velásquez had winter meetings with Jesús Salas and César Chávez, FLOC's strategy became clearer and the influence of UFWOC more specific. The two organizations would cooperate, but would remain independent of each other. FLOC formed as a non-profit organization and started a credit union and a co-op gasoline station. It also intensified its educational and organizational efforts among workers and began to push for legislative reform. It gained support and promises of legal assistance from several established local unions, including the United Auto Workers (UAW), Teamsters, Meat Cutters, Amalgamated Food and Allied Workers, and the Building Trades Council. Most of its material support, however, came from individual contributions of money, food, and time.[94]

In late August FLOC tested its effectiveness in the tomato fields. It twice contacted the growers of Lucas County to request meetings to negotiate contracts for field labor; it was demanding a pay increase from fifteen to nineteen cents per thirty-three-pound hamper and union recognition. After growers failed to respond, FLOC launched its first strike on September 5, directed against James Ackerman and Richard Smarkle. It lowered its demands to a 2-cent-per-hamper increase plus union recognition. This quick action by FLOC surprised Ackerman, who after four days agreed to sign a two-year contract granting a 1.5 cents per hamper increase and union recognition. Family heads received an additional 1 cent per hamper for supervising and 1 cent for loading hampers onto trucks. In return the pickers agreed to take care of and pay for damages to living quarters and to pick any tomatoes designated by the grower. Within the next two weeks, FLOC struck and won agreements with twenty-one tomato growers in the area under terms similar to the first. FLOC also agreed to serve as labor recruiter for the growers, beginning December 31, 1968, technically, but in practice immediately.[95]

Agricultural interests led by the Farm Bureau and grower associations quickly organized a public relations campaign against FLOC, charging that the contract paying workers a penny for two pounds of tomatoes was more than the industry could afford. Paul Slade, head of the Ohio Agricultural Marketing Association and former head of the Ohio Governor's Committee on Migratory Labor and a public relations man, asserted that the new contracts increased growers' labor costs to 48 percent of total receipts. The official Stokeley price to growers was 62.5 cents per ton, of which workers received 18.5 cents for picking, supervision, and loading. Thus total labor costs were 29.1 percent of grower receipts. Slade also contended that "everybody, men, women and children," could pick at least 200 hampers per day, and that many consistently picked 400 and 450 hampers. A 200-hamper day would yield a $33.00 paycheck. Yet testimony and worker receipts indicated that fast workers at harvest peak picked between 80 and 88 hampers, thereby earning roughly $14.00 for a ten-hour day. Individuals could get credit for 200 hampers only by including the entire family on one wage slip.[96]

In addition to publicity, industry sympathizers engaged in other activities to curb FLOC, particularly in the rural counties of Northwestern Ohio. Union members received anonymous phone threats and faced violent challenges to FLOC's vow of nonviolence. In one encounter Putnam County grower Lewis Klass tried to run over Velásquez with his truck when the FLOC organizer was talking with workers in a Klass camp. During the incident Jack Gallion, a Toledo attorney and FLOC supporter, asked Klass if he thought it was funny to run down Velásquez. Klass responded, "Yeah, I think it's funny. . . . Who the hell you working for, the Russians?" Klass then called the police, who arrested Velásquez but refused to administer a breath test on Klass, who had been drinking. Like other farmworker unions, FLOC faced grower threats that law enforcement officials would not control. Local police and sheriffs exacerbated the violence by consistently siding with the growers, tolerating their threatening behavior, and disregarding the workers' freedom of assembly and other constitutional rights.[97]

After the 1968 season FLOC and OU joined forces to organize and recruit workers for their respective states. Their efforts led to the formation of a short-lived organization called the Middle West Federation. Each union was to operate in its own geographic area but to recruit jointly throughout the Rio Grande Valley. The federation, however, collapsed with the demise of OU. FLOC also tried to meet with growers before they contracted with the corporations in an effort to represent workers in negotiations with the corporations to include field labor costs. This effort to refocus the class struggle by convincing farmers to side with the workers rather than with the corporations yielded little success, but FLOC did convince five of the growers with whom it had already won union contracts in March to sign agreements to hire only FLOC-recruited labor.[98]

The following season the Farm Bureau and its allies made a more determined effort to destroy the union. They convinced twelve of the twenty-two growers who had contracted with FLOC the previous year not to plant tomatoes in 1969, in effect canceling the second year of their agreements. Other growers tried to derail the contracts by seeking alternative labor sources, until FLOC threatened to take them to court on the basis of the March, 1969, agreement under which they had agreed to hire only FLOC-recruited workers. Many growers who had not previously signed contracts forestalled the union by increasing wages to a penny more per hamper than the FLOC contracts offered. As a result FLOC had only twelve contracts for the 1969 tomato harvest, with few prospects for the immediate future.[99]

By the end of the decade the growers' campaign drove FLOC out of the fields. Velásquez realized that existing laws would not protect the union and that public agencies, including the Governor's Commission on Migratory Labor, were a voice for the growers. Public programs established in behalf of workers were little more than token efforts that could not alter the balance of power. FLOC retreated to the cities and became involved in organization and civil rights activities on behalf of recently settled farmworkers in Northwestern Ohio and Southeastern Michigan. It proved to be as much a social movement as a labor union and, unlike OU, did not disappear. Its lack of formal ties to organized labor or compromises with federal and state government agencies, as well as its continuous leadership, enabled it to survive the antifarmworker reaction.[100]

National AFL-CIO and UFWOC efforts in the Midwest in the late 1960s were confined to setting up boycott committees in most major and medium-sized cities. This strategy drew the attention of Chicano and non-Chicano volunteer activists away from the region and reduced local union support for organizing in the Midwest. The hesitant national AFL-CIO policy made many midwestern Chicano leaders suspicious of organized labor. The union cause in the region was further hurt by factionalism involving AFL-CIO organizational director Kircher and UAW president Walter Reuther. Kircher criticized the UAW for its support of what the AFL-CIO considered haphazard indigenous efforts in several locations, including Ohio and Wisconsin. The UAW disagreed with the focus on California.[101]

Many local union officials, including John Schmitt, head of the Wisconsin AFL-CIO, also disagreed with the national strategy. He enthusiastically supported OU in his state and argued that farmworker organization could best be achieved by a broad, national effort. In July, 1968, he wrote, "The problem of decent living for migrant workers must be attacked in the nation as a whole since migrant workers must work crops in many states . . . the job will obviously be easier if the labor movement can show these workers how their lot in life can be improved by unions."[102]

As the California farmworker union neared victory in the strike against the table grape growers in 1969, UFWOC began to respond to requests for assistance from farmworkers in the Midwest. UFWOC volunteers Julián Herrera and John Hernández went to Van Buren County that year in an effort they considered "mostly a probe." Growers vigorously resisted their presence and convinced the local

Migrant Ministry to prohibit the union from access to its "Centro Campesino," despite an earlier agreement to allow them space to hold meetings. Later in the summer UFWOC volunteers set up an office in Southeastern Michigan near Erie in Monroe County, but were unable to generate substantial support.[103]

In 1969 local UFWOC volunteers also participated in an organizational effort in the East-Central Michigan sugar beet–growing area. It was initiated by recent settlers and the children of former *betabeleros* involved in the UFWOC Saginaw Boycott Committee and local Brown Berets. Farmworkers recruited by the Michigan Sugar Company discovered on arrival that there were no jobs available. The company encouraged them to wait in the hope that jobs might materialize while they stayed in poorly maintained, crowded, and filthy housing. They approached the Boycott Committee for assistance and together they staged a sit-in at the offices of the Michigan Sugar Company in Saginaw. Michigan Sugar Company vice-president Max Henderson offered to train five hundred workers for the sugar factory. Because the protest demonstration was not well planned and Michigan Sugar had no legal obligation to provide work, the sit-in accomplished little, and the company hastened mechanization of field tasks in order to reduce employment and future conflicts with seasonal workers.[104]

Buoyed by UFWOC victories in 1970, the AFL-CIO announced an organizing drive in Wisconsin, Michigan, Indiana, and Illinois. Chicago boycott coordinator Eliseo Medina stated that "conditions in Illinois make the California problems look like a picnic." Despite the fanfare, organized labor maintained a very low profile in the midwestern fields. UFWOC participated in a strike initiated by workers recruited from South Texas by J. Kenneth Weller, Inc., a Lakeview, Michigan, cucumber grower and processor. The clash stemmed from a state law that raised the minimum wage for agriculture from $1.30 to $1.45 per hour effective July 1, 1970. The workers arrived at the end of June, and began the harvest at the earlier, lower hourly rates. On July 1, Weller switched to piece rates. The state Wage Deviation Board determined that the new minimum piece rate equivalent was 47.5 cents per 5-gallon bucket of the minimum-quality "field run pickles." Weller, however, paid 47.5 cents for 6.5-gallon buckets. He also refused to pay for the largest cucumbers, used for relish, although he required workers to pick them. The workers walked out, demanding the minimum wage as guaranteed by law. Weller refused to discuss the issue and, because they lacked options or money, the strikers returned to work. The next day Weller told his three hundred employees that the harvest was finished, although the season was only three days old. According to one observer, "It seemed to his workers that he wanted silent slaves, or no workers at all."[105]

The workers then requested help from the UFWOC, and a majority signed authorization cards recognizing the union as their sole bargaining agent. On August 4 they demanded union recognition. After Weller refused, several workers, supported by a local priest, Father Joseph Merton, occupied the plant offices, vowing to stay until Weller recognized the union. Weller called the local sheriff to remove and arrest the demonstrators, but when the workers explained the circumstances, the deputy judged their actions reasonable and departed. Weller then decided to sign a UFWOC authorization stipulating that he and the union were to negotiate a wage agreement promptly; apparently, he considered this the only way to stop the demonstration. UFWOC sent the Reverend Jim Drake as negotiator, but at the meeting Weller claimed that the agreement he had signed had no legal binding and he walked out. UFWOC did not test the legality of the agreement and again retreated from the fields. The AFL-CIO drive in 1970 ended almost as inauspiciously as it began.[106]

Conclusion

As the workers' struggle in the Midwest intensified in the 1960s, growers faced a work force that was increasingly Chicano. Euro-Americans, African Americans, and Mexican *braceros* dropped out or were eliminated. The demographic change sharpened the struggle, as growers were less able to apply the traditional strategy of keeping the work force divided by playing off different ethnic groups against each other. At the same time, both the creators of public opinion and the government increasingly stereotyped Chicanos as farmworkers. Government programs worked under a philosophy that jobs would soon be eliminated by mechanization and devised programs aimed at further encouraging settlement.

The effect of mechanization coincided with government policies. The broad range of mechanical and chemical inputs recently introduced in commercial agriculture eliminated thousands of jobs and encouraged workers to settle in the region. As new permanent residents of midwestern communities, they joined the Chicano movement and gained a voice among reformers in public, church, and government circles. At least briefly they shook the bureaucracies from their apathy.

The recent settlers also led farmworker organizing struggles in the region. Organizational drives by the national AFL-CIO and the California-based UFWOC in the region were halting, uninformed, and unable to establish solid bases. The California experience itself suggested that only an indigenous effort could initiate a successful movement. The UFWOC was a useful role model and inspiration, but it was unprepared and unwilling to enter the fray in the Midwest. Furthermore, it was an outsider. The initial success of OU in attracting attention demonstrated that there was widespread support for organizing among farmworkers in the region. It also showed that modest assistance from organized labor and a legal mechanism favorable to farmworker organizing were not sufficient for success. OU's leadership did not establish a solid base of support and became distracted from its goal of organizing farmworkers. Furthermore, its flirtation with workers in the canneries weakened its support within organized labor. FLOC faced many of the same difficulties, but it had greater success, although that success dwindled by the end of the decade. In contrast to the Wisconsin union, however, FLOC's tenacity and consciousness of direction enabled it to survive. In both unions, settled farmworkers formed a bridge between migrant workers and the reformers and were key elements in the farmworker's struggle to break the chains of oppression.

CHAPTER 9

Postscript: Meandering Stream

As the demand for seasonal farmworkers fell in the late 1960s agricultural experts asserted that "the days of migrants [in the Midwest] are numbered." According to Alan Shapley of the Michigan State University Rural Manpower Center, "labor intensive crops are no longer economical." The predictions that the seasonal farm labor force in the region would disappear were based on three interrelated premises: mechanization, heightened competition from other regions, and the disappearance of the labor reserve. The predictions and underlying assumptions that supported them merit further examination.[1]

In the late 1960s experts equated the mechanization of the field labor process with the replacement of workers by mechanical, electronic, and chemical processes. In reality, scientific research and the machinery it created had shaped and transformed the agricultural proletariat continually. Scientific experiments and mechanical innovations stimulated the birth of the sugar beet industry at the end of the nineteenth century. The new sugar beet companies experimented widely before turning to a wage-earning force recruited from the Mexican border, the first permanent agricultural proletariat of the region. Production in the beet fields in the early twentieth century combined hand labor with horses, wagons, and several mechanical devices. Corporations introduced an array of new machines during the next three generations, gradually altering the work process. In the 1920s tractors, conveyors, and bins replaced horses and wagons and reduced the amount of manual labor necessary for loading and hauling. In the 1930s experimentation in new methods of planting and cultivating further reduced the demand for workers and widened the gaps of unemployment between different field tasks. In the 1940s the corporations and the farmers with whom they contracted adopted monogerm seeds and automatic topping machines. In the next two decades they experimented with pesticides and selected herbicides, as well as precision space planters, electronic thinners, and mechanical blocking machines; these innovations eliminated many field tasks. The impact of these changes on seasonal labor was erratic but cumulative. The sugar beet industry in the Great Lakes region offered nearly full-time employment to about forty thousand people for seven to eight months a year in the 1920s. By the early 1970s it provided a few weeks of sporadic employment to fewer than ten thousand.[2]

Mechanization also made possible the appearance of the region's commercial fruit and vegetable industry. During the 1920s and 1930s researchers made great strides in cultivation, refrigeration, canning, and processing techniques. They also induced thousands of farmers to grow the new crops and to sell their produce directly to consumers, store owners, and the small processing plants that appeared throughout the region. The industry depended on mechanized operations, an elaborate infrastructure of highways, automobiles, and trucks for transportation and delivery, and on more sophisticated advertising techniques, which helped increase consumer demand. Application of the new mechanical and scientific techniques also created a growing need for seasonal workers from the 1930s to the early 1960s.

The fruit and vegetable industry created jobs while it promoted mechanization to eliminate them. As in sugar beets, the decline of labor needed for field tasks tended to be gradual, irregular, and partial. The reduction of employment in various tasks had been taking place since the birth of the industry, but it was unprecedented during the late 1960s and the early 1970s, when several types of harvesting machines were perfected and placed into commercial operation. In vegetable production machines cultivated, picked, topped, chopped, and sorted. For the bush and tree crops, shaker and catcher units and other devices picked fruit from the plants, the trees, or from the ground and then sorted it. Consequently, there was a sharp decline in seasonal employment in many major commercial crops, including cherries, blueberries, grapes, tomatoes, cucumbers, and strawberries. In the early 1970s, for example, Michigan State University agricultural engineers developed a strawberry harvester that required seven persons to operate but that performed the same amount of work as one hundred hand laborers.[3]

Mechanization involved more than machines. Sprays and herbicides reduced the time necessary for weeding and thinning crops like sugar beets, mint, and onions. Chemicals that forced simultaneous ripening made it possible to use harvesting machines or fewer hand harvesters in conjunction with harvesting machines. The major thrust of the agricultural engineers during this period, whether concerned about planting, cultivation, or harvesting, was to eliminate hand labor.[4]

The mechanical inputs had several important consequences for field production. Many machines operated economically only on a large scale and thus encouraged larger farms. The tendency toward consolidation was hastened by banking practices adopted in the 1970s. Many financial institutions changed debt repayment policies, demanding that growers repay part of the principal as well as the interest each year; the earlier policy permitted the repayment of interest only in poor years. The new policy forced many growers into bankruptcy. Larger owners bought their lands and hired seasonal workers to run the modern equipment. The increasing use of machines led many experts to predict that the remaining fieldworkers would become skilled machine operators. These predictions largely rang hollow, as most were unskilled operatives working on machines that controlled the pace and nature of work.[5]

Corporations and agricultural experts usually argued that mechanization was necessary because it lowered costs. In many instances, immediate costs were sharply reduced, but in others they were not. In discussing the importance of herbicides to replace hand thinners, in 1970 the head of the Farmers and Manufacturers Beet Sugar Association stated, "You don't save enough to talk about it." John Vandermeer's detailed studies of tomato harvest mechanization revealed that the experts failed to calculate many important costs and that hand harvesting was more profitable than by machine. Vandermeer also criticized agricultural engineers for seldom researching ways to make hand workers' tasks easier. He argued that their primary motivation was to thwart worker organizing by eliminating workers, not necessarily to reduce costs. Vandermeer and other investigators also revealed that mechanization of tomato harvesting did not reduce the price to the consumer, nor did it improve the nutritional quality of the product. He concluded that "it is only under the most favorable of circumstances that the mechanical harvester appears to show a net social advantage over hand harvesting."⁶

A second assumption underlying the argument that the midwestern migrant stream would disappear was the region's inability to compete with other locations, particularly Mexico and California. The experts argued that the Midwest had comparatively unfavorable climatic and soil conditions. Whether regional advantages were permanent remains questionable in light of frequent changes in the site of production and the introduction of commercial crops in recent generations. Furthermore, the Midwest did compete effectively in several crops, even ousting California as the leading grain producer in the late nineteenth and early twentieth centuries.⁷

The Midwest's competitors also faced a potentially fragile political and ecological environment. In the case of Mexico, protectionist pressures in the United States for tariff barriers loomed consistently on the horizon. In addition, the Mexican agricultural industry continued to use dichlorodiphenyltrichloroethane (DDT) and other pesticides and herbicides banned by Mexico's northern neighbor. The consumer movement in the United States, still poorly informed about the use of these dangerous chemicals, represented a serious potential threat to future Mexican production for export to the United States.

In the case of California, the agricultural bonanza was in part the result of a favorable political environment. Massive sums of public monies were devoted to agricultural research and maintenance of agriculture. Future support could not be assured, however, particularly in light of the ecological damage caused by mechanized agriculture in the state. Furthermore, as the water table in the Central Valley and other growing areas fell, the cost of water for irrigation rose. Political resistance both within and outside the state to subsidies to agribusiness for tapping more distant water sources represented an ominous threat.

Some critics of capital-intensive agriculture have predicted doom in California due to ecological considerations. The most important are the destruction of the soil, the widespread abuse of pesticides and herbicides, the decreasing availability of inexpensive water, and the increasing salinity of agricultural land in irrigation. Agriculture in the Golden State contains the roots of a future decline.

Meanwhile, in the Midwest there were plausible reasons to expect an increasing demand for farm labor. One was the introduction of new crops, evident in the 1970s with the expansion of apple, mushroom, and asparagus production in the region. The changes came about partly because agricultural researchers and advertisers continued to change dietary habits. Another force that gained strength in the 1970s was the consumer movement. Consumer groups increasingly criticized food that was artificially ripened, poor tasting, nutritionally unsound, and contaminated by heavy doses of herbicides and pesticides. Midwestern consumers could influence production patterns by demanding fresher, untreated, more healthful, but labor-intensive local crops. Still another possible source of midwestern expansion was experimentation with crop-growing techniques not yet widely popular, including modified greenhouse procedures and intercropping. The former, proven successful in other parts of the world, suggested the possibility of a much longer growing season. The latter involved placing different crops in the same field simultaneously to reduce the costs of fertilizer, pesticides, and herbicides. The experiments represented opportunities for local growers to produce higher-quality food and required a substantial increase in the demand for workers.[8]

The final element in the predicted demise of the agricultural proletariat in the Midwest was that cheap labor was no longer available. In the 1960s the groups that formed the labor reserve employers had tapped for more than a generation were no longer available. Foreign contract workers from Mexico and the Caribbean were cut off by political measures. Euro-American and African American domestic workers from low wage areas in the South found it less expedient to travel such long distances for the poor remuneration offered. Even the Chicanos, who became the bulk of the labor force, were organizing and gaining power and thus becoming less attractive to employers.

The use of an unassimilated labor force recruited from the outside has long been a feature of the Midwest's agricultural proletariat. The first group appeared with the birth of the sugar beet industry at the turn of the twentieth century. It included European-born immigrants and their children, who were beginning to settle in cities but had not yet achieved stability of residence or employment. The sugar beet industry recruited them directly for daily, weekly, and, eventually, seasonal work. Families did not remain long, for they found better opportunities and steadier employment in the cities or the chance to buy farms in the country. They were replaced by other recent arrivals until immigration from Europe ceased at the onset of World War I.

The midwestern beet companies turned to the labor reserve in Mexico that was moving into South Texas. Beet workers spent several months in the Midwest, then returned to their homes in Texas and Mexico, where the cost of living was much lower and where some work was available. Corporate reliance on this labor force continued until the onset of the Great Depression, when a local reserve composed of both recently settled Mexicanos and longer-established Europeans returned to the fields. When faced with an insurgency by these established residents in the late 1930s, the sugar beet companies turned again to South Texas to recruit a new group of workers, U.S. citizens of Mexican descent. The new recruits displaced the older European and Mexican immigrants, who disappeared from the midwestern beet fields.

The expansion of commercial fruit and vegetable production in the Midwest in the late 1920s and the 1930s led to the appearance of another distinct geographic source for the midwestern agricultural proletariat. African Americans and Euro-Americans from the Cotton Belt, particularly its northern fringes, began to work in the Upper Midwest. They were initially recruited by fruit and vegetable growers at a moment of change in labor in cotton production. Citizens from low-wage states to the south continued to form the majority of the agricultural proletariat of the region for more than a generation.

With the onset of World War II, employers discovered additional reserve labor pools in Mexico and the Caribbean. Mexican *braceros*, as well as smaller numbers of Bahamians, Jamaicans, and Puerto Ricans, entered the region to augment the already heterogeneous and ethnically segmented force. Growers separated the groups by task and residence and hired them under distinct contractual arrangements. Employers were able to experiment with and divide the work force more successfully than before, with the assistance of the United States Farm Placement Service. The post–World War II period was a heyday for corporate agriculture in the class struggle.

The system broke down in the 1960s, as the Euro-American and African American citizen labor reserve diminished in size and the federal government abolished or severely reduced foreign worker programs. Employers consequently turned increasingly to Chicanos from South Texas. But they were not as easily manipulated as before. Inspired by national political reforms, the California farmworkers, and the Black Power and Chicano movements, they began to organize to gain a greater voice in the political system and influence on the work process. They and their sympathizers pushed employers on control issues, including better working and living conditions, higher pay, and greater political influence. The labor-organizing efforts of the period are unprecedented in geographic range or intensity in the twentieth century.

A detailed examination of the labor reserve in midwestern agriculture indicates that corporations consciously created and maintained a cultural division of labor. Linguistic, regional, and cultural features distinguished the different groups, but in most cases these differences had little prior meaning, for the groups had only occasional contact with each other until they met in the work setting. Furthermore, despite their different backgrounds, as workers they had much in common. Typically, they traveled long distances from low-wage areas of the United States or foreign countries. They were isolated from the majority resident population in the rural communities where they worked, and they were excluded from participation in mainstream politics in the local, state, and national arenas. Employer strategy played on cultural differences in order to create divisions among workers, maintain control, and keep wages low.

In the 1960s, as employers seemed unable to maintain the ethnic divisions and control of their labor force, they and their allies began to predict the death of the migrant stream. Their talk was premature but it was also political. They sought to reestablish the conditions necessary to regain their hegemony over the workers. First, they tried to undo the political inroads made during the 1960s by weakening agency support for reform. They pressured federal, state, and local governments to withdraw funds, reduce services, and prevent the enforcement of written regulations on housing, wages, and working conditions. Surveys undertaken in the 1970s indicate that they were largely successful. A 1976 Michigan Farm Worker Ministry study showed that most workers surveyed were very poorly housed and earned less than the minimum wage. Ninety percent were unaware of their right to compensation for injury or unemployment, and half did not know whether Social Security was withheld from their paychecks. A Wisconsin study published the following year revealed that the annual earnings of agricultural workers in the state were approximately one-half the official poverty level. An observer suggested that conditions remained tantamount to "modern day slavery." Employers also created a new labor reserve by recruiting workers from Texas and Florida, Puerto Rico, Mexico, Jamaica, and Haiti. Foreign workers were becoming an increasingly important portion of the midwestern seasonal farmworker force.[9]

In fact, the sharp decline in the size of the midwestern agricultural proletariat was concentrated during a short period from the mid-1960s to the early-1970s. During this time perhaps two-thirds of the hand field tasks were mechanized. By the mid-1970s the number of seasonal workers who came to the region each season had fallen to roughly seventy thousand. The numbers later stabilized, and in some locations increased moderately in the late 1970s and early 1980s.[10]

Employer predictions that the seasonal farm work force would disappear were also part of the struggle to counter the efforts to organize farmworkers in the region. If the growers could convince the public

that there would be no farmworkers in the future, support for unionization efforts would diminish. By the end of the 1960s organized
agriculture had successfully defeated organized labor and eliminated Obreros Unidos from the Midwest. It had also pushed the Farm
Labor Organizing Committee out of the fields. Unlike other midwestern labor groups, however, FLOC survived and continued to build
support during the 1970s. It renewed its direct farmworker organizing efforts in 1978, and the following year initiated a major international boycott against the Campbell Soup Company. Its persistence
and its success in gaining public support forced Campbell in 1985 to
allow elections on farms the corporation had contracted in Northwestern Ohio and Southeastern Michigan. FLOC won election victories by a convincing margin, and in 1986 gained union contracts
covering about eight hundred workers involved in various operations in tomato and cucumber cultivation and harvesting employed
by Campbell, its Vlasic subsidiary, and local growers. The following
year it completed successful negotiations and signed three-year contracts for about 750 workers employed in cucumbers by midwestern
growers and Heinz. Although the period was not one of liberal dominance in national public opinion, FLOC was able to gain greater public support and success than at any time in its history. The sporadic
farmworker movement that dated from the early years of the century
finally has established a permanent foothold in the region.[11]

The modest but successful unionization efforts of the 1980s further suggest that the doomsday predictions of the 1960s and early
1970s were not the end of a story. Rather, we have entered a period
of reorganization of farm labor coinciding with a transformation of
the industrial work force. In both capitalist industry and agriculture,
the early 1970s was a period of decay of old forms and simultaneous
exploration of new ones.[12] The changes further suggest that capitalist
agriculture is very creative in its labor relations. Because of historical
and political features of the industry and of the work force, agriculture's labor policies are based on somewhat different premises than
are those of urban factories. Many of its responses to worker resistance have been quite similar to those of urban employers. Both have
adopted repression, flight to new locations, and the hiring of new
labor reserves. Farmworkers have often used established industrial
strategies, but have succeeded best when they have modified them
to meet their own needs. They also had to come to terms with the
reality of the migrant stream to the Midwest, which did not dry up,
as many of their antagonists predicted, but continues to meander.

Notes

Preface

1. Overviews of the Midwest include Gilbert Cardenas, "Los Desarraigados: Chicanos in the Midwestern Region of the United States," 159–160; and Juan R. García, "Midwest Mexicanos in the 1920s: Issues, Questions, and Directions."

2. As examples of the neglect, see David F. Noble, *Forces of Production: A Social History of Industrial Automation*; David M. Gordon, Richard Edwards, and Michael Reich, *Segmented Work, Divided Workers: The Historical Transformation of Labor in the United States*.

1. Factories and the Fields, 1898–1917

1. U.S. Department of Agriculture (hereafter USDA), *Progress of the Beet-Sugar Industry in the United States in 1904*, 38. Many of the details of this chapter are examined in greater depth in Dennis Nodín Valdés, "Betabeleros: The Formation of an Agricultural Proletariat in the Midwest, 1897–1930."

2. U.S. Congress, House, Committee on Ways and Means, *Summary of Tariff Information. 1920 on Tariff of 1922. Schedule 4. Sugar, Molasses and Manufacturers of*, 967.

3. Leonard J. Arrington, "Science, Government, and Enterprise in Economic Development: The Western Beet Sugar Industry," 10; Dan Gutleben, *The Sugar Tramp—1954: Michigan*, 5; *Saginaw News Courier*, March 23, 1925; *Saginaw Daily News*, January 2, 1933; Harry Schwartz, *Seasonal Farm Labor in the United States*, 103.

4. USDA, *Progress of the Beet-Sugar Industry in the United States in 1900*, 6, 19; F. A. Stilgenbauer, "The Michigan Sugar Beet Industry," 494–495; Dan Gutleben, *The Sugar Tramp—1963: Ohio, M.S.G., Indiana, Illinois*, 2; J. Hickman, "Mangold Wurzels and Sugar Beets," 17; H. A. Huston and A. H. Bryan, "The Sugar Beet in Indiana"; U.S. Industrial Commission, *Report on Agriculture and Agricultural Labor*, 10: 535–540; Max Levin, "The Development of Sugar Beet Manufacturing to 1920," NA, RG 69, f. 15, VF 12; USDA, *Progress of the Beet-Sugar Industry in the United States in 1903*, 67; Arrington, "Science," 9–14; David Volkin and Henry Bradford, *American Crystal Sugar: Its Rebirth as a Cooperative*, 1; *Grand Forks Herald*, May 13, 1923; U.S. Congress, House, Select Committee Investigating

National Defense Migration, *National Defense Migration*, 19: 7934 (hereafter the Select Committee, *National Defense Migration*).

5. USDA, *Beet-Sugar Industry . . . 1900*, 19, and idem, *Beet-Sugar Industry . . . 1903*, 33; U.S. Industrial Commission, *Report on Agriculture*, 10: 540–542.

6. Alfred S. Eichner, *The Emergence of Oligopoly: Sugar Refining as a Case Study;* "Data Relating to Mexican Immigration, 1927," f: United States Sugar Association—statistics, NSMC; American Sugar Refining Company, *Annual Report 1918*, MHS, AC, f: American Sugar Refining Co., 1917, 1918, 1925.

7. U.S. Department of Commerce, Bureau of the Census, *Historical Statistics of the United States: Colonial Times to 1970*, 461 (hereafter Bureau of Census, *Historical Statistics*); "Survey of the Middle West," PHS, CWHM, box 21; U.S. Industrial Commission, *Report on Agriculture*, 10:567, 586; U.S. Immigration Commission, *Immigrants in Industries*, Pt. 24, *Recent Immigrants in Agriculture*, 2:570, 571; USDA, *Progress of the Beet-Sugar Industry in the United States in 1901*, 19–24; U.S. Congress, House, Committee on Immigration and Naturalization, *Seasonal Agricultural Laborers from Mexico*, 117, 124 (hereafter Committee on Immigration and Naturalization, *Seasonal Agricultural Laborers*).

8. USDA, *Beet-Sugar Industry . . . 1900*, 8; *Detroit Free Press*, April 7, June 10, 1920; *Scottsbluff Star-Herald*, December 17, 1920; *Isabella County Enterprise*, July 21, 1924; George T. Edson, *Mexicans in Our Northcentral States* (1927), 165, BL.

9. U.S. Immigration Commission, *Immigrants in Industries*, 498; USDA, *Beet-Sugar Industry . . . 1903*, 33.

10. USDA, *Beet-Sugar Industry . . . 1903*, 105; and idem, *Beet-Sugar Industry . . . 1904*, 38; idem, *Progress of the Beet-Sugar Industry in 1905*, 12; U.S. Industrial Commission, *Report on Agriculture*, 10:547, 574; Dan Gutleben, *The Sugar Tramp—Indiana*, 6.

11. U.S. Immigration Commission, *Immigrants in Industries*, 569–573.

12. National Child Labor Committee (hereafter NCLC), "Farm Work and Schools in Kentucky"; Committee on Immigration and Naturalization, *Seasonal Agricultural Laborers*, 154, 177; Theresa Wolfson, "People Who Go to the Beets," 220.

13. U.S. Congress, Senate, Committee on Immigration, *Restriction of Western Hemisphere Immigration*, 139 (hereafter Committee on Immigration, *Restriction*); U.S. Immigration Commission, *Immigrants in Industries*, 496, 565, 574; Wolfson, "People," 225–228; U.S. Department of Labor (hereafter USDL), Children's Bureau, *Child Labor and the Work of Mothers in the Beet Fields of Colorado and Michigan*, 80–119; Walter W. Armentrout, Sara A. Brown, and Charles E. Gibbon, *Child Labor in the Beet Fields of Michigan*, 5–13.

14. USDL, *Child Labor*, 114; Select Committee, *National Defense Migration*, 19:7911; U.S. Immigration Commission, *Immigrants in Industries*, 497; Committee on Immigration, *Restriction*, 138–39; "Survey of the Middle West," PHS, CWHM, box 21; Edson, *Mexicans . . . Northcentral*, 21, BL.

15. Stephan Thernstrom, *The Other Bostonians: Poverty and Progress in the American Metropolis, 1880–1970*, 111–115.

2. Mexican Entry, 1917–1929

1. Committee on Immigration, *Restriction*, 138; Committee on Immigration and Naturalization, *Seasonal Agricultural Laborers*, 113, 154, 177, 180; Wolfson, "People," 226.

2. *Los Angeles Examiner*, May 24, 1917; Edson, Mexicans . . . *Northcentral*, 21, BL; Mark Reisler, *By the Sweat of Their Brow: Mexican Immigrant Labor in the United States, 1900–1940*, 29–35; A. Caminetti, temporary admission of Mexican workers, May 10, 1918, NA, RG 85, 55091/6; Otey M. Scruggs, "The First Mexican Farm Labor Program."

3. W. H. Wallace to Herbert Hoover, May 29, 1918, NA, RG 85, 54261/202; Juan de Negri to Ernesto Garza Pérez, January 17, 1918, 17-14-3, SRE; Committee on Immigration, *Restriction*, 137; U.S. Immigration Commission, *Immigrants in Industries*, 30, 97; J. H. Abel to Francis Key Carey, February 19, 1917, F. C. Carey correspondence, NSMC; Sarah Deutsch, *No Separate Refuge: Culture, Class and Gender on an Anglo-American Frontier in the American Southwest, 1880–1940*, 33–35; *Denver Republican*, April 30, 1902; U.S. Department of Commerce, Bureau of the Census, *13th Census of the United States, 1910: Population*, I: table 37; idem, *15th Census of the United States: 1930, Population*, III: table 21 (hereafter Bureau of Census; *13th Census, 15th Census*); Charles S. Johnson, "The Changing Economic Status of the Negro."

4. R. Artemis to John H. Clark, February 22, 1921, Clark to Caminetti, February 22, 1921, McCall to Caminetti, February 23, 1921, Clark to Caminetti, December 23, 1920, and Clark to Caminetti, February 28, 1921, NA, RG 85, 55091/6.

5. Wolfson, "People," 227; *La Vanguardia*, March 31, 1921; George K. Apple to J. A. Flukey, May 16, 1919, NA, RG 85, 542561/202-H; R. Artemis to John H. Clark, February 22, 1921, NA, RG 85, 55091/6; *Detroit News*, February 15, 1921, November 9, 1932.

6. *Detroit Free Press*, March 20, 1922.

7. McCall to Caminetti, February 3, 1921, Artemis to Clark, February 22, 1921, Francisco Pereda to William Hale Thompson, April 25, 1921, NA, RG 85, 55091/6; *Detroit News*, February 16, 1921; Sáenz to Alvaro Obregón, January 2, 1921, 822-M-1, SRE.

8. John McDowell, *A Study of Social and Economic Factors Relating to Spanish-speaking People in the United States*, 12; interview, Luis García, June 7, 1928, BL, PTRFN, carton 12, f: 3d set; American Beet Sugar Company, "A Nuestros Trabajadores," August 19, 1926, BL, PTCN, f: clipping; *La Prensa* (San Antonio), April 10, 1927; Max Sylvanus Handman, "The Mexican Immigrant in Texas," 334.

9. *Grand Forks Herald*, May 22, 1926; *Moorhead Daily News*, May 8, 1926; *La Prensa* (San Antonio), April 10, 1927; Michigan Sugar Company, "A Nuestros Trabajadores," August 19, 1926, BL, PTCN, f: clipping; Law-

rence Leslie Waters, "Transient Mexican Agricultural Labor," 59; USDL, United States Employment Service, *Report of the Farm Labor Division, 1925*, 1–2.

10. Interviews, Luz and Virginia Campa, Alfonso de León, Sr., Angelo and Marcella Rosendo, and Jesús Méndez, MHS, OH; McDowell, *A Study*, 12, 16; Paul S. Taylor, *Mexican Labor in the United States: Chicago and the Calumet Region*, 35; interview, Mrs. Kembell, June 11, 1928, BL, PTRM, carton 12, f: Paul Taylor's notes; interview, Javier Tovar, July 30, 1928, BL, PTRFN, carton 12, f: Rodrigo's notes.

11. *Des Moines Register*, May 15, 1923; Paul S. Taylor, *Mexican Labor in the United States: Dimmit County, Winter Garden District, South Texas*, 5, 340; Select Committee, *National Defense Migration*, 19: 7875; William John May, Jr., "The Great Western Sugarlands: History of the Great Western Sugar Company," 419–422.

12. "Employment Office—Madison Street–Chicago," January 8, 1928, and "Canal Street Employment District," June 13, 1926, BL, PTRFN, carton 12, f: Rodgrio's notes; "Mexicans in Detroit," October 4, 1926, and "Mexicans in Rural Indiana," n.d., BL, PTCN, f: Midwest; Committee on Immigration, *Restriction*, 122; Committee on Immigration and Naturalization, *Seasonal Agricultural Laborers*, 30.

13. Allen J. Applen, "Migratory Harvest Labor in the Midwestern Wheat Belt, 1870–1940"; Paul S. Taylor, "Migratory Farm Labor in the United States," 538–539; Melvyn Dubovsky, *We Shall Be All: A History of the Industrial Workers of the World*, 313–321.

14. American Beet Sugar Company, *El cultivo del betabel: manual para los trabajadores 1929*, 7, MHS; William T. Ham, "Sugar Beet Field Labor under the AAA," 645; Edson, *Mexicans . . . Northcentral*, 165, BL.

15. U.S. Immigration Commission, *Immigrants in Industries*, 24: 565, 570, 573–574; Michigan Bureau of Labor and Industrial Statistics, *24th Annual Report*, 437; Committee on Immigration, *Restriction*, 138; Wolfson, "People," 226.

16. Schwartz, *Seasonal Farm Labor*, 130; Elmer Cornelius Koch, "The Mexican Laborer in the Sugar Beet Fields of the United States," 47; US Congress, House, Committee on Immigration and Naturalization, *Immigration from Countries of the Western Hemisphere*, 455 (hereafter Committee on Immigration and Naturalization, *Immigration from Countries*); Committee on Immigration, *Restriction*, 137, 139; R. H. Cottrell, ed., *Beet-Sugar Economics*, 192; Edson, *Mexicans . . . Northcentral*, 162, BL.

17. USDL, *Child Labor Colorado and Michigan*, 5; interview, Maude Swett, Wisconsin Industrial Commission, BL, PTRFN, carton 12, f: Chicago-Calumet.

18. Edson, *Mexicans . . . Northcentral*, 153, BL; *La Prensa* (San Antonio), April 10, 1927.

19. Robert N. McLean, *The Northern Mexican*, 18; interview, Trinidad Moreno, June 13, 1984; USDL, *Child Labor Colorado and Michigan*, 117; Minnesota Sugar Company, "Classification of Accounts Report, 1923," f: Minnesota Sugar Company, MHS, AC; "Your Beet Labor," 7.

20. USDL, *Child Labor Colorado and Michigan*, 119; interview, Manuel J. Contreras Prieto, MHS, OH.

21. USDL, *Child Labor Colorado and Michigan*, 80; Armentrout, *Child Labor*, 33; U.S. Immigration Commission, *Immigrants in Industries*, 568; Wolfson, "People," 218.

22. Interviews, Crescencia Rangel and Jesús Méndez, MHS, OH; *Wells Mirror*, May 14, 1924; *Grand Forks Herald*, May 22, 1926; interview, Trinidad Moreno, June 13, 1984; Committee on Immigration and Naturalization, *Seasonal Agricultural Laborers*, 159; "Employment Office—Madison Street–Chicago," BL, PTRFN, carton 12, f: Rodrigo's notes.

23. Interviews, Marcelina Urbina, Luz and Virginia Campa, Manuel J. Contreras Prieto, MHS, OH.

24. Committee on Immigration and Naturalization, *Seasonal Agricultural Laborers*, 162.

25. "Your Beet Labor," 7; American Beet Sugar Company, *El Cultivo*, 11; interview, Trinidad Moreno, June 13, 1984; "Mexicans in Rural Indiana: Northern Sugar Beet Mexicans," February 25, 1927, BL, PTCN, f: Midwest.

26. USDL, *Child Labor Colorado and Michigan*, 90; Esther S. Anderson, "The Beet Sugar Industry of Nebraska as a Response to Geographic Environment," 382.

27. Interview, Manuel J. Contreras Prieto, MHS, OH; "Employment Office—Madison Street–Chicago," PTRFN, carton 12, f: Rodrigo's notes; Jacques E. Levy, *César Chávez: Autobiography of La Causa*, 75.

28. *San Francisco Chronicle*, May 4, 1973; *Fargo Forum*, July 27, 1930; *Grand Forks Herald*, August 3, 1930, *Polk County Leader*, September 11, 1930; Levy, *Chávez*, 74–76.

29. Committee on Immigration and Naturalization, *Immigration from Countries*, 455.

30. USDL, *Child Labor Colorado and Michigan*, 92.

31. Edson, "Northern Sugar Beet Mexicans," BL, PTCN, f: Midwest; Committee on Immigration and Naturalization, *Seasonal Agricultural Laborers*, 166; "Survey of the Middle West," PHS, NCC, DHM, RG 7, box 11, f: 8; Committee on Immigration, *Restriction*, 142; American Sugar-Beet Company, *El Cultivo*, 32–35; interview, Trinidad Moreno, June 13, 1984; M. Colonel Ray to Paul Taylor, March 23, 1927, BL, PTRFN, carton 12, f: 3d set; Koch, "Mexican Laborer," 62; *Child Labor Colorado and Michigan*, 54; interviews, Esiquia Monita and Manuel J. Contreras Prieto, MHS, OH.

32. "Wlad of the Beets"; USDL, *Child Labor Colorado and Michigan*, 4.

33. Edson, *Mexicans . . . Northcentral*, 71, 166, BL; "Northern Sugar Beet Mexicans," BL, PTCN, f: Midwest, 7. See discussion of pattern among migrant workers in Michael Burawoy, "The Functions and Reproduction of Migrant Labor: Comparative Material from Southern Africa and the United States," 1050–1087.

34. Juan de Negri to Ernesto Garza Pérez, January 17, 1918, 17-14-3, SRE; Bureau of Census, *Historical Statistics*, Series A 195–209; "Calling Out the Guard," 437; Juan R. García, "The Mexican in Popular Literature, 1875 to 1925"; Blaine P. Lamb, "The Convenient Villain: The Early Cinema Views

the Mexican-American"; Edson, *Mexicans . . . Northcentral*, 30, BL; R. E. A. Smith, to Alvaro Obregón, October 31, 1922, and Obregón to Smith, November 1, 1922, 822-D-1, SRE; Committee on Immigration and Naturalization, *Seasonal Agricultural Laborers*, 177–178, 271; "Mexicans in Toledo," 2, BL, PTCN, f: Midwest.

35. *Wells Mirror*, July 12, 16, 1922; *Walsh County Record*, August 22, 1926; *Grand Forks Herald*, January 3, 1927; *Warren Sheaf*, June 15, 1927; *Isabella County Enterprise*, August 15, 1924, September 18, 1925; Edson, *Mexicans . . . Northcentral*, 30, 51, BL; interview, Eva Gibbs, BL, PTRFN, carton 12, f: Chicago-Calumet; *Detroit News*, September 5, 1920; McLean, *Northern Mexican*, 52–53.

36. *Grand Forks Herald*, May 13, 1923; U.S. Congress, Senate, Committee on Agriculture and Forestry, *Agricultural Labor Supply*, 90.

37. U.S. Chamber of Commerce, *Mexican Immigration*, 15; Committee on Immigration and Naturalization, *Immigration from Countries*, 557–558; American Crystal Sugar Company, *Beet Labor Information*, 35; Beet Labor Situation, MHS, AC.

38. Interview, Trinidad Moreno, June 13, 1984; American Crystal Sugar Company, *Beet Labor Information*, 35.

39. American Beet Sugar Company, *El Cultivo*, 7–9; interview, Trinidad Moreno, June 13, 1984; Francisco Vásquez to E. P. Kirby Hade, May 19, 1930, IV/241 (73-59)/23, SRE; *La Vanguardia*, March 31, 1921; Ysidro Campos to Alvaro Obregón, November 1, 1928, AGN, OC, 104-M-15; Committee on Immigration, *Restriction*, 142.

40. Edson, *Mexicans . . . Northcentral*, 167, BL; interview, Crescencia Rangel, MHS, OH; American Beet Sugar Company, *El Cultivo*, 14; American Crystal Sugar Company, *Beet Labor Information*, 35; Committee on Immigration, *Restriction*, 141; *Grand Forks Herald*, May 13, 1923; "Your Beet Labor," 7.

41. Interview, Crescencia Rangel, MHS, OH; Informe de Protección, Chicago, 1930, IV/201 (73-10) (03)/2, SRE; *Labor Advocate*, April 17, 1930.

42. E. P. Kirby Hade to Samuel Andrade, March 13, 1931, IV/241 (73-59)/4, SRE; interview, Trinidad Moreno, June 13, 1984; Ysidro Campos to Obregón, November 1, 1928, AGN, OC, 104-T-10; James Ford to Mrs. Kenneth Rich, December 5, 1930, UCC, IPL, Supplement 2, f: 54:A; *La Prensa* (San Antonio), May 25, 1928; Ignacio Batiza to SRE, June 3, 1931, IV/543 (73-34)/5, SRE; Committee on Immigration and Naturalization, *Seasonal Agricultural Laborers*, 273; Committee on Immigration and Naturalization, *Immigration from Countries*, 555; interview, Eva Gibbs, BL, PTRFN, carton 12, f: Chicago-Calumet; Edson, *Mexicans . . . Northcentral*, 72, BL.

43. *Detroit News*, August 1, 1926; *St. Paul Pioneer Press*, December 23, 1926; interview, Eva Gibbs, BL, PTRFN, carton 12, f: Chicago-Calumet; "Mexicans at Galesburg," BL, PTCN, f: Midwest; "Mexicans in Detroit," BL, PTCN, f: Midwest; interview, Javier Tovar, BL, PTRFN, carton 12, f: Rodrigo's notes; *Grand Forks Herald*, August 22, 1926; Ignacio Batiza to delegado de inmigración, Cd. Juárez, December 1, 1930, IV/241 (73-14)/19, SRE.

44. "Child Labor in Michigan Sugar Beet Fields," 3; Edson, *Mexicans . . .*

Northcentral, 66, BL; interview, Maude Swett and Cooper, BL, PTRFN, carton 12, f: Chicago-Calumet; interview, Trinidad Moreno, June 13, 1984.

45. "Editorial Comment on Child Labor Decision"; USDL, *Child Labor Colorado and Michigan*, 96–97; Armentrout, *Child Labor; Mason City Globe Gazette*, January 12, 1924; "Mexicans at Mason City," BL, PTCN, f: Midwest; "Child Labor in Michigan Sugar Beet Fields," 3; "Nineteenth Annual Report of the National Child Labor Committee," 1.

46. Owen R. Lovejoy, "Summing It Up"; "Child Labor in Michigan Sugar Beet Fields," 1–3; Wolfson, "People," 222–224; Harold Curley, "No Chores for Jimmie: He's a Laborer."

47. Select Committee, *National Defense Migration*, 19: 7897; "Child Labor in Michigan Sugar Beet Fields," 1; interview, Trinidad Moreno, June 13, 1984; USDL, *Child Labor Colorado and Michigan*, 76–78, 115; Edson, *Mexicans . . . Northcentral*, 44, BL; Owen R. Lovejoy, "The Child Problem in the Beet Sugar Industry," 30–35; Edward N. Clopper and Lewis W. Hine, "Child Labor in the Sugar-Beet Fields of Colorado," 193; "Northern Sugar Beet Mexicans," BL, PTCN, f: Midwest.

48. Owen R. Lovejoy, "Sugar"; "Michigan Starts Cleaning House"; "In Wisconsin," 5; Lovejoy, "Child Problem," 33: "Labor and Legislation in Michigan."

49. Stilgenbauer, "Michigan Sugar," 502; *Isabella County Enterprise*, September 14, 1924; "Beet Complex"; Owen R. Lovejoy, "Sugar Puzzle Picture—Find the Child."

50. American Beet Sugar Company, *El Cultivo*, 15, 18.

51. Lawrence A. Cardoso, *Mexican Emigration to the United States, 1897–1931*, 57–66; Francisco E. Balderrama. *In Defense of La Raza: the Los Angeles Mexican Consulate and the Mexican Community, 1929 to 1936*.

52. Batiza to Jorge Terrazas, June 5, 1930, IV/241 (73-32)/7, SRE.

53. "Mexicans in Milwaukee, Wisconsin," November 27, 1926, BL, PTCN, f: Midwest; Hade to American Beet Sugar Company, May 18, 1930, and Hade to Samuel Andrade, March 13, 1931, IV/241 (73-59)/4, SRE; Batiza to SRE, June 3, 1931, IV/543 (73-14)/5, SRE; Batiza to SRE, August 20, 1930, IV/241 (73-32)/7, SRE.

54. Edson, *Mexicans . . . Northcentral*, 193, BL; interview, Esiquia Monita and Juanita Morán, MHS, OH; interview, Roberto Cortina, December 1, 1980.

55. *Isabella County Enterprise*, September 18, 1925; Committee on Immigration and Naturalization, *Seasonal Agricultural Laborers*, 273; *Mt. Pleasant Times*, September 17, 1925.

56. Taylor, *Chicago*, 180; interview, Ignacio Vallarta, June 13, 1928, BL, PTRFM, carton 12, f: Paul Taylor's notes, 2d set incomplete; David Montejano, *Anglos and Mexicans in the Making of Texas, 1836–1986*, 106–110. Fine discussions of the internal colony appear in Mario Barrera, *Race and Class in the Southwest*, and Rodolfo Acuña, *Occupied America: A History of Chicanos*.

57. McLean, *Northern Mexican*, 22; American Beet Sugar Company, *El Cultivo*, 8.

58. Taylor, *Chicago*, 35; Edson, *Mexicans . . . Northcentral*, 70–71, BL.

59. Interviews, George Galvin, Manuel J. Contreras Prieto, and Esiquia Monita, MHS, OH.

60. Taylor, *Dimmit County,* 308, 419, 420, 430; David Wigand to E. P. Kirby Hade, November 8, 1930, IV/241.1 (73-59)/9, SRE; interview, Trinidad Moreno, June 13, 1984; interviews, Luz and Virginia Campa, Alfonso de León, Angelo and Marcella Rosendo, MHS, OH; American Beet Sugar Company, *El Cultivo,* 8; Edson, *Mexicans . . . Northcentral,* 156, BL.

61. McLean, *Northern Mexican;* "Mexicans in Saginaw," BL, PTCN, f: Midwest; McDowell, *A Study,* 16; Taylor, *Dimmit County,* 356; Edson, *Mexicans . . . Northcentral,* 4, BL.

62. "Mexicans in Toledo," BL, PTCN, f: Midwest; Anita Edgar Jones, "Conditions Surrounding Mexicans in Chicago," 61; M. R. Ibáñez, "Mexican Work at the University of Chicago Settlement 1930–31," UCC, UCSP, box 21, f: Mexican work; Taylor, *Chicago,* 73; "Mexicans in Milwaukee," "Mexicans at Mason City, Iowa," and "Mexicans in Minneapolis and St. Paul," BL, PTCN, f: Midwest.

63. Committee on Immigration, *Restriction,* 122–123, 140–141; American Beet Sugar Company, *El Cultivo,* 5, 8, 14; Norman D. Humphrey, "Employment Patterns of Mexicans in Detroit," 915–917; interview, Javier Tovar, BL, PTRFN, carton 12: Rodrigo's notes; "Employment Office—Madison Street–Chicago," BL, PTRFN, carton 12, f: Rodrigo's notes; Edson, *Mexicans . . . Northcentral,* 156, BL.

64. "Mexicans in Rural Indiana," BL, PTCN, f: Midwest; interview, W. H. Baird, BL, PTRFN, carton 12, f: Chicago-Calumet; Koch, "Mexican Laborer," 58, n. 78; American Beet Sugar Company, *El Cultivo,* 3–5; "Northern Sugar Beet Mexicans," BL, PTCN, f: Midwest; "Mexicans at Mason City, Iowa," BL, PTCN, f: Midwest.

65. Paul S. Taylor, *Mexican Labor in the United States: Valley of the South Platte, Colorado,* 136–138; *Lincoln State Journal,* May 18, 1934; Colorado State Council, Knights of Columbus, *4th Annual Report of Mexican Welfare Committee,* CSHS; Koch, "Mexican Laborer," 58; "Home Owning, Permanent Beet Labor Colony Is Growing."

66. Montejano, *Anglos and Mexicans,* 159–178.

3. Crisis and Resistance, 1929–1938

1. *Congressional Record,* House, January 8, 1927, 1904; Oswald Ryan, "Who Shall Inherit the United States?"

2. Batiza to Embajada de México, Washington, D.C., March 7, 1930, IV/241 (73-14)/14, SRE; Consulado de México, Detroit, Informe de protección (hereafter Informe), Detroit, December, 1932, to January, 1933; and Informe, Detroit, August to October, 1932, IV/241.04 (73-14)/ "32"/ 1, SRE; Informe, Chicago, January, 1933, IV/241 (04) (73-10) "33"/1, SRE; Select Committee, *National Defense Migration,* 19: 7778; *Saginaw Daily News,* September 3, 1931; *Detroit News,* October 10, 1931; G. M. Greene to Batiza, July 26, 1932, IV/241.2 (73-14)/15, SRE; Mrs. Kenneth Rich, "Memorandum on the Deportation Drive of October–November, 1931, Chicago," UCC, IPL, Supplement

2, f: 54 A; John L. Zubrick to Commissioner General of Immigration, October 20, 1932, NA, RG 85, 55784/585; Norman D. Humphrey, "Mexican Repatriation from Michigan: Public Assistance in Historical Perspective," 500; Stuart Jamieson, *Labor Unionism in American Agriculture*, 380; George C. Kiser and David Silverman, "Mexican Repatriation during the Great Depression."

3. Bertram D. Wolfe, *The Fabulous Life of Diego Rivera*, 202; Hayden Herrera, *Frida: A Biography of Frida Kahlo*, 133; Dennis Nodín Valdés, "Mexican Revolutionary Nationalism and Repatriation during the Great Depression"; Daniel T. Simon, "Mexican Repatriation from East Chicago, Indiana"; Francisco Arturo Rosales, "Mexican Immigration to the Urban Midwest during the 1920s," 229–233; *Minneapolis Tribune*, August 12, 1932; David Stafford Weber, "Anglo Views of the Mexican Immigrant: Popular Perceptions and Neighborhood Realities in Chicago, 1900–1940," 63; "Back to the Homeland."

4. Batiza to Embajada de México, Washington, D.C., March 7, 1930, and Rafael Avereyda to SRE, December 31, 1930, IV/524.5 (73-10)/4, SRE; U.S. Congress, Senate, Committee on Labor and Public Welfare, Subcommittee on Labor-Management Relations, *Migratory Labor 1952*, II: 976 (hereafter Committee on Labor and Public Welfare, *Migratory Labor 1952*); Schwartz, *Seasonal Farm Labor*, 128–130; Select Committee, *National Defense Migration*, 19: 7883; USDA, *Agricultural Statistics 1942*, 130; Jamieson, *Labor Unionism*, 382; "Labor Conditions in Sugar-Beet Fields, and Suggested Remedies," 58; *Detroit News*, November 11, 1932; Rosales, "Mexican Immigration," 229–232.

5. Elizabeth S. Johnson, *Welfare of Families of Sugar-Beet Laborers*, 72; Dorothy Fox to John Thaden, October 30, 1939, MSA, JT, box 227, f: 1; Katherine F. Unroot, "The Migrant Laborer in the Present Rural Situation," February 8, 1936, PHS, CWHM, box 3, f: migrant literature and reports; Stanley V. White to J. L. Steelman, February 27, 1938, NA, RG 280, 196/139; interviews, Angelo and Marcella Rosendo, Leonard López, Marcelina and Carlos Urbina, MHS, OH.

6. *Minneapolis Journal*, August 13, 1931; *St. Paul Pioneer Press*, January 10, 1932; interview, Trinidad Moreno, June 13, 1984; Sidney C. Surfin, "Labor Organization in Agricultural America, 1930–1935," 557.

7. Jamieson, *Labor Unionism*, 380; *Detroit Free Press*, July 24, 1935. Select Committee, *National Defense Migration*, 19: 7886-7887; U.S. Congress, House Select Committee to Investigate the Interstate Migration of Destitute Citizens, *Interstate Migration of Destitute Citizens* (hereafter Select Committee, *Destitute Citizens*). 3: 1134.

8. Select Committee, *National Defense Migration*, 19: 5576. Calculated from Edson, *Mexicans . . . Northcentral*, BL.

9. Gutleben, *Sugar Tramp . . . Michigan*, 8; *Colorado Labor Advocate*, November 22, 1934.

10. "The Story of Beet Sugar and American Crystal Sugar Company," MHS, AC, f: The Story of Beet Sugar; "A Century of Sugar Beets in the United States: Facts about Sugar," 40, 50, MHS, AC, box 156, f: A Century of Sugar Beets.

11. *Saginaw Daily News*, October 6, 1932, November 17, 1933; Farmers and Manufacturers Beet Sugar Association, *Facts about Beet Sugar*, SOM.

12. "Labor Conditions in Sugar Beet Fields," 58; Kent Hendrickson, "The Sugar-Beet Laborer and the Federal Government: An Episode in the History of the Great Plains in the 1930s," 50.

13. Select Committee, *National Defense Migration*, 19: 7998; Allen D. Ochs to Chet Darby, July 20, 1934, NA, RG 59, FERA state files, Ohio, f: 1.

14. C. C. Stillman to Aubry Williams, August 6, 1934, NA, RG 59, Ohio Reports, 401.3, f: 1; "Survey of the Middle West," PHS, NCC, DHM, RG 7, box 11, f: 8; Charles E. Gibbons, "The Onion Workers."

15. Select Committee, *National Defense Migration*, 19: 7999. Hardin County Relief Commission, "Marion Township—Report on Education, 1934," NA, RG 280, 176/1691; Ochs to Darby, July 20, 1934, and Hardin County Relief Administration, "Relief Families on Scioto Marsh," NA, RG 59, FERA state files, Ohio, f: 1.

16. "Developing Michigan Fruitlands"; "Expansion of Northwestern Michigan Fruit Agency"; G. P. Marston to Mrs. Jefferson Butler, September 28, 1922, f: Michigan agriculture, misc. material, BHC; *Detroit News*, July 25, 1937; *Detroit Free Press*, December 4, 1935.

17. "Survey of the Middle West," PHS, NCC, DHM, RG7, box 11, f: 8; R. L. B., "Berry Picking"; Select Committee, *Destitute Citizens*, 3: 1231.

18. John DeWilde et al., "Migratory Workers in Southwestern Michigan," August 5, 1940, SCUCLA, CM, box 14, f: migratory labor—Mich.; Paul Taylor, *Adrift on the Land*, 7; R. G. Fuller, *Children in the Strawberries*.

19. Orlando Tusler, "Report of a Survey Made of Traverse City, Michigan, 1940," PHS, CWHM, box 21, f: Michigan; *Detroit News*, August 7, 1938; *Traverse City Record-Eagle*, July 14, 1939, July 24, 1940; Select Committee, *Destitute Citizens*, 3: 1130.

20. Department of Commerce, U.S. Bureau of the Census, *16th Census of the United States: 1940, Agriculture*, III: 838; *Detroit News*, July 9, 1932.

21. *Detroit News*, July 9, August 9, 1932, September 11, 1938.

22. Michigan Study Committee on Migratory Labor, "Report of Field Trip to Keefe Blueberry Plantation at Grand Junction, July 23, 1952," WPR, EJ, box 1, f: 6.

23. Select Committee, *National Defense Migration*, 19: 7921; DeWilde et al., "Migratory Workers in Southwestern Michigan," August 5, 1940, SCUCLA, CM, box 14, f: migratory labor—Mich.; Daniel O'Connor to Frances Perkins, December 12, 1940, NA, RG 174, f: migratory labor, 1940; W. V. Allen, "Agricultural Crop and Labor Survey: State of Michigan, September 1940," NA, RG 211, f: Michigan; "Report on Migratory Workers in Michigan and Wisconsin Region II FSA," SCUCLA, CMNC.

24. White House Conference on Child Health and Protection, Committee on the School Child, Sub-Committee on the Migrant School Child, "Report," 16, UIL; Mervin George Smith, "An Economic Analysis of Tomato Production in Indiana," 1–7.

25. Select Committee, *Destitute Citizens*, 3: 983–990; Smith, "An Economic Analysis of Tomato Production in Indiana," 2–3; F. C. Gaylord and

K. I. Fawcett, *A Study of Grade, Quality and Price of Canned Tomatoes Sold at Retail in Indiana*, 5.

26. *Indianapolis Star*, August 17, 1938, August 19, 1939; Select Committee, *Destitute Citizens*, 3: 979.

27. Ham, "Sugar Beet Field Labor"; Elizabeth Johnson, "Wages, Employment Conditions, and Welfare of Sugar Beet Laborers," 339; Cletus E. Daniel, *Bitter Harvest: A History of California Farmworkers, 1870–1941*, 259–260.

28. The most important extant studies of Mexicano agricultural unionism during the 1930s include parts of Jamieson, *Labor Unionism*; Schwartz, *Seasonal Farm Labor*; Daniel, *Bitter Harvest*; Carey McWilliams, *Factories in the Field: The Story of Migratory Farm Labor in California*; Linda C. Majka and Theo J. Majka, *Farm Workers, Agribusiness and the State*; Sam Kushner, *Long Road to Delano*.

29. *Labor Advocate*, April 17, 1930; Anastacio Rodríguez to Alfredo C. Vásquez, April 10, 1930, IV/662.1 (73-25)/1, SRE.

30. Bernard Sternsher, "Scioto Marsh Onion Workers Strike, Hardin County, Ohio, 1934"; Taylor, *Adrift on the Land*, 26; Jim Rizor to Frances Perkins, July 24, 1934, Robert C. Fox to H. L. Kerwin, January 11, 1936, and Hardin County Relief Commission, "Marion Township Survey, 1934," NA, RG 280, 176/1691; interview, Henry Pomerenck, October 18, 1939, MSA, JT, box 227, f: 4; Otto W. Brach to William Green, July 21, 1934, NA, RG 280, 176/1691; Ohio State Federation of Labor, *1934 Proceedings*, 101–102.

31. Interview, Harry Bubaven, June 5, 1941, BL, SJFN, f: 13; Carl Drumm, *A Complete History of the Scioto Marsh*, 62; J. B. Stambaugh *vs.* J. M. Rizor, June 29, 1934, EL, box 23, f: 1; Otto Brach to William Green, July 21, 1934, and Robert C. Fox to H. L. Kerwin, August 27, 1934, NA, RG 280, 176/1691.

32. Allen D. Ochs to Chet Darby, July 20, 1934, NA, RG 59, FERA state file, Ohio, f: 1.

33. Robert C. Fox to H. L. Kerwin, August 27, 1934, NA, RG 280, 176/1691.

34. *Toledo Blade*, August 26, 28, September 21, 1934, April 3, 1935; American Civil Liberties Union, *The Struggle for Civil Liberty on the Land*, 25–28.

35. *Toledo Blade*, September 10, 12, November 23, December 22, 1934, September 11, 1935; *Rural Worker*, December 1935.

36. Ochs to Darby, July 20, 1934, NA, RG 59, FERA state file, Ohio, f: 1; Select Committee, *Destitute Citizens*, 3: 1131; Barbara Stokes, "Report of Field Investigation, June 21–July 5, 1937," PHS, CWHM, box 21, f: Michigan; "The Transient Labor Problem in Stockbridge and Vicinity," MSA, JT, box 226, f: 7; Robert E. Lucas and Willah Weddon, *Muck Farmers, Farmers Week: 50th Annual Meeting*, 1–8; *Rural Worker*, April 1936.

37. Sternsher, "Scioto Marsh Onion Workers," 81; *Toledo Blade*, June 10, June 22, 26, July 5, 1935.

38. *Rural Worker*, August, 1935; *Lima News*, January 4, 1936; *Findlay Republican Courier*, June 22, 1935.

39. Stanley V. White, "Toledo, Ohio Sugar Beet Wage Hearings," February 28, 1938, NA, RG 280, 196/139; Surfin, "Labor Organization," 557; *Rural*

Worker, May, June, October, 1936; Johnson, "Wages," 339; USDA, Annual Crop Summary, 1935, 39; Informe, Detroit, April, 1935, IV/241.04 (73-14)/"35"/1, SRE; Informe, Chicago, June, 1935, IV/241 (04) (73-10) "35"/1, SRE.

40. J. E. O'Connor, "Preliminary Report, Blissfield," NA, RG 280, 176/2321; Rural Worker, November, 1935, January, 1936; Toledo Blade, June 19, 1935.

41. C. P. Milham to Beet Growers, May 13, 1935, NA, RG 280, 176/2321; J. E. O'Connor, "Summary of Final Report, Blissfield," NA, RG 280, 176/2321; Informe Detroit, April, 1935, IV/241.04 (73-14)/"35"/1, SRE; Johnson, Welfare of Families, 92.

42. Toledo Blade, June 3, 4, 10, 24, 26, 1935; Rural Worker, January, 1936; Findlay Republican Courier, June 24, 25, 26, 1935.

43. Rural Worker, June, October, 1936.

44. Jamieson, Labor Unionism, 384.

45. Fort Lupton Press, November 17, 1938; Johnson, "Wages," 332; Thaden, "Mexican Migratory Laborers in the Sugar Beet Fields of Michigan," 22, MSA, JT, box 223, f: 2.

46. "Toledo Hearings," and White to J. L. Steelman, November 1, 1937, February 27, 1938, and Steelman to Henrik Shipstead, March 26, 1938, NA, RG 280, 196/139; Bay City Times, February 25, 1938.

47. Select Committee, National Defense Migration, 19: 7803.

48. Ibid., 24: 9255, and 19: 7805; Thaden, "Mexican Migratory Laborers," 31, MSA, JT, box 223, f: 2.

49. Detroit Free Press, May 20, 1938; W. P. Knapp to District Director, I.N.S., May 16, 1934, NA, RG 174, f: employment—labor policies; Robert M. Pilkington, "Progress Report," May 24, 1938, NA, RG 280, 199/1985.

50. Detroit News, April 9, May 5, 1935; Detroit Free Press, April 10, 1935; Select Committee, National Defense Migration, 19: 7912–7913; George Kaplan to Cordell Hull, May 11, 1935, NA, RG 59. 311.1215/81; Informe, Detroit, April, 1935," IV/241.04 (73-14)/"35"/1, SRE; Lincoln Star, April 20, 1936; Denver Post, March 13, 1936.

51. Select Committee, Destitute Citizens, 3: 1272, and 4: 1830; Detroit Labor News, June 5, 1938, SCUCLA, CMNC; Francis J. Dillon to Frances Perkins, May 18, 1938, NA, RG 280, 199/1985; J. H. Bond, "Statement on Problems of USDL," J. H. Bond to John Thaden, August 6, 1941, MSA, JT, box 227, f: 1; USDA and Michigan Department of Agriculture, Annual Crop Summary, 1939, 45; Select Committee, National Defense Migration, 19: 7779; Dillon to Perkins, May 18, 1938, NA, RG 280, 199/1985; Thaden, "Mexican Migratory Laborers," 54, MSA, JT, box 223, f: 2; Carey McWilliams, "Mexicans to Michigan"; J. F. Thaden, Field Notes on Migratory Beet Workers, MSA, JT, box 222, f: 3. On Associated Farmers' fascism, see McWilliams, Factories in the Field, 231–263.

52. Robert M. Pilkington, "Blissfield Progress Report," May 24, 1938, NA, RG 280, 199/1985; U.S. Congress, Senate, Committee on Education and Labor, Violations of Free Speech and Rights of Labor, Report no. 398, pt. 4, 1601–1603; Dillon to Perkins, May 18, 1938, NA, RG 280, 199/1985; "Want, Terror Ride through Michigan Sugar Beet Fields Like Four Horsemen," clip-

ping, June 17, 1938, SCUCLA, CMNC; *Toledo Blade*, May 20, 1938: *Detroit Free Press*, May 21, 1938; Jamieson, *Labor Unionism*, 386.

53. Pilkington to Perkins, May 19, 1938, NA, RG 280, 199/1985.

54. Pilkington to Steelman, June 1, 1938, NA, RG 280, 199/1985.

55. Jamieson, *Labor Unionism*, 387; *Detroit News*, March 13, 1941; David Brown to Stanley White, September 23, 1938, and White, Final Report, October 6, 1938, NA, RG 280, 195/2465; White to Steelman, October 2, 1938, NA, RG 280, 199/2465; Emilia Angela Rojo, "Between Two Cultures: A Phenomenological Participatory Investigation of the Enduring Struggle of a Mexican-American Community," 36, 54.

56. Hendrickson, "Sugar Beet Laborer," 46–57; Reisler, *By the Sweat*, 248.

57. Mark Reisler, "Mexican Unionization in California Agriculture," 578.

58. *Greeley Tribune*, October 12, 13, 14, 1938; *Pueblo Chieftain*, May 2, 1939; *Trinidad Chronicle Gazette*, October 12, 1938; *Rocky Mountain News*, May 21, 1938; interview, Thomas Mahoney, September 25, 1940, f: 5. BL, SJFN.

4. A Midwestern Grapes of Wrath, 1938–1942

1. Walter J. Stein, *California and the Dust Bowl Migration*, 91; Select Committee, *Destitute Citizens*, 3: 1324; Report of Migrant Work in Mid-Western Area, Helen White, Supervisor, July, August, September, 1942, PHS, HMC, box 41, f: Midwest 1940s.

2. Migrant Survey, Brown City, Michigan, PHS, HMC; box 50, interview, Cecundino Reyes, December 25, 1983.

3. Interviews, Patterson, Santos Vásquez, and Clay Cochran, BL, SJFN, f: 6; Selden C. Menefree, *Mexican Migratory Workers of South Texas*; Texas State Employment Service (hereafter TSES), Unemployment Compensation Division, *Annual Report of the Farm Placement Service, Texas, 1939*, 17; John Thaden to C. E. Marcum, November 14, 1940, MSA, JT, box 227, f: 1; Survey Analysis: Mid-West Area, 1943, PHS, HMC, box 41, f: Midwest 1940.

4. Selden C. Menefree and Orin C. Cassmore, *The Pecan Shellers of San Antonio*; interview, Juan Luna, December 25, 1983; "The Mexican Pecan Shellers," BL, SJFN, f: 6; Julia Kirk Blackwelder, *Women of the Depression: Caste and Culture in San Antonio, 1929–1939*, 141–151.

5. Select Committee, *Destitute Citizens*, 5: 1919; interviews, Andrew Anguiano, June 21, 1984, and Juan Luna, December 25, 1983.

6. Menefree, *Mexican Migratory Workers*, 29; Johnson, "Wages," 335–337; Beet Worker Statements, 1939, MSA, JT, box 226, f: 10.

7. Montejano, *Anglos and Mexicans*, 208, 210–213; TSES, "Supplement to Origins and Problems of Texas Migratory Farm Labor," 16, TSA; Texas Bureau of Labor Statistics, *Texas Laws concerning Employment and Emigrant Agencies*.

8. T.Y. Collins to Ben L. Owens, April 23, 1940, LMT, f: 3.

9. Select Committee, *Destitute Citizens*, 3: 1272–1273, and 5: 1846–1848; Thaden, "Mexican Migratory Laborers," 31, MSA, JT, box 223, f: 2;

interview, Andrew Anguiano, June 21, 1984; McWilliams, "Mexicans to Michigan", 5–9.

10. Thaden, "Mexican Migratory Laborers," 73, MSA, JT, box 223; f: 2; Select Committee, *National Defense Migration*, 19: 7796–7800.

11. McWilliams, "Mexicans to Michigan," 6–11; interview, Juan Luna, August 31, 1982.

12. W. V. Allen, "Agricultural Crop and Labor Survey: State of Michigan, September 1940," NA, RG 211, WMC Bureau of Placement, Rural Industries Division, f: Michigan; Thaden, "Mexican Migratory Laborers," 73; *Migration*, 5: 1848–1850.

13. U.S. Congress, House, Committee on Labor, *To Regulate Private Employment Agencies*, 22; interview, Efraín Marínez, June 6, 1984; "AFL Asks U.S. to Stop Importation of Mexican Labor," June 3, 1938, SCUCLA, CMNC; interview, Juan Luna, August 31, 1982.

14. Select Committee, *Destitute Citizens*, 5: 1843.

15. Ibid., 1848–1850; interviews, Cecundino Reyes, December 25, 1983, and Juan Luna, August 31, 1982.

16. Katherine F. Unroot, "The Migrant Laborer in the Present Situation," February 8, 1936, 2, PHS, CWHM, box 2, f: migrant literature and reports; TSES, Farm Placement Division, "Supplement to Origins," 30, TSA; "Will Prosecute for Hauling Mexicans: I.C.C. Will Act under Common Carrier Laws," clipping, June 24, 1938, SCUCLA, CMNC.

17. Interview, Juan Luna, August 31, 1982.

18. Interviews, Regina Anguiano, June 21, 1984, Juan Luna, August 31, 1982; Forrest G. Brown, Department of Labor and Industry, Lansing, Michigan, May 13–14, 1938, SCUCLA, CM, box 16, f: minorities—Mexican.

19. Select Committee, *Destitute Citizens*, 3: 1303; F. B. O'Connell, Investigation of Mexicans Entering Michigan by Truck, May 8, 1938, SCUCA, CM, box 16, f: minorities—Mexican; Jarrard Potter to L. A. Lyons, May 13, 1938, SCUCLA, CM, box 16, f: minorities—Mexican; "Trucks Bootleg Mexican Labor into State Beet Fields While Jobless Rolls Grow," clipping, June 5, 1938, SCUCLA, CMNC.

20. J. H. Bond to John Thaden, August 6, 1941, MSA, JT, box 227, f: 1; Migrant Survey, Brown City, PHS, HMC, box 50; TSES, Farm Placement Division, "Supplement to Origins," 26, TSA.

21. Paul S. Taylor, "Migratory Farm Labor, 541; Select Committee, *Destitute Citizens*, 3: 1232–1233, 1337–1338; John DeWilde et al., "Migratory Workers of Southwestern Michigan," August 5, 1940, 2–3, SCUCLA, CM, box 14, f: migratory labor—Mich.; Report of the Work with Migrants, Villa Ridge, Illinois, 1942, PHS, HMC, box 41, f: Illinois.

22. Charles T. Bush, "Migrant Southern Labor," 1942, MSA, JT, box 226, f: 2; Orlando Tusler, Survey of Hart, Michigan, PHS, CWHM, box 21, f: Michigan; Select Committee, *National Defense Migration*, 19: 7949.

23. Select Committee, *National Defense Migration*, 19: 7918–7927.

24. De Wilde et al., "Migratory Workers in Southwestern Michigan," August 5, 1940, 1, SCUCLA, CM, box 14, f: migratory labor—Mich.; Schwartz, *Seasonal Farm Labor*, 62; Select Committee, *National Defense Migration*,

19: 7925, 7949; USDA, Farm Security Administration, "Summary of a Field Survey of Migrant Farm Labor in Berrien County, Michigan, 1940," MSA, JT, box 225, f: 4.

25. *Lansing State Journal*, March 13, 1941; *Benton Harbor News-Palladium*, July 24, 1940; Select Committee, *National Defense Migration*, 19: 7949; Erdmann Doane Benyon, "The Southern White Laborer Migrates to Michigan," 340–342.

26. Select Committee, *Destitute Citizens*, 3: 1302, Select Committee, *National Defense Migration*, 19: 7948–7950; Thaden, "Mexican Migratory Laborers," 3, MSA, JT, box 223, f: 2.

27. "Migrant Service in the Mid-West," September 1941, and Report of Migrant Work in Mid-Western Area, Helen White, July–September, 1942, PHS, HMC, box 41, f: Midwest 1940s.

28. Select Committee, *Destitute Citizens*, 5: 1808–1809; Select Committee, *National Defense Migration*, 19: 7946, and 23: 9258; Susan Fisher Burns Migrant Center, PHS, HMC, box 41, f: Midwest 1940s; "Mid-West Work in Michigan," PHS, HMC, box 50.

29. Select Committee, *Destitute Citizens*, 3: 1104; Thaden, "Migratory Agricultural Workers in Michigan, August 18, 1949," 5, MSA, box 223, f: 3.

30. Menefree, *Mexican Migratory Workers*, 25; interview, Trinidad Moreno, June 13, 1984.

31. Thaden, "Mexican Migratory Workers," 58, MSA, JT, box 223, f: 2; interviews, Juan Luna, August 31, 1982, Regina Anguiano, June 22, 1984, Efraín Marínez, June 6, 1984.

32. Mid-West Work: Blissfield, Michigan, 1942, PHS, HMC, box 50, PHS; interview, Regina Anguiano, June 22, 1984.

33. Select Committee, *National Defense Migration*, 19: 7941–7943; "Florence Brooks, Brown City, Mich.," and K. B. Clark to John Thaden, December 22, 1942, MSA, JT, box 225, f: 4, MSA; interview, Juan Luna, August 31, 1982; "The Story of the Román Family," PHS, CWHM, box 42, f: Michigan; "Church of the Brethren Shepherd Work Camp," PHS, HMC, box 49; Report of Mrs. Winnie Lende, Indiana, Sept. 1–Sept. 19, 1941, PHS, HMC, box 41, f: Indiana, 1940s.

34. Orlando Tusler, "Survey of Traverse City, Michigan," PHS, CWHM, box 21, f: Michigan; *Detroit News*, August 7, 1938; *Traverse City Record-Eagle*, July 24, 1940; "Report on Migratory Workers in Michigan and Wisconsin Region II FSA," SCUCLA, CM, box 14, f: migratory labor—Mich.; Barbara Stokes, "National Child Labor Committee, Report of Field Investigation, June 21–July 5, 1937," PHS, CWHM, box 21, f: Michigan.

35. Villa Ridge, 1942, PHS, HMC, box 41, f: Illinois; Select Committee, *National Defense Migration*, 19: 7924, and 23: 9236; W. V. Allen, "Agricultural Crop and Labor Survey Michigan," September, 1940, NA, RG 211, Bureau of Placement, Rural Industries Division, f: Michigan.

36. USES, *Michigan Labor Market Bulletin*, 1942, series no. 1, NA, RG 183, f: Michigan 1941–1945; Allen, "Agricultural Crop and Labor Survey," NA, RG 211, f: Michigan; Farm Security Administration (FSA), "Report on Migratory Workers in Michigan and Wisconsin," SCUCLA, box 14, f: migra-

tory labor—Michigan; Select Committee, *Destitute Citizens*, 3: 1130; Select Committee, *National Defense Migration*, 23: 9249.

37. *Migration*, 19: 7924; interview, Andrew Anguiano, June 21, 1984; interview, Cecundino Reyes, December 25, 1983.

38. Select Committee, *Destitute Citizens*, 3: 978; Select Committee, *National Defense Migration*, 19: 7928–7931, 7946; "Migrant Survey, Brown City," PHS, HMC, box 50.

39. Menefree, *Mexican Migratory Workers*, xiii–xv; Select Committee, *National Defense Migration*, 19: 7855–7862, 7952–7953; Thaden, "Mexican Migratory Laborers," 70, MSA, JT, box 223, f: 2.

40. TSES, Farm Placement Division, "Supplement to Origins," 16, TSA; Select Committee, *National Defense Migration*, 19: 7945; Forrest G. Brown, Investigation of Mexican Laborers, Lansing Michigan, May 13–14, 1938, SCUCLA, CM, box 16, f: minorities—Mexican.

41. Select Committee, *National Defense Migration*, 23: 9257–9258; interview, L. W. Erickson, February 10, 1939, MSA, JT, box 227, f: 1; Thaden, "Mexican Migratory Laborers," 62–64, MSA, JT, box 223, f: 2; Migrant Problem at Barryton, Michigan, PHS, CWHM, box 21, f: Michigan.

42. Thaden, "Mexican Migratory Laborers," 53, 64–65, MSA, JT, box 223, f: 2; Tusler, "Survey of Traverse City," PHS, CWHM, box 21, f: Michigan; interview, Trinidad Moreno, June 13, 1984.

43. Migrant Service in Villa Ridge, Illinois, May–June 1941, PHS, HMC, box 41, f: Illinois, 1940s; Berrien and Van Buren County, PHS, HMC, box 49; Select Committee, *Destitute Citizens*, 3: 1264.

44. Select Committee, *National Defense Migration*, 19: 7951; "Migrant Survey Brown City," PHS, HMC, box 50; Daniel T. O'Connor, "Migratory Labor in Berrien County," 7, SCUCLA, CM, box 14, f: migratory labor—Michigan; Winnie Lende, Michigan Territory, PHS, HMC, box 50; De Wilde et al., "Southwestern Michigan, SCUCLA, CM, box 14, f: migratory labor—Mich.; "Migratory Workers in Michigan and Wisconsin," SCUCLA, CM, box 14, f: migratory labor—Mich.; Traverse City, July–August, 1942, PHS, HMC, box 50.

45. Tusler, "Survey of Traverse City," PHS, CWHM, box 21, f: Michigan, Daniel O'Connor to Frances Perkins, December 10, 1940, NA, RG 174, f: migratory labor, 1940.

46. Modest Caluwe to Frances Perkins, November 16, 1937, NA, RG 280, 196/139; Tusler, "Survey of Traverse City," PHS, CWHM, box 21, f: Michigan; Select Committee, *Destitute Citizens*, 3: 1257, and 19: 7949; De Wilde et al., "Southwestern Michigan," 8, SCUCLA, CM, box 14, f: migratory labor—Mich.; O'Connor to Perkins, December 10, 1940, NA, RG 174, f: migratory labor, 1940; interview, Woodman, November 27, 1941, MSA, JT, box 227, f: 1; Mid-West Work: Michigan, Arthur Eikamp, Community Worker, summer, 1942, PHS, HMC, box 50.

47. Traverse City, July–August, 1942, and Work with Migrants, Leelanau County, Michigan, 1942, PHS, HMC, box 50; interviews, Regina Anguiano, June 21, 1984, and Cecundino Reyes, December 25, 1983.

48. Select Committee, *Destitute Citizens*, 3: 979–980, 993–996.

49. Select Committee, *National Defense Migration*, 23: 9245; Arthur Ei-kamp, "Mid-West Work in Michigan, summer 1942," PHS, HMC, box 50; Il-linois Church Council, *Illinois Neighbors—1941*, MSA, JT, box 230, f: 2; FSA, "Survey Berrien County," MSA, JT, box 225, f: 4; O'Connor, "Migra-tory Labor in Berrien County," 11–14, SCUCLA, CM, box 14, f: migratory labor—Mich.

50. Traverse City, July–August, 1942, PHS, HMC, box 41, f: Midwest 1940s; Migrant Work in Mid-Western Area, July–September, 1942, PHS, HMC, box 41, f: Midwest 1940s.

51. Interview, Bill Reimer, December 6, 1941, MSA, JT, box 226, f: 3; Mid-West Work in Michigan, summer 1942, PHS, HMC, box 50.

52. Interview, Mrs. Due Norton, MSA, JT, box 227, f: 1; "County by County Study, 1937," SCUCLA, CM, box 14, f: migratory labor—Mich.; Sur-vey Analysis: Mid-West Area, 1943, PHS, HMC, box 41, f: Midwest 1940s; Florence Brooks, "Abuses Connected with the Seasonal Migration of Mexi-cans to Michigan," PHS, HMC, box 50.

53. Interview, Ronald C. Wagner, January 1, 1941, MSA, JT, box 227, f: 1; "Survey Analysis: Midwest Area, 1943," PHS, HMC, box 41, f: Midwest 1940s.

54. Brooks, "Abuses Connected with the Seasonal Migration of Mexicans to Michigan," PHS, HMC, box 50; Report of the Mexican Children's Center, Alma, Michigan, 1940, PHS, CWHM, box 21, f: Michigan; Thaden, "Mexican Migratory Laborers, " 74 MSA, JT, box 223, f: 2.

55. Bureau of Employment Security (hereafter BESC), "Farm Labor Mar-ket Conditions, September 15–October 15, 1941," 5, 16, 17, RG 10, SG 3, f: 523; Report Breckenridge, Michigan, 1942, PHS, HMC, box 50; Report of Migrant Work in Mid-Western Area, July–September, 1942, PHS, HMC, box 41, f: Midwest 1940s; Survey Analysis: Mid-West Area, 1943, PHS, HMC, box 41, f: Midwest 1940s; *Migration*, 4: 1409.

56. Robert Lincoln Kelley to A. J. Ballard, January 23, 1937, PHS, CWHM, box 21, f: Michigan; Villa Ridge, 1942, PHS, HMC, box 41, f: Illinois.

57. Select Committee, *Destitute Citizens*, 3: 1264.

58. De Wilde et al., "Southwestern Michigan," 7, SCUCLA, CM, box 14, f: migratory labor—Mich.

59. Ibid., 12; Arthur Eikamp, in "Mid-West Work in Michigan, summer, 1942," PHS, HMC, box 50.

60. *Indianapolis News*, August 23, 1938; Select Committee, *Destitute Citizens*, 3: 1128.

61. *Indianapolis Star*, August 16, 17, 19, 1939; *Franklin Evening Star*, August 16, 1939.

62. Interviews, Andrew Anguiano, June 21, 1984, and Efrain Marínez, June 6, 1984; O'Connor, "Migratory Labor in Berrien County," 9, SCUCLA, CM, box 14, f: migratory labor—Mich.; Breckenridge, 1942, PHS, HMC, box 50; Migrant Problem at Barryton, Michigan, PHS, CWHM, box 21, f: Michigan.

63. *Lansing State Journal*, July 6, 1941; interviews, Andrew Anguiano, June 21, 1984, and Trinidad Moreno, June 13, 1984.

64. Select Committee, *National Defense Migration,* 19: 7977, and 23: 9244; Benyon, "Southern White Laborer," 340–342.

65. Select Committee, *Destitute Citizens,* 3: 1087–1093, 1336.

66. Thaden field notes, MSA, JT, B 222, f: 3; Thaden to Florence Brooks, January 26, 1941, MSA, JT, box 225, f: 4; interview, María Castellanos, June 8, 1984.

67. Interviews, Rev. Alberto Moreno, MSA, JT, box 227, f: 1; Juan Luna, August 31, 1982.

68. Thaden to Brooks, January 26, 1941, MSA, JT, box 225, f: 4; Select Committee, *Destitute Citizens,* 5: 1830, 1927; interview, María Castellanos, June 8, 1984.

69. Thaden, "Mexican Migratory Laborers," 8, MSA, JT, box 223, f: 2; Select Committee, *Destitute Citizens,* 3: 1293.

70. Select Committee, *Destitute Citizens,* 3: 1298; McWilliams, "County by County Survey," SCUCLA, CM, box 14, f: migratory labor—Mich.; Thaden, "Mexican Migratory Laborers," 49, MSA, JT, box 223, f: 2; interview, Ramiro González, June 7, 1984.

71. TSES, "Supplement to Origins," 16, TSA; "The Story of the Román Family," PHS, CWHM, box 21, f: Michigan; Brooks, "Abuses," PHS, HMC, box 50; Committee on Labor, *Private Employment Agencies,* 22–23; "AFL Asks U.S.," SCUCLA, CMNC; interview, Efraín Marínez, June 6, 1984.

72. Select Committee, *National Defense Migration,* 19: 7796–7855.

73. Ibid., 7800, 7816–7834.

74. John Thaden to Carey McWilliams, October 18, 1941, MSA, JT, box 224, f: 4.

75. TSES, "Supplement to Origins," 8, TSA; Select Committee, *Destitute Citizens,* 5: 1964.

76. Interviews, Andrew Anguiano, June 21, 1984, Juan Luna, August 31, 1982.

77. Brooks, "Abuses," PHS, HMC, box 50; "Krogstad Gives Michigan Sugar Firm Ultimatum: Charges of Abuses of Labor Brings Orders from State Department to 'Clean House' in Two Weeks," September 7, 1937, SCUCLA, CMNC; Majka and Majka, *Farm Workers,* 108–112; TSES, *Farm Placement Service, Texas, 1939,* 10; O'Connor, "Migratory Labor in Berrien County," 14, SCUCLA, CM, box 14, f: migratory labor—Mich.; Select Committee, *National Defense Migration,* 19: 7951–7952, 7958–7963; Thaden, "Mexican Migratory Laborers," 38, MSA, JT, box 223, f: 2.

78. *Detroit News,* March 13, 1941; *Lansing State Journal,* March 13, 1941; *Benton Harbor News-Palladium,* June 15, 1951; "On Worker Camps," MSA, JT, box 222, f: 3; Select Committee, *National Defense Migration,* 19: 7962; Majka and Majka, *Farm Workers,* 108–111, 127, 129.

79. O'Connor, "Migratory Labor in Berrien County," 9, SCUCLA, CM, box 14, f: migratory labor—Mich.; *Lansing State Journal,* March 13, 1941; Select Committee, *National Defense Migration,* 19: 7962–7963.

80. Select Committee, *National Defense Migration,* 19: 7958; *Lansing State Journal,* March 13, 1941; Galarza, *Farm Workers,* 129–132.

81. Moorhead Children's Center, 1942, PHS, HMC, box 41, f: Minnesota reports 1940s; Florence Brooks to Thaden, n.d., MSA, JT, B 225, f: 4; Select Committee, *National Defense Migration*, 3: 1340, and 19: 7952; "Shepherd Work Camp," PHS, HMC, box 49.

82. De Wilde et al., "Southwestern Michigan," 9, SCUCLA, CM, box 14, f: migratory labor—Mich.; Select Committee, *Destitute Citizens*, 3: 1257, 1265; "Offer Farm Labor Plan: Ban Mexicans—Use Labor from North," SCUCLA, n.d., CMNC.

83. L. H. Gaston to C. D. Barrett, September 13, 1937, SCUCLA, CM, box 16, f: minorities—Mexican; C. C. Slemans, "Health Problems Created by Importation of Labor from Southern States for Work in Sugar Beet Fields," Michigan Department of Public Health (hereafter MDPH), October 22, 1937, SCUCLA, CM, box 16, f: minorities—Mexican.

84. Select Committee, *National Defense Migration*, 19: 7793.

85. MDPH, news release, MDPH (Acc 70-9) lot 11, box 1, SCUCLA, CM, f: 6; Select Committee, *National Defense Migration*, 19: 7791, 7792; Mid-West Work: Blissfield, Michigan, 1942, PHS, HMC, box 50; MDPH, *70th Annual Report of the Commissioner*, 73.

86. Select Committee, *Destitute Citizens*, 3: 1317–1319, and 19: 7794–7796; Floyd R. Town, Isabella County Health Department, September 25, 1937, SCUCLA, CM, box 16, f: minorities—Mexican.

87. Thaden, "Mexican Migratory Laborers," 91, MSA, JT, box 223, f: 2.

88. Select Committee, *National Defense Migration*, 19: 7795; MDPH, *70th Annual Report*, 73; interviews, Juan Luna, December 25, 1983, Andrew Anguiano, June 21, 1984.

89. Thaden Field Notes, 1942, MSA, JT, box 225, f: 4; MDPH, news release, February 19, 1942, MSA, MDPH (Acc 70-9), lot 11, box 1, f: 5; MDPH, news releases, June 14, 1942, April 6, 1943, MSA, MDPH, lot 11, box 1, f: 6; Anthony Calomeni, "Fluoroscopic Examination of the Migratory Sugar Beet Workers for 1942," MSA, JT, box 227, f: 3.

90. Select Committee, *National Defense Migration*, 19: 7554.

91. Select Committee, *Destitute Citizens*, 3: 1320.

92. Ibid., 1323; interview, Trinidad Moreno, June 13, 1984.

93. Dorothy Fox to Thaden, October 30, 1939, MSA, JT, box 227, f: 1; Select Committee, *National Defense Migration*, 19: 7787; Select Committee, *Destitute Citizens*, 3: 992, 1134.

94. Select Committee, *Destitute Citizens*, 3: 867–869, 1104, 1131.

95. Report of Reverend Emmett B. Waite, July 30, 1942, PHS, HMC, box 50; O'Connor, "Migratory Labor in Berrien County," SCUCLA, CM, box 14, f: migratory labor—Mich.

96. Fox to Thaden, MSA, JT, box 227, f: 1; O. B. Moore to Thaden and Thaden notes, MSA, JT, box 227, f: 4.

97. Select Committee, *Destitute Citizens*, 3: 1104; Select Committee, *National Defense Migration*, 19: 7903–7904.

98. Select Committee, *Destitute Citizens*, 19: 7903–7904.

99. Thaden, "Mexican Migratory Laborers," 82, MSA, JT, box 223, f: 2;

McWilliams, "County by County Study," SCUCLA, CM, box 14, f: migratory labor—Mich.; Select Committee, Destitute Citizens, 3: 1338; Field Notes, MSA, JT, box 222, f: 3.

100. Thaden, "Mexican Migratory Laborers," 83, MSA, JT, box 233, f: 2.

101. Select Committee, National Defense Migration, 19: 7911; Thaden, "Mexican Migratory Laborers," 76, 80, MSA, JT, box 223, f: 2.

102. "Shepherd Work Camp," PHS, HMC, box 49; Select Committee, National Defense Migration, 19: 7915–7917, 7949; "County by County Study, 1937," SCUCLA, CM, box 14, f: migratory labor—Mich.; V. K. Volk to C. D. Barrett, October 13, 1937, SCUCLA, CM, box 16, f: minorities—Mexican.

103. CWHM, Minutes of Committee on Migrant Work, February 6, 1939, PHS, CWHM, box 1, f: Council of Women—minutes of Committee on Migrant Work; Community Center for Mexican Sugar Beet Workers, PHS, HMC, box 49; Michigan Christian Advocate, November 25, 1941; interview, Trinidad Moreno, June 13, 1984; Migrant Work in Michigan, PHS, CWHM, box 21, f: Michigan.

104. Report of Michigan Migrant Center, June 6 to August 6, 1938, PHS, HMC, box 49; Mexican Children's Center at Mt. Pleasant, Michigan, season of 1940, PHS, CWHM, box 21, f: Michigan reports 1935–1940; Report of a Summer's Work in Migrant Camps, 1937, PHS, CWHM, box 2; interview, Trinidad Moreno, June 13, 1984.

105. Report of the Michigan Migrant Center, PHS, HMC, box 49; Michigan Christian Advocate, November 25, 1941; interview, Trinidad Moreno, June 13, 1984.

106. Migrant Work in Mid-Western Area, July–September, 1942, PHS, HMC, box 41, f: Midwest 1940s; Mexican Children's Center, Alma, Michigan, 1940, PHS, CWHM, box 21, f: Michigan reports, 1935–1940; Lansing State Journal, June 18, 1940; Tusler, Survey of Hart, PHS, CWHM, box 21, f: Michigan; Migrant Survey, Brown City, PHS, HMC, box 50.

107. Mt. Pleasant Migrant Report, 1941, and Mid-West Work: Blissfield, Michigan, summer 1942, PHS, HMC, box 50; interview, Trinidad Moreno, June 13, 1984.

108. E. B. Hill, George A. Brown, H. C. Rather, R. V. Gardner, criticisms of Thaden ms., MSA, JT, box 229, f: 3.

5. Foreign Workers and Control, 1942–1950

1. Majka and Majka, Farm Workers, 137.

2. A. B. Love and H. P. Gaston, Michigan's Emergency Farm Labor 1943–1947; L. G. Sorden, Erven Long, and Margaret Salock, Wisconsin Farm Labor Program, 1943–1947.

3. Carey McWilliams, "California and the Wetback," 19.

4. Ernesto Galarza, "Program for Action," 31; Hank Hasiwar, "The Corporate Farmer: Agriculture's Newest Blight," 16.

5. Alan Clive, "The Michigan Farmer in World War II," 314; Bay City Times, May 14, 1943; Detroit News, November 5, 1942; U.S. Bureau of the Census, Census of Agriculture, 1950.

6. Grant County, Indiana, 1943, PHS, HMC, box 50; Smith, "Economic Analysis," 7–9.

7. Rochelle, Illinois, June–August, 1949, PHS, HMC, box 41, f: Illinois, 1940s; J. Z. Rowe, "Migrant Farm Labor in Indiana," 1; *Bay City Times*, April 10, 1943.

8. Statement on Policy, NA, RG 174, f: War Manpower Commission—recruitment of domestic and Mexican agricultural workers; Farm Placement Activities of USES, Ohio, February 6, 1942, NA, RG 211, f: Ohio; Schwartz, *Seasonal Farm Labor*, 71–72; *Detroit Free Press*, July 12, 1942; *Lansing State Journal*, March 13, 1941, October 5, 1942; Daniel M. Tracy to Frank P. Fenton, May 20, 1942, NA, RG 174, f: migratory labor 1942; Walter Erb to J. L. Taylor, June 4, 1943, NA, RG 224, f: farm labor 53—certification (Michigan); N. Gregory Silvermaster to Wayne H. Darrow, n.d., NA, RG 224, f: farm labor-7; Arthur A. Schupp to Wayne H. Darrow, April 10, 1943, and Farmers and Manufacturers Beet Sugar Association, "Migratory Agricultural Labor Requirements in the East North Central States," NA, RG 224; f: farm labor 9-1; *Bay City Times*, October 28, 29, 1942; *Detroit News*, December 15, 1942; W. R. Frey to Harry F. Kelly, MSA, HK, box 64, f: 4; Kay Diekman Willson, "The Historical Development of Migrant Labor in Michigan Agriculture," 62; U.S. Congress, House, Subcommittee of the Committee on Appropriations, *Farm Labor Program, 1944*, 87; Love and Gaston, *Michigan's Emergency Farm Labor*, 5–10.

9. J. Z. Rowe and J. B. Kohlmeyer, *Migrant Farm Labor in Indiana*, 2; U.S. Subcommittee of the House Committee on Appropriations, *Farm Labor Program, 1944*, 111–112; *Lansing State Journal*, June 17, 1944.

10. James W. Coddington to August Ludwig, May 18, 1943, NA, RG 224, f: farm labor—7 (transportation); Edmundo Flores, "Mexican Migratory Workers in Wisconsin: A Study of Some Aspects of the War Food Administration Program for the Use of Mexican Agricultural Workers during 1945 in the State of Wisconsin," 37; *Lansing State Journal*, June 17, 1944, February 16, 1947; U.S. Congress, Senate, Committee on Appropriations, *Farm Labor Program, 1943*, 71–72, 87.

11. Michigan State Employment Service (hereafter MESC), Farm Placement Section, "Plan of Operations," WPR, CK, f: 1947–1948 affidavits; US, President's Commission on Migratory Labor (hereafter PCML), *Migratory Labor in American Agriculture*, 62–63, 96; *Indianapolis Star*, January 28, 1948; Luther Youngdahl to Paul D. Robinson, December 31, 1947, MHS, LY, executive letters, 1948, f: Farm Employment Advisory Committee; *Lansing State Journal*, February 16, 1947; *Indianapolis Star*, January 28, 1948; Committee on Labor and Public Welfare, *Migratory Labor 1952*, 1: 832.

12. Love and Gaston, *Michigan's Emergency Farm Labor*, 10; R. G. Coke to California Field Crops, September 22, 1942, NA, RG 211, Bureau of Placement, Files of the Chief, f: Mexican; Michigan Annual Report of Non-Profit Corporations—1946 Report of Michigan Field Crops Inc., Acc. 70-35, lot 15, box 315, MSA; *Fargo Forum*, September 16, 1948; A. G. Quamme, "Statement to Growers of Sugar Beets in the Mason City, Iowa, Territory"; Edgar Johnston, "Michigan's Step Children: The Social and Educational Status of

Migrant Children of Mexican Descent in Michigan," 115, PCML, box 14, f: Saginaw, Michigan, September 11, 12, 1950; Volkin and Bradford, *American Crystal*, 1.

13. Love and Gaston, *Michigan's Emergency Farm Labor*, 10; PCML, *Report of Proceedings*, 9: 249 (stenographic copy at WHS); Michigan Canner's Association to Paul V. McNutt, November 10, 1942, MSA, HK, box 54, f: 4.

14. PCML, *Migratory Labor*, 33, 98, 101; Ernesto Galarza, *Merchants of Labor: The Mexican Bracero Story*, 122, 127–130; Hoopeston, Illinois, September, 1948, PHS, HMC, box 41, f: Illinois, 1940s; U.S. Congress, Senate, Committee on Agriculture and Forestry, *Farm Labor Supply Program, 1947*, 69; Jack D. Brock and M. C. Henderson, "Migratory Labor—Its Problems and Their Solution," MHS, AC, 15.1, 10.4 F.

15. Michael Hechter, "Group Formation and the Cultural Division of Labor"; Alejandro Portes and Robert L. Bach, *Latin Journey: Cuban and Mexican Immigrants in the United States*, 3–20; Manuel García y Griego, "The Importation of Mexican Contract Laborers to the United States, 1942–1964: Antecedents, Operation and Legacy," 55–76; Juan R. García, *Operation Wetback: The Mass Deportation of Mexican Undocumented Workers in 1954*, 18–61; Richard B. Craig, *The Bracero Program: Interest Groups and Foreign Policy*; Coke to California Field Crops, NA, RG 211, Bureau of Placement, files of the Chief, f: Mexican; USDA, "Individual Work Agreement, 1943" SCSU, EG, box 18, f: 9; National Citizens Council for Migrant Labor, "Analysis of Agreement Signed February 17, 1948," WPR, CK, f: affidavits 1947–1948; Midwest Agricultural Workers Association, NA, RG 224, f: laborers 3—Mexicans; Barrera, *Race and Class in the Southwest*.

16. *Bay City Times*, April 7, 1943; Robert L. Wilson to George W. Hill, July 13, 1943, NA, RG 224, f: farm labor 4-1 Germans; Meeting for Joint Consideration by the Sugar Interests and the Railroads, March 22, 1943, MHS, GNVP, f: employing Mexican and Jap labor; Rojo, "Between Two Cultures," 38, 53; Rochelle, Illinois, April–May, 1948, PHS, HMC, box 41, f: Illinois, 1940s; Informe José Pérez Morales, May 22, 1946, WPR, CK, f: 1945–1946 affidavits.

17. Max E. Egloff, "British West Indian Workers in the United States," January 2, 1951, HST, PCML, box 15, f: staff studies, Nov. 1950–Feb. 1951; Committee on Appropriations, *Farm Labor Program, 1943*, 211; Wayne Darrow to Earl G. Harrison, March 24, 1943, NA, RG 224, Office of Labor, General Correspondence, f: farm labor 3: Bahamas.

18. Egloff, "British West Indian Workers in the United States," January 2, 1951, HST, PCML, box 15, f: staff studies, Nov. 1950–Feb. 1951; *Denver Post*, October 23, 1944; George W. Hill to Clarence Hurt, June 9, 1943, NA, RG 224, f: farm labor 53—certification (Minnesota); Hill to Hurt, June 18, 1943, NA, RG 224, f: farm labor 53—certification (Wisconsin); Herbert G. MacDonald to Philip G. Bruton, June 25, 1943, and Arthur A. Schupp to W. H. Talbert, June 9, 1943, NA, RG 224, f: farm labor 3:4 Jamaican; *Bay City Times*, May 21, June 3, June 24, 1943; *South Bend Tribune*, April 17, 1945; *Lansing State Journal*, June 17, 1944; Committee on Appropriations, *Farm Labor Program, 1943*; *Traverse City Record-Eagle*, July 19, 1943.

19. Dorothy Knowles, April Report, 1945, Minnesota, PHS, HMC, box 41, f: Midwest 1940s; PCML Proceedings, 9: 326, WHS; USES, Foreign Labor Program, November 1, 1948, HST, PCML, box 94, f: migratory labor— foreign, general; "Local employment agent," April 30, 1947, MHS, MAC, f: migrants, 3; *Indianapolis News,* May 14, 1944.

20. Minnesota, Governor's Interracial Commission, *The Mexican in Minnesota,* 16, 18; Max Howard Leftwich, "The Migratory Harvest Labor Market: An Illinois Case Study," 75, 94–98, 146–148; Robert L. Wilson to George W. Hill, July 13, 1943, NA, RG 224, f: farm labor 4-1; PCML Proceedings: 9: 100–103, WHS.

21. Leftwich, "Migratory Harvest Labor," 30, 44, 134; Minnesota Migrant Reports: Summary of 1944 Activities, and Quarterly Report on Migrant Work Midwestern Area: April–June, 1948, PHS, HMC, box 41, f: Midwest 1940s; PCML Proceedings: 9: 209–212, WHS; Rowe, "Migrant Farm Labor," 12–14.

22. Philip G. Bruton to H. J. Reed, July 26, 1943, NA, RG 224, Farm Labor 4-4; *Lansing State Journal,* June 17, 1944; Clive, "Michigan Farmer," 308–309; Grant County 1943, PHS, HMC, box 50; Arnold Krammer, *Nazi Prisoners of War in America,* vii, 83, 107; Leftwich, "Migratory Harvest Labor," 131.

23. Arnold Krammer, "Japanese Prisoners of War in America," 81–83; Leftwich, "Migratory Harvest Labor," 131–132; Krammer, *Nazi Prisoners,* 91–92, 107; Virgil L Bankson to N. Gregory Silvermaster, June 3, 1943, NA, RG 224, f: M 26, war prisoners; John Burkes to James W. Coddington, June 6, 1943, NA, RG 224, f: farm labor 4-1 Germans.

24. R. C. Lott to Claude Wickard, March 23, 1943, NA, RG 224, f: farm labor 5—recruitment, May, 1943; *Bay City Times,* February 18, 1943; *Detroit News,* February 10, 1943; Report on Migrant Projects in Mid-West Area, 1943, PHS, HMC, box 41, f: Midwest 1940s; Minnesota Migrant Report, 1943, MHS, CWUM, f: migrants, 1944–1947.

25. Clare E. Hoffman to George W. Hill, May 10, 1943, NA, RG 224, f: farm labor 5-2; Flores, "Mexican Migratory Workers," 40–42; George W. Hill to Clarence Hurt, June 9, 1943, RG 224, f: farm labor 53—certification (Minnesota); Michigan Migrant Report: Summary of 1944 Activities, PHS, HMC, box 50; Summary of Churches Program for Migrant Labor in Minnesota Summer 1946, MHS, CWUM, f: migrants 1944–1947.

26. Baldwin to Philip G. Bruton, July 13, 1943, NA, RG 224, f: farm labor 53—certification, Michigan; "Survey Analysis: Mid-West Area, 1943," PHS, HMC, box 41, f: Midwest 1940s; *Bay City Times,* July 11, 1943, June 14, October 10, 1946; WHS, PCML Proceedings: 9: 209–210, 558–560; Michigan Unemployment Compensation Commission (hereafter MUCC), *Post Season Farm Labor Report, 1949,* 20; *Saginaw News,* July 2, 1948; Rochelle, Illinois, 1948, PHS, HMC, box 41, f: Illinois, 1940s; Migrant Survey Work Southern Minnesota, 1943, PHS, HMC, box 41, f: Midwest 1940s; MUCC, Farm Placement Section, "Characteristics of Migratory Farm Labor in Michigan, 1949," HST, PCML, box 114, f: Saginaw, Michigan, September 11–12, 1950, #2; "Analysis of Information from North Central Area," SCSU, EG,

box 11, f: 11; USDA, *Preliminary Survey of Major Areas Requiring Outside Labor*, 82, 84, 88–96, 101.

27. Rowe, "Migrant Farm Labor," 17; Rowe and Kohlmeyer, *Migrant Farm Labor*, 19; Michigan Migrant Report 1944, PHS, HMC, box 50; WHS, PCML Proceedings, 9: 21–23.

28. Madison and Tipton counties, Indiana: August 30 to October 2, 1945, PHS, HMC, box 50; Migrants around Marion, Indiana, September 6–24, 1949, PHS, HMC, box 50; Reports, Rochelle, Illinois, April–May, 1948 and June–August, 1949, PHS, HMC, box 41, f: Illinois, 1940s; WHS, PCML Proceedings, 9: 255.

29. *South Bend Tribune*, May 12, November 21, 1946; *Rocky Mountain News*, June 13, 1948; Needs of Mexican Contract Laborers, November 19, 1945, CHS, WCMC, box 147, f: 4; *New York Times*, May 13, 1948; *Chicago Tribune*, August 12, 1945.

30. Hart Stilwell, "The Wetback Tide," 6; Midwestern Area: Quarterly Report, April–June, 1947, PHS, HMC, box 41, f: Midwest 1940s.

31. William H. Metzler, "The Migratory Worker in the American Agricultural Economy," WPR, EJ, box 4, f: 4; Brown City 1942, PHS, HMC, box 50; Herbert A. Bahr, Summary Report of Illinois, 1945, PHS, HMC, box 41, f: Illinois, 1940s; Minnesota Migrant Reports: Summary of 1944 Activities, October 1944, PHS, HMC, box 41: f: Midwest 1940s.

32. Michigan Migrant Committee, April 13, 1945, MSA, JT, box 225, f: 2; Migrant Work—Midwestern Area, June–September, 1947, and April–June, 1948, and Report of Dorothy Knowles, Supervisor in Minnesota, July and August, 1945, PHS, HMC, box 41, f: Midwest 1940s; Louisa R. Shotwell, "A Look at the Migrant Outlook," 42; *Bay City Times*, March 13, 1949; Byron Mitchell to J. Otis Garber, December 31, 1948, HST, PCML, box 14, f: staff studies, November, 1950 to February, 1951.

33. Study State Migrant Committees, April, 1950, PHS, HMC, box 49; MUCC, "Characteristics of Migratory Farm Labor in Michigan," 4, HST, PCML, box 114, f: Saginaw, Michigan; idem, *Post Season . . . 1949*, 13; Sebastián Joseph Hernández, "The Latin American Migrant in Minnesota," 32–33; Love and Gaston, *Michigan's Emergency Farm Labor*, 21; Peter John Huber, "Migratory Agricultural Workers in Wisconsin," 13, 16; David E. Henley and Mrs. David E. Henley, *Minnesota and Her Migratory Workers: Land of Promises—Partially Fulfilled*, 1; Analysis of Information from North Central Area, SCSU, EG, box 11, f: 11.

34. Governor's Interracial Committee, *Mexican in Minnesota, 1948*, 13; MESC, Farm Placement Section, Minutes, State Farm Advisory Committee Meeting, February 6, 1948, WPR, CK, f: 1947--1948, affidavits; Informe, Rito Herrera H., May 23, 1946, and Informe, Angel G. Contreras, WPR, CK, f: 1945–1946 affidavits; Galarza, *Merchants of Labor*, 86; Informe, Tomás Ledesma, WPR, CK, f: 1947–1948.

35. "Caso en Millinton," WPR, CK, f: 1945–1946 affidavits; Antonio Islas to Consul General of Mexico, Chicago, June 7, 1945, informe sobre la situación, SCSU, EG, box 18, f: 9.

36. Informe, Angel Contreras, WPR, CK, f: 1945–1946 affidavits; Michi-

gan Migrant Report 1944, PHS, HMC, box 50; Flores, "Mexican Migratory Workers," 24, 26–28; Emilio Aldama Report, February 24, 1945, SCSU, EG, box 18, f: 8; *Detroit Free Press*, July 22, 1945.

37. J. Jesús Ramírez to J. J. Rangel, November 8, 1946, MHS, SMBRA, f: Francisco Rangel correspondence; Individual Work Agreement, 1943, SCSU, EG, box 17, f: 9; Informe, Gerardo Hernández Paul, September 15, 1948, WPR, CK, f: affidavits 1947–1948; Flores, "Mexican Migratory Workers."

38. Flores, "Mexican Migratory Workers," 30, 32, 48; John A. Wright to Francisco Rangel, September 6, 1945, MHS, SMBRA, f: Francisco Rangel correspondence; *Detroit Free Press*, July 22, 1945; Octavio García Padilla to Luis Fernández del Campo, and N. Lovelette to William G. Winemiller, July 25, 1945, SCSU, EG, box 18, f: 9; Clement Kern to Ernesto Galarza, July 12, 1945, SCSU, EG, box 5, f: 8.

39. Flores, "Mexican Migratory Workers," 33, 42, 49; E. Laveaga, "Work in the Beetfields," WPR, CK, f: 1945–1946 affidavits; Ernesto Laveaga to Consul General Chicago, June 30, 1945, SCSU, EG, box 18, f: 9.

40. "Caso en Millinton," WPR, CK, f: 1945–1946, affidavits.

41. Informe Gerardo Hernández Paul and Eduardo Morales Poot, September 15, 1948, WPR, CK, f: affidavits, 1947–1948; Flores, "Mexican Migratory Workers," 28.

42. Flores, "Mexican Migratory Workers," 20; "Diario de un Bracero," WPR, CK, f: affidavits, 1945–1946.

43. Kern to Galarza, SCSU, box 5, f: 8; Flores, "Mexican Migratory Workers," 29; "Guarde esta carta en su persona," WPR, CK, f: affidavits, 1945–1946; Lovelette to Winemiller, July 25, 1945, SCSU, EG, box 18, f: 9.

44. Treatment of Workers in Rosemont Cannery, Faribault, Minnesota (1947), NA, RG 224, Laborers 1; Francisco Espinosa Q. and Uvaldo García R., to Marcelino B. Mendoza, July 8, 1946, WPR, CK, f: affidavits, 1945–1946; Flores, "Mexican Migratory Workers," 50.

45. "Caso en Millinton," WPR, CK, f: 1945–1946, affidavits; Kern to Ernesto Galarza, SCSU, box 5, f: 8; Robert G. Smith to William F. Murphy, February 19, 1947, MSA, KS, box 14, f: 13; Ricardo B. Pérez to R. L. Hertzer, August 20, 1945, and Emilio Aldama to Ralph E. Gates, September 15, 1945, SCSU, EG, box 19, f: 1; Byron Mitchell to J. Otis Garber, HST PCML, box 15, f: Mexican farm labor, 1945–1950.

46. Emilio Aldama Report, October 5, 1944, SCSU, EG, box 18, f: 8; Ernesto Laveaga to Consul General Chicago, SCSU, box 18, f: 9; *Detroit Free Press*, July 22, 1945; Flores, "Mexican Migratory Workers," 33.

47. Michigan Migrant Report, PHS, HMC, box 50; 1944, Grant County 1943, and Veda Burge, Elwood, Indiana, 1944, PHS, HMC, box 50.

48. Wisconsin, Governor's Commission on Human Rights, *Migratory Workers in Wisconsin: A Problem in Human Rights*, 23.

49. *Detroit News*, July 11, 1943; H. Frosman to Harry F. Kelly, April 25, 1944, MSA, HK, box 64, f: 4; Huber, "Migratory Agricultural Workers," 80, 82; Report, Joseph L. Quinn, July 7, 1943, NA, RG 224, f: M 18 medical care; Report of the Mid-West Supervisor, April–September, 1945, PHS, HMC, box 41, f: Midwest, 1940s; WHS, PCML Proceedings, 9: 111.

50. Migrant Survey Work, Southern Minnesota, 1943, and Report of Dorothy Knowles, Minnesota: July, August, 1945, PHS, HMC, box 41, f: Midwest 1940s.

51. Huber, "Migratory Agricultural Workers," 46–48, 86; John McGrath, "Lessons for Liberals"; Wisconsin Legislative Reference Library, *Wisconsin Blue Book 1954*, 342; WHS, PCML Proceedings, 9: 358.

52. Huber, "Migratory Agricultural Workers," 80, 86–87.

53. *Bay City Times*, August 5, 6, 13, 18, 21, 1948; *Detroit Times*, June 14, 1950.

54. Clinton M. Fair to G. Mennen Williams, June 3, 1949, MHC, GMW, Press Office topical files, f: Migratory Labor; Mid-West Work in Michigan: summer 1942, PHS, HMC, box 50; *Bay City Times*, June 15, 1950.

55. Report Northport, Michigan, 1943, PHS, HMC, box 50; Michigan Migrant Report 1944, PHS, HCM, box 50; Work in Midwestern Area, October–December, 1946 and July–September, 1947, PHS, HMC, box 41, f: Midwest 1940s.

56. Edgar Johnston, "Statement on Migratory Labor in Michigan," WPR, EJ, box 4, f: 3; George W. Hill, "Texas-Mexican Migratory Agricultural Workers in Wisconsin," WPR, EJ, box 2, f: 9.

57. Michigan Migrant Report 1944, PHS, HMC, box 50; Frances E. Mueller to Kim Sigler, February 13, 1947, and Robert G. Smith to William F. Murphy, February 19, 1947, MSA, KS, box 14, f: 13; Summary Report, Illinois, 1945, PHS, HMC, box 41, f: Illinois 1940s; Michigan Migrant Committee, Summer 1946, MSA, JT, box 223, f: 12.

58. Susan Fisher Brown Children's Center 1942, PHS, HMC, box 41, f: Midwest 1940s; G. G. Bourg to T. G. Maynard, June 4, 1945, NA, RG 224, f: laborers.

59. Mid-West Area, June 23, 26, 29, 1945, and July–September, 1944, PHS, HMC, box 41, f: Midwest 1940s; Robert G. Smith to William F. Murphy, February 19, 1947, MSA, KS, f: Michigan Governor's Study Commission, 1947; Johnston, "Michigan's Step Children," HST, PCML, box 14, f: Saginaw, Michigan; Grant County, 1943, PHS, HMC, box 50; U.S. Congress, House, Committee on Agriculture, *Permanent Farm Labor Supply Program, 1947*, 53.

60. Treatment of Workers in Rosemont, NA, RG 224, f: laborers 1; Report of Migrant Survey Work: Southern Minnesota, 1943, PHS, HMC, box 41, f: Midwest 1940s; Bay County, Munger, Traverse City, Au Gres, Michigan, 1949, Battle Creek, 1949, and Leelanau County, Michigan, Summer, 1943, PHS, HMC, box 50; WHS, PCML Proceedings, 9: 396–397; *Detroit Free Press*, May 31, 1948; interviews, Sister Lucía Medina, June 8, 1984, and Raquel Moreno, June 13, 1984.

61. *Indianapolis Times*, October 1, 1948; interview, Mario Compeán, December 18, 1983.

62. Southern Minnesota, 1943, PHS, HMC, box 41, f: Midwest 1940s; WHS, PCML Proceedings, 9: 245; Lucas, *Muck Farmers*, 8.

63. Kokomo, Indiana, September 1945, PHS, HMC, box 41, f: Midwest 1940s; Brooks, "Abuses," PHS, HMC, box 50; Migrant Work Mid-Western Area, July–September, 1944, PHS, HMC, box 41, f: Midwest 1940s; inter-

view, Jesús Méndez, MHS, OH; "A Field and Program Survey of the Backgrounds and Trends of Migratory Labor," January 1, 1944, 26–27, PHS, HMC, box 49, f: migrant survey, 1940s; Rowe and Kohlmeyer, *Migrant Farm Labor*, 28; *Detroit News*, November 5, 1942; Governor's Interracial Commission, *Mexican in Minnesota, 1948*, 61; Wisconsin Governor's Commission, *Migratory Agricultural Workers*, 35.

64. Report of Migrant Work in Mid-Western Area, July–September, 1944, PHS, HMC, box 50; *Midwest Review: 1945 Fall Bulletin*, MSA, JT, box 225, f: 2; Rowe and Kohlmeyer, *Migrant Farm Labor*, 26; WHS, PCML Proceedings, 9: 535.

65. *Detroit Free Press*, May 30, 31, 1948; James A. Hickey to William Murphy, January 29, 1947, MSA, KS, box 14, f: 13; *Saginaw News*, February 12, 1950; Joseph Cantavella to William A. Murphy, July 20, 1945, f: Mexican Apostolate, DS; interview, Sister Lucía Medina, June 8, 1984; Diocese of Saginaw, "Historical Facts," 60, LAAD; *Chicago Sun*, June 17, 1946; *Saginaw Catholic Weekly*, June 11, July 2, 1950; U.S. Congress, Senate, Committee on Labor and Public Welfare, Subcommittee on Migratory Labor, *Migratory Labor (1959)*, 216; interview, Msgr. Clement Kern, July 31, 1980.

66. *Saginaw News*, October 25, 1947; Margaret Rogan to James A. Hickey, November 19, 1951, and Saginaw Foundation, Mission Sisters of the Holy Ghost, f: Mexican Apostolate, DS; "What Prompted Catholic Cooperation As a Problem?" MHS, CWUM, f: migrants 1944–1947; Governor's Interracial Commission, *Mexican in Minnesota, 1948*, 45.

67. Migrant Work in Minnesota, 1946, and Contacts with Migrant Work in Mid-West Area, June 23, 26, 29, 1945, PHS, HMC, box 41, f: Midwest 1940s; Brown City Report, 1943, PHS, HMC, box 50; Survey Analysis: Mid-West Area, 1943, PHS, HMC, box 49; Michigan Migrant Committee, November 1, 1950, MSA, JT, box 223, f: 4.

68. Michigan Migrant Report 1944, PHS, HMC, box 50; Report, Dorothy Knowles, July, August, 1945, PHS, HMC, box 41, f: Midwest, 1940s.

69. Quarterly Report, Midwestern Area, April–June and October–December, 1947, and April–June, 1948, Migrant Work in Mid-West Area, June 23, 26, 29, 1945, PHS, HMC, box 41, f: Midwest 1940s; "What Prompted Catholic Cooperation As a Problem?" MHS, CWUM, f: migrants 1944–1947.

70. *Saginaw News*, September 9, 1945; *Chicago Tribune*, August 12, 1945; Mexican Civic Committee, Subcommittee on Services to Mexican Migratory Workers, Minutes, March 3, 1947, CHS, WCMC, box 147, f: 4; Carl Allsup, *The American G.I. Forum: Origins and Evolution*, 98; interviews, Efraín Marínez, June 6, 1984, and Ramiro González, June 7, 1984.

71. Saint Paul International Institute and Neighborhood House, "A Study of the Mexican Community in St. Paul," September, 1946, 3, 8, 9; James A. Hickey to William Murphy, January 29, 1947, MSA, KS, f: Michigan Governor's Study Commission; interview, María Castellanos, June 8, 1984; Case Study of the Flores Family, PHS, NCC, RG 7, box 9, f: 14; Report on the Mexican American in Chicago, May 22, 1949, WCMC, box 147, f: 4, CHS; David J. Saposs, Survey of Resident Latin-American Problems, April 3, 1942, CHS, CAP, box 89, f: 1.

72. Interview, Isabel Salas, August 13, 1980; Florence Cassidy, Social and Educational Work With Mexicans in Southeastern Michigan, January 1, 1945, to June 30, 1945, SCSU, EG, box 10, f: 10; Jane W. Piojan, Report on Field Trip to Detroit Area, February 10–13, 1944, SCSU, EG, box 58, f: 6; Report: Texas—Ohio, May, 1947, PHS, HMC, box 41, f: Midwest 1940s; interviews, Juan Luna, August 31, 1982, and Henry Miranda, August 27, 1982; NA, RG 211, f: monthly operating reports, April, 1944; Elizabeth R. Fotia and Richmond Calvin, *The Mexican-American of the South Bend–Mishawaka Area*, 9.

73. Interviews, Juan Luna, August 31, 1982, Henry Miranda, August 27, 1982, and Israel Leyton, August 13, 1980; Robley Alexander to Mrs. Rich, June 24, 1943, UCC, IPL, f: 74.

74. Robert G. Smith to William F. Murphy, February 19, 1947, MSA, KS, box 14, f: 13; Flores, "Mexican Migratory Workers," 24, 25, 28; interview, Jane Gonzales, MHC; Majka and Majka, *Farm Workers*, 137; H. L. Mitchell, "Migrant Farm Labor," PHS, HMC, box 34.

75. Grant County, 1943, PHS, HMC, box 50; Edgar C. Johnston, "The Education of Children of Spanish-speaking Migrants in Michigan," 513; *Appleblossom*, May 31, 1944; Committee on Labor and Public Welfare, *Migratory Labor 1952*, 1: 786.

76. Edwin C. Pendleton and Joe Clifton, "Child Labor and Education," January 2, 1951, PCML, box 15, f: staff studies, November 1950–February, 1951; Johnston, "Michigan's Step Children," 93–105, HST, PCML, box 14, f: Saginaw, Michigan; Migrant Report 1943, MHS, CWUM, box 1, f: migrant literature for promotion; Survey Analysis: Mid-West Area, 1943, PHS, HMC, box 49; WHS, PCML Proceedings, 9: 363; Brooks, "Abuses," HMC, box 50.

77. G. B. Erskine to Schwellenbach, April 15, 1945, and March 3, 1947, NA, RG 174, Files of Secretary of Labor, f: Committee on Migratory Labor; Harry S. Truman, Establishment of President's Commission on Migratory Labor, MHC, GMW, General Subjects, 1950, f: migrant labor.

78. WHS, PCML Proceedings, 9: 198–199; "Interdepartmental Committee Recommends Appointment of a Study Commission on Migrant Labor," Lansing, 1947, MSA, KS, box 14, f: 13; Michigan Governor's Committee on the Education, Health and Welfare of Migrant Workers to G. Mennen Williams, February 28, 1949, MSA, JT, box 223, f: 4; Lee M. Thurston to Eugene Elliott, February 26, 1947, MSA, KS, box 14, f: 13; *Lansing State Journal*, August 13, 1949; Michigan, House of Representatives, Committee to Investigate Problems of Migrant Workers, Minutes, August 12, 1949, MHC, GMW, General Subjects, 1949, f: migrant labor; Wisconsin Governor's Commission, *Migratory Workers*, 6, 47; State Agencies and the Migrant Labor Problem in Wisconsin in 1954, DDE, PCML, box 4, f: Wisconsin; Governor's Interracial Commission, *Mexican in Minnesota*, 1948, 3–5; Committee on Labor and Public Welfare, *Migratory Labor 1952*, 1: 606–607; Wisconsin, Interdepartmental Committee on Migratory Labor, Minutes, August 4, 1950, WHS.

79. Raymond J. Bernard, "Run-Around for Migrants," 353–354; *Lansing State Journal*, August 13, 1949; Michigan House of Representatives, Com-

mittee to Investigate the Problems of Migrant Workers, Minutes, October 10, 1949, MHC, GMW, General Subjects, 1949, f: migrant labor.

80. Analysis of Information from North Central Area, SCSU, EG, box 11, f: 11; Shiawassee County, 1943, PHS, HMC, box 50; Mid-West Area, 1943, PHS, HMC, box 49.

81. Hill, "Texas-Mexican," WPR, EJ, box 2, f: 9; WHS, PCML Proceedings, 9: 429; Committee on Agriculture, *Permanent Farm Labor Program 1947*, 56.

82. Louise Año Nuevo Kerr, "Mexican Chicago: Chicano Assimilation Aborted, 1939–1954"; *Detroit Free Press*, June 1, 1948. For more on these subjects, see Acuña, *Occupied America*; Mauricio Mazón, *The Zoot-Suit Riots: The Psychology of Symbolic Annihilation*; Carey McWilliams, *North from Mexico: The Spanish-speaking People of the United States*; Arturo Madrid-Barela, "In Search of the Authentic Pachuco: An Interpretive Essay."

83. Carey McWilliams, *North from Mexico*, 202.

84. *Mears Newz*, October 20, 27, 1944; Enrique Gonzales Martínez to Fidel Velásquez, November 27, 1944, AGN, MAC, 575.1/84.

85. J. Vásquez to Miguel Alemán Valdés, December 13, 1946, AGN, MAV, 575.1/5; Ofelia Mendoza to Ernesto Galarza, August 12, 1945, SCSU, EG, box 17, f: 9.

86. Hechter, "Group Formation."

6. Operation Farmlift: Bootstrap to the Midwest, 1950

1. *Bay City Times*, August 5, 6, 13, 17, 1948, and June 2, 18, 1950; *Detroit Times*, June 14, 1950; WHS, *PCML Proceedings*, 9: 24, 152, 557, 576–577.

2. James L. Dietz, *Economic History of Puerto Rico: Institutional Change and Capitalist Development*, 31, 204–205, 227; Sidney Mintz, *Worker in the Cane: A Puerto Rican Life History*, 20–21; William L. Connolly to Fernando Sierra Berdecia, December 17, 1947, DDE, PCML, box 94, f: migratory labor—Mexican.

3. Edwin Maldonado, "Contract Labor and the Origins of Puerto Rican Communities in the United States"; Max A. Egloff, "Puerto Rican Agricultural Workers in the Continental United States," 1–8, HST, PCML, box 15, f: staff studies; Fernando Sierra Berdecia, *Protegiendo 686,000 trabajadores*; Centro de Estudios Puertorriqueños, *Sources for the Study of Puerto Rican Migration*, 45–64, 183–193; Edward D. Beecher, *Working in Hawaii: A Labor History*; McDowell, *A Study*, 11; Edwin Charles Pendleton, "History of Labor in Irrigated Arizona Agriculture," 160–179.

4. Max Egloff, "British West Indian Agricultural Workers," HST, PCML, box 15, f: staff studies, 6–7; J. S. Russell to J. L. Taylor, June 11, 1943, NA, RG 224, f: farm labor 3:2 Mexican.

5. Fernando Sierra Berdecia to Maurice J. Tobin, December 16, 1949, NA, RG 174, Files of John W. Gibson, f: migratory labor, 1950; Egloff, "Puerto Rican Agricultural Workers," 3–7, HST, PCML, box 15, f: staff studies; Agreed Puerto Rican Statement on Policy, DDE, PCML, box 94, f: migratory labor—Puerto Rican; Puerto Rico Bureau of Employment Security, *Annual*

Agricultural and Food Processing Report, 1961, Table 14; Puerto Rico Department of Labor, *Nineteenth Annual Report of the Commissioner of Labor,* 57; O. J. Fjetland to G. Mennen Williams, June 14, 1950, MHC, GMW, General Subjects 1950, f: migrant labor.

6. "The True Story of Crystal White Sugar Company," MHC, FLC, f: Michigan Sugar Beet Company papers; WHS, PCML Proceedings, 9: 5; interview, Msgr. Clement Kern, July 30, 1980; *Puerto Rican World Journal,* June 19, 1943.

7. *Bay City Times,* June 17, July 1, 1950; Thomas Hayes, "Sugar and Vinegar," *El Mundo,* n.d., WPR, CK, f: 1950 correspondence, accounts; Gutleben, *Sugar Tramp . . . Michigan,* 8–9; *Congressional Record,* House, June 20, 1950, 9375–9376; *Puerto Rican World Journal,* June 5, 1943.

8. Egloff, "Puerto Rican Agricultural Workers," 3, 7, HST, PCML, box 15, f: staff studies; Michigan Field Crops Incorporated (hereafter MFCI), Contract 1950, MHC, GMW, box 30, General Subjects 1950, f: migrant labor.

9. MFCI, Contract 1950, MHC, GMW, box 30, General Subjects 1950, f: migrant labor; Informe, Tiburcio Torres, WPR, CK, f: 1950 affidavits.

10. *Bay City Times,* June 18, 1950; Puerto Rico Department of Labor, *Nineteenth Annual Report,* 57; Robert Krause, "Report to Michigan State Farm Labor Advisory Council," March, 1950, WPR, MAFL, series 3, box 138, f: 1; MUCC, Farm Placement Service, Weekly In-Season Agricultural and Food Processing Report, May 22–May 26, 1950, WPR, MAFL, series 3, box 138, f: 1.

11. Max Henderson to Maurice T. Van Hecke, October 23, 1950, HST, PCML, box 13, f: Saginaw, Michigan; *Bay City Times,* August 7, 1950; Informe, Eduardo Vásquez, Juan Marcano, Pablo Tirado, and Eleno Torres, June 30, 1950, WPR, CK, f: 1950 affidavits.

12. Krause, "Report to Michigan State Farm Labor Advisory Council," March, 1950, WPR, MAFL, series 3, box 138, f: 1.

13. *Bay City Times,* June 2, 18, 1950; interview, Ruperto Muñoz, February 8, 1981.

14. *Bay City Times,* June 6, 7, 8, 9, 14, 1950; *Detroit Free Press,* September 13, 1950; WHS, PCML Proceedings, 9: 455; Puerto Rico Department of Labor, *Nineteenth Annual Report,* 57; *New York Times,* June 6, 7, 1950.

15. *Bay City Times,* June 9, 14, 15, 1950; *New York Times,* June 8, 9, 1950; US Civil Aeronautics Board, *Accident Investigation Report: Aviation Corporation of Seattle (Westair Transport) 300 Miles East of Melbourne, Florida, June 5, 1950* (Adopted July 9, 1951).

16. *New York Times,* June 10, 13, 18, 1950; *Bay City Times,* June 10, 13, 16, 1950; *Detroit Times,* June 14, 1950; *Detroit News,* August 27, 1950.

17. *Saginaw Catholic Weekly,* June 18, 1950; *Bay City Times,* July 1, 1950.

18. *Bay City Times,* July 22, 1950; Informe, Eduardo Vásquez, Tiburcio Torres, and Jesús Nieves et al., WPR, CK, f: 1950 affidavits.

19. Informe, Octavio Baez Rivera, Juan Marcano, Tiburcio Torres, and Santos Flores, WPR, CK, f: 1950 affidavits.

20. Informe, Primitivo Padilla and Octavio Báez Rivera, and Rogelio Polo

López, WPR, CK, f: 1950 affidavits; interview, Ruperto Muñoz, February 8, 1981; WHS, PCML Proceedings, 9: 449.

21. Informe, Santos Flores, Pablo Tirado, Jesús Nieves et al., and Manuel Acevedo, n.d., WPR, CK, f: 1950 affidavits; *Bay City Times*, August 6, 1950.

22. Informe, Pedro Angel Colón, Rogelio Polo López, Santos Flores, Pablo Tirado, and Severo Ortiz, July 16, 1950, WPR, CK, f: 1950 affidavits; *Bay City Times*, August 8, 1950; Molly Frazer Durham, "Down to Earth with the Migrants," HST, PCML, box 13, f: Saginaw.

23. Informe, Jesús Nieves et al., Juan Serrano, and Pablo Tirado, July 3, 1950, WPR, CK, f: 1950 affidavits; Durham, "Down to Earth with the Migrants," HST, PCML, box 13, f: Saginaw.

24. Migrant Work Mid-Western Area, 1950, and Report, Donald L. West: summer and fall, 1950, PHS, HMC, box 41, f: Midwest 1940s; Informe, Juan Marcano, Rogelio Polo López, Santos Flores, and Angel Fuentes, August 7, WPR, 1950, CK, f: 1950 affidavits; Manuel Cabranes to Eulalio Torres, October 11, 1950, WPR, CK, f: 1950 correspondence, accounts.

25. *Bay City Times*, July 14, August 8, 1950; WHS, PCML Proceedings, 9: 266–267.

26. Informe, Juan Marcano; Durham, "Down to Earth with the Migrants," HST, PCML, box 13, f: Saginaw.

27. Interview, Ruperto Muñoz, February 8, 1981; *Bay City Times*, August 6, 7, 1950; Informe, Tiburcio Torres, Pedro Lopez Ríos, Primitivo Padilla, Rogelio Polo López, Jesús Nieves et al., and Roberto Torres Jiménez, WPR, CK, f: 1950 affidavits.

28. Informe, Jesús Nieves et al., July 3, 1950, WPR, CK, f: 1950 affidavits; interview, Clement Kern, July 30, 1980.

29. Interviews, Clement Kern, July 30, 1980, Ruperto Muñoz, February 8, 1981.

30. Informe, Eleno Torres, WPR, CK, f: 1950, affidavits; interview, Clement Kern, July 30, 1980.

31. Eulalio Torres to Clement Kern, November 15, 1950, WPR, CK, f: 1950 correspondence, accounts; WHS, PCML Proceedings, 9: 455; interview, Clement Kern, July 30, 1980.

32. "Migratory Workers—A Major Social and Economic Problem," 3; *Saginaw News*, September 13, 1950; *El Mundo*, September 14, 1950; WHS, PCML Proceedings, 9: 420–424, 455; "Excerpts from Frank Edwards' Broadcast, July 12, 1950, WPR, CK, f: 1950 correspondence, accounts; *Gothic*, December, 1950; *Detroit News*, August 27, 1950.

33. *Bay City Times*, July 22, 1950; *Detroit Times*, July 16, 17, 22, 1950; *Wage Earner*, August, 1950.

34. *Detroit Times*, July 16, 17, 22, 1950; *Detroit Free Press*, July 22, 1950.

35. *Detroit Free Press*, August 5, 1950; *Bay City Times*, August 8, 14, 15, 1950; WHS, PCML Proceedings: 1: 117; Luis Muñoz Marín, open letter, August 25; 1950, HST, PCML, box 13, f: Saginaw; Report, Donald L. West, summer and fall, 1950, HST, PHS, HMC, box 41, f: Midwest 1940s.

36. *Bay City Times*, August 20, 22, 1950; statement Max Henderson,

WHS, PCML Proceedings 9: 152; Hayes, "Sugar and Vinegar," *El Mundo* (n.d.), WPR, CK, f: 1950, correspondence, accounts.

37. *Detroit Free Press*, September 14, 1950; *Saginaw News*, August 13, September 13, 1950; *Detroit News*, September 13, 1950; "Beet Workers Defense Committee Organized," WPR, CK, f: 1950 correspondence, accounts; interview, Clement Kern, July 30, 1980.

38. *Saginaw News*, September 12, 13, 1950; *New York Times*, September 13, 1950; *Detroit Free Press*, September 12, 13, 1950; *El Mundo*, September 14, 29, 1950.

39. *Bay City Times*, July 28, August 21, 1950; *Detroit Free Press*, September 12, 1950; MUCC, Farm Placement Section, "Characteristics of Migratory Farm Labor in Michigan," (1950), HST, PCML, box 114, f: Saginaw; *Saginaw News*, November 9, 1950; *Ingham County News*, July 21, 1950.

40. *Gothic*, December, 1950.

41. *Saginaw News*, September 12, October 4, 1950; *Detroit Times*, September 2, 1950; *New York Times*, September 13, 1950; WHS, PCML Proceedings, 9: 235.

42. US Civil Aeronautics Board, *Accident Investigation Report*.

43. *Catholic Weekly*, July 23, 1950.

44. Eulalio Torres to Clement Kern, November 15, 1950, WPR, CK, f: 1950 correspondence, accounts; "Following the Crops"; *Detroit News*, March 5, 1951; interviews, Clement Kern, July 30, 1980, Anastacio Muñoz, November 12, 1980, and Ruperto Muñoz, February 8, 1981.

45. *Bay City Times*, June 13, August 8, 1950; *Saginaw News*, April 11, 1951; Migrant Work Midwestern Area—1950, PHS, HMC, box 41, f: Midwest, 1940s; *Detroit News*, August 27, 1950.

46. *Detroit News*, March 5, 1951; García, *Operation Wetback*, 40–41; García y Griego, "Importation," 63; interview, Jane Gonzales, MHC.

7. Age of Illusions, 1950–1959

1. Cottrell, *Beet-Sugar Economics*, 198; Clarence Edmund Johnson, "The Influence of New Sugar Beet Production Methods on Time and Cost Requirements in Michigan, 1946," 11; MESC, *Post Season Farm Labor Report 1956*, 4.

2. Committee on Labor and Public Welfare, *Migratory Labor 1952*, 2: 992; "Michigan Résumé on the Migrant Situation 1954," PHS, NCC, RG 7, box 10, f: 1; E. S. Willis, "The Trend toward More Acres per Worker"; "Local Beet Fields Look Good," 37; Johnson, "The Influence," 11; John Thaden, "Migratory Agricultural Workers in Michigan: The Origin of the Problem," MSA, JT, box 223, f: 3.

3. C. W. Doxtator, "Sugar Beet Yields from Mechanical and Hand Thinning"; Robert A. Young, *An Economic Study of the Eastern Sugar Beet Industry*, 94; WHS, PCML Proceedings, 9: 326.

4. Minnesota Governor's Farm and Migratory Labor Advisory Committee, Meeting, April 8, 1958, MHS, OCF, f: Migratory Labor Commission, 1958; Hernández, "Latin American Migrant," 85; Young, *Economic Study*,

35; O. J. Fjetland to G. Mennen Williams, May 15, 1951, MHC, GMW, General Subject Files, 1951, f: migrant labor; *Detroit News*, March 5, 1951.

5. Leftwich, "Migratory Harvest Labor, 118.

6. Rossville, Illinois, 1953, PHS, NCC, RG 7, box 10, f: 14; WHS, PCML Proceedings, 9: 107; "Michigan Résumé on the Migrant Situation 1954," PHS, NCC, RG 7, box 10, f: 1; Minnesota Governor's Farm and Migratory Labor Advisory Committee, Meeting, April 12, 1956, MHS, OCF, f: Farm and Migratory Labor Advisory Committee, 1955–1956; Lewis Levine, "Migrant Farm Workers: The Economy Lies Ahead," DDE, PCML, box 37, f: migrant ministry meeting, February 19, 1959; *Cleveland Plain Dealer*, May 29, 1959; Hernández, "Latin American Migrant," 49.

7. Michigan Governor's Interagency Committee on Migratory Labor, Meeting, March 24, 1952, WPR, EJ, box 1, f: Governor's Interagency Committee on Migrant Labor; *Detroit Free Press*, February 10, 1954; Saint Joseph County Council of Community Services, Community Services to Migrant Workers, December 18, 1958; DDE, PCML, box 5, f: Indiana; *Michigan Farmer*, July 4, 1959; Thelma Harper, "Our Trip to Wisconsin," October 30, 1958, DDE, PCML, box 6, f: Wisconsin; Joe R. Motheral and Ruben W. Hect, "Projected Estimates of Migratory Farm Labor Needs, Southwestern Michigan, September 21, 1956, DDE, PCML, box 56, f: publications—Michigan; MESC, *Post Season Farm Labor Report 1952*, 20; Committee on Labor and Public Welfare, *Migratory Labor 1952*, 1: 368.

8. Alfred Robert Koch, "Interregional Competition in the Tomato Processing Industry," xiv; Alvar W. Carlson, "Specialty Agriculture and Migrant Laborers in Northwestern Ohio," 298; Lucas County Child Welfare Board, "Curtis Day Care Center, 1957," DDE, PCML, box 59, f: publications—Ohio; Ohio Legislative Service Commission, *Migrant Workers in Ohio*, 16; Noel W. Stuckman, *Michigan Pickling Cucumbers—the Grower, the Picker, and the WYRF*, 2–3; Willson, "Historical Development," 79; *Ingham County News*, July 31, 1952.

9. Michigan Governor's Interagency Committee, Meeting, March 24, 1952; interview, Andrew Anguiano, June 21, 1984; WHS, PCML Proceedings, 9: 267; Hernández, "Latin American Migrant," 46; Committee on Labor and Public Welfare, *Migratory Labor 1952*, 2: 993.

10. Sanilac County, Michigan, 1954, MMC, box 93C, MHC; Committee on Labor and Public Welfare, *Migratory Labor 1959*, 200; Field Trip to Grant Community, WPR, EJ, box 1, f: 6; "Michigan Résumé on the Migrant Situation 1954," PHS, NCC, RG 7, box 10, f: 1.

11. Meeting, Michigan Governor's Interagency Committee on Migratory Labor, March 24, 1952; Committee on Labor and Public Welfare, *Migratory Labor 1952*, 2: 992; *Detroit Free Press*, May 18, 1952.

12. Thaden, "Migratory Agricultural Workers," 6, MSA, JT, box 223, f: 3; "It Happened in Michigan," PHS, NCC, RG 7, box 10, f: 1; Wood County, Ohio, 1952, PHS, NCC, RG 7, box 10, f: 16; Texas Council on Migrant Labor, "Mechanization and the Texas Migrant," DDE, PCML, box 35, f: Texas Committee on Migrant Farm Workers; Huron-Tuscola County, Michigan, 1959, MHC, MMC, box 93C; Galarza, *Farm Workers*, 69–70.

13. John Zuckerman, "The Impact of Public Law 78 on Migrant Labor," November 21–22, 1959, DDE, PCML, box 77, f: National Conference to Stabilize Migrant Labor; Galarza, *Farm Workers*, 214, 216.

14. "Michigan Résumé on the Migrant Situation 1954," PHS, NCC, RG 7, box 10, f: 1; Michigan Governor's Study Commission on Migratory Labor and the Interagency Committee on Migratory Labor, *Migrants in Michigan*, 12; "Great Lakes States Cooperative Agreement," WPR, CK, f: 1950 correspondence; Minnesota Governor's Farm and Migratory Labor Advisory Committee, meeting, April 12, 1956, DDE, PCML, box 2, f: Minnesota; Galarza, *Farm Workers*, 43, 45.

15. Shirley E. Greene, *The Education of Migrant Children: A Study of the Educational Opportunities and Experiences of the Children of Agricultural Migrants*, 2; Illinois State Report, 1950, PHS, HMC, box 49; Illinois State Report, 1957, PHS, NCC, RG 7, box 9, f: 14; *Chicago Daily News*, July 27, 1959; Indiana State Report, 1954, PHS, NCC, RG 7, box 9, f: 15; State Reports for Indiana, Ohio, Minnesota, Wisconsin and Indiana, 1958, DDE, PCML, box 34, f: National Council of Churches—Migrant Ministry state reports; *Toledo Blade*, October 8, 1959; Wisconsin Final Report, summer, 1951, PHS, NCC, RG 7, box 11, f: 8.

16. Greene, *Education*, 2; MDPH, "A Study of Non-Settled Tuberculosis Patients Hospitalized in Michigan, 1952," MSA, JT, box 224, f: 1; Michigan State Reports, 1958 and 1960, MHC, MMC, box 93C; Michigan State Report, October, 1956, PHS, NCC, RG 7, box 10, f: 1; *Saginaw News*, April 12, 1951; Berrien County, Michigan, 1956 and 1959, Huron-Tuscola, Michigan, 1959, MHC, MMC, box 93C; MESC, *Post Season Farm Labor Report 1960*, 10.

17. Ohio Legislative Service Commission, *Migrant Workers in Ohio*, 6; Galarza, *Farm Workers*, 42–46; Jerome G. Manis, *A Study of Migrant Education: Survey Findings in Van Buren County, Michigan*, 7–8; Texas Legislative Council, Commission on Transportation, *Transportation of Migrant Labor in Texas*, 15; Michigan Report of Projects, 1954, PHS, NCC, RG 7, box 10, f: 2; Saint Joseph County Council of Churches, "Community Services," DDE, PCML, box 5, f: Indiana; Wisconsin 1957 State Report, PHS, NCC, RG 7, box 11, f: 8.

18. Tipton County, Indiana, August 13–September 3, PHS, NCC, RG 7, box 9, f: 15; Hector, Minnesota, July 18, 1958, PHS, NCC, RG 7, box 10, f: 3; Bay County Board of Education, "Bay County School for Migrant Children, July and August, 1956," MHC, GMW, General Subject File, f: migrant labor, 1956; Mrs. Morgan to G. Mennen Williams, October 1, 1959, MHC, GMW, General Subject File, f: migrant labor 1959; WHS, PCML Proceedings, 9: 478; Committee on Labor and Public Welfare, *Migratory Labor 1952*, 1: 786; idem, *Migratory Labor 1959*, 1: 166–167.

19. Thompson, North Dakota, summer, 1951, PHS, NCC, RG 7, box 10, f: 4; Michigan State Report, 1960, MHC, MMC, box 93C; *Saginaw News*, April 1, 1953; Minnesota State Report, 1957, PHS, NCC, RG 7, box 10, f: 3.

20. Interview, Jane Gonzales, MHC; Michigan Study Commission on Migratory Labor, March 24, 1952, WPR EJ, box 1, f: minutes; "Mexican American Council of Chicago, July 1951–January, 1952, CHS, CAP, box 88, f: 11;

Committee on Labor and Public Welfare, *Migratory Labor 1952*, 1: 177; interview, Andrew Anguiano, June 21, 1984; Juan Ramón García, "Operation Wetback: Midwest Phase."

21. John Thaden, "Migratory Agricultural Laborers in Michigan," April, 1953, WPR, EJ, box 1, f: Governor's Interagency Committee; Wisconsin Final Report, summer, 1951, PHS, NCC, RG7, box 11, f: 8; Oceana and Ingham County, Michigan, 1954, MHC, MMC, box 93C; "Keefe Blueberry Plantation," WPR, EJ, box 1, f: 6.

22. Camp Warren, Coloma, Michigan, July 7, 1952, Mason, Michigan, July 6, 1952, Lacota, Michigan, August 9, 1952, and Northport, Michigan, August 1, 1952, PHS, NCC, RG 7, box 10, f: 2; Illinois Migrant Ministry, State Report 1957, PHS, NCC, RG 7, box 9, f: 14.

23. Morris, Illinois, July 27–August 16, 1953, PHS, NCC, RG 7, box 9, f: 14; Huntington County, Indiana, August 18–October 4, 1951, PHS, NCC, RG 7, box 9, f: 15; Huron-Tuscola, Michigan, 1954, and Michigan State Report, 1958, MHC, MMC, box 93C; Lucas County Child Welfare Board, "Curtis Day Care Center," DDE, PCML, box 59, f: publications—Ohio; Greene, *Education*, 44.

24. Rossville, Illinois, 1953, PHS, NCC, RG 7, box 10, f: 14; Upland, Indiana, August 15, 1952, PHS, NCC, RG 7, box 9, f: 15; Wade H. Andrews and Saad Z. Nagi, *Migrant Agricultural Labor in Ohio*, 13–14; Temporary South Cook County Commission for Migrants, Census of Agricultural Migrant Workers in South Cook County, October, 1956, DDE, PCML, box 5, f: Illinois; Committee on Labor and Public Welfare, *Migratory Labor 1959*, 1: 247, 368; Hector-Gibbon, Minnesota, July 10, 1958, PHS, NCC, RG 7, box 10, f: 3.

25. Henley and Henley, *Minnesota and Her Migratory Workers*, 7; Galarza, *Farm Workers*.

26. R. C. Rudy Mayan to Alvin Bentley, January 5, 1954, MHC, AB, Congressional Files, Topical file 1954, f: Chicano farm labor; Carl D. Davenport to Alvin Bentley, February 4, 1958, and Millard Brazington to Bentley, March 29, 1958, MHC, AB, Congressional Files, Topical Files 1958, f: Chicano farm labor–2; Eugene Committee for the Defense of Domestic Workers, "From the Sands of the Rio Grande to the Michigan Shores," PHS, NCC, RG 7, box 10, f: 1.

27. Galarza, *Merchants of Labor*, 239; Brazington to Bentley, March 29, 1958, MHC, AB, Congressional Files, Topical Files 1958, f: Chicano farm labor–2; Eugene Committee for the Concern of Domestic Migrant Workers, "Excerpts," PHS, NCC, RG 7, box 10, f: 1.

28. Arthur H. Wright et al. to Patrick V. McNamara, July 17, 1956, MHC, GMW, General Subject Files, f: migrant labor 1956; Allegan County, Michigan, 1956, box 93C, MHC, MMC, Alvin Bentley to Frederick Loss, May 7, 1958, MHC, AB, Congressional Files, Topical Files 1958, f: Chicano farm labor–2; "From the Sands of the Rio Grande to the Michigan Shores," PHS, NCC, RG 7, box 10, f: 1.

29. Montcalm and Bay County, Michigan, 1959, MHC, MMC, box 93C; interview, Andrew Anguiano, June 21, 1984; "From the Sands of the Rio Grande to the Michigan Shores," PHS, NCC, RG 7, box 10, f: 1; *Migratory*

Labor 1959 1: 200; Ellis W. Hawley, "The Politics of the Mexican Labor Issue, 1950–1965," 174; U.S. Congress, Senate, Subcommittee of Committee on Agriculture and Forestry, Extension of Mexican Farm Labor Program, 93–97.

30. Saginaw News, September 13, 1951, March 25, 1952; Lansing State Journal, March 7, 1952; Grand Rapids Herald, March 4, 1953; Michigan State Report, 1958, MHC, MMC, box 93C; J. F. Thaden, Formation of the Michigan Study Commission on Migratory Labor, 1953, MSA, JT, box 223, f: 3; Michigan Governor's Study Commission on Migratory Labor, Meeting, May 27, 1952, MHC, GMW, General Subject Files, f: migrant labor 1952; Charles S. Brown to G. Mennen Williams, November 16, 1959, MHC, GMW, General Subject Files, f: migrant labor 1959.

31. Rebecca Barton, "Relationship of the Governor's Commission on Human Rights to the Migrant Labor Problem," September 30, 1959, DDE, PCML, box 76, f: Wisconsin (general); Ohio Governor's Committee on Migrant Labor, Migratory Labor in Ohio (1960), 5; Ohio Governor's Committee on Migrant Labor, December 4, 1956, DDE, PCML, box 3, f: Ohio.

32. Naomi Heitt to Frank Potter, March 12, 1959, DDE, PCML, box 20, f: Illinois Committee; Illinois Commission on Children, "Programs for Agricultural Migrants and Their Families," July, 1952, DDE, PCML, box 56, f: publications Illinois; Minnesota Governor's Interracial Commission, The Mexican in Minnesota (1953), 4, 9–12.

33. Saginaw News, July 16, 1953; Michigan State Report, October 15, 1957, PHS, NCC, RG 7, box 10, f: 1, Hector, Minnesota, July 12, 1958, PHS, NCC, RG 7, box 10, f: 3; Lansing State Journal, September 24, 1955; Detroit Free Press, May 30, 1954; Indianapolis Star, September 15, 1957; P. H. Evelken to James P. Mitchell, June 21, 1957, DDE, PCML, box 4, f: Wisconsin; Texas Legislative Council Commission on Transportation, Transportation of Migrant Labor in Texas, 37; Lansing State Journal, June 25, 1954; Edgar Johnston, "Statement on Migratory Labor in Michigan," March 11, 1952, WPR, EJ, box 4, f: 3; US Bureau of Labor Standards, Transportation Accidents to Migrants, October 29, 1958, DDE, PCML, box 100, f: ML-2-accidents.

34. Galarza, Merchants of Labor, 144–150; Al Craig to Max Horton, August 23, 1954, and John Thaden to Sweeney, October 14, 1955, MHC, GMW, General Subject Files, f: migratory labor, 1955; interview, Vicenta Velásquez, August 27, 1982.

35. Stuckman, Michigan Pickling Cucumbers, 18; James J. Savron to G. Mennen Williams, August 5, 1957, MHC, GMW, General Subject Files, f: migrant labor 1958; Committee on Labor and Public Welfare, Migratory Labor 1959, 1: 202; interview, Mario Compeán, December 18, 1983.

36. Committee on Labor and Public Welfare, Migratory Labor 1959, 1: 200; Lloyd H. Gallardo, "Economics of the Demand for Harvest Labor by the Individual Farm Enterprise," 192–194.

37. Eugene Committee, "Excerpts," PHS, NCC, RG 7, box 10, f: 1; Stuckman, Michigan Pickling Cucumbers, 19, 23; Rev. Joseph H. Crosthwait,

"Excerpts from Report of Field Trip into Northern States," SCSU, EG, box 13, f: 5.

38. Stuckman, *Michigan Pickling Cucumbers*, 3–7, 18.

39. Carl D. Davenport to Frank E. Johnston, December 3, 1958, MHC, AB, Congressional Files, f: Chicano farm labor–1.

40. Consumers League of Michigan, *Bulletin* 9 (August 17, 1951); Evelken to Mitchell, June 21, 1957, DDE, PCML, box 4, f: Wisconsin; Huber, "Migratory Agricultural Workers," 59.

41. Committee on Labor and Public Welfare, *Migratory Labor 1959*, 1: 201; Charles S. Brown to G. Mennen Williams, August 21, 1958, MHC, GMW, Executive Files, Charles S. Brown, f: migrant labor; Eugene Committee, "Excerpts," PHS, NCC, RG 7, box 10, f: 1; "From the Sands of the Rio Grande to the Michigan Shores," PHS, NCC, RG 7, box 10, f: 1.

42. Herbert H. Lindsey and Thomas W. Walton, *Spatial and Temporal Patterns of the Movement of Seasonal Agricultural Migrant Children into Wisconsin*, 6–7.

43. Leftwich, "Migratory Harvest Labor," 158–161; Subcommittee on Employment and Transportation, December 10, 1957, DDE, PCML, box 29, f: Ohio (committee); Lindsay and Walton, *Spatial and Temporal Patterns*, 6–7; Ohio Governor's Committee on Migrant Labor, *Migratory Labor in Ohio, 1960*, 3, 8; Minnesota Governor's Human Rights Commission, Migrant Worker Subcommittee, *Annual Report 1958*, MHS, OCF, f: human rights, July–December, 1958; Evelken to Mitchell, June 21, 1957, DDE, PCML, box 4, f: Wisconsin; Frank E. Johnston to Ed Guggenheim, February 2, 1959, MHC, AB, box 26, Topical Files 1959, f: Chicano farm labor; Ohio Legislative Commission, *Migrant Workers in Ohio*, 31; *Cleveland Plain Dealer*, May 29, 1959; Andrew Kramarz to Roscoe Walters, August 8, 1958, MHC, GMW, General Subject Files, f: migrant labor 1959; *Christian Science Monitor*, June 22, 1959.

44. *Saginaw News*, May 23, 1951; Andrews and Nagi, *Migrant Agricultural Labor*, 20; Martin and Faribault County, Minnesota, August 12, 1958, PHS, NCC, RG 7, box 10, f: 3; Joint Committee of the Governor's Study Commission on Migratory Labor and the Inter-Agency Committee on Migratory Labor, Saginaw, October 20, 1954, DDE, PCML, box 2, f: Michigan; Michigan Governor's Study Commission on Migratory Labor, Recommendations, January, 1955, DDE, PCML, box 28, f: Michigan committees.

45. National Advisory Committee on Farm Labor (hereafter NACFL), *Report on Farm Labor*; U.S. Department of Health, Education and Welfare (hereafter HEW), *Children of Migrant Families*, 39; Edward Duff, S.J., "The Plight of Migrant Labor."

46. *Detroit Free Press*, August 28, 1955; Consumer's League of Michigan, *Bulletin*, August 17, 1951; Rossville, Illinois, 1953, PHS, NCC, RG 7, box 10, f: 4; Upland, Red Key, Eaton, Fowlerton, and camp on route 22, Indiana, August 6–September 1, 1951, PHS, NCC, RG 7, box 9, f: 15; *Michigan Catholic*, August 25, 1954; *Detroit Times*, August 25, 1954; Minnesota Subcommittee on Migrant Workers, Report, April 19, 1956, MHS, OCF, f: Human

Rights Interracial Commission 1956; James O'Connor to Ford Foundation, January 16, 1956, MHS, OCF, f: Farm and Migratory Labor Advisory Committee, 1955–1956; *Chicago Daily News*, July 24, 27, 1959; Committee on the Problems of Agricultural Migrant Workers, May 26, 1955, DDE, PCML, box 2, f: Illinois; Evelken to Mitchell, June 21, 1957, DDE, PCML, box 4, f: Wisconsin; Wood County, Ohio, 1952, PHS, NCC, RG 7, box 10, f: 16; Ingham County, Michigan, 1954, MHC, MMC, box 93C; "Case Stories of Migrant Families," PHS, NCC, RG 7, box 9, f: 14; Savron to Williams, MHC, GMW, General Subject Files, f: migrant labor, 1958; June Cedarleaf to A. E. Ramberberg, June 27, 1957, MHS, OCF, f: Farm and Migratory Labor Advisory Committee, 1957; "Family Case Study," PHS, NCC, RG 7, box 10, f: 14; Gaston Indiana, August 6, 1952, PHS, NCC, RG 7, box 9, f: 15; Sandusky County, Ohio, 1952, and Ohio State Report, 1957, PHS, NCC, RG 7, box 10, f: 16; Sheboygan County, Wisconsin, June 15–July 28, 1953, PHS, NCC, RG 7, box 11, f: 8; Nancy Stockham to John Thaden, May 18, 1953, MSA, JT, box 226, f: 9; *Detroit Times*, August 25, 1954; Michigan Committee to Investigate Problems of Migrant Workers, Meeting, June 1, 1950, MHC, GMW, General Subject Files, f: migrant labor 1950.

47. "Family Case Study," PHS, NCC, RG 7, box 10, f: 14; Wood County, Ohio, 1952, PHS, NCC, RG 7, box 10, f: 16; G. H. Agate and C. C. Crumley, "Field Report: Lewis Myers Farm, Iosco Twp., Livingston County, August 5, 1954, MHC, MMC, box 93C; *Saginaw News*, April 12, 1951; Michigan Welfare Conference, Status of Migrant Children, November 12, 1952, MHC, GMW, General Subject Files, f: migrant labor 1952; Mason-Stockbridge Area, Michigan, 1954, MHC, MMC, box 93C; *La Prensa* (New York City), October 27, 1957; Minnesota Farm and Migratory Labor Advisory Committee, Meeting, June 7, 1957, DDE, PCML, box 28, f: Minnesota Committee.

48. *Ann Arbor News*, January 10, 1951; Minnesota Governor's Human Rights Commission, Migrant Worker Subcommittee, Annual Report, 1958, MHS, OCF, f: human rights, July–December, 1958; "Keefe Blueberry Plantation," WPR, EJ, box 1, f: 6; Kenneth Cory to Patrick V. McNamara, March 2, 1959, WPR, PUM, box 330, f: labor—farm workers; *Berrien Springs Journal-Era*, March 2, 1956; Minnesota Governor's Farm and Migratory Labor Advisory Committee, meeting, April 8, 1958, MHS, OCF, f: Migratory Labor Commission, 1958; *Cleveland Plain Dealer*, June 2, 1959; Hale and Beatrice Thorton to Max Henderson, April 29, 1959, MHC, AB, Congressional Files, f: Chicano farm labor–1, 1959; Committee on Labor and Public Welfare, *Migratory Labor 1959* 1: 147–148, 161, 203, 267–268, 271–273, 276–278, 349, 401–402.

49. Migrant Housing Regulations, 1957, and State Migratory Committee, April 1, 1958, DDE, PCML, box 30, f: Wisconsin (committee); Wisconsin Interdepartment Committee on Migratory Labor, August 4, 1950, WHS; Committee on Labor and Public Welfare, *Migratory Labor 1959*, 227–232.

50. State Agencies and the Migrant Labor Problem in Wisconsin, and Elizabeth Brandeis to Clara M. Beyer, January 5, 1955, DDE, PCML, box 4, f: Wisconsin; Ted E. Moses to F. A. Potter, June 3, 1959, and State Migratory

Committee Minutes, April 1, 1958, DDE, PCML, box 30, f: Wisconsin (committee); Huber, "Migratory Agricultural Workers," 103–109.

51. Blue Earth, Minnesota, August 10, 1958, PHS, NCC, RG 7, box 10, f: 3; Cedarleaf to Ramberberg, June 27, 1957, MHS, OCF, f: Farm and Migratory Labor Advisory Committee, 1957; Minnesota Governor's Commission on Human Rights, *The Migrant Worker in Minnesota (1958)*, 4; Committee on Labor and Public Welfare, *Migratory Labor 1959*, 1: 359–360.

52. Eugene Committee for the Betterment of Migrants, "Citizens versus Foreign Workers in Agriculture," DDE, PCML, box 5, f: Michigan; Crosthwait, "Excerpts from Report of Field Trip into Northern States," SCSU, EG, box 13, f: 5.

53. Ohio Migrant Ministry Confidential Report, PHS, NCC, RG 7, box 10, f: 16; Savron to Williams, MHC, GMW, general subject files, f: migrant labor, 1958; G. Mennen Williams to Editors of *The Reporter*, January 21, 1959, MHC, GMW, General Subject File, f: migrant labor 1959; Andrews and Nagi, *Migrant Agricultural Labor*, 17; interview, Clement Kern, August 7, 1980, Thompson, North Dakota, summer, 1951, PHS, NCC, RG 7, box 10, f: 4.

54. Minnesota Governor's Commission on Human Rights, *The Migrant Worker in Minnesota (1956)*, 6; HEW, *Children of Migrant Families*, 39; Committee on Labor and Public Welfare, *Migratory Labor, 1959*, 1: 125; Wisconsin Department of Welfare, Division for Children and Youth, *Migrant Agricultural Workers in Door County.*

55. "Michigan Résumé on the Migrant Situation 1954," PHS, NCC, RG 7, box 10, f: 1; Austin L. Pino to O. K. Fjetland, June 4, 1954, MSA, JT, box 223, f: 4; Ohio Migrant Ministry, State Report, 1957, PHS, NCC, RG 7, box 10, f: 15.

56. Indiana State Report, 1954, PHS, NCC, RG 7, box 9, f: 15; Status of Migrant Children, November 12, 1952, MHC, GMW, General Subject Files, f: migratory labor, 1952; Stockham to Thaden, February 11, 1953, MSA, JT, box 226, f: 9; *South Bend Tribune*, June 18, 1955; Johnston, "Statement on Migratory Labor, 1952," WPR, EJ, box 4, f: 3.

57. "Special Migrant Summer Schools Make News"; Henry J. Ponitz to Curtis Catlan et al., July 18, 1956, and "Bay County School for Migrant Children, July and August, 1956," MHC, GMW, General Subject Files, f: migrant labor, 1956; Sam Rabinovitz, "Michigan Migrants and the NCLC"; Bay County Board of Education, "Bay County School for Children, July 3–July 5, 1957," MHC, GMW, General Subject Files, f: migrant labor, 1957.

58. Rebecca Barton, "Relationship of the Governor's Commission on Human Rights to the Migrant Problem," DDE, PCML, box 76, f: Wisconsin (general); Greene, *Education*, 155, 158; Ohio Governor's Committee, *Migratory Labor in Ohio (1960)*, 7–8.

59. James O'Connor to Ford Foundation, January 16, 1956, MHS, OCF, f: Farm and Labor Advisory Committee, 1955–1956; *Migratory Labor Notes* 4 (April 1, 1958); Minnesota Governor's Commission on Human Rights, Migrant Worker Subcommittee, *Annual Report 1958*, MHS, OCF, f: human rights, July–December 1958.

60. Michigan Department of Public Instruction, "Migrants in Bay County

in 1954," and "Migrants in Van Buren County in 1954," MSA, JT, box 227, f: 5; Manis, *Study of Migrant Education*, 8; MESC, "Parents of Children Attending Summer School for Migrants in Bay County, Michigan (1957)" MSA, JT, box 223, f: 4.

61. Gratiot County, Michigan, 1959, MHC, MMC, box 93C; Ohio Migrant Ministry, "Survey of Mexican People Toledo, Ohio, Area," PHS, NCC, RG 7, box 13, f: 5; *Chicago Daily News*, July 27, 1959; June Cedarleaf to Industrial Commission of Minnesota, June 3, 1958, DDE, PCML, box 5, f: Minnesota; Ned S. Baker and Elizabeth S. Magee, "Agricultural Migrant Workers in Ohio," 10; William L. Connolly to Ruth Woods, April 24, 1952, DDE, PCML, box 94, f: migratory labor—children; Field Trip to Grant, WPR, EJ, box 1, f: 6; WHS, PCML Proceedings, 1: 20–21.

62. Shirley E. Greene, "The Iron Curtain in Berrien County," February 18, 1953, PHS, NCC, RG 7, box 10, f: 2; Ray DeWitt to editor, *Michigan Christian Advocate*, April 21, 1953, MHC, GMW, General Subject Files, f: migrant labor 1953.

63. Greene, "The Iron Curtain in Berrien County," February 18, 1953, PHS, NCC, RG 7, box 10, f: 2; William E. Schoules to Edith Lowry, April 15, 1953, PHS, NCC, RG 7, box 8, f: 16; Shirley E. Greene, *Education*, 5.

64. *Migratory Labor Notes* 10 (July–September, 1959); M. C. Henderson to Alvin Bentley, March 29, 1954, MHC, AB, Congressional Files, f: Chicano farm labor 1954; Robert G. Goodwin to Alvin Bentley, March 13, 1958, and Donald O. Brown to Robert Goodwin, February 12, 1958, MHC, AB, Congressional Files, f: Chicano farm labor 1954; *Toledo Blade*, October 8, 1959; C. W. Meyers to Walter H. Judd, March 19, 1959, MHS, WHJ, f: Labor and Public Welfare Committee, January, 1958–July, 1959; U.S. Congress, House, Committee on Agriculture, Subcommittee on Equipment, Supplies, and Manpower, *Mexican Farm Labor Program*, 196; *Congressional Record*, House, March 2, 1954, 2358; *Benton Harbor News-Palladium*, September 30, 1959.

65. "Migrant Reforms Urged"; Bernard, "Run-Around," 353; *Berrien Springs Journal-Era*, March 2, 1956; Edgar Johnston to John Sweeney, October 26, 1955, MHC, GMW, General Subject File, f: migrant labor, 1955; *Lansing State Journal*, September 24, 1955; *Detroit News*, February 25, 1956; Report of Legislative Committee to Study Problems of Migratory Labor, 1955, MSA, JT, box 223, f: 4.

66. John Sweeney to Edgar Johnston, October 12, 1955, MHC, GMW, General Subject Files, f: migrant labor, 1955; *Lansing State Journal*, September 24, 1955; Ralph Seitz to Patrick V. McNamara, March 28, 1950, WPR, PVM, box 512, f: labor–migrants, May 25, 1950.

67. Summaries of Michigan Migrant Ministry Projects, summer 1956, and Michigan State Report, October 15, 1957, PHS, NCC, RG 7, box 10, f: 1; Minnesota State Report, 1957, PHS, NCC, RG 7, box 10, f: 3; Ohio State Report, 1957, PHS, NCC, RG 7, box 10, f: 16; Wisconsin State Report, 1957, PHS, NCC, RG 7, box 11, f: 8; Minnesota Governor's Farm and Migratory Labor Advisory Committee, meeting, April 8, 1958, MHS, OCF, f: Migratory Labor Commission, 1958; Health and Activities, DDE, PCML, box 2, f: Illinois.

68. "Good-Will Gesture to Migrants Pays Off in Michigan"; Martin and

Faribault County, Minnesota, August 12, 1958, PHS, NCC, RG 7, box 10, f: 3; *Migratory Labor Notes* 7 (September–December, 1958); *Lansing State Journal,* July 5, 1952; Huber, "Migratory Agricultural Workers," 74, 76; MESC, *Post Season 1956,* 19.

69. Michigan Commission on Migratory Labor, meeting, March 24, 1952, WPR, EJ, box 1, f: minutes; Camp Warren, Coloma, Michigan, Report, July 7, 1952, PHS, NCC, RG 7, box 10, f: 2; Polk County, Minnesota, Report, 1956, PHS, NCC, RG 7, box 10, f: 3; Albert Ralston to Clare E. Hoffman, MHC, GMW, General Subject Files, f: migratory labor, 1953; Field Trip to Grant, WPR, EJ, box 1, f: 6; A. W. Bolan to G. Mennen Williams, July 19, 1958, MHC, GMW, General Subject Files, f: migrant labor, 1958.

70. Bay County, Michigan, 1955, MHC, MMC, box 93C, Barbara June Macklin, *Structural Stability and Culture Change in a Mexican-American Community,* 35–38; Comments, County Extension Directors, 1958, MHC, GMW, Executive Office, Charles Brown, f: migrant labor; *Lansing State Journal,* May 25, 1952; Minnesota Governor's Farm and Migratory Labor Advisory Committee, meeting, April 8, 1958, MHS, OCF, f: Migratory Labor Commission, 1958.

71. *Saginaw News,* May 13, 1953; Minnesota Farm and Migratory Labor Advisory Committee, meeting, November 22, 1957, MHS, OCF, f: Farm and Migratory Labor Advisory Committee, 1957; *Cleveland Plain Dealer,* May 31, 1959; *New World,* October 31, 1952; Mrs. Margaret Rogan to James Hickey, November 19, 1951, f: Mexican Apostolate, DS; Crosthwait, "Excerpts from the Report of Field Trip into Northern States," SCSU, EG, box 13, f: 5.

72. "Study of State Migrant Committees, PHS, HMC, box 49; Michigan State Report, October, 1956, PHS, NCC, RG 7, box 10, f: 1; Michigan Summaries of Projects, 1956, PHS, NCC, RG 7, box 10, f: 1; Lutheran Church Ministry to Migrants in the Red River Valley, 1958, MHS, OCF, f: migrant labor committees, 1958; *Port Huron Times,* June 25, 1950; Holland, Michigan, 1959, MMC, box 93C; *South Bend Tribune,* June 16, 1959; Minnesota Governor's Commission, *Migrant Worker in Minnesota (1956),* 9; Mason County, Michigan, Report, 1959, MHC, MMC, box 93C.

73. Michigan Area Reports, 1957, and Bay County, 1959, MHC, MMC, box 93C; Upland, Indiana, State Report, 1957, August 15, 1952, PHS, NCC, RG 7, box 9, f: 15; Indiana State Report, 1957, PHS, NCC, RG 7, box 9, f: 15; Wisconsin State Report, 1957, PHS, NCC, RG 7, box 11, f: 8; Ohio State Report, 1957, PHS, NCC, RG 7, box 10, f: 16.

74. Lacota, Michigan, 1956, PHS, NCC, RG 7, box 10, f: 2; Ohio State Report, 1957, PHS, NCC, RG 7, box 10, f: 16; "Confidential Report," PHS, NCC, RG 7, box 10, f: 16; Schoules to Lowry, PHS, NCC, RG 7, box 8, f: 16; Blue Earth, Minnesota, Report, August 10, 1958, PHS, NCC, RG 7, box 10, f: 3.

75. Berrien County, Michigan, 1959, MHC, MMC, box 93C; Indiana State Report, 1957, PHS, NCC, RG 7, box 9, f: 15; Blue Earth, Minnesota, August 10, 1958, PHS, NCC, RG 7, box 10, f: 3; Martin and Faribault County, Minnesota, August 12, 1958, PHS, NCC, RG 7, box 10, f: 3.

76. Ohio State Report, 1957, PHS, NCC, RG 7, box 10, f: 16; Montcalm

County, Michigan, Report 1954, MHC, MMC, box 93C; Summaries of Migrant Ministry Projects, summer, 1956, PHS, NCC, RG 7, box 10, f: 1.

77. *Wage Earner,* July 1951; Al Craig to Max Horton, August 23, 1954, MHC, GMW, General Subject Files, f: migratory labor, 1955; *Lansing State Journal,* February 26, 1953; M. C. Henderson to Steven Woznicki, May 6, 1958, and James L. Vizzard to Woznicki, September 10, 1959, f: Mexican Apostolate, DS; *Saginaw News,* February 16, 1953; *Catholic Weekly,* May 4, 1958.

78. *Work,* September, 1956; *Cleveland Union Leader,* October 5, 1956.

79. Consumers League of Michigan, *Bulletin* 9 (August 17, 1951); Gabriel Torres to Adolfo Ruiz Cortines, August 19, 1953, 546.6/109, AGN, ARC; *Ann Arbor News,* December 1, 1951; interview, Msgr. Clement Kern, August 7, 1980.

80. *Detroit Free Press,* September 14, 1950; Galarza, *Farm Workers,* 107, 307; *Saginaw News,* February 16, 1953.

81. Committee on Labor and Public Welfare, *Migratory Labor 1959,* 1:301.

82. *Economic Outlook* 13 (April 1952): 26; *CIO Constitutional Convention,* November 5–9, 1951, DDE, PCML, box 63, f: migratory labor, 1952; AFL-CIO Executive Council, "Migratory Agricultural Labor," August 13, 1957, SCSU, EG, box 19, f: 9.

83. Macklin, *Structural Stability,* ii; Alvar W. Carlson, "The Settling Process of Mexican-Americans in Northwestern Ohio"; John R. Weeks and Joseph Spielberg Benítez, "The Cultural Demography of Midwestern Chicano Communities," 229–231; Minnesota Governor's Interracial Commission, *Mexican in Minnesota (1953),* 6–9; Fotia and Richmond, *Mexican-American of the South Bend,* 5–6.

84. *Detroit Free Press,* August 28, 1955; Waupun Council on Human Relations, Waupun Migrant Project, 1951, WPR, EJ, box 2, f: 9, WPR; interviews, Andrew Anguiano, June 21, 1984, Efraín Marínez, June 6, 1984, Mario Compeán, December 18, 1983; Janet M. Jorgensen, David E. Williams, and John H. Burma, *Migratory Agricultural Workers in the United States.*

85. Michigan Governor's Study Commission, November 12, 1952, MHC, GMW, General Subject Files, f: migrant labor 1952; interviews, Andrew Anguiano, June 21, 1984, Juan Luna, August 31, 1982, Mario Compeán, December 18, 1983, Cata Estrada, August 25, 1982.

86. *Detroit Free Press,* August 28, 1955; Nancy Stockham, "Statistical-Narrative Study of Resident-Migrant Mexican Labor in Gratiot County," 1952, MSA, JT, box 226, f: 9; Gratiot County, Michigan, 1956, MHC, MMC, box 93C, "Family Case Study," PHS, NCC, RG 7, box 10, f: 14; Survey of Mexican People, Toledo, PHS, NCC, RG 7, box 13, f: 5.

87. Minnesota Farm and Migratory Labor Advisory Committee, meeting, November 22, 1957, MHS, OCF, f: Farm and Migratory Labor Advisory Committee; Minnesota Governor's Interracial Commission, *Mexican in Minnesota (1953),* 30, 48; Norman S. Goldner, "The Mexican in the Northern Urban Area: A Comparison of Two Generations," 42–45; Miriam J. Wells,

"Oldtimers and Newcomers: The Role of Context in Mexican American Assimilation," 280−281.

88. Chicago Heights Program, August 1−August 30, DDE, PCML, box 2, f: Illinois; Illinois Commission on Children, "Program for Agricultural Migrants and Their Families," Springfield, July, 1952, DDE, PCML, box 56, f: publications, Illinois; Chicago Research Group, "Study of Mexican-American Community," 1957, CHS, WCMC, box 147, f: 4; HEW, Harvey District Office, "Project to Reach Agricultural Migrant Workers," December, 1959, CHS, WCMC, box 402, f: 6; Juan R. García, "History of Chicanos in Chicago Heights," 299−301.

89. Committee on Labor and Public Welfare, *Migratory Labor 1960*, 1: 301; Fotia and Richmond, *Mexican-American of the South Bend*.

90. Michigan Study Commission on Migratory Labor, March 24, 1952, WPR, EJ, box 1, f: minutes; Stockham, "Statistical-Narrative Study of Resident-Migrant Mexican Labor in Gratiot County," 1952, WPR, JT, EJ, box 2, f: 6; Lenawee County, Michigan, 1959, MHC, MMC, box 93C, "Michigan Résumé on the Migrant Situation, 1954," PHS, NCC, RG 7, box 10, f: 1; William Kerns to Donovan, March 17, 1954, f: correspondence, 1953−1954, AD; Dennis Nodín Valdés, *El Pueblo Mexicano en Detroit y Michigan: A Social History*, 51−66; interview, Juan J. Castillo, June 12, 1984.

91. Survey, Mexican People, Toledo, PHS, NCC, RG 7, box 13, f: 5; Ohio Migrant Ministry, Sandusky County Report, June 25−September 3, 1951, PHS, NCC, RG 7, f: 3; interviews, Henry Miranda, August 27, 1982, Juan Luna, August 31, 1982, and December 25, 1983, Vicenta Velásquez, August 27, 1982; Macklin, *Structural Stability*, 31−32.

92. Stockham, "Statistical-Narrative Study of Resident-Migrant Mexican Labor in Gratiot County," 1952, MSA, JT, box 226, f: 9; June Macklin, *Americans of Mexican Descent: A Toledo Study*, 3, 5, 13.

93. Henley and Henley, *Minnesota And Her Migratory Workers*, 25; interviews, Israel Leyton, August 13, 1980, Juan Luna, August 31, 1982, and December 25, 1983.

94. Gratiot County, Michigan, 1957, MHC, MMC, box 93C; Macklin, *Structural Stability*, 49; idem, *Americans*, 16, 20; Clifford E. Rucker, Activities Report, August 30, 1954, MHS, EA, f: Interracial Commission; interviews, Henry Miranda, August 27, 1982, Juan Luna, August 25, 1981, and December 25, 1983, María Castellanos, June 8, 1984.

8. Breaking Chains, 1960−1970

1. *Detroit Free Press*, August 20, 1969.

2. *Lansing State Journal*, August 2, 1966; Karl T. Wright, Dennis Fisher, and Myron P. Kelsey, *Agricultural Employment and Income in Michigan*, 1.

3. David Cormier and Arnold Mauricio, "Indiana Farm Labor Scene," MCLR, box 11, f: 21; Interview, Jesús Salas, December 21, 1983; Oceana County, Michigan, 1960, MHC, MMC, box 93C; MESC, *Farm Labor Report: Post Season 1962*, 35; Myrtle Reul, *Territorial Boundaries of Rural Poverty*;

Profiles of Exploitation, 327; Indiana State Employment Service (hereafter ISES), *Indiana Farm Labor Report 1962*, 11; Willson, "Historical Development," 99; Leftwich, "Migratory Harvest Labor," 112.

4. J. Craig Jenkins and Charles Perrow, "Insurgency of the Powerless: Farm Worker Movements (1946–1972)," 259; *NACFL Information Letter #12* (November 1960); Allsup, *G.I. Forum*, 124–125; Galarza, *Farm Workers*, 315–320; Majka and Majka, *Farm Workers*, 156.

5. *Saginaw Journal*, September 13, 1964; MESC, *Post Season Farm Labor Report 1961*, 17; idem, *Post Season Farm Labor Report 1964*, 33; New Hudson Farm Bureau to Patrick McNamara, February 23, 1962, and Victor Anderson to McNamara, February 15, 1962, WPR, PVM, box 534, f: labor—migrant workers, S. 1129; George Dupont to Dwight D. Eisenhower, September 13, 1960, and Charles B. Shuman to Eisenhower, September 2, 1960, DDE, CFGF, box 968, f: 126-J-4 (migratory labor, 4); Willard Wirtz, *Year of Transition: Seasonal Farm Labor, 1965*, 25.

6. Mildred Gladstone to Fay Bennett, April 14, 1965, MHC, MMC, box 93C; *Detroit Free Press*, September 25, 1965; *Detroit News*, May 18, 1965; Philip Fell to MacNamara, April 21, 1965, and Francis Janicke to McNamara, March 10, 1965, WPR, PVM, box 562, f: labor—braceros; "Final Report of the Michigan Farm Labor Panel to the Secretary of Labor, Willard Wirtz" (Detroit, 1965), 13, SOM; U.S. Congress, Senate, Committee on Agriculture and Forestry, *Extension of Mexican Farm Labor Program*, 126.

7. *Saginaw News*, August 6, 1965; *Detroit News*, May 18, July 4, 25, 1965, August 31, 1966; *State Journal*, January 12, 1966; *Bay City Times*, August 21, 1966, March 15, 1967.

8. *Bay City Times*, December 13, 1963; North Montcalm and Saint Joseph County, Michigan, Reports, 1964, MHC, MMC, box 93C; *Saginaw Journal*, September 13, 1964; MESC, *Post Season Farm Labor Reports 1964*, 45: *Lansing State Journal*, September 8, 9, 1964.

9. *Bay City Times*, January 30, July 30, 1967; Willson, "Historical Development," 84; MESC, *Post-Season 1964*, 11.

10. F. M. Mitchell to Mildred Gladstone, November 16, 1964, MHS, MMC, box 93C; Michigan Migrant Ministry (hereafter MMM), *Annual Reports, 1961–1966, 1969*, MHS, MMC, box 93C; MESC, *Post Season Farm Labor Reports, 1964*, 10, and *1965*, 10, and *1968*, 10; Wisconsin, Governor's Committee on Migratory Labor, *Report for 1966 and 1967*, 5; Minnesota, Department of Employment Security (hereafter MDES), *Post-Season Agricultural and Food Processing Report, 1964*, 8, 27; ISES, *Indiana Farm Labor Report, 1964*, 43, and *1967*, 39, and *1968*, 34, and *1969*, 29; Illinois Commission on Children, Committee on Agricultural Migrant Workers, *County Profile of Agricultural Migrant Workers in Illinois 1967*; "Illinois Fact Sheet," f: Chicago, SSCC.

11. Michigan Civil Rights Commission (hereafter MCRC), *1969 Report and Recommendations: A Field Study of Migrant Workers in Michigan*, 8; United Migrant Opportunity Services (UMOS), "Annual Report—1968," 3, WHS.

12. Jenkins and Perrow, "Insurgency"; Kushner, *Long Road*; Galarza,

Farm Workers; Max J. Pfeffer, "The Labor Process and Corporate Agriculture: Mexican Workers in California."

13. Veril Baldwin to Glen Johnson and J. Elterich, October 11, 1962, WPR, MWL, box 41, f: Michigan Citizen's Committee on Agricultural Labor; NACFL, *Agribusiness and Its Workers*, 3; Rankin Lyman to Patrick McNamara, February 24, 1962; PVM, box 534, f: labor—migrant workers, WPR, *Detroit Free Press*, February 27, 1963; Michigan House and Senate Labor Committees, "Migrant Labor Report, November, 1965," 8–9, MSA, RCK, box 4, f: 9; U.S. Congress, Senate, Committee on Labor and Public Welfare, Subcommittee on Migratory Labor, *To Stabilize the Domestic Farm Labor Force*, 763; W. L. Maitland to George Romney, January 15, 1963, MHC, GR, box 34, General Subject Files, f: migrant labor, 1963; Dorothy Spiker to Walter Mikesell, April 29, 1964, CHS; WCMC, box 402, f: 6.

14. *NACFL Information Letter #32* (December, 1966); *Saginaw News*, March 20, 22, April 30, 1966; Edgar Johnston, *Migrant Workers in the State of Michigan*, 16.

15. Ohio, Senate, *Ohio's Migrant Workers, June, 1980–April, 1981*, 16, FLOC; Midwestern Regional Office, Division for the Spanish-speaking, Department of Social Services, *Newsletter* 3 (October, 1970); *Cleveland Plain Dealer*, March 2, 1961; Ohio, Governor's Committee on Migratory Labor, *Migratory Labor in Ohio (1964)*, 5; Thomas Stewart to William Kircher, April 26, 1967, WPR, WK, box 22, f: 11.

16. Rebecca Tompkins to H. Rubenstein, July 10, 1962, WPR, MWL, box 41, f: MCCAL; *Lansing State Journal*, November 15, 1964; *Chicago Star*, July 6, 1962; South Cook Council for Migrants (hereafter SCCM), August 28, 1961, CHS, WCMC, box 402, f: 6; *Toledo Blade*, June 13, 16, August 20, 1962; *Toledo Catholic Chronicle*, August 30, 1963.

17. Ohio Governor's Committee on Migrant Labor, *Migratory Labor in Ohio (1965)*, 16; Leelanau County, Michigan, 1960, and Mildred Gladstone to Ester, November 15, 1965, MHC, MMC, box 93C.

18. Gladstone to Mrs. U. G. Collins, April 12, 1965, Michigan Migrant Ministry *Annual Reports, 1966, 1967, 1968*, MHC, MMC, box 93C; John Adams, "Goals of the Migrant Ministry," August 4, 1969, MFWM; Ohio Governor's Committee on Migrant Labor, *Migratory Labor in Ohio (1965)*, 15–16.

19. Bay County, 1960, Lenawee County, Michigan, 1963, and Mildred Gladstone to Mary H. Goddess, April 13, 1965, MHS, MMC, box 93C; *Lansing State Journal*, April 13, 1967; *Indianapolis Star*, September 17, 1961; *Indianapolis Times*, December 17, 1962; statement, Gilbert Cardenas, *The Status of Agricultural Workers in Indiana* (South Bend, 1974), 13, MCLR, box 11, f: 13; *Milwaukee Journal*, July 1, 1966; *Toledo Blade*, April 13, 1967; *Toledo Catholic Chronicle*, April 22, 1966.

20. Allsup, *G.I. Forum*, 124–125; Galarza, *Farm Workers*, 315–320; *Indianapolis Times*, December 17, 1962; *Indianapolis Star*, February 14, 1963; Willis W. Velte to Walter Judd, June 12, 1961, MHS, WHJ, f: Labor and Public Welfare Committee, March, 1961; Wisconsin Governor's Committee, *Report 1966 and 1967*, 8–9; *Detroit Free Press*, August 18, 1969.

21. *Bay City Times*, August 16, 1970; Mitzi Cohen, *Migrant Health in*

Monroe County, 2–3; U.S. Congress, Senate, Committee on Labor and Public Welfare, Subcommittee on Migratory Labor, *Migrant Health Services,* 152–153; Wisconsin Governor's Commission on Human Rights, *Migrant Labor in Wisconsin,* 3; *Minneapolis Star,* August 1, 1968; *Toledo Blade,* June 27, 1963.

22. *Cleveland Plain Dealer,* December 25, 1960, March 2, 1961; Rev. and Mrs. Carl Staser, *The Frankfort Child Care Center,* MHC, MMC, box 93C; Wisconsin Governor's Committee on Migratory Labor, *Report to the Governor, 1964,* 3, WHS; *Detroit Free Press,* August 18, 1969.

23. *Bay City Times,* July 28, 1968; MMM, *Annual Reports, 1967, 1969,* MHC, MMC, box 93C; *Saginaw News,* May 18, 1965, June 4, 1970; *Lansing State Journal,* March 28, 1965, June 30, 1966, June 21, November 15, 1970; James D. Howell, Bernard L. Erven, and John S. Bottum, *Migrant Farm Workers in Northwestern Ohio,* 19; Wisconsin Governor's Commission on Human Rights, *Proceedings of the Migrant Labor Conference, December 4, 1964* (Madison, 1965), 7, 27, WHS.

24. Harvey M. Choldin and Grafton D. Trout, *Mexican-Americans in Transition: Migration and Employment in Michigan Cities,* 224; UMOS, *Annual Report–1968,* 3.

25. MMM, *Annual Report, 1968,* MHC, MMC, box 93C; Ohio Governor's Committee on Migratory Labor, *Migratory Labor in Ohio (1965),* 14. *Indianapolis News,* April 20, 1967; Amendment of the Articles of Incorporation of AMOS, Inc., MCLR, box 44, f: AMOS; *South Bend Tribune,* July 4, 1965; "UMOS," f: Green Bay, SSCC; Illinois Commission on Children, *County Profile,* 8; *Minneapolis Star,* July 30, 1968; *Toledo Catholic Chronicle,* April 22, 1966; UMOS, *Annual Report–1968,* 3, 16–17; US Congress, Senate, Committee on Labor and Public Welfare, Subcommittee on Migratory Labor, *Migrant and Seasonal Farmworker Powerlessness,* IV-B, 1901; interview, Henry Miranda, August 27, 1982; USDL News Release, August 1, 1976, NA, RG 174, W. J. Usery papers, f: farm labor, May–December 1976; National Migrant Ministry Section, Executive Committee, meeting, May 7, 1970, PHS, NCC, RG 6, box 61, f: 3.

26. *UMOI Newsletter* 4 (October, 1968), 6 (March, 1969); *Indianapolis Star,* December 29, 1966, April 17, 1968; *Indianapolis News,* April 21, 1967, March 30, 1972; UMOS, *Annual Report–1968,* 3, 24; *Detroit Free Press,* June 26, 30, 1970; William Benallack to Stanley Powell, November 11, 1969, MSA, SMP, box 4, f: 3.

27. Johnston, *Migrant Workers,* 27; *Saginaw News,* August 23, 1969; *UMOI Newsletter* (March, 1969); Duane Lindstrom, *Indiana Migrants: Blighted Hopes, Slighted Rights,* 27; *Indianapolis Star,* July 16, 1967; *South Bend Tribune,* November 11, 1968; UMOS, *Annual Report–1968,* 3.

28. MMM, *Annual Report, 1969,* MHC, MMC, box 93C; Carol Berry, *A Survey of the Holland Spanish-speaking Community,* 54; UMOI, *Compendium of College Student Employees,* MCLR, box 11, f: 13.

29. Michigan Farm Worker Ministry (hereafter MFWM), "Michigan Farm Worker Ministry, 1973–1974," MFWM; Testimony, Carlos Sundermann, 1973, MSA, JS, box 4, f: 5; *Wall Street Journal,* April 4, 1973.

30. *Indianapolis Star*, December 29, 1966; Leftwich, "Migratory Harvest Labor," 81; John F. Heathershaw to Mrs. Vincent C. Oltman, November 18, 1960, DDE, PCML, box 72, f: Illinois, general; *Columbus Union-Republican*, May 31, 1962; Welfare Council of Metropolitan Chicago (hereafter WCMC), "Services to Children of Migrants," September 14, 1964, 6, CHS, WCMC, box 624, f: 6; U.S. Civil Rights Commission, *The Fifty States Report: Submitted to the Commission on Civil Rights by the State Advisory Committees, 1961*, 280; *Bay City Times*, October 2, 1966; MMM, *Annual Reports, 1966, 1967*, MHC, MMC, box 93C; *Lansing State Journal*, February 26, 1978; Willson, "Historical Development," 116–118. Johnston, *Migrant Workers*, 23–24; *Detroit Free Press*, August 18, 1969.

31. UMOI, University-affiliated Migrant Research and Service, MSA, JS, box 4, f: 5; *Indianapolis News*, October 6, 1970; Michigan Civil Rights Commission, *Report and Recommendations (1969)*, 9; *Houston Post*, September 1, 1963; *Ave Maria*, October 10, 1966; *Detroit Free Press*, August 17, 20, 1969; *Toledo Blade*, August 4, 1961; *Columbus Citizen-Journal*, October 3, 1969; *Wall Street Journal*, September 19, 1969.

32. MMM, *Annual Report, 1967*, MHC, MMC, box 93C; *Detroit Free Press*, August 17, 1969; *Houston Post*, September 1, 1963; *Dayton Daily News*, June 3, 1968.

33. UMOI, University-affiliated Migrant Research and Service, MSA, JS, box 4, f: 5; Lenawee County, Michigan, 1961, MHC, MMC, box 93C; Wisconsin, Governor's Committee, *Report for 1966 and 1967*, 23; *Milwaukee Sentinel*, September 8, 1967; *Detroit Free Press*, August 17, 1969; *Madison Capital Times*, July 31, 1967; *Toledo Blade*, August 4, 1961.

34. Sanilac County and Tri-County, Michigan, 1962, MHC, MMC, box 93C; "Health Care for Migrants"; *Toledo Blade*, August 4, 1961; *Migrant Health Services*, 152; *Ave Maria*, December 10, 1966; Cohen, *Migrant Health in Monroe County*, 5–6.

35. Oceana County, Michigan, 1963, MMC, box 93C; MMM, *Annual Report, 1969*, MHC, MMC, box 93C; *Saginaw News*, July 24, 1970; *Detroit Free Press*, July 2, 1970.

36. MMM, *Annual Report, 1969*, MHC, MMC, box 93C.

37. *Migratory Labor Notes* 13 (November, 1960); Lindstrom, *Indiana Migrants*, 22; South Cook Council for Migrants, (SCCM), minutes, August 22, October 3, 1960, CHS, WCMC, box 402, f: 7; Heathershaw to Oltman, DDE, PCML, box 72, f: Illinois.

38. MMM, *Annual Report, 1967*, MHC, MMC, box 93C; *Lansing State Journal*, August 27, 1971; *Migratory Labor Notes* 12 (August, 1960); John W. Schmitt to William Kircher, July 9, 1968, WPR, WK, box 23, f: 13.

39. *Detroit Free Press*, August 22, 1970; Dennis U. Fisher, "The State vs. the Federal Minimum Wage and Michigan Farm Employers," 1; Schmitt to Kircher, July 9, 1968, WPR, WK, box 23, f: 13; *Detroit Free Press*, August 18, 1969.

40. *Detroit Free Press*, August 18, 1969; NACFL, *Information Letter # 32*; *Madison Capital Times*, May 27, 1968; *Wisconsin State Journal*, May 28, 1968.

41. Walter D. Krech to Arthur S. Fleming, May 11, 1960, DDE, PCML, box 72, f: Illinois (general); *Wisconsin State Journal*, June 28, 1968; *Detroit Free Press*, August 18, 1969; *Minneapolis Star*, July 29, 1968.

42. MCRC, *1969 Report*, 4.

43. University of Wisconsin Institute for Research on Poverty, *A Study of Migratory Workers in Cucumber Harvesting: Waushara County, Wisconsin, 1964*, 58; Wirtz, *Year of Transition*, 11; John Adams, "A Background Paper for the Reconsideration of the Goals of the Migrant Ministry," MFWM; "Health Care for Migrants"; *Lansing State Journal*, March 28, 1965; United States Catholic Conference, News Release, December 9, 1974, f: legislation, AD.

44. MMM, *Annual Report, 1967*, MHC, MMC, box 93C; Daniel W. Sturt, "Workmen's Compensation and Michigan Farm Employers," 1–2; Roy O. Fuentes, *An Assessment of the Problems of Migrant Workers in Michigan* (Lansing, 1968), 15, JJC; Donald L. Uchtman, *Agricultural Labor Laws in Illinois*, 5; Wisconsin Governor's Commission on Human Rights, *Migrant Labor in Wisconsin*, 4; University of Wisconsin Institute for Research on Poverty, *Cucumber Harvesting*, 1; *Detroit Free Press*, August 18, 1969.

45. *Detroit Free Press*, August 17, 18, 1969; *Wall Street Journal*, September 19, 1969; MCRC, *Report and Recommendations on the Status of Migrant Farm Labor in Michigan 1968*, 7.

46. *Lansing State Journal*, April 25, 1968; Ohio, Senate, *Ohio's Migrant Workers: Senate Investigation of Living and Working Conditions*, June, 1980–April, 1981, FLOC; Stanley M. Powell to Dan E. Reed, March 13, 1968, and Powell to Lorraine Beebe, October 16, 1969, MSA, SMP, box 4, f: 3; Arthur Schoules to Alvin Bentley, January 21, 1960, MHC, AB, box 26, f: Chicano farm labor 1; Mr. and Mrs. Ralph Alkire to George Romney, March 10, 1966, and Davis Farm Bureau, to Romney, March 28, 1966, MHC, GR, box 145, f: agricultural workers, A–F; New Hudson Farm Bureau to McNamara, WPR, PVM, box 534, f: labor—migrant workers; *Indianapolis Star*, February 14, 1963; Dorothy Spiker to SCCM, December 7, 1960, CHS, WCMC, box 402, f: 6; *Detroit Free Press*, August 18, 1969; *Toledo Blade*, August 9, 1969.

47. John S. Kramek to Patrick V. McNamara, November 30, 1960, and Elizabeth M. Munger to McNamara, March 5, 1960, WPR, PVM, box 409, f: labor—migrant worker; *Indianapolis Star*, December 29, 1966; *South Bend Tribune*, December 27, 1966; *Columbus Union-Republican*, May 31, 1962; *Minneapolis Star*, July 30, 1968.

48. Arthur C. and Lillian J. Thade to McNamara, February 13, 1962, and Lawrence to McNamara, February 20, 1962, and Arthur Thomas to McNamara, February 22, 1962, WPR, PVM, box 534, f: labor–migrant workers.

49. Lenawee County, 1961 and 1964, Midland County, Michigan, 1964, MHC, MMC, box 93C; *Lansing State Journal*, August 6, 1969; *Indianapolis News*, October 9, 1971; Howell et al., *Migrant Farm Workers*, 21; Rankin Lyman to James L. Vizzard, November 25, 1964, SCSU, JLV, box 8, f: 9.

50. James Riddle Hundley, Jr., *A Study of Interpersonal Relations among*

Managers and Employers of Fruit and Vegetable Farms, 46; Edgar Johnston, *Migrant Workers in the State of Michigan,* 26; Sheldon Geller and Raymond R. Leal, "The Wretched of the Earth Revisited: The Case of Indiana's Migrant Laborers," MCLR, box 11, f: 25; UMOS, *Annual Report—1968,* 24; Wisconsin Governor's Commission on Human Rights, *Migrant Labor in Wisconsin,* 2; *Wall Street Journal,* September 19, 1969; *Madison Capital Times,* July 27, 1967; *Columbus Citizen-Journal,* October 3, 1968.

51. *Lansing State Journal,* October 4, 1971; *Detroit Free Press,* August 17, 1969; George Gutiérrez et al. v. Joseph Hassle and Harriet Hassle, MCLR, box 39, f: 3; statement, Alicia Gutiérrez, MCLR, box 10, f: 4; *Detroit Free Press,* July 26, 1970.

52. Statement, Alicia Gutiérrez, MCLR, box 10, f: 4; *Lansing State Journal,* April 14, July 8, 1971.

53. *Lansing State Journal,* April 17, July 8, 1971; *Detroit Free Press,* August 17, 1969; statement, Alicia Gutiérrez, MCLR, box 10, f: 4.

54. *Lansing State Journal,* April 14, July 8, October 4, 1971; Gutiérrez et al. v. Hassle and Hassle; Geller and Leal, "Wretched of the Earth," 8, MCLR, box 11, f: 25; Cormier and Mauricio, "Indiana Farm Labor Scene," MCLR, box 11, f: 21; Ohio Senate, *Migrant Workers,* 2–3, FLOC; Ohio House, Select Committee on Migrant Workers in Ohio, *Final Report, December, 1981,* FLOC; *Indianapolis News,* March 30, 1972.

55. *Lansing State Journal,* November 15, 1964, August 6, 1969; Ohio Governor's Committee on Migratory Labor, *Migratory Labor in Ohio (1965),* 13; Roy O. Fuentes, "An Assessment of the Problems of Migrant Workers in Michigan" (Lansing, 1968), 4–5, 7, JJC; MCRC, *Report and Recommendations 1968,* 7; UMOI, "Compendium of College Student Employees," MCLR, box 11, f: 13; *Detroit Free Press,* April 2, 1969; Ohio, House, *Final Report,* 21.

56. Leelanau (Northport) and Lenawee County, 1960, and North Montcalm, Michigan, 1961, MMM, *Annual Report, 1969,* MHC, MMC, box 93C; *Lansing State Journal,* November 15, 1964; SCCM, meeting, August 14, 1961, CHS, WCMC, box 402, f: 7.

57. MMM, *Annual Report, 1969,* MHC, MMC, box 93C; *Detroit Free Press,* August 17, 1969, July 2, 1970; Committee on Labor and Public Welfare, *Powerlessness,* 7-B: 4552; MCRC, *Report and Recommendations 1968,* 13, 15.

58. MCRC, *Report and Recommendations,* 9; Reul, *Territorial Boundaries,* 332; *Lansing State Journal,* November 15, 1964; SCCM, June 26, 1961, CHS, WCMC, box 402, f: 7; *Toledo Blade,* July 9, 1963.

59. Manistee County, Michigan, 1960, MHC, MMC, box 93C; Illinois Committee on Children, March 8, 1962, CHS, WCMC, box 402, f: 6; Marilyn McGee to Charles O. Ross, June 26, 1967, CHS, WCMC, box 624, f: 2; *Houston Post,* September 1, 1963.

60. Ohio Governor's Committee on Migratory Labor, *Migratory Labor in Ohio 1965,* 7.

61. *Indianapolis Star,* August 6, 1967; Cardenas, "The Status," 15; Mid-

west Council on La Raza Information, MCLR, box 58, f: 2; Choldin and Trout, *Mexican-Americans*, 26, 105; Carlson, "Settling Process"; La Raza Unida of Michigan to Ford Foundation, 1970, JJC; *Detroit Free Press*, August 20, 1969.

62. *Lansing State Journal*, May 29, 1966; WCMC, "Background Paper"; *Toledo Blade*, August 1, 1964; *South Bend Tribune*, August 3, 1975.

63. Lenawee and Gratiot County, 1960, and Bay, Lenawee, Oceana, and Ottawa County, 1961, Mason County, Michigan, 1964, MHC, MMC, box 93C; Doris P. Slesinger and Eileen Muirragui, *Migrant Agricultural Labor in Wisconsin: A Short History*, 15; MMM, *Annual Report, 1969*, MHC, MMC, box 93C; *Detroit Free Press*, September 14, 1980; Choldin and Trout, *Mexican-Americans*, 226; Eldon E. Snyder and Joseph B. Berry, Jr., "Farm Employer Attitudes toward Mexican-American Migrant Workers."

64. Carlson, "Settling Process," 36–37; Archdiocese of Milwaukee, "Cristo Rey Pastoral Center," MCLR, box 37, f: 43; Wells, "Oldtimers and Newcomers," 282, 288; Lenawee and Oceana County, 1960, and Bay County, Michigan, 1961, MHC, MMC, box 93C; Gloria Cárdenas to George Romney, December 11, 1965, MHC, GR, box 135, 1966, f: Civil Rights Commission, A–F, and Fred R. Comer to George Romney, February 11, 1962, MHC, GR, box 34, f: migrant labor, 1963; Mr. and Mrs. John Walper to Patrick McNamara, November 25, 1960, WPR, PVM, box 512, f: labor—migrant workers, 1960; *South Bend Tribune*, August 3, 1975; SCCM, meeting, December 5, 1960, CHS, WCMC, box 402, f: 2; Duane Boudreaux, "Chicken and Militants," DDE, PCML, box 72, f: Indiana (general); *Toledo Blade*, August 1, 1964.

65. MMM, *Annual Report, 1968*, MHC, MMC, box 93C; Lindstrom, *Indiana Migrants*, 22–23; *Action*, February 22, 1969; *South Bend Tribune*, June 16, 1974; *La Raza Unida of Michigan*, 18, 20, 32; Ohio Governor's Committee on Migratory Labor, *Migratory Labor in Ohio, 1964*, 12–15; Jim D. Faught, "Social and Economic Characteristics of the Spanish Origin Population in South Bend, Indiana" (Notre Dame: Centro de Estudios Chicanos e Investigaciones Sociales, 1974), 37, 39, MCLR, box 37; interview, Juan J. Castillo, June 12, 1984; *Detroit News*, March 27, 1967; *Madison Capital Times*, July 31, 1967; Berry, *Holland Spanish-speaking*, 16; Rubén Alfaro, "Concerned Citizens for Migrant Workers," WPR, WK, box 21, f: 10.

66. Berry, *Holland Spanish-speaking*, 4; John R. Weeks, "The Impact of Neo-Pentacostalism on Spanish-speaking Catholic Families: The Case of Fremont, Ohio," 1–2, SSCC, f: Toledo, Ohio.

67. *Saginaw News*, January 30, 1968, *Detroit Free Press*, April 2, 1969; Lansing Catholic Diocese, Bishop's Committee for the Spanish-speaking, *1962 Summary*, and Saginaw Catholic Diocese, Bishop's Committee for the Spanish-speaking, *1969 Summary*, and Saginaw Catholic Diocese, "Latin American Affairs Department," LAAD; Harold J. Brown to Stephen S. Woznicki, March 17, 1965, DS, f: Mexican Apostolate; *Action*, February 22, 1969.

68. MMM, *Annual Report, 1969*, MHC, MMC, box 93C; *Lansing State Journal*, April 13, 1967; Saginaw Diocese, Bishop's Committee for the Spanish-speaking, *1968 Handbook*, LAAD; *Perspectives—UCS* 1 (October 1965), MCLR, box 20, f: 1; Barbara Driscoll, *Newspaper Documentary His-*

tory of the Chicano Community of South Bend, Indiana, 10; *South Bend Tribune,* May 22, 1964.

69. Willson, "Historical Development," 107; *Lansing Labor News,* May 2, 1968; *Lansing State Journal,* April 13, 1967; *Detroit Free Press,* March 25, 1967; *Detroit News,* March 27, 1967; Michigan, Department of Social Services, Midwestern Regional Office, Division for the Spanish Speaking, *Newsletter* 3 (October, 1970); Roy O. Fuentes, "An Assessment of the Problems of Migrant Workers in Michigan," 16, JJC; Meeting with Dan Healy and Quality Products Association, July 2, 1969, WPR, WK, box 21, f: 8; William Benallack to R. Alfaro et al., December 8, 1967, and Eugene Boutilier to William Benallack, January 9, 1968, WPR, WK, box 21, f: 12; *Toledo Blade,* April 13, 1967; *Michigan AFL-CIO News,* March 29, 1967; interview, Juan J. Castillo, June 12, 1984.

70. Lenawee, Manistee, and Ottawa County, Michigan, 1961, MHC, MMC, box 93C; MFWM, "Summary, 1973–1974"; *Detroit Free Press,* August 27, 1968, September 14, 1980; Comer to Romney, MHC, GR, box 135, f: Civil Rights Commission, A–F; MCRC, *Report and Recommendations 1968,* 11.

71. Lenawee County, Michigan, 1960, MHC, MMC, box 93C; Wells, "Old-timers and Newcomers," 288; *Detroit Free Press,* September 14, 1980; Vicente T. Jiménez to George Romney, January 2, 1963, and Víctor Hernández to Walter DeVries, September 5, 1963, MHC, GR, box 34, f: migrant labor, 1963; Lindstrom, *Indiana Migrants,* 18; UMOI, "Compendium" MCLR, box 11, f: 13; MCRC, *Report and Recommendations 1968,* 15; *Milwaukee Journal,* July 26, 1967; *Madison Capital Times,* July 27, 1967.

72. Leelanau (Northport), Lenawee, and Manistee, 1960, and Oceana and Ottawa County, Michigan, 1961, MHC, MMC, box 93C; *Detroit Free Press,* September 14, 1980; Committee on Labor and Public Welfare, *Powerlessness,* 7-B: 4554; Michigan Commission of the Spanish-speaking, "Report to Governor Milliken, 1973," JJC; statement, Mrs. A. Went, SSCC, f: Indiana, South Bend; Cárdenas to Romney, December 11, 1965, MHC, GR, box 135, 1966, f: Civil Rights Commission, A–F.

73. *Bay City Times,* August 13, 1967; interview, Juan J. Castillo, June 12, 1984.

74. *Industrial Worker,* August 5, 1964.

75. *Bay City Times,* September 6, 1966; Michigan Migrant Ministry, MMM, *Annual Report, 1966,* MHC, MMC, box 93C; Stewart to Kircher, WPR, WK, box 22, f: 11.

76. Dan Healy to Kircher, May 15, 1970, WPR, WK, box 23, f: 13; Kircher to Healy, November 16, December 14, 1966, WPR, WK, box 21, f: 11; Boutilier to Benallack, January 9, 1968, WPR, WK, box 21, f: 12; Healy to Kircher, October 22, 1969, WPR, WK, box 21, f: 14.

77. Miguel Arias to Charles Heymanns, September 1, 1966, WPR, WK, box 23, f: 9; Kircher to files, March 29, 1967, WPR, WK, box 21, f: 10; Kircher to Healy, November 16, 1966, WPR, WK, box 21, f: 11; Napuk to Kircher, November 9, 1966 and John A. Armendáriz to Kircher, November 12, 1966, WPR, WK, box 21, f: 11; Healy to Kircher, October 22, 1969, WPR, WK, box

21, f: 14; Healy to Kircher, December 14, 1966, WPR, WK, box 21; Boutilier to Benallack, January 9, 1968, WPR, WK, box 21, f: 12.

78. Interview, Jesús Salas, December 21, 1983; *South Bend Tribune*, May 1, 1967; Kerry Napuk to Ralph Helstein, September 30, 1966, WPR, WK, box 23, f: 9; *Milwaukee Journal*, September 7, 1969; *Madison Capital Times*, July 31, 1967.

79. Wisconsin Governor's Committee, *1966 and 1967 Report*, 31; *NACFL Information Letter # 31* (September, 1966); Arias to Heymanns, September 1, 1966, WPR, WK, box 23, f: 9; *La Voz Mexicana*, July 14, August 19, 1967; *Milwaukee Sentinel*, August 15, 17, 18, 1966.

80. Interview, Jesús Salas, December 21, 1983; Wisconsin Migrant Ministry, *Annual Report 1966*; Wisconsin Governor's Committee, *1966 and 1967 Report*, 31; Napuk to Helstein, WPR, WK, box 23, f: 9; *Waushara Argus*, October 13, 1966; Obreros Unidos, "The Migrant Workers Strike in Almond, Wisconsin," WPR, WK, box 23, f: 10.

81. Obreros Unidos, "Migrant Workers Strike," WPR, WK, box 23, f: 10; *Wisconsin State Journal*, October 9, 1966; *Milwaukee Journal*, October 13, 16, 1966.

82. Heymanns to Kircher, October 13, 1967, WPR, WK, box 23, f: 12; Obreros Unidos, "Justification of Proposed Budget," WPR, WK, box 23, f: 10; John W. Schmitt to Robert Durkin, July 19, 1967, WPR, WK, box 23, f: 11; *Milwaukee Journal*, October 13, 1966, January 15, 1967; *Milwaukee Journal*, August 9, 1967; *Madison Capitol Times*, June 14, 1967.

83. Obreros Unidos, "Migrant Workers Strike," WPR, WK, box 23, f: 10; *Wisconsin State Journal*, October 9, 1966; *Milwaukee Journal*, October 16, 1966; *La Voz Mexicana*, July 14, 1967; Committee on Labor and Public Welfare, *Powerlessness*, 4-B: 1900.

84. *Waushara Argus*, August 18, December 1, 8, 1966; Obreros Unidos, "The Case against Howard Dutcher," January 12, 1967, and idem, "Projected 1967 Summer Budget," WPR, WK, box 23, f: 10.

85. *Madison Capital Times*, August 24, 1967, June 29, 1968; *Milwaukee Labor Press*, December 21, 1967; Committee on Labor and Public Welfare, *Powerlessness*, 4-B: 1901–1902.

86. *Milwaukee Labor Press*, January 11, 1968; *Madison Capital Times*, January 17, 18, 1968.

87. Committee on Labor and Public Welfare, *Powerlessness*, 4-B: 1902; *Wisconsin State Journal*, January 17, 18, May 29, 1968.

88. Schmitt to Kircher, July 9, 1968, Manuel Salas to Kircher, May 12, 1970, and Healy to Kircher, May 15, 1970, WPR, WK, box 23, f: 13.

89. Interview, Jesús Salas, December 21, 1983, Wisconsin Governor's Committee on Migratory Labor, *Report to the Governor*, 7; Manuel Salas to Kircher, May 12, 1970 and César Chávez to Manuel Salas, May 22, 1970, WPR, box 23, f: 13.

90. Interview, Baldemar Velásquez, August 27, 1982; *Toledo Blade*, September 7, 1967; *Toledo Catholic Chronicle*, October 20, 1967.

91. Interview, Baldemar Velásquez, August 27, 1982; *Toledo Blade*, Sep-

tember 7, 1967; *Bluffton News*, September 7, 1967; *Toledo Catholic Chronicle*, October 20, 1967.

92. *Toledo Blade*, September 7, 1967; *Findlay Republican Courier*, September 12, 1967; *Bluffton News*, September 14, 1967.

93. *Lima News*, September 20, 1967; *Toledo Blade*, September 15, 1967; *Findlay Republican Courier*, September 15, 1967; *Bluffton News*, September 21, October 19, 1967; *Toledo Catholic Chronicle*, October 20, 1967.

94. E. S. H. to Kircher, September 12, 1967, WPR, WK, box 22, f: 11; *Findlay Republican Courier*, September 15, 1967; *UAW Solidarity*, November, 1967; *Dayton Daily News*, June 24, 1968; "How to Unpollute the Migrant Stream"; *Celina Daily Standard*, September 10, 1969; *Toledo Blade*, September 15, 1968, November 5, 1969.

95. *Putnam County Sentinel*, August 29, 1968; *Toledo Blade*, September 7, 15, 1968; *Celina Daily Standard*, September 7, 1968; *Ohio Christian News*, October, 1968; *Celina Daily Standard*, September 9, 1968; *Oregon News*, September 12, 1968; *Ohio Christian News*, October, 1968; *Toledo Times*, September 9, 1968.

96. *Toledo Blade*, September 15, October 27, 1968; *Columbus Citizen-Journal*, October 3, 1968; *Celina Daily Standard*, October 30, 1968.

97. *Dayton Daily News*, June 24, 1968; *Cleveland Plain Dealer*, June 24, 1968; *Farmland News*, July 9, 1968; *Celina Daily Standard*, July 2, 1968.

98. *Toledo Blade*, September 15, October 9, 1968, August 29, 1969; Elena Macías, "Application for Community Organization Program," f: FLOC, SSCC.

99. *Packer*, September 13, 1969; *Toledo Blade*, August 9, 20, 29, September 6, 26, 1969.

100. *Celina Daily Standard*, June 8, 1968, February 19, 1970; *Toledo Catholic Chronicle*, March 6, 1970; *Toledo Blade*, July 19, September 29, 1970.

101. Thomas Stewart to Kircher, April 26, 1967, WPR, WK, box 22, f: 11; *Milwaukee Labor Press*, December 21, 1967; Boutilier to Benallack, January 9, 1968, WPR, WK, box 21, f: 12; Healy to Kircher, October 22, 1969, WPR, WK, box 21, f: 14; Kircher to Lupe Anguiano, November 27, 1968, WPR, WK, box 21, f: 12; Kircher to Healy, April 3, 1969, WPR, WK, box 21, f: 13.

102. Schmitt to Durkin, WPR, WK, box 23, f: 11; Schmitt to Kircher, WPR, WK, box 23, f: 13; *Milwaukee Journal*, August 9, 1967; interview, Jesús Salas, December 21, 1983.

103. *Saginaw News*, July 21, 1969; MMM, *Annual Report 1969*, MHC, MMC, box 93C; *Detroit Free Press*, August 19, 1969.

104. *Saginaw News*, July 21, 1969; MMM, *Annual Report, 1969*, MHC, MMC, box 93C; Willson, "Historical Development," 125; *Lansing State Journal*, July 16, 1969.

105. *Chicago Tribune*, August 6, 1970; Rep. Sprenkle to John F. Schreier, August 17, 1970, WPR, WK, box 21, f: 10; Concerned Citizens about Migrant Workers, "Weller Pickle Company Cheats Migrant Workers," WPR, WK, box 21, f: 15.

106. *Detroit Free Press*, August 6, 1970; Sprenkle to Schreier, August 17, 1970, WPR, WK, box 21, f: 10; Concerned Citizens about Migrant Workers, "Weller Pickle Company Cheats," WPR, WK, box 21, f: 15.

9. Postscript: Meandering Stream

1. *Bay City Times*, July 8, 1969, July 9, 1970; *Saginaw News*, June 17, 1973; *Detroit News*, July 19, 1973; *Lansing State Journal*, June 21, 1973; MDPH, "Summary Report 1966–1976," SOM; *Toledo Blade*, December 8, 1968.

2. *Detroit News*, June 8, 1969; *Bay City Times*, October 18, 1970, July 16, 1975; Michigan, Farm Labor and Rural Manpower Service Section, *1969 Post-Season Farm Labor and Rural Manpower Report*, 40; Farmers and Manufacturers Beet Sugar Association, *Michigan and Ohio Beet Sugar Production*, 7.

3. *Bay City Times*, July 8, 1969, October 18, 1970; *Saginaw News*, October 8, 1970; MESC, *Post-Season Farm Labor Report*, *1959*, 22; *Detroit Free Press*, August 27, 1979; *Detroit News*, July 19, 1973; Michigan, *1969 Post-Season*, 40; Michigan, Bureau of Community Social Services, *1972 Migrant Services Report*, 19; Latin American Affairs Department (hereafter LAAD), Catholic Diocese of Saginaw, "Final Report of LAAD Summer Program, Summer, 1972," LAAD; Slesinger and Muirragui, *Migrant Agricultural Labor*, 9; Willson, "Historical Development," 95–96; MDPH, "Summary Report 1966–1976," 7; *Toledo Blade*, December 8, 1968.

4. Michigan, *1969 Post-Season*, 40; Slesinger and Muirragui, *Migrant Labor*, 13; Willson, "Historical Development," 95; *Bay City Times*, July 8, 1969; *Saginaw News*, October 18, 1970.

5. MDPH, "Summary Report 1966–1976," 7; interview, Andrew Anguiano, June 21, 1984; *Toledo Blade*, December 8, 1968; *Bay City Times*, August 21, 1966, August 20, 1967; Peter H. Rosset and John H. Vandermeer, "The Confrontation between Labor and Capital in the Midwest Tomato Industry and the Role of the Agricultural Research Establishment," 7.

6. LAAD, Saginaw, "Final Report of LAAD Program, Summer, 1972," LAAD; John H. Vandermeer, "Mechanized Agriculture and Social Welfare: The Tomato Harvester in Ohio," 6–7; idem, "Science and Class Conflict: The Role of Agricultural Research in the Midwestern Tomato Industry," 48–57; MESC, *1972 Post-Season Rural Manpower Report*, 27; *Detroit Free Press*, October 31, 1982; Committee on Labor and Public Welfare, *Powerlessness*, 7-B: 4549–4550.

7. *Bay City Times*, March 17, 1967; *Detroit News*, July 19, 1973.

8. MDPH, "Summary Report 1966–1976," 10; *Detroit News*, May 16, June 27, 1971; *Detroit Free Press*, November 22, 1970; Michigan, Department of Agriculture, *Michigan Food Facts*, 10; Vandermeer, "Science," 53; Peter Kropotkin, *Fields, Factories and Workshops Tomorrow*, 47.

9. *Bay City Times*, August 22, 1978; *Lansing State Journal*, May 6, 1977, August 27, 1979; *Detroit News*, September 9, 1976; MFWM, "Michigan Farm Worker Ministry, 1973–1974," MFWM; Ohio House, *Final Report December*

1981, FLOC; Ohio Senate, *Ohio's Migrant Workers*, FLOC; MCRC, "Report and Recommendations on the Status of Mushroom Workers in Michigan," JJC; *Wisconsin State Journal*, July 9, 1976; Anne Ferguson, Jane Haney, and Timothy Ready, *Culture, Environment and Work: A Study of Health and Health Care among Spanish-speaking Migrant Workers in the Mid-Michigan Area*; Ness Flores and Daniel Hannigan, *Report on Migratory Labor in Wisconsin*, 14; *Hope College Anchor*, April 22, 1974; Fred Ezminda Johannes to Gene Conzemius, December 4, 1978, f: La Crosse, SSCC.

10. *Detroit News*, July 19, 1973, September 6, 1978, September 13, 1981; *Lansing State Journal*, June 14, 1970, April 7, 1977, February 1, 1978; *Detroit Free Press*, March 9, 1971, October 31, 1982; Flores and Hannigan, *Migratory Labor*, 16.

11. *FLOC Boycott Update*, October, 1985, May 1987; *National Farm Worker Ministry Newsletter*, Spring, 1986, Spring, 1987; *Cleveland Plain Dealer*, February 20, 1986; *Toledo Blade*, March 1, 1987; *Detroit Free Press*, April 10, 1987.

12. Rural America, *Where Have All the Farmworkers Gone? The Statistical Annihilation of Hired Farmworkers*, viii–xi; Gordon et al., *Segmented Work*, 215–216.

Bibliography

AD	Archives of the Archbishopric of Detroit
AGN	Archivo General de la Nación, Mexico City
	AR—Fondo Abelardo Rodríguez
	ARC—Fondo Adolfo Ruiz Cortines
	DT—Fondo Departamento de Trabajo
	LC—Fondo Lázaro Cárdenas
	MAC—Fondo Manuel Avila Camacho
	MAV—Fondo Miguel Alemán Valdés
	OC—Fondo Alvaro Obregón–Plutarco Elías Calles
	POT—Fondo Pascual Ortiz Rubio
BHC	Burton Historical Collections, Detroit Public Library
BL	Bancroft Library, University of California, Berkeley
	PTCN—Paul Taylor Papers, collection of notes, etc., concerning Mexican labor in the United States
	PTRFN—Paul Taylor Papers, reports and field notes
	PTRM—Paul Taylor Papers, research materials collection
	SJFN—Stuart Jamieson Papers, field notes
CHS	Chicago Historical Society
	CAP—Chicago Area Project Papers
	JK—John Kearney Papers
	WCMC—Welfare Council of Metropolitan Chicago Papers
CSRC	Chicano Studies Research Center, University of California, Los Angeles
DDE	Dwight D. Eisenhower Library, Abilene, Kansas
	PCML—President's Commission on Migratory Labor
	CFGF—Central Files, General Files
DNPL	Denver Public Library
	WHD—Western History Department
DS	Archives of the Diocese of Saginaw, Michigan
EL	Edward Lamb Papers, Center for the Archival Collections, Bowling Green State University
FLOC	Farm Labor Organizing Committee files, Toledo, Ohio

HST	Harry S. Truman Library, Independence, Missouri
	PCML—President's Commission on Migratory Labor
ISL	Indiana State Library, Indianapolis
JJC	John J. Castillo personal files, Michigan Civil Rights Commission, Lansing
LAAD	Latin American Affairs Department files, Saginaw Diocese, Saginaw, Michigan
LMT	Labor Movement in Texas Collection, Barker Texas History Center, University of Texas at Austin
MCLR	Midwest Council on La Raza Papers, Archives of the University of Notre Dame, Notre Dame, Indiana
MFWM	Michigan Farm Worker Ministry files, Lansing
MHC	Michigan Historical Collections, Bentley Historical Library, Ann Arbor

AB—Alvin M. Bentley Papers
FLC—Frederick Lewis Crawford Papers
GMW—G. Mennen Williams Papers
GR—George Romney Papers
MMC—Michigan Migrant Committee Papers

MHS   Minnesota Historical Society, Archives and Manuscripts Division, St. Paul

AC—American Crystal Sugar Company Papers
CWUM—Church Women United in Minnesota Papers
EA—Elmer C. Andersen Papers
EJM—Eugene J. McCarthy Papers
GNVP—Great Northern Railroad Papers, vice-presidential subject files
LY—Luther Youngdahl Papers
MAC—Mexican American Community of St. Paul Papers
OCF—Orville C. Freeman Papers
OH—Collection of oral history interviews
SMBRA—Sociedad Mutua Beneficia Recreativa Anáhuac, St. Paul, Papers

MSA   Michigan State Archives, Lansing

HK—Harold F. Kelley Papers
JS—Joel Sharkey Papers
JT—John Frederick Thaden Papers
KS—Kim Sigler Papers
MCRC—Michigan Civil Rights Commission Papers
MD—Michael Divley Papers
MDPH—Michigan Department of Public Health Papers
MWL—Michigan Welfare League Papers
RCK—Raymond C. Kehrese Papers
SMP—Stanley M. Power Papers

NA   National Archives, Washington, DC

RG 59—Department of State (Federal Employment Relief Administration)

	RG 69—Works Progress Administration
	RG 85—Bureau of Immigration
	RG 174—Department of Labor
	RG 183—United States Employment Service
	RG 211—War Manpower Commission
	RG 224—War Food Administration
	RG 280—US Mediation and Conciliation Service

NSMC National Sugar Manufacturing Company Papers, Colorado State Historical Society

OHS Ohio Historical Society, Columbus

PHS Presbyterian Historical Society, Philadelphia

CWHM—Church Women Home Missions Papers (unprocessed)

HMC—Home Missions Council of North America Papers (unprocessed)

NCC—National Council of Churches, Division of Home Missions Papers (unprocessed)

RG 10 US Department of Labor, Nebraska State Historical Society, Lincoln

SCMSU Special Collections, Michigan State University Library, East Lansing

SCSU Special Collections, Stanford University, Stanford, California

EG—Ernesto Galarza Papers

JLV—James L. Vizzard Papers

SCUCLA Special Collections, University of California, Los Angeles

CM—Carey McWilliams Collection Papers

CMNC—Carey McWilliams Collection Papers, newspaper clippings, box 16, f: migratory workers—Mexican

SOM State of Michigan Library, Lansing

SRE Archivo Histórico de la Secretaría de Relaciones Exteriores, Mexico City

SSCC Spanish-speaking Catholic Commission files, Notre Dame, Indiana

TPL Toledo and Lucas County, Ohio, Public Library

TSA Texas State Archives, Lorenzo de Zavala Archives and Library Building, Austin

UCC Archives of the University of Illinois-Chicago

IPL—Immigrants Protective League Papers

UCSP—University of Chicago Settlement Papers

UIL University of Illinois Library, Urbana

WHS Wisconsin Historical Society, Madison

OU—Obreros Unidos microprint

PCML—President's Commission on Migratory Labor, 1950

WPR Walter P. Reuther Library of Labor and Urban Affairs, Wayne State University, Detroit, Michigan

CK—Clement Kern Papers (unprocessed)

EJ—Edgar Johnston Papers

ID—Irwin L. DeShetler Papers
MAFL—Michigan AFL-CIO Papers, series 3
MWL—Michigan Welfare League Papers
PVM—Patrick V. McNamara Papers
UFWOP—United Farm Workers, Office of the President
   Papers
WDL—Workers Defense League Papers
WK—William Kircher Papers

Newspapers and Newsletters

Action (Detroit), 1969
Ann Arbor News, 1951
Appleblossom (Mt. Pleasant, Michigan), 1944
Bay City Times (Michigan), 1938–1978
Benton Harbor News-Palladium (Michigan), 1940–1959
Berrien Springs Journal-Era (Michigan), 1956
Bluffton News (Ohio), 1967
Celina Daily Standard (Ohio), 1968–1970
Chicago Daily News, 1959
Chicago Star, 1962
Chicago Sun, 1946
Chicago Tribune, 1945–1970
Christian Science Monitor, 1959
Cleveland Plain Dealer, 1959–1986
Cleveland Union Leader, 1956
Colorado Labor Advocate (*See* Labor Advocate–Denver)
Columbus Citizen-Journal (Ohio), 1968–1969
Columbus Union-Republican (Indiana), 1969
Dayton Daily News (Ohio), 1968
Denver Post, 1936
Denver Republican, 1902
Des Moines Register (Iowa), 1923
Detroit Free Press, 1922–1987
Detroit Labor News, 1938
Detroit News, 1920–1976
Detroit Times, 1950–1954
Fargo Forum (North Dakota), 1930–1948
Farmland News (Archbold, Ohio), 1968
Findlay Republican Courier (Ohio), 1935–1967
FLOC Boycott Update (Toledo, Ohio), 1985–1987
Fort Lupton Press (Colorado), 1938
Franklin Evening Star (Indiana), 1939
Gothic (Detroit), 1950
Grand Forks Herald (North Dakota), 1923–1930
Grand Rapids Herald (Michigan), 1953
Greeley Tribune (Colorado), 1938

Hope College Anchor (Holland, Michigan), 1974
Houston Post, 1963
Indianapolis News, 1938–1972
Indianapolis Star, 1938–1968
Indianapolis Times, 1948–1962
Ingham County News (Michigan), 1950–1952
Isabella County Enterprise (Michigan), 1924–1925
Labor Advocate (Denver), 1930
Lansing Labor News (Michigan), 1968
Lansing State Journal (Michigan), 1940–1979
Lima News (Ohio), 1936–1967
Lincoln Star (Nebraska), 1936
Lincoln State Journal (Nebraska), 1934
Los Angeles Examiner, 1917
Madison Capital Times (Wisconsin), 1967–1968
Mason City Globe Gazette (Iowa), 1924
Mears Newz (Michigan), 1944
Michigan AFL-CIO News (Detroit), 1967
Michigan Catholic (Detroit), 1954
Michigan Christian Advocate (Adrian), 1941
Michigan Farmer (Middleburg Heights), 1959
Migratory Labor Notes (Washington, DC), 1960
Milwaukee Journal, 1966–1969
Milwaukee Labor Press, 1967–1968
Milwaukee Sentinel, 1966–1967
Minneapolis Journal, 1931
Minneapolis Star, 1968
Minneapolis Tribune, 1932
Moorhead Daily News (Minnesota), 1926
Mt. Pleasant Times (Michigan), 1925
El Mundo (San Juan, PR), 1950
National Advisory Committee on Farm Labor Information Letter, 1960–1966
National Farm Worker Ministry Newsletter, 1986–1987
New World (Cleveland, Ohio), 1952
New York Times, 1948–1950
Ohio Christian News (Columbus), 1968
Oregon News (Ohio), 1968
Packer (Kansas City), 1969
Polk County Leader (Minnesota), 1930
Port Huron Times, 1950
La Prensa (New York City), 1957
La Prensa (San Antonio, Texas), 1927–1928
Pueblo Chieftain (Colorado), 1939
Puerto Rican World Journal (San Juan), 1943
Putnam County Sentinel (Ohio), 1968
Rocky Mountain News (Denver), 1938–1948

Rural Worker (Philadelphia), 1935–1936
Saginaw Catholic Weekly (Michigan), 1950–1958
Saginaw Daily News (Michigan), 1931–1933
Saginaw Journal (Michigan), 1964
Saginaw News (Michigan), 1945–1973
Saginaw News Courier (Michigan), 1925
San Francisco Chronicle, 1973
Scottsbluff Star-Herald (Nebraska), 1920
South Bend Tribune (Indiana), 1945–1975
St. Paul Pioneer Press (Minnesota), 1926–1932
Toledo Blade (Ohio), 1934–1987
Toledo Catholic Chronicle (Ohio), 1963–1970
Toledo Times (Ohio), 1968
Traverse City Record-Eagle (Michigan), 1939–1943
Trinidad Chronicle Gazette (Colorado), 1938
UAW Solidarity (Detroit), 1967
UMOI Newsletter (Mt. Pleasant, Michigan), 1968–1969
La Vanguardia (Austin, Texas), 1921
La Voz Mexicana (Wautoma, Wisconsin), 1967
Wage Earner (Detroit), 1950–1951
Wall Street Journal, 1969–1973
Walsh County Record (North Dakota), 1926
Warren Sheaf (Minnesota), 1927
Waushara Argus (Wisconsin), 1966
Wells Mirror (North Dakota), 1922–1924
Wisconsin State Journal (Madison), 1966–1976
Work (Detroit), 1956

Interviews

Andrew Anguiano. Interview with author, June 21, 1984.
Regina Anguiano. Interviews with author, June 21, 22, 1984.
Rosa Arenas. Interview with author, June 18, 1984.
María Castellanos. Interview with author, June 8, 1984.
Juan J. Castillo. Interview with author, June 12, 1984.
Mario Compeán. Interview with author, December 18, 1983.
Carmen Cortina. Interview with Guadalupe Luna, December 1, 1980.
Roberto Cortina. Interview with Guadalupe Luna, December 1, 1980.
Cata Estrada. Interview with author, August 25, 1982.
Fernando Cuevas, Sr. Interview with author, August 26, 1982.
Ramiro González. Interview with author, June 7, 1984.
Msgr. Clement Kern. Interviews with author, July 30, August 7, 1980.
Israel Leyton. Interview with author, August 13, 1980.
Juan Luna. Interviews with author, August 31, 1982, December 25, 1983.
Efraín Marínez. Interview with author, June 6, 1984.

Sister Lucía Medina. Interview with author, June 8, 1984.
Henry Miranda. Interview with author, August 27, 1982.
Raquel Moreno. Interview with author, June 13, 1984.
Trinidad Moreno. Interview with author, June 13, 1984.
Anastacio Muñoz. Interview with Delfín Muñoz, November 12, 1980.
Ruperto Muñoz. Interview with Delfín Muñoz, February 8, 1981.
Cecundino Reyes. Interview with author, December 25, 1983.
Isabel Salas. Interview with author, August 13, 1980.
Jesús Salas. Interview with author, December 21, 1983.
Mike Uriegas. Interview with author, June 22, 1984.
Baldemar Velásquez. Interview with author, August 27, 1982.
Vicenta Velásquez. Interview with author, August 27, 1982.

Works Consulted

Acuña, Rodolfo. *Occupied America: A History of Chicanos.* 3d ed. New York: Harper & Row, 1988.

Allsup, Carl. *The American G.I. Forum: Origins and Evolution.* Monograph no. 6. Austin: Center for Mexican American Studies, University of Texas, 1982.

American Beet Sugar Company. *El Cultivo de Betabel: Manual para los Trabajadores.* N.p., 1929.

American Civil Liberties Union. *The Struggle for Civil Liberty on the Land.* New York, 1935.

Anderson, Esther S. "The Beet Sugar Industry of Nebraska as a Response to Geographic Environment." *Economic Geography* 1 (October 1925): 372–386.

Andrews, Wade H., and Saad Z. Nagi. *Migrant Agricultural Labor in Ohio.* Research Bulletin no. 780. Wooster: Ohio Agricultural Experiment Station, 1956.

Applen, Allen J. "Migratory Harvest Labor in the Midwestern Wheat Belt, 1870–1940." Ph.D. dissertation, Kansas State University, 1974.

Armentrout, Walter W., Sara A. Brown, and Charles E. Gibbon. *Child Labor in the Beet Fields of Michigan.* New York: National Child Labor Committee, 1923.

Arrington, Leonard J. "Science, Government, and Enterprise in Economic Development: The Western Beet Sugar Industry." *Agricultural History* 41 (January 1967): 1–18.

B., L. R. "Berry Picking." *Rural New Yorker* 77 (1928): 1049.

"Back to the Homeland." *Survey* 69 (January 1933): 39.

Baker, Ned S., and Elizabeth S. Magee. "Agricultural Migrant Workers in Ohio." *Ohio's Health* 6 (October 1954): 9–11.

Balderrama, Francisco E. *In Defense of La Raza: The Los Angeles Mexican Consulate and the Mexican Community, 1929 to 1936.* Tucson: University of Arizona Press, 1982.

Barrera, Mario. *Race and Class in the Southwest: A Theory of Racial In-equality.* Notre Dame, Ind.: University of Notre Dame Press, 1979.

Beecher, Edward D. *Working in Hawaii: A Labor History.* Honolulu: University of Hawaii Press, 1985.

"Beet Complex." *The American Child* 5 (June 1923): 2.

Benyon, Erdmann Doane. "The Southern White Laborer Migrates to Michigan." *American Sociological Review* 3 (June 1938): 333–343.

Bernard, Raymond, S. J. "Run-Around for Migrants." *Social Order* 1 (October 1951): 353–360.

Berry, Carol. *A Survey of the Holland Spanish-speaking Community.* East Lansing: Deparment of Sociology and Institute of Community Development, Michigan State University, 1970.

Blackwelder, Julia Kirk. *Women of the Depression: Caste and Culture in San Antonio, 1929–1939.* College Station: Texas A&M University Press, 1984.

Burawoy, Michael. "The Functions and Reproduction of Migrant Labor: Comparative Material from Southern Africa and the United States." *American Journal of Sociology* 81 (March 1976): 1050–1087.

"Calling Out the Guard." *World's Work* 32 (August 1916): 437–452.

Cardenas, Gilbert. "Los Desarraigados: Chicanos in the Midwestern Region of the United States." *Aztlán* 7 (Summer 1976): 153–186.

Cardoso, Lawrence A. *Mexican Emigration to the United States, 1897–1931.* Tucson: University of Arizona Press, 1980.

Carlson, Alvar W. "Specialty Agriculture and Migrant Laborers in Northwestern Ohio." *Journal of Geography* 75 (May 1976): 292–310.

———. "The Settling Process of Mexican-Americans in Northwestern Ohio." *Journal of Mexican-American History* 5 (1975): 24–42.

Centro de Estudios Puertorriqueños. *Sources for the Study of Puerto Rican Migration.* New York, 1982.

"Child Labor in Michigan Sugar Beet Fields." *The American Child* 5 (March 1923): 1–4.

Choldin, Harvey M., and Grafton D. Trout. *Mexican-Americans in Transition: Migration and Employment in Michigan Cities.* East Lansing: Rural Manpower Center and Department of Sociology, Michigan State University, 1969.

Clive, Alan. "The Michigan Farmer in World War II." *Michigan History* 60 (Winter 1976): 291–314.

Clopper, Edward N., and Lewis W. Hine. "Child Labor in the Sugar-Beet Fields of Colorado." *Child Labor Bulletin* 4 (February 1916): 176–206.

Cohen, Mitzi. *Migrant Health in Monroe County.* Ann Arbor: Comprehensive Health Planning Council of Southeastern Michigan, 1974.

Cottrell, R. H., ed. *Beet-Sugar Economics.* Caldwell, Idaho: Caxton Printers, 1952.

Craig, Richard B. *The Bracero Program: Interest Groups and Foreign Policy.* Austin: University of Texas Press, 1971.

Curley, Harold. "No Chores for Jimmie: He's a Laborer." *Colliers* (11 August 1923): 11.

Daniel, Cletus E. *Bitter Harvest: A History of California Farmworkers, 1870–1941.* Ithaca, N.Y.: Cornell University Press, 1981.

Deutsch, Sarah. *No Separate Refuge: Culture, Class, and Gender on an Anglo-American Frontier in the American Southwest, 1880–1940.* New York: Oxford University Press, 1987.

"Developing Michigan Fruitlands." *The Detroiter* 2 (June 1912): 20–21, 29.

Dietz, James L. *Economic History of Puerto Rico: Institutional Change and Capitalist Development.* Princeton, N.J.: Princeton University Press, 1986.

Doxtator, C. W. "Sugar Beet Yields from Mechanical and Hand Thinning." *Crystallized Facts* 1 (June 1947): 7–8.

Driscoll, Barbara. *Newspaper Documentary History of the Chicano Community of South Bend, Indiana.* Notre Dame, Ind.; Centro de Estudios Chicanos e Investigaciones Sociales, 1978.

Drumm, Carl, *A Complete History of the Scioto Marsh.* Kenton, Ohio: Kenton Republican Company, 1940.

Dubovsky, Melvyn. *We Shall Be All: A History of the Industrial Workers of the World.* New York: Quadrangle, 1969.

Duff, Edwards, S.J. "The Plight of Migrant Labor." *Social Order* 10 (January 1960): 1–2.

"Editorial Comment on Child Labor Decision." *The American Child* 4 (August 1922): 91–96.

Eichner, Alfred S. *The Emergence of Oligopoly: Sugar Refining as a Case Study.* Baltimore: Johns Hopkins University Press, 1969.

"Expansion of Northwestern Michigan Fruit Agency." *Michigan Factorer and Financial Record* 15 (June 19, 1915): 25.

Farmers and Manufacturers Beet Sugar Association. *Michigan and Ohio Beet Sugar Production.* Saginaw, Mich.: Farmers and Manufacturers Beet Sugar Association, n.d.

Ferguson, Anne, Jane Haney, and Timothy Ready. *Culture, Environment, and Work: A Study of Health and Health Care among Spanish-speaking Migrant Workers in the Mid-Michigan Area.* East Lansing: College of Human Medicine, Michigan State University, 1974.

Fisher, Dennis U. "The State vs. the Federal Minimum Wage and Michigan Farm Employers." Mimeograph no. 18. East Lansing: Rural Manpower Center, Michigan State University, 1970.

Fisher, Dennis U., and Myron P. Kelsey. "Manpower, Employment, and Income in Michigan." Report no. 27. East Lansing: Rural Manpower Center, Michigan State University, 1972.

Flores, Edmundo. "Mexican Migratory Workers in Wisconsin: A Study of Some Aspects of the War Food Administration Program for the Use of Mexican Agricultural Workers during 1945 in the State of Wisconsin." M.A. thesis, University of Wisconsin, 1945.

Flores, Ness, and Daniel Hannigan. *Report on Migratory Labor in Wisconsin.* Madison: Governor's Committee on Migratory Labor, 1977.

"Following the Crops." *National Consumer's League for Fair Labor Standards Bulletin* 2 (Fall 1950): 1–2.

Fotia, Elizabeth R., and Richmond Calvin. *The Mexican-American of the South Bend–Mishawaka Area.* South Bend: Indiana University–South Bend, 1975.

Fuller, R. G. *Children in the Strawberries.* New York: Child Labor Committee, 1940.

Galarza, Ernesto. *Farm Workers and Agri-business in California.* Notre Dame, Ind.: University of Notre Dame Press, 1977.

———. *Merchants of Labor: The Mexican Bracero Story.* Charlotte & Santa Barbara: McNally & Loftin, 1964.

———. "Program for Action." *Common Ground* 9 (Summer 1949): 27–38.

Gallardo, Lloyd H. "Economics of the Demand for Harvest Labor by the Individual Farm Enterprise." *Western Economic Journal* 2 (Summer 1964): 183, 194.

García, Juan Ramón. "History of Chicanos in Chicago Heights." *Aztlán* 7 (Summer 1976): 291–306.

———. "The Mexican in Popular Literature, 1875 to 1925." In *Down Mexico Way,* edited by Teresa L. Turner, pp. 3–13. Tuscon: Tuscon Public Library and Arizona Historical Society, 1984.

———. "Midwest Mexicanos in the 1920s: Issues, Questions, and Directions." *Social Science Journal* 19 (April 1982): 89–99.

———. "Operation Wetback: Midwest Phase." Presented at National Association for Chicano Studies, Midwest Foco Conference, November 1981.

———. *Operation Wetback: The Mass Deportation of Mexican Undocumented Workers in 1954.* Westport, Conn.: Greenwood Press, 1980.

García y Griego, Manuel. "The Importation of Mexican Contract Laborers to the United States, 1942–1964: Antecedents, Operation and Legacy." In *The Border That Joins: Mexican Migrants and U.S. Responsibility,* edited by Peter J. Brown and Henry Shire, pp. 49–98. Totowa, N.J.: Rowan & Littlefield, 1983.

Gaylord, F. C., and K. I. Fawcett. *A Study of Grade, Quality, and Price of Canned Tomatoes Sold at Retail in Indiana.* Bulletin no. 48. West Lafayette, Ind.: Purdue Agriculture Experiment Station, 1939.

Gibbons, Charles E. "The Onion Workers." *The American Child* 1 (February 1920): 406–418.

Goldner, Norman S. "The Mexican in the Northern Urban Area: A Comparison of Two Generations." M.A. thesis, University of Minnesota, 1960.

"Good-Will Gesture to Migrants Pays Off in Michigan." *The American Child* 38 (May 1956): 6.

Gordon, David M., Richard Edwards, and Michael Reich. *Segmented Work, Divided Workers: The Historical Transformation of Labor in the United States.* Cambridge: Cambridge University Press, 1982.

Greene, Shirley E. *The Education of Migrant Children: A Study of the Educational Opportunities and Experiences of the Children of Agricultural Migrants.* Washington: National Council on Agricultural Life and Labor, 1954.

Gutleben, Dan. *The Sugar Tramp—Indiana.* Walnut Creek, Calif.: Dan Gutleben, 1958.

————. *The Sugar Tramp—1954: Michigan*. Walnut Creek, Calif.: Dan Gutleben, 1954.

————. *The Sugar Tramp—1963: Ohio, M.S.G., Indiana, Illinois*. Walnut Creek, Calif.: Dan Gutleben, 1963.

Ham, William T. "Sugar Beet Field Labor under the AAA." *Journal of Farm Economics* 19 (May 1937): 643–647.

Handman, Max Sylvanus. "The Mexican Immigrant in Texas." *Proceedings of the National Conference on Social Work* 53 (1926): 332–339.

Hasiwar, Hank. "The Corporate Farmer: Agriculture's Newest Blight." *New Leader* 35 (January 21, 1952): 15–18.

Hawley, Ellis W. "The Politics of the Mexican Labor Issue, 1950–1965." *Agricultural History* 40 (July 1966): 157–176.

"Health Care for Migrants." *Michigan's Health* (January–February 1965): 22.

Hechter, Michael. "Group Formation and the Cultural Division of Labor." *American Journal of Sociology* 84 (September 1978): 293–318.

Hendrickson, Kent. "The Sugar-Beet Laborer and the Federal Government: An Episode in the History of the Great Plains in the 1930s." *Great Plains Journal* 3 (Spring 1964): 44–59.

Henley, David E., and Mrs. David E. Henley. *Minnesota and Her Migratory Workers: Land of Promises—Partially Fulfilled*. Minneapolis: Minnesota Council of Churches and Home Missions Council, 1950.

Hernández, Sebastián Joseph. "The Latin American Migrant in Minnesota." M.A. thesis, McAlister College, 1960.

Herrera, Hayden. *Frida: A Biography of Frida Kahlo*. New York: Harper & Row, 1983.

Hickman, J. Fremont. "Mangold Wurzels and Sugar Beets." *Bulletin of the Ohio Agriculture Experiment Station*, 2d series, no. 5 (February 1892): 17–33.

"Home Owning, Permanent Beet Labor Colony Is Growing." *Monthly Labor Review* 11 (July 1923): 15.

Howell, James D., Bernard L. Erven, and John S. Bottom. *Migrant Farm Workers in Northwestern Ohio*. Wooster: Ohio Agricultural Research and Development Center, 1971.

"How to Unpollute the Migrant Stream." *Discovery* 2 (October 1968): 1.

Huber, Peter John. "Migratory Agricultural Workers in Wisconsin." M.A. thesis, University of Wisconsin, 1967.

Humphrey, Norman D. "Employment Patterns of Mexicans in Detroit." *Monthly Labor Review* 61 (November 1945): 913–924.

————. "Mexican Repatriation from Michigan: Public Assistance in Historical Perspective." *Social Service Review* 15 (September 1941): 497–513.

Hundley, James Riddle, Jr. *A Study of Interpersonal Relations among Managers and Employers of Fruit and Vegetable Farms*. East Lansing: Rural Manpower Center and Department of Sociology, Michigan State University, 1968.

Huston, H. A., and A. H. Bryan. "The Sugar Beet in Indiana." *Indiana Agriculture Experiment Station Bulletin* 75 (January 1899): 3–8.

Illinois Commission on Children. Committee on Agricultural Migrant Workers. *County Profile of Agricultural Migrant Workers in Illinois.* Springfield, 1967.

Indiana. State Employment Commission. *Indiana Farm Labor Report 1967.* Indianapolis: Indiana State Employment Commission, 1968.

———. *Indiana Farm Labor Report 1968.* Indianapolis: Indiana State Employment Commission, 1969.

———. *Indiana Farm Labor Report 1969.* Indianapolis: Indiana State Employment Commission, 1970.

———. State Employment Service. *Indiana Farm Labor Report 1962.* Indianapolis: Indiana Employment Security Service, 1963.

———. *Indiana Farm Labor Report, 1964.* Indianapolis: Indiana Employment Security Service, 1965.

"In Wisconsin." *The American Child* 5 (November 1923): 2.

Jamieson, Stuart. *Labor Unionism in American Agriculture.* Department of Labor Bulletin no. 836. Washington: GPO, 1945.

Jenkins, J. Craig, and Charles Perrow. "Insurgency of the Powerless: Farm Worker Movements (1946–1972)." *American Sociological Review* 42 (April 1977): 249–267.

Johnson, Charles S. "The Changing Economic Status of the Negro." *Annals of the American Academy of Political and Social Science* 145 (November 1928): 128–137.

Johnson, Clarence Edmund. "The Influence of New Sugar Beet Production Methods on Time and Cost Requirements in Michigan, 1946." M.S. thesis, Michigan State College, 1947.

Johnson, Elizabeth S. "Wages, Employment Conditions, and Welfare of Sugar Beet Laborers." *Monthly Labor Review* 46 (February 1938): 332–340.

———. *Welfare of Families of Sugar-Beet Laborers.* U.S. Department of Labor, Children's Bureau Pub. no. 247. Washington: GPO, 1939.

Johnston, Edgar. "The Education of Children of Spanish-speaking Migrants in Michigan." *Papers of the Michigan Academy of Science, Arts, and Letters* 32 (April 1946): 509–520.

———. *Migrant Workers in the State of Michigan.* Detroit: MACSD, 1971.

Jones, Anita Edgar. "Conditions Surrounding Mexicans in Chicago." M.A. thesis, University of Chicago, 1928.

Jorgensen, Janet M., David E. Williams, and John H. Burma. *Migratory Agricultural Workers in the United States.* Grinnell, Iowa: Grinnell College, 1961.

Kerr, Louise Año Nuevo. "Mexican Chicago: Chicano Assimilation Aborted, 1939–1954." In *The Ethnic Frontier: Essays in the History of Group Survival in Chicago and the Midwest,* edited by Melvin G. Holli and Peter d'A. Jones, pp. 293–328. Grand Rapids, Mich.: William B. Eerdmans, 1977.

Kirstein, Peter. *Anglo over Bracero: A History of the Mexican Worker in the United States from Roosevelt to Nixon.* San Francisco: R&E Research Associates, 1977.

Kiser, George C., and David Silverman. "Mexican Repatriation during the

Great Depression." *Journal of Mexican American History* 3 (1973): 139–164.

Koch, Alfred Robert. "Interregional Competition in the Tomato Processing Industry." Ph.D. dissertation, Purdue University, 1959.

Koch, Elmer Cornelius. "The Mexican Laborer in the Sugar Beet Fields of the United States." Ph.D. dissertation, University of Illinois, 1927.

Krammer, Arnold. "Japanese Prisoners of War in America." *Pacific Historical Review* 52 (February 1983): 67–91.

———. *Nazi Prisoners of War in America*. New York: Stein & Day, 1979.

Kropotkin, Peter. *Fields, Factories, and Workshops Tomorrow*. Edited by Colin Ward. New York: Harper & Row, 1974.

Kushner, Sam. *Long Road to Delano*. New York: International Publishers, 1975.

"Labor and Legislation in Michigan." *The American Child* 5 (June 1923): 6.

"Labor Conditions in Sugar-Beet Fields, and Suggested Remedies." *Monthly Labor Review* 42 (July 1934): 55–60.

Lamb, Blaine P. "The Convenient Villain: The Early Cinema Views the Mexican-American." *Journal of the West* 14 (October 1975): 75–81.

Leftwich, Max Howard. "The Migratory Harvest Labor Market: An Illinois Case Study." Ph.D. dissertation, University of Illinois-Urbana, 1975.

Levy, Jacques E. *César Chávez: Autobiography of La Causa*. New York: W. W. Norton, 1975.

Lindsey, Herbert H., and Thomas W. Walton. *Spatial and Temporal Patterns of the Movement of Seasonal Agricultural Migrant Children into Wisconsin*. Madison: University of Wisconsin Cooperative Educational Research and Services, 1962.

Lindstrom, Duane. *Indiana Migrants: Blighted Hopes, Slighted Rights*. Indianapolis: Indiana Advisory Committee to U.S. Commission on Civil Rights, 1975.

"Local Beet Fields Look Good." *The Sugar Beet* 7 (August 1930): 36–37.

Love, A. B., and H. P. Gaston. *Michigan's Emergency Farm Labor, 1943–1947*. Bulletin no. 288. East Lansing: Michigan State College Extension Service, 1947.

Lovejoy, Owen R. "The Child Problem in the Beet Sugar Industry." In *U.S. Bureau of Labor Statistics Bulletin no. 323*, pp. 27–37. Washington: GPO, 1923.

———. "Sugar." *The American Child* 5 (May 1923): 1.

———. "Sugar Puzzle Picture—Find the Child." *The American Child* 5 (October 1923): 2.

———. "Summing It Up." *The American Child* 5 (June 1923): 3, 5.

Lucas, Robert E. *Muck Farmers, Farmers Week: 50th Annual Meeting*. East Lansing: Soil Science Department, Michigan State University, 1968.

McDowell, John. *A Study of Social and Economic Factors Relating to Spanish-speaking People in the United States*. New York: Home Missions Council, n.d.

McGrath, John. "Lessons for Liberals." *The Progressive* 13 (October 1949): 24.

Macklin, Barbara June. *Americans of Mexican Descent: A Toledo Study*. Toledo: Toledo Board of Community Relations, 1958.

———. *Structural Stability and Culture Change in a Mexican-American Community*. New York: Arno, 1976.

McLean, Robert N. *The Northern Mexican*. New York: Home Missions Council, 1930.

McWilliams, Carey. "California and the Wetback." *Common Ground* 9 (Summer 1949): 15–20.

———. *Factories in the Field: The Story of Migratory Farm Labor in California*. Santa Barbara & Salt Lake City: Peregrine, 1971.

———. "Mexicans to Michigan." *Common Ground* 2 (Autumn 1941): 5–17.

———. *North from Mexico: The Spanish-speaking People of the United States*. New York: Greenwood, 1968.

Madrid-Barela, Arturo. "In Search of the Authentic Pachuco: An Interpretive Essay." *Aztlán* 4 (Spring 1973): 31–60.

Majka, Linda C., and Theo J. Majka. *Farm Workers, Agribusiness, and the State*. Philadelphia: Temple University Press, 1982.

Maldonado, Edwin. "Contract Labor and the Origins of Puerto Rican Communities in the United States." *International Migration Review* 13 (Spring 1979): 103–121.

Manis, Jerome G. *A Study of Migrant Education: Survey Findings in Van Buren County, Michigan*. Kalamazoo: Western Michigan University Press, 1958.

May, William John, Jr. "The Great Western Sugarlands: History of the Great Western Sugar Company." Ph.D. dissertation, University of Colorado, 1982.

Mazón, Mauricio. *The Zoot-Suit Riots: The Psychology of Symbolic Annihilation*. Mexican American Monograph no. 8. Austin: University of Texas Press, 1984.

Menefee, Selden C. *Mexican Migratory Workers of South Texas*. Work Projects Administration, Division of Research. Washington: GPO, 1941.

Menefee, Selden C., and Orin C. Cassmore. *The Pecan Shellers of San Antonio*. Work Projects Administration, Division of Research. Washington: GPO, 1940.

Michigan. Bureau of Community and Social Services. Division of Family and Children Services. Migrant Services Program Unit. *1972 Migrant Services Report*. Lansing, 1972.

———. Bureau of Labor and Industrial Statistics. *24th Annual Report*. Lansing: Wynkoop, Hallenback & Crawford, 1907.

———. Civil Rights Commission. *1969 Report and Recommendations: A Field Study of Migrant Workers in Michigan*. Lansing, 1970.

———. *Report and Recommendations on the Status of Migratory Farm Labor in Michigan 1968*. Lansing, 1969.

———. Department of Agriculture. *Michigan Food Facts*. Lansing, 1975.

———. Department of [Public] Health. *70th Annual Report of the Commissioner*. Lansing, 1942.

———. *Summary Report 1966–1976.* Lansing, 1976.

———. Employment Security Commission. *Post Season Farm Labor Report 1952.* Detroit, 1953.

———. *Post Season Farm Labor Report 1956.* Detroit, 1957.

———. *Post Season Farm Labor Report 1959.* Detroit, 1960.

———. *Post Season Farm Labor Report 1960.* Detroit, 1961.

———. *Post Season Farm Labor Report 1961.* Detroit, 1962.

———. *Post Season Farm Labor Report 1962.* Detroit, 1963.

———. *Post Season Farm Labor Report 1964.* Detroit, 1965.

———. *Post Season Farm Labor Report 1965.* Detroit, 1966.

———. *Post Season Farm Labor Report 1968.* Detroit, 1969.

———. *Post Season Rural Manpower Report 1972.* Detroit, 1973.

———. Farm Labor and Rural Manpower Service Section. *1969 Post-Season Farm Labor and Rural Manpower Report.* Detroit: Central Manpower Division, 1970.

———. Governor's Study Commission on Migratory Labor and the Interagency Committee on Migratory Labor. *Migrants in Michigan.* Lansing, 1954.

———. Unemployment Compensation Commission. *Post Season Farm Labor Report 1949.* Detroit, 1949.

"Michigan Migrants and the NCLC." *The American Child* 39 (January 1957): 7–9.

"Michigan Starts Cleaning House." *The American Child* 5 (November 1923): 2.

"Migrant Reforms Urged." *The American Child* 38 (March 1956): 7.

"Migratory Workers—A Major Social and Economic Problem." *The American Child* 32 (October 1950): 1–4.

Minnesota. Department of Employment Security. *Post Season Agricultural and Food Processing Report, 1964.* Minneapolis, 1965.

———. Governor's Commission on Human Rights. *The Migrant Worker in Minnesota (1956).* St. Paul, 1956.

———. *The Migrant Worker in Minnesota (1958).* St. Paul, 1958.

———. Governor's Interracial Commission. *The Mexican in Minnesota (1948).* St. Paul, 1948.

———. Governor's Interracial Commission. *The Mexican in Minnesota (1953).* St. Paul, 1953.

Mintz, Sidney. *Worker in the Cane: A Puerto Rican Life History.* New Haven, Conn.: Yale University Press, 1960.

Montejano, David. *Anglos and Mexicans in the Making of Texas, 1836–1986.* Austin: University of Texas Press, 1987.

National Advisory Committee on Farm Labor. *Agribusiness and Its Workers.* New York: National Advisory Committee on Farm Labor, 1963.

———. *Report on Farm Labor.* New York, 1959.

National Child Labor Committee. "Farm Work and Schools in Kentucky." *Child Labor Bulletin* 5 (February 1917): 173.

"Nineteenth Annual Report of the National Child Labor Committee." *The American Child* 6 (January 1924): 1–4.

Noble, David F. *Forces of Production: A Social History of Industrial Automation.* Oxford: Oxford University Press, 1986.

Ohio. Governor's Committee on Migrant Labor. *Migratory Labor in Ohio (1960).* Columbus: Ohio Division of Labor Statistics, 1960.

———. *Migratory Labor in Ohio (1964).*Columbus: Ohio Department of Industrial Relations, 1964.

———. *Migratory Labor in Ohio (1965).* Columbus: Ohio Department of Industrial Relations, 1965.

———. Legislative Service Commission. *Migrant Workers in Ohio.* Research Report no. 49. Columbus: Ohio Legislative Service Commission, 1961.

Ohio State Federation of Labor. *1934 Proceedings.* Columbus, 1935.

Pendleton, Edwin Charles. "History of Labor in Irrigated Arizona Agriculture." Ph.D. dissertation, University of California–Berkeley, 1950.

Pfeffer, Max J. "The Labor Process and Corporate Agriculture: Mexican Workers in California." *Insurgent Sociologist* 10 (Fall 1980): 25–44.

Portes Alejandro, and Robert L. Bach. *Latin Journey: Cuban and Mexican Immigrants in the United States.* Berkeley & Los Angeles: University of California Press, 1985.

Puerto Rico. Bureau of Employment Security. *Annual Agricultural and Food Processing Report, 1961.* San Juan, 1961.

———. Department of Labor. *Nineteenth Annual Report of the Commissioner of Labor.* San Juan: Government Service Office, 1951.

Quamme, A. G. "Statement to Growers of Sugar Beets in the Mason City, Iowa, Territory." *Crystallized Facts* 1 (March 1947): 5.

Rabinovitz, Sam. "Michigan Migrants and the NCLC." *The American Child* 39 (January 1957): 7, 9.

Reisler, Mark. *By the Sweat of Their Brow: Mexican Immigrant Labor in the United States, 1900–1940.* Westport, Conn.: Greenwood Press, 1976.

———. "Mexican Unionization in California Agriculture, 1927–1936." *Labor History* 14 (Fall 1973): 562–579.

Reul, Myrtle. *Territorial Boundaries of Rural Poverty: Profiles of Exploitation.* East Lansing, Mich.: Center for Rural Manpower and Public Affairs, 1974.

Rojo, Emilia Angela. "Between Two Cultures: A Phenomenological Participatory Investigation of the Enduring Struggle of the Mexican-American Community." Ph.D. dissertation, University of Michigan, 1980.

Rosales, Francisco Arturo. "Mexican Immigration to the Urban Midwest during the 1920s." Ph.D. dissertation, Indiana University, 1978.

Rosset, Peter H., and John H. Vandermeer. "The Confrontation between Labor and Capital in the Midwest Tomato Industry and the Role of the Agricultural Research and Extension Establishment." Unpublished. University of Michigan Division of Biological Sciences, 1983.

Rowe, J. Z. "Migrant Farm Labor in Indiana." M.S. thesis, Purdue University, 1947.

Rowe, J. Z., and J. B. Kohlmeyer. *Migrant Farm Labor in Indiana.* Bulletin no. 543. West Lafayette: Purdue Agricultural Experiment Station, 1949.

Rural America. *Where Have All the Farmworkers Gone: The Statistical An-nihilation of Hired Farmworkers.* Washington: Rural America, 1977.

Ryan, Oswald. "Who Shall Inherit the United States?" *Michigan Educational Journal* 5 (January 1928): 291.

Schwartz, Harry. *Seasonal Farm Labor in the United States: With Special Reference to Hired Workers in Fruit and Vegetable and Sugar Beet Production.* New York: Columbia University Press, 1945.

Scruggs, Otey M. "The First Mexican Farm Labor Program." *Arizona and the West* 2 (Winter 1960): 319–326.

Shotwell, Louisa R. "A Look at the Migrant Outlook." *The Women's Press* 41 (December 1947): 14–15, 42–43.

Sierra Berdecia, Fernando. *Protegiendo 686,000 trabajadores.* San Juan: Departamento de Trabajo de Puerto Rico, 1949.

Simon, Daniel T. "Mexican Repatriation in East Chicago, Indiana." *Journal of Ethnic Studies* 2 (Summer 1974): 11–23.

Slesinger, Doris P., and Eileen Muirragui. *Migrant Agricultural Labor in Wisconsin: A Short History.* Madison: Department of Sociology, University of Wisconsin, 1979.

Smith, Mervin George. "An Economic Analysis of Tomato Production in Indiana." Ph.D. dissertation, Purdue University, 1940.

Snyder, Eldon E., and Joseph B. Berry, Jr. "Farm Employer Attitudes toward Mexican-American Migrant Workers." *Rural Sociology* 35 (June 1970): 244–252.

Sorden, L. G., Erven Long, and Margaret Salock. *Wisconsin Farm Labor Program, 1943–1947.* Madison: University of Wisconsin Agriculture Extension Service. 1948.

"Special Migrant Summer Schools Make News." *The American Child* 38 (November 1956): 1, 6.

Stein, Walter J. *California and the Dust Bowl Migration.* Contributions in American History, no. 21. Westport, Conn.: Greenwood Press, 1973.

Sternsher, Bernard. "Scioto Marsh Onion Workers Strike, Hardin County, Ohio, 1934." *Northwest Ohio Quarterly* 85 (Spring/Summer 1986): 39–92.

Stilgenbauer, F. A. "The Michigan Sugar Beet Industry." *Economic Geography* 3 (October 1927): 486–506.

Stilwell, Hart. "The Wetback Tide." *Common Ground* 9 (Summer 1949): 3–14.

Stuckman, Noel W. *Michigan Pickling Cucumbers—the Grower, the Picker, and the WYRF.* Bulletin no. 42: 1. East Lansing: Michigan State University Agriculture Experiment Station, 1959.

Sturt, Daniel W. "Workmen's Compensation and Michigan Farm Employers." Mimeograph no. 12. East Lansing: Rural Manpower Center, Michigan State University, 1970.

Surfin, Sidney C. "Labor Organization in Agricultural America, 1930–1935." *American Journal of Sociology* 43 (January 1938): 544–559.

Taylor, Paul S. *Adrift on the Land.* New York: Public Affairs Committee, 1940.

————. *Mexican Labor in the United States: Chicago and the Calumet Region.* University of California Publications in Economics, vol. 7, no. 2. Berkeley & Los Angeles: University of California Press, 1932.

————. *Mexican Labor in the United States: Dimmit County, Winter Garden District, South Texas.* University of California Publications in Economics, vol. 6, no. 5. Berkeley & Los Angeles: University of California Press, 1930.

————. *Mexican Labor in the United States: Valley of the South Platte, Colorado.* University of California Publications in Economics, vol. 6, no. 2. Berkeley & Los Angeles: University of California Press, 1929.

————. "Migratory Farm Labor in the United States." *Monthly Labor Review* 44 (March 1937): 537–549.

Texas. Bureau of Labor Statistics. *Texas Laws Concerning Employment and Emigrant Agencies.* Austin: State of Texas, 1941.

————. Legislative Council. Commission on Transportation. *Transportation of Migrant Labor in Texas.* Report no. 54–4. Austin, 1956.

————. State Employment Service. Unemployment Compensation Division. *Annual Report of the Farm Placement Service, Texas, 1939.* Austin: State of Texas, 1940.

Thaden, J. F. *Mexican Beet Workers in Michigan.* Special Bulletin 316–339. East Lansing: Michigan Agriculture Experiment Station, Section of Sociology, 1942.

Thernstrom, Stephan. *The Other Bostonians: Poverty and Progress in the American Metropolis, 1880–1970.* Cambridge, Mass.: Harvard University Press, 1973.

Thomas, Robert J. "The Social Organization of Industrial Agriculture." *Insurgent Sociologist* 10 (Winter 1980): 5–24.

Uchtman, Donald L. *Agricultural Labor Laws in Illinois.* Urbana: University of Illinois Cooperative Extension Service, 1977.

United States. Chamber of Commerce. *Mexican Immigration.* Washington, 1930.

United States. Civil Aeronautics Board. *Accident Investigation Report: Aviation Corporation of Seattle (Westair Transport) 300 Miles East of Melbourne, Florida, June 5, 1950 (Adopted July 9, 1951).* Washington: Civil Aeronautics Board, 1951.

————. Civil Rights Commission. *The Fifty States Report: Submitted to the Commission on Civil Rights by the State Advisory Committees, 1961.* Washington: GPO, 1961.

————. House of Representatives. *Congressional Record.* 69th Cong. 2d Sess. January 18, 1927, p. 1904.

————. *Congressional Record.* 81st Cong. 2d Sess. June 20, 1950, pp. 9375–9376.

————. *Congressional Record.* 83d Cong. 2d Sess. March 2, 1954, p. 2358.

————. Committee on Agriculture. *Permanent Farm Labor Supply Program, 1947.* 80th Cong. 1st Sess. Washington: GPO, 1947.

————. Subcommittee on Equipment, Supplies, and Manpower. *Mexican Farm Labor Program.* 84th Cong. 1st Sess. Washington: GPO, 1955.

———. *Extension of Mexican Farm Labor Program.* 87th Cong. 1st Sess. Washington: GPO, 1961.

———. Committee on Immigration and Naturalization. *Seasonal Agricultural Laborers from Mexico.* 69th Cong. 1st Sess. Washington: GPO, 1926.

———. *Immigration from Countries of the Western Hemisphere.* 70th Cong. 1st Sess. Washington: GPO, 1928.

———. Committee on Labor. *To Regulate Private Employment Agencies.* 77th Cong. 1st Sess. Washington: GPO, 1941.

———. Committee on Ways and Means. *Summary of Tariff Information, 1920 on Tariff of 1922. Schedule 4. Sugar, Molasses, and Manufacturers of.* Washington: GPO, 1929.

———. Select Committee Investigating National Defense Migration. *National Defense Migration.* 24 vols. (numbered 11–34). 77th Cong. 1st Sess. Washington: GPO, 1941.

———. Select Committee to Investigate the Interstate Migration of Destitute Citizens. *Interstate Migration of Destitute Citizens,* 10 vols. 76th Cong. 3d Sess. Washington: GPO, 1940–1941.

———. Senate. Committee on Agriculture and Forestry. *Agricultural Labor Supply.* 71st Cong. 2d Sess. Washington: GPO, 1930.

———. *Farm Labor Supply Program, 1947.* 80th Cong. 1st Sess. Washington: GPO, 1947.

———. Committee on Agriculture and Forestry. *Extension of Mexican Farm Labor Program.* 87th Cong. 1st Sess. Washington: GPO, 1961.

———. Committee on Appropriations. *Farm Labor Program, 1943.* 78th Cong. 1st Sess. Washington: GPO, 1943.

———. *Farm Labor Program, 1944.* 78th Cong. 2d Sess. Washington: GPO, 1944.

———. Committee on Education and Labor. *Violations of Free Speech and Rights of Labor.* Report no. 398, pt. 4. 78th Cong. 2d Sess. Washington: GPO, 1941.

———. Committee on Immigration. *Restriction of Western Hemisphere Immigration.* 70th Cong. 1st Sess. Washington: GPO, 1928.

———. Committee on Labor and Public Welfare. Subcommittee on Labor-Management Relations. *Migratory Labor (1952).* 2 vols. 82d Cong. 2d Sess. Washington: GPO, 1952.

———. Subcommittee on Migratory Labor. *Migrant and Seasonal Farmworker Powerlessness.* 8 pts. in 16 vols. 91st Cong. 1st and 2d Sess. Washington: GPO, 1970–1971.

———. *Migrant Health Services.* 90th Cong. 1st Sess. Washington: GPO, 1968.

———. *Migratory Labor (1959–1960).* 86th Cong. 1st Sess. Washington: GPO, 1960.

———. *To Stabilize the Domestic Farm Labor Force.* 87th Cong. 1st and 2d Sess. Washington: GPO, 1962.

———. Committee on Labor. *To Regulate Private Employment Agencies.* 77th Cong. 1st Sess. Washington: GPO, 1941.

————. Department of Agriculture. *Agricultural Statistics 1942.* Washington: GPO, 1943.

————. *Preliminary Survey of Major Areas Requiring Outside Labor.* Extension Farm Circular 38. Washington, 1947.

————. *Progress of the Beet-Sugar Industry in the United States in 1900.* Washington: GPO, 1901.

————. *Progress of the Beet-Sugar Industry in the United States in 1901.* Washington: GPO, 1902.

————. *Progress of the Beet-Sugar Industry in the United States in 1903.* Washington: GPO, 1904.

————. *Progress of the Beet-Sugar Industry in the United States in 1904.* Washington: GPO, 1904.

————. *Progress of the Beet-Sugar Industry in the United States in 1905.* Washington: GPO, 1906.

United States. Department of Agriculture, and Michigan Department of Agriculture. *Annual Crop Summary, 1935.* Lansing: USDA and Michigan Department of Agriculture, 1936.

————. *Annual Crop Summary, 1939.* Lansing: USDA and Michigan Department of Agriculture, 1940.

————. Department of Commerce. *Mexican Immigration.* Washington: GPO, 1930.

————. Bureau of the Census. *Census of Agriculture, 1950.*

————. *Historical Statistics of the United States: Colonial Times to 1970.* Washington: GPO, 1970.

————. *13th Census of the United States, 1910.*

————. *14th Census of the United States, 1920.*

————. *15th Census of the United States, 1930.*

————. *16th Census of the United States, 1940.*

————. Department of Health, Education, and Welfare. *Children of Migrant Families.* Washington: GPO, 1960.

————. Department of Labor. Employment Service. *Report of the Farm Labor Division, United States Employment Service, 1925.* Washington: GPO, 1925.

————. Children's Bureau. *Child Labor and the Work of Mothers in the Beet Fields of Colorado and Michigan.* Bureau Pub. no. 115. Washington: GPO, 1923.

————. Immigration Commission. *Immigrants in Industries.* 25 vols. Pt. 24. 61st Cong. 1st & 2d Sess. *Recent Immigrants in Agriculture.* Washington: GPO, 1910–1911.

————. Industrial Commission. *Report on Agriculture and Agricultural Labor.* 19 vols. 57th Cong. 1st Sess. Washington: GPO, 1901–1902.

————. President's Commission on Migratory Labor. *Migratory Labor in American Agriculture.* Washington: GPO, 1951.

University of Wisconsin. Institute for Research on Poverty. *A Study of Migratory Workers in Cucumber Harvesting: Waushara County, Wisconsin, 1964.* Madison: Institute for Research on Poverty, 1964.

Valdés, Dennis Nodín. "Betabeleros: The Formation of an Agricultural Proletariat in the Midwest, 1897–1930." *Labor History* 30 (Fall 1989): 536–562.

———. "Mexican Revolutionary Nationalism and Repatriation during the Great Depression." *Mexican Studies/Estudios Mexicanos* 4 (Winter 1988): 1–23.

———. *El pueblo mexicano en Detroit y Michigan: A Social History.* Detroit: College of Education, Wayne State University, 1982.

Vandermeer, John H. "Mechanized Agriculture and Social Welfare: The Tomato Harvester in Ohio." Unpublished. University of Michigan Division of Biological Sciences, 1983.

———. "Science and Class Conflict: The Role of Agricultural Research in the Midwestern Tomato Industry." *Studies in Marxism* 12 (1982): 41–57.

Volkin, David, and Henry Bradford. *American Crystal Sugar: Its Rebirth as a Cooperative.* Farmer Cooperative Service Information Bulletin no. 98. Washington: GPO, 1975.

Waters, Lawrence Leslie. "Transient Mexican Agricultural Labor." *Southwest Social Science Quarterly* 22 (June 1941): 49–66.

Weber, David Stafford. "Anglo Views of the Mexican Immigrant: Popular Perceptions and Neighborhood Realities in Chicago, 1900–1940." Ph.D. dissertation, Ohio State University, 1982.

Weeks, John R., and Joseph Spielberg Benítez. "The Cultural Demography of Midwestern Chicano Communities." In *The Chicano Experience,* edited by Stanley A. West and June Macklin, pp. 229–251. Boulder, Colo.: Westview Press, 1979.

Wells, Miriam J. "Oldtimers and Newcomers: The Role of Context in Mexican Assimilation." *Aztlán* 11 (Autumn 1980): 271–295.

———. "Social Conflict, Commodity Constraints, and Labor Market Structure in Agriculture." *Comparative Studies in Society and History* 23 (October 1981): 679–704.

Willis, E. S. "The Trend toward More Acres per Worker." *Through the Leaves* 48 (March–April 1960): 36–37.

Willson, Kay Diekman. "The Historical Development of Migrant Labor in Michigan Agriculture." M.A. thesis, Michigan State University, 1977.

Wirtz, Willard. *Year of Transition: Seasonal Farm Labor, 1965.* Washington: GPO, 1965.

Wisconsin. Department of Welfare. Division for Children and Youth. *Migrant Agricultural Workers in Door County.* Madison, 1951.

———. Governor's Commmision on Human Rights. *Migratory Workers in Wisconsin: A Problem in Human Rights.* Madison, 1950.

———. *Migrant Labor in Wisconsin.* Madison, 1965.

———. Governor's Committee on Migratory Labor. *Report for 1966 and 1967.* Madison: Department of Industry, Labor, and Human Relations, 1968.

———. *Report to the Governor, 1964.* Madison: Governor's Commission on Human Rights, 1964.

———. *Report to the Governor, January, 1971.* Madison: Governor's Commission on Human Rights, 1971.

————. Legislative Reference Library. *Wisconsin Blue Book 1954*. Madison, 1954.

"Wlad of the Beets." *New Republic* 35 (August 8, 1923): 285.

Wolfe, Bertram D. *The Fabulous Life of Diego Rivera*. New York: Stein & Day, 1969.

Wolfson, Theresa. "People Who Go to the Beets." *The American Child* 1 (November 1919): 217–239.

Wright, Karl T., Dennis Fisher, and Myron P. Kelsey. *Agricultural Employ-ment and Income in Michigan*. Report no. 27. East Lansing: Center for Rural Manpower and Public Affairs, Michigan State University, 1972.

Young, Robert A. *An Economic Study of the Eastern Beet Sugar Industry*. Research Bulletin no. 9. East Lansing: Michigan Agriculture Experiment Station, 1964.

"Your Beet Labor." *The Sugar Beet* 6 (April 1929): 7–8.

Index